Unexpected Prosperity

Unexpected Prosperity

How Spain Escaped the Middle Income Trap

OSCAR CALVO-GONZALEZ

OXFORD
UNIVERSITY PRESS

OXFORD
UNIVERSITY PRESS

Great Clarendon Street, Oxford, OX2 6DP,
United Kingdom

Oxford University Press is a department of the University of Oxford.
It furthers the University's objective of excellence in research, scholarship,
and education by publishing worldwide. Oxford is a registered trade mark of
Oxford University Press in the UK and in certain other countries

© Oscar Calvo-Gonzalez 2021

The moral rights of the author have been asserted

First Edition published in 2021

Published in the United States of America by Oxford University Press
198 Madison Avenue, New York, NY 10016, United States of America

British Library Cataloguing in Publication Data
Data available

Library of Congress Control Number: 2021942701

ISBN 978–0–19–885397–8

DOI: 10.1093/oso/9780198853978.001.0001

Printed and bound by
CPI Group (UK) Ltd, Croydon, CR0 4YY

To Christina, Beatrice, and Hugo

Acknowledgements

This book is about how Spain became a prosperous and open society in the second half of the twentieth century. It is a case study of economic development. As such I owe the greatest debt to all the political, economic, and business historians which have uncovered the bulk of the primary evidence on which the argument draws. Some of those great historians also helped me directly. I am particularly thankful to Leandro Prados de la Escosura and Albert Carreras for advice and encouragement over the years. I am also grateful to all those who taught me economic history, and especially to Nick Crafts.

I am also grateful to the archivists that facilitated my research at Spain's Ministry of Foreign Affairs, Bank of Spain, the General Archive of the Administration of Spain, the Historical Archive of the European Union, the Bank of England, the US National Archives at College Park, the International Monetary Fund, and, especially, to Bertha Wilson at the World Bank.

As this book is intended for a broad audience interested in development, there was much of *what* happened in Spain that needed to be presented to non-specialists in the history of the country. I thank William Chislett, Doug Irwin, and Riccardo Trezzi for their help in this regard. My gratitude also goes to Adam Swallow and Henry Clarke at OUP for their guidance and patience. The thoughtful copy-editing by Phil Dines and the work by Carlos Reyes on the figures greatly improved the final product. In thinking about how Spain's path to prosperity may be relevant for development I have benefited from many conversations over the years with numerous World Bank colleagues, including Zeina Afif, Rodrigo Chaves, Andrea Coppola, Barbara Cunha, María Dávalos, Anna Fruttero, David Gould, Marco Hernández, Arturo Herrera, Camino Hurtado, Felipe Jaramillo, Fernando Jiménez Latorre, Ole Jorgensen, Fritzi Koehler-Geib, Daniel Lederman, Humberto López, Luis-Felipe López-Calva, Bill Maloney, Denis Medvedev, Lars Moller, Ambar Narayan, Marcin Piatkowski, Ana Revenga, Rashmi Shankar, Carlos Silva-Jáuregui, and Steve Webb. I owe special thanks to three anonymous referees for their constructive suggestions and to Axel Eizmendi for his help undertaking the topic modeling of Franco's speeches. Jeremy Adelman, Thomas Christiansen, Olga Christodoulaki, Jordi Domènech, Jesús Fernández-Villaverde, Nur Gryskiewicz, Alfonso Herranz-Loncán, Víctor Lapuente, Arnaud Mehl, Francisco Meneses, José Navarro de Pablo, Mar Rubio, and Anna Spadavecchia all helped at different points of the research and writing; most commented on lengthy excerpts of the manuscript.

I ask the reader forgiveness for my having included throughout the text a handful of footnotes with my own family story. As the writer Sergio del Molino put it, childhood is a powerful homeland and the childhood of one's parents even more so. It is the generation of my parents, Aurora and Domiciano, that collectively achieved a prosperity that was unimaginable when they were children. In addition to inspiration, my parents also provided me with decades-long support and an example to follow. I am grateful to them, as well as to Elena, Clive, Irene, Hernán, and Guiomar, for their help, especially during a particularly intense stretch of drafting. My thanks also to my mother-in-law, Vijaya, who has been a cornerstone of our family for years. My wife, Christina, encouraged and supported my writing, lent her clinical eye to the manuscript, and was a role model herself on getting a project like this one done while meeting numerous other professional demands. There is no one else I would rather get stuck with during a lockdown. To her and to our marvelous children, Beatrice and Hugo, I dedicate this book.

Rights and Permissions

Contents

List of Figures

List of Tables

Introduction

"Everyone is starving," the innkeeper said. "The rations we get aren't enough to keep a dog alive and who but the rich can afford to buy in the black market?," she asked. These were the desperate words of an elderly woman in charge of a guesthouse in the small town of Aguilar de la Frontera, 30 miles south of the Andalusian city of Córdoba. It was 1949 and her interlocutor was Gerald Brenan, a British writer who had produced an influential account of the origins of the Spanish Civil War (1936–9). Brenan was traveling back to Spain after an absence of over a decade. Throughout his journey, he felt besieged by people anxious to express their views. He turned the diary of his trip into a poignant exposé of life in Spain under the regime of General Francisco Franco, who had emerged victorious from the Civil War. Brenan's narrative is full of vivid first-hand accounts: "[t]he working classes are dying of hunger," said a shopkeeper; "General Franco is teaching Spaniards how to live without eating," protested a man on a bus.[1]

Hunger was but the most life-threatening of the many problems affecting the Spanish economy at around the mid-point of the twentieth century. Almost half of the economically active population was engaged in agriculture. Productivity was so low that the agricultural sector, despite its large workforce, accounted for less than a third of GDP.[2] As many developing countries in later decades, Spain had to import basic foodstuffs to feed itself. At times food aid proved to be a temporary respite, as in the case of grain sent by Argentina in the late 1940s. Electricity shortages crippled industrial sectors like textiles, forcing factories to operate at severely reduced schedules of two to three days a week. The country had adopted a policy of economic autarky and state controls determined nominal prices and wages in much of the economy. The government had also set up numerous state-owned enterprises geared towards achieving self-sufficiency. Most such efforts had not borne fruit. Thus, the government's poor management, including a bad use of scarce foreign exchange, added to a vicious circle of low productivity and state interventionism.

---

[1] Brenan (1951, pp. 48, 57–8, 106). The great Hispanist Sir Raymond Carr put it this way: "Between us, Gerald Brenan and I visited most of the Spanish provinces between 1949 and 1950. Everywhere we detected the sullen resentment of poverty and bitter criticism of the corruption that a highly regulated economy inevitably fosters" (Carr, 1994).

[2] Statistical information in this paragraph and, unless otherwise noted, throughout the introduction is from the monumental "Estadísticas históricas de España, siglos XIX y XX" edited by Albert Carreras and Xavier Tafunell (2005) and Prados de la Escosura (2017).

Unexpected Prosperity: How Spain Escaped the Middle Income Trap. Oscar Calvo-Gonzalez, Oxford University Press.
© Oscar Calvo-Gonzalez 2021. DOI: 10.1093/oso/9780198853978.003.0001

Complaints about corruption were widespread. On occasion they even surfaced publicly despite the censorship practiced by the Franco regime. Almost at the very same time that Gerald Brenan was traveling through the south of Spain, a young bishop in Catalonia, Vicente Enrique Tarancón, released a pastoral letter titled "Our daily bread, give it to us today." The text, which would be widely circulated in early 1950, presented a sharp indictment of the corrupt management of food rationing and placed the blame squarely on the Franco regime. The ensuing consequence, the bishop warned, was "suspicion, mistrust, and resentment" against the government.[3]

Spain in 1950 was also a country afflicted by fragility, conflict, and violence. The Civil War had arguably caused limited damage to physical capital, but it had left a devastating death toll in its wake, causing an estimated 200,000 deaths in battle plus a similar number of extrajudicial killings in a country of less than 25 million people. The atrocities were so widespread that one of the leading historians of the period has gone as far as labeling it a holocaust (Preston, 2012). The loss of human life was aggravated by the exodus of skilled labor and a politics of revenge that did not end when the war was over. On the contrary, it escalated. The repression by the victors was harsh and fear was the dominant social sentiment of Spain in the 1940s. After the war ended, tens of thousands of people were executed and the prison population swelled to over a quarter million people of all walks of life.[4]

The repressive nature of the Franco regime took up significant resources of an otherwise small and low-capacity state. In 1950, the taxes collected by the government barely reached 10 percent of GDP. Public spending priorities were clear: Around one-third of all public spending was devoted to defense. In contrast, spending on education and health accounted for a combined 7 percent of the public budget. It is no surprise that access to education was low: Only 6 percent of youth aged 14–19 years were enrolled in secondary education, with heavy bias favoring boys.

The insufficiency of a social safety net meant that families were on their own to weather any shocks. The consequences were often tragic. Preventable death was common. Gerald Brenan, in his journal, tells of a young woman under 30 who told him that she had been ill "after the birth of a child, which had died because her milk had dried up."[5] This was far from an isolated case. For every 1,000 babies born in 1950, 70 would not live through their first birthday (a rate more than double that of the UK or the US).

---

[3] Enrique Tarancón (1950). Tarancón, as he was known, was prompted to take this unusual step after receiving around a thousand letters complaining about the situation (Enrique Tarancón, 1996, p. 110).

[4] Richards (1998, p. 11). In the aftermath of the Civil War some 170,000 people were incarcerated, adding to the 100,000 prisoners that were already in jail by the end of the war. My own maternal grandmother, María, was one of those imprisoned in 1939.

[5] Brenan (1951, p. 34).

Brenan's informants were not the only ones that, in 1950, were pessimistic about the future of Spain. Those in the business of making projections were also doubtful about Spain's potential. The Central Intelligence Agency, which—like other American agencies—had been tasked with assessing Spain's economy and its potential contribution to the defense of Western Europe, concluded that "the principal obstacle to a considerable program of US economic aid to Spain is in the nature of the Franco regime." The CIA analysts believed that the regime was "too corrupt and incompetent" to successfully carry through a program of economic recovery and development.[6]

Against the odds, over the next quarter century, Spain would go on to become one of the fastest growing economies in the world. Within three decades, Spain's real per capita income quadrupled—for comparison, it had taken the entire previous century to double. More impressively, real per capita income caught up 30 percentage points in relation to the US: Spain's per capita income went from 27 to 57 percent of that in the US between 1950 and 1980. The country graduated as a borrower from the World Bank in 1977. Convergence went beyond measures of income. By 1980 Spain had caught up with both the US and the UK in infant mortality rates. Not only was growth unexpected, but it translated into a broadly shared prosperity which was sustained over time. Rapid urbanization was managed without, by and large, the by-product of slums and shantytowns—at least not to the extent that are common in many middle income countries today.

With the advent of democracy in 1975, the incipient welfare state was much developed, providing universal access to health and education, making for a more level playing field across the income distribution. As a result, Spain became one of the countries where reaching the top end of educational achievement was not particularly dependent on the level of education of one's parents.[7] This emerging welfare state was only possible because of a sharp rise in government revenues, from less than 10 percent of GDP in 1950 to over 30 percent in the 1980s. Informality was greatly reduced. Income inequality decreased for much of the period and the reduction in regional income disparities was particularly pronounced.[8] And all this was achieved without creating much public debt.

By the turn of the twenty-first century, Spain was solidly among the high-income economies and in the top tier of broader measures of well-being like the Human Development Index. The story of this striking turnaround is the subject of this book. Surprisingly, while well documented in the economic

---

[6] CIA, Office of National Estimates, "NIE-34: Spain's Position in the East-West Struggle (Working Draft)," July 5, 1951. Documents such as this one are now increasingly being made available online through https://www.cia.gov/readingroom/home (accessed February 11, 2021).

[7] The specific indicator is the share of those born in 1980 into the bottom half who have made it to the top quartile of their generation (World Bank, 2018a).

[8] For a discussion on the evolution of inequality see Prados de la Escosura (2008). Regional disparities are analyzed in Martinez-Galarraga et al. (2015).

historiography, this is a success story that has received relatively little attention in the broader literature on economic development policy, especially when compared to other successes like that of South Korea—which is much more accessible to a global audience.[9] Before addressing some of the causes of its reversal of fortunes it is worth pausing momentarily to examine the extent to which Spain's economic rise can be characterized as a success as well as dispelling some common misconceptions about Spain's path. This introductory chapter then discusses the relevance of the Spanish case to economic development in the twenty-first century and concludes with a brief sketch of the main argument of the book.

How much of a success?

The rapid and broad spread of prosperity was unexpected not only from the perspective of those alive in 1950 but also in a statistical sense. Spain is one of a handful of countries that has successfully transitioned from middle income to high-income status in recent decades. Of over a hundred middle income countries in 1960 only a dozen had become high income by the turn of the century. The finding—that it is relatively rare to see countries transition into high-income status—was so remarkable that it led those that uncovered it to coin the phrase "middle income trap" (Gill and Kharas, 2007). Much has been written about this phenomenon, but let me stress at the outset that even if you consider that "trap" is an incorrect label to characterize any stage of the development process, the insights from Spain's rise to high-income status are still worthwhile and largely unharvested. The fact that today's high-income economies spent decades as middle income, as documented by Jesús Felipe and coauthors (2017), is in some sense a further reason to look at their experience for lessons that may be relevant for the middle income countries of today.

Whether one sees middle income countries as more prone to being stuck or not, Spain's path was relatively unlikely in a comparative perspective. We can best show this in graphical form, using a scatterplot in which each dot represents a country and where the horizontal axis shows that country's real per capita GDP in 1950 and, on the vertical axis, the corresponding value for 2000 (Figure 0.1). The dotted-line oval corresponds to countries that started with similar per capita GDP but have done better than Spain. What is notable is how few countries had a higher growth than Spain. Only five economies fall in this category, four of the

[9] In addition to an abundant literature in English there is also a massive open online course (MOOC) on South Korea's development: World Bank and Korea Development Institute, "Policy Lessons of Korea's Development" available at https://olc.worldbank.org/content/policy-lessons-korea%E2%80%99s-development (accessed February 18, 2018).

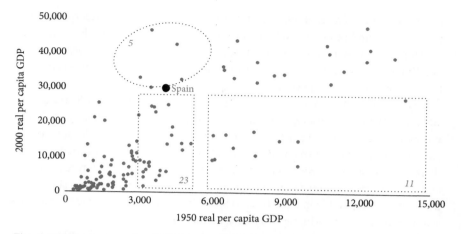

Figure 0.1 Real per capita GDP in 1950 and 2000 across countries

Note: Real GDP per capita in 2011US$. Norway, Switzerland, and the United States have real per capita GDP outside the ranges shown. The shaded vertical bar represents countries that had a real GDP per capita close to that of Spain in 1950 (±$1,100). Among this group of 28 comparators, Spain did better than 23 economies, shown within the dotted-line rectangle. Spain also overtook 11 economies, shown in the solid-line rectangle, that had a clearly higher real GDP per capita in 1950.

Source: Maddison Project Database (Bolt, Inklaar, de Jong, and van Zanden, 2018).

original East Asian "tigers"—Hong Kong, Japan, Taiwan, and Singapore—and oil-rich Oman.[10]

In contrast, there were many more countries that performed worse than Spain. This is shown in the dotted-line rectangle in Figure 0.1, which encompasses 23 countries that had a similar per capita GDP to Spain in 1950 (plus or minus $1,100) but had fallen behind Spain 50 years later. Moreover, Spain surpassed the per capita GDP of 11 countries that had a significantly higher per capita GDP in 1950, shown in the solid-line rectangle in Figure 0.1. When we combine the numbers in the two rectangles, there are a total of 34 countries that did worse than Spain while only 5 countries did better. This underscores what a remarkable growth trajectory Spain had in the second half of the twentieth century.

Amongst those 11 countries that started with a higher real per capita GDP than Spain but which Spain surpassed, there is a diverse set of economies such as Argentina, Chile, Hungary, New Zealand, South Africa, Uruguay, and Venezuela. For example, New Zealand had three times the real per capita GDP of Spain in 1950 but had been overtaken by 2000. And the analysis above is rather conservative in identifying countries that have performed worse than Spain among the

---

[10] South Korea could be added to this list. In Figure 0.1 it lies just outside the top shaded area because by 2000 it had only reached a real per capita income of $21.4 thousand compared to $29.5 thousand for Spain.

richer countries. For example, we did not include Britain as underperforming relative to Spain because in 2000 it still had a real per capita GDP that was 7 percent higher than Spain's. As Britain's real per capita GDP had been over two and a half times larger than that of Spain in 1950, the catching up by Spain was particularly intense during this period.

Traditionally, the economic history literature has benchmarked Spain against advanced Western European countries like Britain, France, Germany, or Italy.[11] But Figure 0.1 warns us against jumping into those comparisons without a pause. Among the 28 countries that had a comparable per capita output to Spain in 1950, there were only four European countries in this group: Portugal, Greece, Cyprus, and Poland. Spain would go on to do better than all of them. The full list of countries with a comparable income level to Spain in 1950 is not the type of countries against which the historiography typically benchmarks Spain.[12]

The catching up was not only unexpected but was also fast. In the 30 years that followed 1950, Spain grew its real per capita GDP by an average rate of 4.8 percent annually. To understand what an anomaly such a fast and sustained growth episode is, we can re-examine the Maddison Project cross-country data referred to in Figure 0.1. A simple exercise is to check what was the average growth rate of a country in the 30 years after it reaches the real per capita GDP that Spain had in 1950. This allows us to compare Spain's performance with other countries at a similar stage of development regardless of when that happened. For example, if a country reached that level in 1960, we look at its economic growth in the 30-year period after 1960.[13] Overall, there are 82 countries that have at some point in time reached the level of output per capita that Spain achieved in 1950. When we take those 82 cases together, we observe that their mean growth rate over the following 30-year period was 2.5 percent, around half that of Spain.

Perhaps middle income countries in the 1950s enjoyed advantages given that the world economy was embarking on an unusual "Golden Age" of economic

---

[11] Notably Prados de la Escosura and Zamagni (1992) provide a detailed comparative account of Spain and Italy's falling behind in the nineteenth century and catching up in the second half of the twentieth century. More broadly, while the literature has moved beyond the idea of Spain's historical path as exceptional, systematic comparative perspectives are still rare (Townson, 2015).

[12] The full list of the 28 comparator eonomies is: Bolivia, Chile, Colombia, Costa Rica, Cuba, Cyprus, Djibouti, Ecuador, Egypt, El Salvador, Greece, Guatemala, Hong Kong, Iran, Israel, Japan, Jordan, Mexico, Namibia, Nicaragua, Oman, Peru, Poland, Portugal, Puerto Rico, Seychelles, Singapore, and Trinidad and Tobago. If we had set the criterion for inclusion in this list as the per capita GDP to Spain in 1950 plus or minus $1,000 (instead of $1,100), both Japan and Chile would drop out of our list. Since these two countries are successful examples I decided to include them among the comparators.

[13] I choose a 30-year period for three reasons. First, it is long enough to speak to long-term trends while being short enough that we can use data for countries which crossed the threshold in the 1970s. Second, given that Spain's growth was fastest in the 1960–74 period, including the early 1950s and the late 1970s in Spain avoids cherry-picking a time frame that would overstate Spain's success. Third, by using a thirty-year window Spain's period ends by 1980, thus helping to highlight that the catching up was an ongoing process well before Spain's membership in the then European Economic Community.

growth (Crafts and Toniolo, 1996). To test this theory, we repeat the simple exercise of computing 30-year growth averages but this time only for those countries that had reached Spain's 1950 real per capita GDP during the 1950s and 1960s—and hence would have enjoyed the very favorable external conditions of the period. When we do so, we still find that Spain's 4.8 percent annual growth rate over 30 years substantially exceeds the average of 3.3 percent for those countries that also benefited from being middle income during the Golden Age of economic growth. It is hard not to conclude that Spain's economic rise was fast even by the standards of the Golden Age. Thus, the first question we need to address is: Why did growth take off?[14]

One additional way to determine how much of a success Spain's economic performance was in the second half of the twentieth century is to compare it with a case of unquestionable success, such as that of South Korea. As shown in Figure 0.2, Spain was substantially richer than South Korea during the first half of the twentieth century, although in both cases we observe a virtually flat line indicative of a very low real economic growth on a per capita basis. Spain took off earlier than South Korea, which did not reach Spain's 1950 real per capita output until 1974. Notably, the pace of growth was not much lower in Spain, as shown in Figure 0.2 by a similarly sloped curve in the cases of both South Korea and Spain.

Prosperity in Spain was not only fast and unexpected, but also sustained. Figure 0.2 illustrates this point. The fastest economic growth period of Spain was from 1959 to 1974, when per capita growth reached annual rates that exceeded 6 percent on average. And while growth slowed down in the late 1970s, it remained positive and resumed vigor in the mid-1980s, with further accelerations in the late 1990s and early 2000s. Growth decelerations hit Spain, in what Eichengreen et al. (2012) characterize as a two-step deceleration in 1974 and 1990, but the economy avoided getting stuck—at least until the early part of the twenty-first century. The case of Spain in the second half of the twentieth century shows the importance of sustaining growth over several decades and avoiding relapses.[15] Thus, the second question we need to address is: How was growth sustained for an extended time?

Our starting point of Spain as an economic success story is not standard fare—which is why we went through the above discussion in detail. This is in part

---

[14] The term "take off" was popularized by Walt Rostow in his landmark *The Stages of Economic Growth* (1960). While Rostow's model fails at recognizing that there is no single path to development, his most significant yet underappreciated contribution—and what motivates the use of the term take off here—was the idea that policies that promote growth in one stage may be different from those that promote growth in other stages; see Costa et al. (2016).

[15] Spain was not included among the cases studied by the Growth Commission led by Nobel laureate Michael Spence (2008). It was so because Spain was not one of the countries with a highest growth spell over two and a half decades. Over time, however, it has proven to be more sustainable than some of the purely high-growth episodes studied by the Growth Commission, like that of Brazil.

Figure 0.2 Spain and South Korea's real per capita GDP over the last century
Source: Maddison Project Database (Bolt, Inklaar, de Jong, and van Zanden, 2018).

because the development of the Spanish economy has attracted only limited attention—especially when compared to the overwhelming interest in other epi-sodes of Spain's history such as the Spanish Civil War, which has generated over fifteen thousand books.[16] Moreover, some of the best-known traits of Spain's economy, such as persistently high unemployment, are decidedly not a cause for celebration. The decade that followed the global economic crisis of 2008 has been particularly painful—as can be seen in Figure 0.2. It is of course true that Spain suffers from traditionally high unemployment, as well as many other problems. But we should not fall for this "single story" view of Spain's economy. This is not to say that many development goals, like learning outcomes in the case of educa-tion, cannot be improved. Any country, at any time, can do better on many dimensions. The point remains, however, that the very substantial progress achieved merits a close look.

An inevitable catch-up?

To the extent that Spain is considered a success story, it is often misunderstood. Looking back from the standpoint of the early twenty-first century, the turn-around of Spain seems inevitable. We should resist this temptation for what it is, a

---

[16] By the count of Graham (2005). Franco's biographies are also plentiful and provide the focal point of the literature that covers the time period where Spain's rise to prosperity took place.

case of what psychologists would call hindsight bias. One common misconception is that Spain's prosperity was largely due to its joining what is now the European Union.[17] Generous structural and cohesion funds have certainly benefited Spain, and the EU provides for the largest domestic market in the world. The main problem of a simplistic EU-centric view of Spain's economic rise is that the timeline is inconsistent with it: Spain joined the European Economic Community (EEC) in 1986 well after its most intense period of catching up. Spain had initially applied to be associated with the EEC in 1962, but a preferential trade agreement was not even signed until 1970—again, too late to account directly for the economic takeoff. The key contribution of the European integration process to Spain's prosperity would not be the fiscal transfers received or even access to the single market. But the *idea* of Europe played a significant role in shaping a consensus view on the direction in which economic and political institutions ought to evolve.

Another common misunderstanding is that Spain had been a developed economy in the past and hence there is little to explain other than a return to a trend. One common argument is to explain much of Spain's backwardness in 1950 on account of the Civil War and the disastrous Francoist policies implemented in the immediate postwar period. And it is true that the period 1935–50 represented a lost decade and a half in terms of growth. It is also true that the century prior to 1950 had seen some economic growth. But growth before 1950 had been generally modest and resulted in a relative decline vis-à-vis the leading economies of the world. As shown in Figure 0.3, Spain's per capita output expressed as a share of that of the US had dropped from 71 percent in 1850 to 27 percent in 1950. Perhaps the comparison with the US, which was undergoing a rapid transformation at the time, is not particularly helpful as the US economy was leaving every other country behind. But Figure 0.3 also shows a stagnant share of Spain's per capita output relative to that of Britain over the century prior to 1950—no convergence there either.

Even more important is to compare Spain's long-term performance with a similar country like Poland—which is also shown in Figure 0.3 on the right axis. This is not a comparison that is usually presented in the literature, but it is more revealing than simply comparing Spain to the most advanced country of the day.[18] Poland is a particularly relevant comparator for Spain since it is a country

---

[17] On the occasions in which the literature on middle income traps identifies Spain as a useful case, it is common to overlook the period on which we focus. Foxley and Sossdorf (2011) is one example where the swift modernization of the Spanish economy—and therefore the start in the search for lessons—is ascribed to Spain's transition to democracy and its subsequent accession to the European Union.

[18] The relevance of Spain's growth experience for Poland in the early twenty-first century was nevertheless explored by Caselli and Tenreyro (2005).

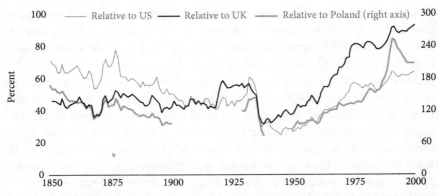

Figure 0.3 Spain's real per capita GDP relative to the US, UK, and Poland, 1850–2000
Source: Maddison Project Database (Bolt, Inklaar, de Jong, and van Zanden, 2018).

that has similar characteristics in terms of population size and proximity to Western European markets. The hundred years before 1950 show Spain's disappointing performance relative to Poland. In the middle of the nineteenth century, Spain had a per capita income that was around 60 percent higher than that of Poland. By 1900, Spain's underperformance meant that Poland had closed the gap. While data for Poland is sketchy for the early part of the twentieth century, it shows that it had a similar income level as Spain by 1950. Then, until the twenty-first century, Spain overtakes Poland decisively.[19]

But do these trends hold up if we take a broader comparative perspective? To answer this question, we benchmark Spain against all countries for which the Maddison Project has data at the following points in time: 1850, 1900, 1950, and 2000. This comparison, shown in Figure 0.4, suggests that over the century before 1950 Spain had been losing relative ground not only against the best performing country but also against the median country. Overall, Figures 0.3 and 0.4 show two broad sweeps of Spanish economic history over the last century and a half: divergence at varying speeds until 1950 and convergence since that time until at least the early twenty-first century.[20]

It may be argued that these long-term trends suggest that the catching up observed after 1950 was some type of return to "normal." In fact, if we look at Spain's per capita GDP relative to the richest economy, it is the case that from a long-run perspective Spain has simply returned to its initial position. The

---

[19] The rapid catch-up of Poland in the last 15 years or so provides a useful case study of development (Piatkowski, 2018).
[20] While worrying, it is too early to tell whether the last decade represents a change in the trend.

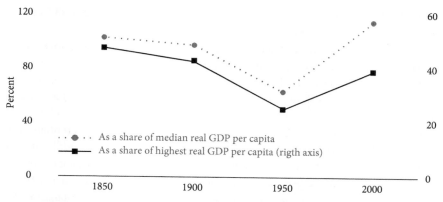

Figure 0.4 Spain's real GDP per capita relative to that of 34 countries with data for 1850, 1900, 1950, and 2000

Source: Author's elaboration based on Maddison Project Database.

possibility that this was merely the economy "bouncing back" therefore deserves due attention.

On closer inspection, however, three reasons suggest that a bouncing back explanation does not fully account for the observed performance. The first reason is the persistence of the high rates of economic growth in the catching-up phase after 1950. This has been shown in detail by the work of economic historians Leandro Prados de la Escosura and Joan Rosés (2009). The growth rates of per capita GDP in the 1951–74 period stood at 5.5 percent, compared to an average of 0.8 percent over the previous century. Before 1950, the sub-period closest to having sustained fast rates of economic growth was 1921–9, which posted rates of 2.8 percent, or about half as fast as in 1951–74, and lasted less than half as long. If catching up after 1950 had simply been the result of some sort of bounceback, we would not have expected it to last for around a quarter of a century. From a comparative perspective, sustaining a growth acceleration over such an extended period is rare (Hausmann, Pritchett, and Rodrik, 2005).

The second and even more important reason that suggests the post-1950 period is not a simple bounceback is that the sources of growth changed. Prados de la Escosura and Rosés (2009) have definitively shown that, while factor accumulation dominated long-run growth up to 1950, it was total factor productivity that led the way in the following quarter century. During the period 1951–74, total factor productivity grew by 3.7 percent annually (compared to 0.3 percent over the previous century and to 1.1 percent during the previous high watermark in 1921–9). Total factor productivity growth remained high at 3.4 percent from 1975 to 1986. This very significant increase in total factor productivity came on top of increased factor accumulation, which was also significantly higher after 1950 than it had been before. Thus, the three decades after 1950 show a remarkable confluence where, as Prados de la Escosura and Rosés (2009) put it, capital accumulation and efficiency gains appear as complementary.

The third reason why the catching-up period is more than just a bounceback to normal is the significant difference in the frequency and intensity of economic contractions after 1950. By focusing on economic "shrinking" and not only on economic growth, we follow the lead of Stephen Broadberry and John Wallis (2017), who have documented the importance of reducing spells of negative growth and their intensity in explaining long-run performance differentials. This issue remains of relevance to development today, including for middle income countries, and has attracted increasing attention in explaining the lack of convergence. For example, Argentina has spent one-third of the time since 1950 in economic contractions, a fact that is pointed to as the main explanation for the country's relatively poor economic performance over the long run (World Bank, 2018b).

Spain fits particularly well the global pattern uncovered by Broadberry and Wallis. In the century before 1950, the Spanish economy spent 40 percent of the time suffering declines in real per capita GDP. In the three decades after 1950, it would shrink in only 10 percent of the years. The declines were also much milder after 1950, averaging an annual drop of 2.1 percent in per capita GDP in the years in which it shrank compared with a much higher average annual decline of 4.1 percent when it shrank over the previous century.

Notably, the reduction in the frequency of shrinking did not come about in a steady fashion. On the contrary, it was a sudden phenomenon. As we can see from Figure 0.5, the decades after 1950 stand out even when we take each quarter century at a time. The quarter century after 1950 has a relatively high average growth rate when the economy is growing (4.9 percent) but even more importantly it is the period with the lowest frequency of shrinking. It is also the period with the lowest rate of economic decline (–2.1 percent) when the economy was shrinking. A relevant question for the literature is therefore how the economy reduced the frequency and intensity of shrinking.

It is therefore reasonable to question the view, discussed above, that in the absence of the Civil War and the distortionary early Franco period, Spain's catching up would have been on its way. Our argument for focusing on the period after 1950 does not merely rest on the fact that we see a faster rate of economic growth—an acceleration that was nevertheless substantial enough to be detected econometrically as a rare upwards break in the trend (Prados de la Escosura, 2017). If that was the only reason to focus on the decades after 1950, a legitimate counterargument would be that other periods in Spanish history also saw robust economic growth and accelerations of total factor productivity growth, for example during the 1920s. In fact, in contrast with an earlier literature that had squarely focused on the "failure" of Spanish industrialization (Nadal, 1975),

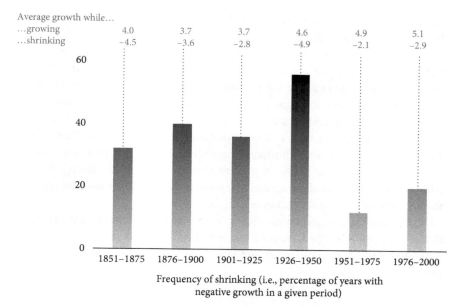

Figure 0.5 Spain's frequency of economic contractions and average growth while growing and shrinking
Source: Author's elaboration based on the Maddison Project Database.

subsequent quantitative economic historians have been able to demonstrate a more nuanced record.

The central question, as Albert Carreras and Xavier Tafunell (2004) put it, remains not whether Spain's economy had grown, but whether or not the economy had grown fast enough to converge with the most advanced economies. Taking this comparative lens, the only two periods before 1950 which showed catching up vis-à-vis the US were 1868–77 and 1918–33—as shown in Figure 0.3. These periods were much too short and sporadic to consider them sustained episodes of convergence.

And what about if we think in terms of an even longer historical perspective? Those familiar with the Empire-building days of the conquest of the Americas or the Spanish Armada may wonder how that history fits into our narrative. Spain had been a relatively rich country and a world power in the fifteenth and sixteenth centuries. Through 1600, it had in fact a similar income per capita as Britain. But in the following two and a half centuries, Spain fell behind, and a wide gap emerged. Regional fragmentation within Spain limited the size of the domestic market, the fiscal capacity of the state, and undermined trade and ultimately economic growth (Grafe, 2012). In a remarkable reversal of fortunes, by 1850 Spain's real per capita GDP was less than half of Britain. Thus, the very long-term economic performance of Spain can only be thought of as subpar. Strikingly, pre-1350 per capita income was only to be exceeded by 1820 (Alvarez Nogal and Prados de la Escosura, 2013).

Across other socioeconomic indicators Spain fell behind its competitors for political influence in the world stage as early as the seventeenth century. By 1650, over half of the population in both Britain and what is now the Netherlands was literate. The corresponding figure in Spain was in the single digits. It would only be in the mid-nineteenth century that more Spaniards knew how to read and write than not, lagging a full two centuries behind Britain and the Netherlands. Regional fragmentation also undermined trade and ultimately economic growth. Low urbanization rates, below 20 percent until the nineteenth century, coupled with a high share of landless agricultural workers, implied that few had access to the opportunities needed to improve their lot.

As we have seen, the economic rise of Spain was unexpected from the perspective of those in 1950. We have seen that it was unlikely in a statistical sense, and moreover, that it was also unexpected in a historical sense. What made this possible?

The argument in brief

This book is concerned with two main questions about Spain's unexpected prosperity. First, why did economic growth take off around the early 1950s? Addressing this first question also implies tackling an earlier one about what may have held Spain back before then. Second, what made it possible to sustain this growth over time?

The question of why growth took off is intriguing given the previous history of failed starts and long spells of relative decline. In this regard, Spain is not that dissimilar from the story of many emerging economies today. From a growth accounting perspective, the answer to why growth resumed is relatively straightforward. After years in which gross capital formation had been at most 15 percent of GDP, it shot up 10 percentage points during the 1950s and stayed at around 25 percent of GDP thereafter. Given the limited size of the state, this was largely private investment. The question therefore becomes what prompted such a sharp supply-side response.

We begin our effort to tackle these questions by reflecting on a characteristic that Spain, until 1950, shared with many developing countries today: fragility, conflict, and violence. At its core, the argument revolves around the inability of the state to effectively control the use of violence for political purposes through all the nineteenth century and well into the twentieth century—a context which is explored in Chapter 1. Political instability had been a feature of Spain not just in the 1930s and 1940s but going all the way back to the early nineteenth century.

From 1812 to 1935 there were a total of 53 *pronunciamientos* or *coups d'état* in Spain (of which 14 successful), seven different constitutions, three civil wars, and two successful but short-lived efforts to install a republican regime.

What helped Spain break out of this situation of political instability? As with any complex historical episode, multiple factors came into play, which are the subject of Chapters 2 and 3. To simplify, a critical element was exogenous to Spain: The new world order around the Cold War made the US reconsider Spain as a potential ally in the defense of the West and led it to throw its support behind the Franco regime. The combination of weak internal opposition—the result of the brutal repression—and a willingness of the population to never repeat the devastation of the Civil War put the Franco regime in the unexpected position of being the guarantor of peace and political stability.

Political stability on its own may not have been enough for the economy to take off. Macroeconomic management became increasingly predictable. Not overnight or fully, but in discernible ways for economic agents to take note and act upon. There were of course specific moments in which reforms took a greater impetus, like around the 1959 Stabilization Plan, but perhaps even more important was the absence of significant backtracking, as discussed in Chapters 4 and 5. In making this argument I differ from the existing literature on the political economy of the Franco regime, which has tended to emphasize reforms as being induced by crisis and adopted reluctantly. This may have been the case early on, but not so by the 1950s or 1960s. While others see a series of discontinuities, I put the emphasis on the continuity of reforms in the direction of more predictable macroeconomic management.

Policy reforms over time tilted the balance towards greater openness to the outside world and, importantly, towards more contestability in markets. Again, this was neither overnight nor full but nevertheless happened in a meaningful way. The economy was beginning to transition, to use the framework of Nobel laureate Douglass North and his coauthors John Wallis and Barry Weingast (2009), from a limited access order to a more open access one. I track this evolution, which can also be interpreted through the lens of inclusive institutions put forward by Daron Acemoglu and James Robinson (2012).

Greater contestability, beyond market entry, is also an important element when answering the second question addressed by this book: What made growth sustainable? Thinking about the proximate sources of growth, the answer is again relatively straightforward: There were plenty of opportunities to catch up technologically. Given the low base of imports and inflows of foreign direct investment, the potential for growth driven by sheer technology transfer was high—as discussed in Chapters 6, 7, and 8. Productivity growth ensued. Growth in this period, like perhaps in other countries during the Golden Age, was overdetermined: Even in the absence of a significant increase in investment, there was a decently sized growth dividend to be had by shifting workers from low productive agriculture to urban activities.

Underpinning this process was a long-term view that put great emphasis on the role of technocracy. The Franco dictatorship came to adopt developmentalism as its source of legitimacy. But many regimes try to follow a similar strategy yet fail. What made technocratic planning successful in Spain? This is a relatively under-researched area in Spanish economic history. I argue that the variety of technocratic planning that was implemented got the basics right—things like urban planning, water, and sanitation—while it also tolerated a greater contest-ability of ideas, allowing for much of development to really take place *outside* of the plan. As competition increased, even if in an uneven form, the process of pro-ductivity gains from structural transformation gave way to those arising from intra-sectoral technological change. The economy was therefore able to increase the complexity of the products it produced and increase its competitiveness, just as the excess supply of agricultural labor was dwindling.

Spain's story of economic success is also of interest because it translated into a broad prosperity. Growth was enjoyed across the income distribution and, as we have seen, even territorial disparities were reduced. Improved access to health, education, housing, and social protection proved critical in allowing the country to catch a second and third wave of growth in the late 1980s and 1990s. The investments in education paid off, a generation later, in allowing Spanish workers and firms to continue to move up the technology ladder and avoid the middle income trap.

Chapter 9 explores how ideas about the future of Spain as a society, and particularly its aspiration to join the European integration process, played a role throughout Spain's economic rise. In answering the question on how growth was sustained I also explore the role of aspirations and the part they played in phenomena such as the rural–urban migration, the decisions of families to invest in educating their children, and the role of women. In short, we observe significant shifts in social norms, but it is prudent to acknowledge that how these changes of social norms contributed to economic development remains insufficiently understood.

The last chapter takes us back to the first issue we addressed: politics. Most authors point to the Franco regime as deficient not only politically but also in terms of its record of economic achievements. The Spanish historian Javier Tusell, one of the most accomplished of his generation, put it clearest: "Francoism can be blamed for delaying a national economic development that could have occurred earlier."[21] Statements like this are true but miss an important point. In terms of

---

[21] Tusell (2011, p. 7). This type of handicapping is also found among the best economic historians: "despite growth which was rapid by the standards of their own historical record, we find distinctly adverse judgements [...] on 1950s Spain [...] because opportunities for better performance were missed" (Crafts and Toniolo, 1996, p. 577).

economic development, the main indictment against the Franco regime is not that growth could have perhaps started five or ten years earlier. Rather, from the perspective of economic performance, an overlooked charge against the Franco regime is that because of its personalistic nature, succession could only imply uncertainty and instability, putting at risk the hard-earned prosperity. It was inevitable that the regime would have a succession problem. For all the economic policies supporting economic growth adopted during the Franco years, the nature of the regime implied that transitioning to a post-Franco regime would carry a risk that could not be hedged and that could have had serious consequences for the prosperity of the country.

We now know that the political transition to democracy turned out well, indeed better than initially expected. The political transition to democracy has been widely praised and labeled as a model in part because it was rather unlikely that it would turn out as well as it did. In fact, there were many instances in which the transition could have been derailed. Spain's economic development under Franco can be likened to a game of Russian roulette: Just because a player got lucky and did not shoot himself, it does not mean that playing Russian roulette is a good idea.

Relevance for the twenty-first century

Every imperfect institution is imperfect in its own way. It is by getting to the bottom of those imperfections and understanding how they played out that we get a sense of how a country grows. Spain's economic rise illustrates that development happens with imperfect institutions. For example, Spain's story shows how greater contestability spreads through different spheres, often reinforcing each other. Sequencing looms large in our story. Because we track in some detail Spain's development over half a century, we can show the dynamic aspects of institutional development with some precision. Sometimes, what was once helpful became hurtful. In the case of Spain, what proved critical to kick-start economic growth—the stability guaranteed by the political regime—turned over time into a liability as the regime was unable to ensure succession at its helm without uncertainty and instability. This speaks directly to a growing literature on how development *actually* happens without adopting perfect institutions.[22]

How Spain sustained its growth spurt is relevant for discussions on the prospects for middle income countries today because many of the challenges Spain faced remain relevant. This is not to say that challenges today are exactly the same. Technological change is perhaps of a qualitatively different nature today

---

[22] As Yuen Yuen Ang (2016) puts it: "What is harder and more useful, instead, is to explain why some nations succeed *despite* ominous starting points and daunting odds" (p. 3).

and, together with a more open trading system, may have combined for pushing still developing economies towards a premature deindustrialization (Rodrik, 2015). At the same time, many of the issues that Spain faced resemble those that occupy the policymakers of today's middle income countries. These include, among others, how to increase tax revenues, provide universal health care and education, and foster competition and productivity. While there is an abundant literature on the middle income trap, it tends to focus on cross-country analyses of a few indicators.[23] By providing a country case study, I hope to show in some detail the importance of the institutional-political framework, as called for in some of the literature on the middle income trap (Agénor, 2016). My argument is not that the specifics of Spain's path to prosperity offer a best practice solution. Rather, the value of this analysis is precisely to document how Spain's economic policies operated within imperfect institutions and, despite their flaws, often supported growth. This is relevant to middle income countries, which face the need to implement policies within institutional settings that are far from the frontier.

Lastly, the insights from Spain's rise in the second half of the twentieth century may also be relevant to Spain's current and future development. Much of the attention today is devoted to explaining a disappointing economic performance in the last couple of decades. It responds to a justified preoccupation about the fact that the catching-up curve had flattened, even before the Great Recession came into the picture. The challenge has only grown bigger with the impact of the global health pandemic in 2020. The context is certainly different than it was while Spain successfully converged, seemingly suggesting that there is little to gain from looking back. That would be a missed opportunity. The great Austrian economist Joseph Schumpeter argued that "most of the fundamental errors currently committed in economic analysis are due to lack of historical experience more often than to any other shortcoming of the economist's equipment."[24] In our case, to follow his lead, we would need to ask ourselves: Do the insights about the role of increasing openness and contestability apply in today's Spain? What role do we anticipate that expectations and aspirations will play in the 30 years after 2020?

Despite having written a critical account of the Franco regime, Gerald Brenan was able to return to live in Spain in 1953, where he settled permanently. At the time of his death in 1987, Spain had been transformed beyond any reasonable expectation he could have had when he crisscrossed the country in 1950. This is a transformation that is worthy of our attention.

---

[23] Despite the popularity of the concept of the middle income trap, it is important to acknowledge that there is no consensus on how to define it. Moreover, different definitions used give rise to rather different sets of countries considered to be in a middle income trap (Glawe and Wagner, 2016) which complicates the ability to draw lessons from cross-country analyses (Im and Rosenblatt, 2015). And some authors, noting that some middle income countries seem to be enjoying the highest rates of growth among all countries, have not only questioned the existence of a "trap" but wondered whether there may not be a "middle income trampoline" (Patel et al., 2018).

[24] Joseph A. Schumpeter (1994[1954]), p. 13.

PART I
FOUNDATIONS

1

The Control of Violence

On his deathbed, General Ramón María Narváez, who had led Spain's government a record seven times in the period from 1844 to 1868, was asked by the priest administering the last rites: "Does Your Excellency forgive all his enemies?" The dying statesman is said to have replied: "I have no enemies. I have had them all shot."[1] This story, true or not, is a fitting image of the predicament affecting Spanish politics during the entire nineteenth century and the first half of the twentieth century. From 1812 to 1935 there were a total of 53 *pronunciamientos* or *coups d'état* in Spain (of which 14 successful), three civil wars, and two successful efforts to install a republican regime.[2] Violence became the norm to resolve political disputes in Spain in the 150 years before 1950. It seemed so entrenched that, from the perspective of 1950, repeated bouts of political violence appeared to be inevitable. Brenan, the British writer that we met in the Introduction, had intended to go back to Spain to write on the essence of the Spanish character, tired as he was of the "hopeless politics of Spain."[3] Breaking out of that cycle of political violence would prove the cornerstone for the country's prosperity in the decades after 1950. To grasp the contrast and the implications of this change, we need first to take a close look at why politics had become so disheartening.

Violence or the threat of it was often present in the way governments changed in the century and a half before 1950. This typically took the form of a *pronunciamiento* by one or more military officers who would publicly proclaim their rebellion against the ruling government. If the rest of the military backed the insurgent, the previous government would leave office and often the country or else suffer a violent end. If the military failed to back the uprising its leaders would typically be executed—something which happened in around 20 separate failed *pronunciamientos* or revolutionary uprisings during the nineteenth century. Regardless of whether a coup succeeded or failed, it was marked by the potential for violence. It was those with the means for violence—military men—that played a critical role in changes in government.

---

[1] As recounted by one of the greatest Spanish intellectuals of all time, Salvador de Madariaga (1958), p. 66. Ironically, Narváez was the leader of the "moderates." A more charitable account of Narváez can be found in Pabón (1983).

[2] A recent synthesis of modern Spain thus concluded that "[w]hat really dominated nineteenth-century Spain was political instability." (Shubert and Álvarez Junco, 2018, p. 3).

[3] Brenan (1951, p. viii).

Unexpected Prosperity: How Spain Escaped the Middle Income Trap. Oscar Calvo-Gonzalez, Oxford University Press.
© Oscar Calvo-Gonzalez 2021. DOI: 10.1093/oso/9780198853978.003.0002

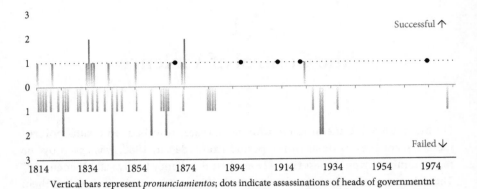

Vertical bars represent *pronunciamientos*; dots indicate assassinations of heads of governmentnt

Figure 1.1 *Pronunciamientos* (*coups d'état*) and assassinations of heads of government, 1814–1984

Note: The pronunciamientos include a variety of military uprisings.

Source: Own elaboration with data from Linz, Montero, and Ruiz (2005) on pronunciamientos and Martorell and Juliá (2012) on assassinations. The *coup* that led to the Civil War (1936-1939) is shown as a failed one since its original aim was to gain power instantly.

The recurrent nature of such *pronunciamientos* meant that violence was never far from politics. In the 60 years after 1814 there were over 40 uprisings, or an average of one every 18 months. Importantly, these were spread throughout the entire period, as shown in Figure 1.1. The figure displays the number of *pronunciamientos* and other types of uprisings, whether successful (shown above the *x* axis) or failed (below the *x* axis). For example, in 1844 there were a record number of three failed uprisings representing the whole political spectrum of progressive, liberal, and traditionalist forces that resulted in dozens of their leaders executed.

The decades after 1940 during the Franco dictatorship also stand out as the longest period being free from violent changes of government since the beginning of the nineteenth century. When the Franco regime set out to celebrate its "Twenty-Five Years of Peace" in the 1960s it was, as the political opposition stressed, a "peace of the cemeteries," but it was also a break with the history of the previous century and a half. This is not to say that there was no political violence during the Franco period. The repression of the Franco regime was brutal, especially in the 1940s. But it was largely state violence. In the decades after 1950, the state effectively secured for itself the exclusive use of force to keep the peace and enforce the law, something that had proven elusive for the Spanish state since the beginning of the nineteenth century. As happened in other countries, the control of violence and the ensuing political stability underpinned the process of economic development.

Why is the control of violence central to economic development?

The control of violence as a core function of the state has long been recognized by thinkers of different traditions. Peace and a tolerable administration of justice were two of three ingredients—the other being easy taxes—that Adam Smith identified as true prerequisites for prosperity. The phrase "the monopoly on the use of violence" was introduced by Max Weber, who went as far as saying that the group that has such monopoly on the legitimate use of violence *is* the state (Weber, 1919[2004]). More recently, the criticality of violence control for political and economic development has been emphasized by a diverse range of authors such as Mancur Olson (2000), Francis Fukuyama (2011, 2014), and Nobel laureate Douglass North and his coauthors John Wallis and Barry Weingast (2009). These contributions are particularly relevant for shedding light on Spain's path to prosperity because of their explicit link between violence, the state, and markets.

To the extent that violence reduces rents, groups with violence potential that benefit from rents have incentives to refrain from violence. Controlling access to rents is how limited access social orders solve the problem of violence. This insight is also at the heart of what Daron Acemoglu and James Robinson (2012) refer to as extractive political and economic institutions. It is also, as Francis Fukuyama (2014) points out, what an older political science literature referred to as neopatrimonialism. Regardless of one's preferred label, a common element in these explanatory frameworks is that in a limited access order, or under extractive institutions, competition runs counter to the logic that sustains the polity.

In contrast, in open access orders the problem of violence is solved through competition. The state has a monopoly on the use of violence both in theory and in practice, and power is contested openly. All citizens have the right to form political or economic organizations, as long as they are not violent. Open access helps sustain both economic and political competition as well as an active civil society. Competition in the marketplace, whether it be for products, ideas, or policies, generates the conditions for Schumpeterian creative destruction to take hold. As a result, economic growth is more likely to be sustained and to be spread widely in a society under open access order.

This does not necessarily mean that economic growth will always be higher under open access orders. Economic growth can happen for many reasons within a limited access order. The elite in control has an incentive to increase the monopolistic rents which it is enjoying, provided that any such measures do not undermine their privileged position. As such, economic growth in limited access orders is likely to be less inclusive and, depending on how unstable the ruling coalition is, it may be marked by reversals of fortunes.

The conceptual framework of North and coauthors is particularly helpful for understanding Spain's path to prosperity. To anticipate the argument, the three decades after 1950 can be thought of as the moment in which Spain's limited access order matured and reached the threshold of an open access order. This is what makes the decades after 1950 qualitatively different from previous episodes of economic growth and what sets the foundation for prosperity to be sustained. The framework of closed and open access orders has proven useful to analyze the transitions of early developed countries like Britain or Germany (North et al., 2009) and subsequently has also been applied to the process of economic development, but not yet to Spain.[4]

Applying this framework to our case involves, above all, addressing three basic questions to the historical record. The first question explores how effectively did the state control violence. The second and third questions revolve around the extent to which open competition or monopolistic practices ruled the economy and the polity. In answering these questions, we distinguish four periods in Spanish political and economic development since 1800 (see Table 1.1). We will flesh out the argument below, but a first broad-brush picture of the four periods is in order, especially since breaking down Spain's modern history in this way is not necessarily standard in the existing literature.[5]

Table 1.1 From a closed to an open access order

	Does the state control political violence?	Is access to political organizations open?	Is access to economic organizations open?
1800–75	No	No	No
1875–1950	Partially. Less frequent but highly significant episodes of violence (e.g., political assassinations, coups, Civil War 1936–39)	No, except for short periods (1931–36)	No
1950–80	Yes, except for instances associated with the transition from the dictatorship	No before 1977. Yes after 1977	Increasingly so
Since 1980	Yes	Yes	Yes

Note: The date of 1980 as the beginning of the open access order is approximate as it could have been thought to begin with the approval of the democratic constitution in 1978 or the peaceful change in government that took place after the 1982 elections.

Source: Author's own elaboration.

[4] Interestingly, it was applied to South Korea's development as one of nine country case studies in North et al. (2013) that illustrate how the framework of limited and open access orders sheds lights on the challenges of promoting economic development.

[5] While our approach is new, it is not at odds with more traditional ones. For example, the discussion in Shubert and Álvarez Junco (2018) is arranged as follows: crisis of the old regime (1808–33),

The first period was marked by fragility—the era of the *pronunciamientos* and civil wars. Violence was not fully controlled by the state. Violent changes in government were commonplace throughout this first period, as we saw in Figure 1.1. This led to volatile changes in institutions and large swings in access to political power, while access to economic organizations remained largely closed. A much lower prevalence of political violence characterized the second period, which started around 1876 with a relatively stable "Restoration" of the Bourbon monarchy and a pact between the two main political parties of the time to peacefully take turns in government. Violence was reduced through political and economic institutions that remained dominated by entrenched narrow interests. In the terminology of North and coauthors, Spain evolved from a fragile to a basic limited access order during the century and a half before 1950.

In contrast, after 1950 we saw not only the control of violence by the state but also the maturing of a limited access order where elites increasingly competed nonviolently with each other for economic and political power and were increasingly subject to the rule of law. Access to economic opportunities went beyond elites and became increasingly open. Competition eventually also reached the political marketplace, culminating in a transition to an open access order. The distinction between closed and open access orders makes it clear how critical the years from 1950 to 1980 were and suggests that we focus on this period to understand Spain's *unexpected prosperity*.

But before doing so we need to provide the necessary historical context for the argument that will follow. Our effort, as in a growing economics literature that finds that institutional arrangements from the distant past have long-lasting implications, is to search for clues that will help understand both why economic development may have been delayed and why it happened when it did.[6] Therefore, our historical account will focus only on the most critical issues. Our guide for deciding what to cover is the framework by North and coauthors presented above. As with any analytic narrative, this means that our account will necessarily be a simplification of reality. Our explanation should be no more complex than it needs to but without falling into excessive simplification. The rest of this chapter tries to strike that balance.

---

liberalism (1833–74), Restoration (1874–1914), quest for modernization (1914–36), Civil War (1936–9), Franco dictatorship (1939–75), and democratic transition to consolidation (1975–96). We lump together the first two periods (1808–33 and 1833–74) on account of how widespread was violence throughout. Our second period covers a larger set of "traditional" periods which have typically focused on key events like the Civil War or political regimes like the Franco dictatorship in their approach to periodization.

[6] In the case of Spain, for example, the role of the *Reconquest* of Muslim-held territory from 800 to 1492 has been found to have effects on the location of economic activity in today's Spain (Oto-Perarías and Romero-Ávila, 2016).

Why was political violence so persistent?

The fact that violence had been a persistent force in political life in Spain in the century and a half before 1950 begs the question why this was the case. Surprisingly, this has not been a central question in the historiography of Spain until recently. Even then, most of the effort has been concentrated on explaining violence in specific instances as opposed to the central role played by violence in politics at large.[7] In short, the answer offered here is related to the long undoing of the absolutist regime in place until the early nineteenth century. The challenge of replacing the absolutist monarchy with a new regime was not exclusive to Spain. Most European countries struggled with fundamental questions such as the source of sovereignty or to what extent the political franchise ought to be enlarged. In the case of Spain, frustrated attempts at creating a liberal-constitutional order consumed much of the nineteenth century. There were repeated violent fights, and the use of violence became entrenched as the norm to resolving fundamental political disputes. As a result, instability remained the norm.

A fragile state, 1800–75

Since the beginning of the nineteenth century, the most extreme political violence took the form of civil wars. Most people today identify "the" Spanish Civil War with the conflict from 1936 to 1939. But this was not the only such civil war that affected Spain in modern history. Even more deadly, in relation to the country's population at the time, was the war fought from 1833 to 1840 between supporters of Queen Isabella II and the pretender *Infante* Charles, her uncle. The *Infante* challenged the legitimacy of the Queen as successor to her father Ferdinand VII, who had died in 1833 without any male offspring.[8] But this first *carlista* war—there would be two more such wars later in the century—was much more than a dynastic battle. It was a fight between two concepts of how inclusive the political order should be. Those on the side of Queen Isabella II defended a more liberal regime and those in the *Infante* Charles camp sought a return to a traditional absolutist monarchy.

As in the case of the civil war a hundred years later, repression against civilians was brutal. Women were often targeted, and, on the battlefront, prisoners were

---

[7] The historian Julio Aróstegui, in an edited volume (1994) on violence and politics in Spain, noted the paradox of few studies on the topic compared to its historical importance. While there has been a burgeoning of case studies since then, especially on the repression after the Civil War, Aróstegui's prescient warning that such studies need to be guided by a clear conceptual framework remains valid (p. 15).

[8] Deaths totaled 150,000 in a total population of less than 15 million.

routinely executed. After some early victories by the *carlistas*, the superior forces of the loyalists put them in an advantageous position. The war ended with an agreement by which the *carlistas* gave up their demands in exchange for being incorporated into the Spanish army with their rank and honors preserved. How this agreement to end the war came to be provides another example of the role that violence played in settling disputes: The leader of the *carlista* army executed those of his fellow rebel army generals that were against the deal; with those opposed to the agreement killed, he went on to sign the peace. The fact that this civil war ended not with the crushing defeat of the *carlistas* but with a settlement that accommodated the losing side was evidence of the relatively weak position of liberals. Arguably, it helped entrench violence in Spanish politics as the *carlistas* themselves remained a force in Spanish society for over a century, causing two additional wars in the nineteenth century. This is in line with cross-country empirical evidence that suggests that wars that end with a decisive military victory for one side lead to a more stable peace (Page Fortna, 2004; Toft, 2009). Spain in the nineteenth century saw no such decisive victories for either side and the country lurched from left to right, in what a historian decried as "too much backtracking."[9]

The political back and forth—with violence—was a constant during the nineteenth century. The dismantling of the absolutist regime had taken several decades and a great deal of violence even before the first *carlista* war. The process started in 1808 when Napoleon, for whom the control of the Iberian Peninsula was a strategic objective in support of his imperial ambitions, first sent armies into Spain. Napoleon then forced the Spanish King Charles IV and his successors to abdicate to him. Having secured the dynastic rights from Charles IV, Napoleon appointed his brother Joseph as King of Spain. These events led to a popular uprising in Spain against the occupying French army. The ensuing war, which lasted until 1814, is referred to in Spain as the "War of Independence" and elsewhere as the "Peninsular War." But it was more than a war of independence or the backdrop to a bigger geopolitical conflict between France and Britain.

Importantly, there were elements of a civil war also in the 1808–14 confrontation. With the defeat of the French in 1814 and the return of Ferdinand VII as an absolutist king, the modernizing Spanish liberals who, during the war, had created a liberal constitutional order had to go on exile. Thereafter, a frequent back-and-forth would ensue. In 1820, on the back of a successful *pronunciamiento*, the absolutist king was forced to take his oath to the liberal constitution to remain in power, only to be restored yet again as absolutist king in 1823 with the help of

---

[9] The phrase ("*demasiados retrocesos*" in Spanish) is by Ramón Carande, one of the greatest Spanish historians of all time, who coined it when asked by a journalist to sum up Spanish history in two words. The phrase has stuck, and other great historians like Josep Fontana or Borja de Riquer have referred to it as a way of capturing the essence of the nineteenth and first part of the twentieth centuries.

100,000 French troops. Over the next decade there would be repeated conflicts, culminating upon the death of Ferdinand VII in a somewhat more liberal regime under his daughter by Isabella II and the civil war—discussed above—between loyalists and *carlistas* that ended with the defeat of the traditionalists in 1840. After 1840 the fight nevertheless continued, now among the liberals who had been themselves divided between moderates and progressives since 1812.

How open would the political process be remained at the core of disputes between moderates and progressives. One sticking point was the extent of the electoral franchise. In another example of the lurching between extremes that represented the nineteenth century, there was much backtracking in the extent of the electoral franchise. The 1812 Constitution had been one of the earliest in the world to grant indirect universal male suffrage but would soon be reversed, the first of several drastic swings throughout the nineteenth and twentieth centuries on the extent of the franchise (Figure 1.2).

The country was not unique in having a limited electoral franchise; in fact, Spain was not far from the median of 20 European countries, and at times it was well above (Figure 1.2). But more unusual were the large swings, especially the reversals, in the extent of the electoral franchise. This backtracking contrasts with the experience of other European countries, like Britain or Sweden, in which the extension of the franchise was more gradual (Acemoglu and Robinson, 2000). Spain was the only European country where, after having been enlarged, the electoral franchise would be cut by more than 10 percentage points. Using the dataset compiled by Robert Goldstein (1983), which provides data at five-year intervals for 20 European countries from 1815 to 1915, out of the top ten episodes of

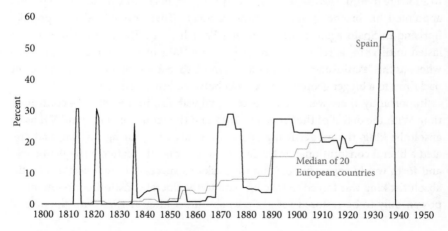

Figure 1.2 The expansion of the electoral franchise, 1800–1950

Source: Goldstein (1983) for European countries (Austria, Belgium, Bulgaria, Denmark, Finland, France, Germany, Greece, Hungary, Italy, Netherlands, Norway, Portugal, Romania, Russia, Serbia, Spain, Sweden, Switzerland, and United Kingdom) and Linz, Montero, and Linz et al. (2005) for Spain.

franchise reductions in 1815–1915, Spain accounted for four. In fact, reductions in the electoral franchise were relatively rare in the rest of Europe.

Another sticking point between Spanish moderates and progressives throughout the nineteenth century was the source of national sovereignty and what this meant for personal liberty. Moderates insisted that national sovereignty was shared between the monarch and the people. The progressive position stated that the monarchy derived its legitimacy in the sovereignty of the people and called for a division of powers, legal equality, and personal liberty. In a pattern that would by now be familiar to the reader, individual liberties would be constitutionally enshrined and subsequently rescinded several times throughout the nineteenth century.

Moderates and progressives also disagreed about the role of the Catholic Church and what to do with its lands. The Church had become a vast landowner following centuries of accumulating lands, often through bequeaths to the Church. Much land held by religious orders and monasteries was not farmed but by law could not be sold or transferred. The disentailment of Church lands, to be followed by sale in public auction, had been advocated since the late eighteenth century as a measure to boost agricultural productivity. Disentailment was also a way to raise public revenues that could ease the burden of public debt. Some expected a new middle class of property owners to arise. However, when the disentailment of Church lands took place in the mid-nineteenth century it did not alter the structure of land ownership in a significant sense. About one-quarter of land changed hands, yet the landless remained so. The sale of municipal lands did not benefit the poorest peasants who had traditionally complemented their earnings by foraging and collecting wood in commons now privatized. In fact, the commons had played a range of positive roles in rural areas. For example, commons have been shown to contribute to social capital formation as well as to higher life expectancy and heights, as well as helping poorer households in affording sending their children to school (Beltrán Tapia, 2012, 2013, and 2015).

These cleavages over the openness of political and economic institutions were not unique to Spain, but the role that violence and the military played in them was particularly salient. This was the case even during periods of apparent political stability. For example, General Narváez, with whom we started this chapter as someone who had earned his reputation for a ruthless exercise of power, ordered at least 400 executions of those involved in uprisings against his rule. Narváez led a government based on a narrow coalition of wealthy landowners and industrialists. He was also responsible for banning all workers' societies and for creating in 1844 the Civil Guard, a new police force tasked with policing the countryside and which would become central to the repression of peasants for over a century.

Intense political instability would make another comeback from 1868 to 1876. In those eight years the country rejected a monarch who was forced into exile, called in a foreign king to head a constitutional monarchy, and installed and quickly dismantled a republic. All this was followed by two *pronunciamientos* that paved the way for the return of the Bourbon dynasty in the person of King Alfonso XII. During this chaos, the traditionalists saw an opening and assembled 50,000 armed men who fought in yet another *carlist* civil war (1872–6). What stands out in the case of Spain is not the difficulty of replacing the absolutist regimes with a more open political one or that there was a counterrevolutionary movement, but that the latter retained throughout this period the capacity "to undertake extensive political violence" (Romeo, 2015, p. 49).

While political instability marked this period, there was nevertheless some economic growth. From 1850 to 1883, real per capita GDP grew 1.3 percent annually, roughly twice the 0.6 percent annual growth that it would register from 1883 to 1929. Thus, as perceptively asked by the great economic historian Leandro Prados de la Escosura, how can we square the fact of economic growth from 1850 to 1883 with our characterization of Spain being a fragile state in this period?[10]

The presence of growth under fragility is not at odds with the theoretical framework of access regimes that we have adopted here. Growth can happen even in a fragile setting for a variety of reasons, including external factors such as terms of trade shocks or technology diffusion. The apparent paradox of growth under fragility is more widespread than one may imagine. But fragile countries tend not to be able to sustain this growth (McKechnie et al., 2018). Moreover, economic growth under fragility is typically low quality in the sense that it is often concentrated in a few sectors, subject to significant shocks, and is typically not inclusive (McMillan et al., 2017).

The spurts of economic growth of Spain in the mid-nineteenth century fit the above description of unsustainability and low quality. First, growth was concentrated in a few years.[11] Combined with the fact that structural change did not contribute to an increase in labor productivity growth during the period,[12] it suggests that growth in some periods of the mid-nineteenth century may not have fully qualified as "modern economic growth," understood as a sustained process that moves labor and other resources from lower to higher productivity activities. The limited extent of urbanization reinforces the view that those spurts of growth throughout the nineteenth century did not amount to an extensive economic transformation.

---

[10] As he put it "contrary to common economic wisdom, robust economic performance took place in a context of political instability which included the 1854 liberal uprising and the 1868 Glorious Revolution." (Prados de la Escosura, 2017, p. 18).

[11] As Prados de la Escosura (2017) himself points out, economic growth was concentrated even within the 1850–83 period: 2.1 percent in 1850–5, 0.4 percent in the longer 1855–66 period, 2.9 percent in 1866–73, and 0.6 percent in the longer 1873–83 period.

[12] Also shown by Prados de la Escosura (2017, p. 31) and, for inequality, (Prados de la Escosura, 2008).

A limited access order, 1875–1950

By the late nineteenth century, there was a widespread recognition that political instability had taken its toll on the country. Speaking in the Senate floor in 1876, the politician and writer Juan Valera captured the mood when he called for "the end of the era of the pronunciamientos, for the law to prevail, and for a country with a stable government."[13] A pact was reached between the Liberal and Conservative parties to limit political competition in exchange for stability. The two main parties agreed to simply alternate in office, a corrupt arrangement that served well the respective elites. The regime would come to be known as the Restoration since it involved the return of the Bourbon dynasty to the throne.

Spain under the Restoration proved to be a model example of a limited access order. Above all, the fact that the arrangement became known contemporaneously as the "peaceful turn" ("*el turno pacífico*") leaves little doubt as to its fundamental objective being the reduction of violence.[14] As expected in a limited access order, political power was shared only within a restricted group. The liberal and conservative parties that took turns in power excluded from power factions both on the right (antiliberal Catholics and traditionalists) and on the left (republicans and revolutionaries).

The achievements in terms of the reduction of political violence were remarkable at first. There were 13 peaceful transitions of power as envisaged by the "turn" from 1876 to 1910. And there were no *pronunciamientos* from the mid-1880s to 1923, as we saw in Figure 1.1. The political system was formally a parliamentary constitutional monarchy and therefore the "turn" required the large-scale manipulation of elections. In practice, it was done as follows. When it was time for a change in party, the outgoing prime minister would resign and the king would nominate a new prime minister from the opposing party. Local and provincial authorities would be replaced and new elections would be called that would be sure to return a parliamentary majority to the new government because the two parties would have previously agreed on who would be the official candidate in each electoral circumscription. This type of electoral manipulation, while centrally orchestrated, required the cooperation of local strongmen, *caciques*, who engaged in vote-buying and outright fraud to ensure that the winner was in fact the desired candidate.

The extraction of rents, and their allocation through patronage networks, was essential to the system—much in line with the stylized description of a limited access order by North and coauthors. In such settings, rents can play a positive

---

[13] As quoted in Martorell and Juliá (2012), p. 136.

[14] While there is a vast literature on the Restoration, I am not aware of any efforts at interpreting it through the lens of the limited and open access order framework. For an account of the period in English see Moreno-Luzón (2018), who incorporates in his synthesis the great progress made in understanding the nuances of this period made by researchers in recent years.

short-term role since they help control violence and align incentives of a variety of actors. Such was the case of Spain as the nineteenth century progressed. Industrialization, despite its late start, resulted in increases in factory jobs. Manufacturing as a share of GDP rose from 18 percent in 1870 to 27 percent in 1900. Improvements in transport were notable, contributing to increased market integration for commodities and shifts in the geography of economic activity (Tirado et al., 2002; Rosés, 2003; Rosés and Sánchez-Alonso, 2004). As trade integration proceeded, regional specialization took place (Rosés et al., 2010). Cities grew, moderately at first and substantially in the three decades after 1900.[15] The density of the paved road network more than doubled from 1876 to 1900. Railroads, which had seen a major construction push already in the 1860s, significantly increased from around 6,000 kilometers of track in 1876 to over 11,000 by the end of the century.

While there was economic growth during this period, access to economic opportunities remained limited. A law that had mandated school enrollment for children between 6 and 9 years of age remained unenforced, as evidenced by the fact that the gross enrollment rate of boys in primary education barely edged up from 48 to 52 percent from 1860 to 1900. Economic power remained concentrated. A variety of interests colluded to secure oligopolistic rents. Railroad companies managed to obtain favorable concessions and financial bailouts when needed, so that profits to the investors did not depend on the operational success of the railroads (Cuéllar, 2018). Protectionism was on the rise (Fraile, 1991 and Tortella, 1994), with a resulting lack of competitiveness in international markets of most industrial products that were produced domestically.

Political and economic power were inseparably linked. The richest man in Spain in the nineteenth century, José de Salamanca, made his fortune in rent-extracting activities like arranging a foreign loan to the state, the monopolies on salt and tobacco, and railroad concessions (Tortella, 2011). Salamanca was known, even at the time, for shady deals and conflicts of interests. He had business dealings with Narváez, was accused of having financially benefited during his tenure as Minister of Finance, and even helped the Regent with stock market tips.[16] While an earlier literature may have underappreciated the economic transformation of the late nineteenth and early twentieth centuries, its characterization of the political economy was essentially correct: "an alliance of minorities that held power [. . . by] manipulating a parliamentary monarchy to maintain their

---

[15] The share of the urban population increased from 23 percent in 1860 to 29 percent by 1900 and 37 percent by 1930. Significantly, thanks to an increase in housing supply and urban infrastructure, rents were relatively affordable and helped avoid the proliferation of slums around the cities (Carmona et al., 2017; note that, while their urbanization rates differ from the ones shown here on account of different thresholds used, the trends of urbanization are the same). All data in this paragraph is from Carreras and Tafunell (2005).

[16] A biography of Salamanca, who would receive the noble title of marquis from the monarch, carries the revealing subtitle of "the great rascal" (Rico, 1994).

positions."[17] In our conceptual framework, the difficulty distinguishing between economic and political organizations is an indication of fragility of the political order.

The assessment of the liberal reforms in the nineteenth century in the current literature is therefore mixed. On one hand, liberal reforms are acknowledged as well-meaning efforts to better define property rights and reduce transactions costs, at least on paper. As such, these reforms are widely seen as positive for growth, even if their impact is hard to quantify. On the other hand, the literature points out that there were deficiencies in the implementation of reforms, instances where elites benefited from departures between *de jure* equality and *de facto* practices. Such deficiencies are sometimes seen as having resulted in "smaller gains for economic growth than might have been expected" from the range of reforms adopted (Tedde de Lorca, 1994).

This assessment can be taken a step further by drawing on an important insight from the explanatory framework used here, namely that rents will either hurt or help economic growth depending on the starting conditions. If rents contribute to reduce violence, they may not hurt but help the expansion of economic activity. The "deficiencies" in the implementation of reforms may have been essential to bring about a decline in violence and thus they may have supported, instead of hampered, growth. The critical question to ask is as follows: What is a realistic counterfactual in the absence of such "deficiencies" in the institutional framework, one closer to the conditions of a perfectly competitive market economy or one closer to a situation that slides back into violence? If we think the latter, there is little point lamenting the detrimental impact on growth of a far from perfectly competitive set of institutions. As the development policy practice shows, simply transplanting institutions from developed to developing countries often fails to produce the desired results. This is why, as North et al. (2013) argue, the principal problem of development is making improvements within the limited access order, moving away from fragility and towards more mature versions of limited access orders.

But not all regimes based on rents evolve in a similar manner. Importantly, in the case of Spain in the late nineteenth and early twentieth century, the economic rents that fueled political stability did not induce increases in economic efficiency. Total factor productivity grew at a paltry 0.2 percent per year in 1880–1920, while the rate of growth of the capital stock also failed to accelerate (Prados de la Escosura and Rosés, 2009). The case of infrastructure investment in Spain under the Restoration is a particularly good example of how rents—while serving well

---

[17] Herr (1974, p. 99). Herr sees much continuity in the broad outlines of the political economy of Spain throughout the nineteenth and early twentieth centuries, arguing that effectively the absolute monarchy had been replaced by "a kind of joint stock company in which the monarch held some of the shares but not the controlling interest."

the logic of a limited access order—may not support long-term economic development. In fact, infrastructure investment in large nationwide networks did not have a positive effect on the country's economic growth between 1850 and 1935 (Herranz-Loncán, 2007). This seemingly puzzling result is explained in part by the importance of pork barrel politics in road expenditure distribution, which resulted in wasteful spending (Curto-Grau et al., 2012). These roads were often redundant or located in areas of little economic dynamism.

The stability of the order under the Restoration would come under pressure in exactly the way that our explanatory framework would suggest. As groups excluded from the power-sharing agreement grew in significance, the ability of the two parties to command enough control was eroded. The recent historiography on the period has stressed that society was far from being stuck. For example, urban workers gained strength because of the incipient transformation of the economy. It is precisely because of this economic and social transformation that the Restoration regime became unsustainable. The underlying balance of power shifted, and the transacting elites could no longer deliver on the original bargain.

Political leaders were fully aware of the growing tensions but proved unable to address them. The principal architect of the peaceful turn and six-time prime minister, Antonio Cánovas del Castillo, would come to conclude that the "social problem" of poor living conditions had become a political problem. For the conservative Cánovas, this meant that the state ought to "intervene in the growing conflicts between capital and labor."[18] Across the political aisle, the Liberals shared in the concern. José Canalejas, who would rise through the ranks of the Liberal party to become its leader, worried that the common people had begun to question the regime. Canalejas worried explicitly about the potential for violence, asking himself: "How can we be surprised that the classes that are sidelined appeal to force, as they have always done, as a last resort?" Despite these diagnoses, little was done in practice to address these concerns. Universal male suffrage was reintroduced in 1890 but did not imply significant changes in the working and living conditions of most of the population. A Commission for Social Reform created in 1883 was largely limited to collecting information with only a trickle of social legislation, as the ruling parties shied away from intervening in the labor market (Domènech, 2011). Even for a Liberal like Canalejas, an overriding principle was "not to replace the tyranny of the few with the tyranny of the many."[19]

Very much in line with a limited access order, few protections were accorded to workers. A comparative perspective will help to illustrate what this meant for workers. We can in fact benchmark Spain against 17 European countries on labor

---

[18] Speech before the *Ateneo* of Madrid on November 10, 1890, as quoted in Seco Serrano (2000, p. 258).
[19] Quotes by Canalejas in this paragraph are from his speech before the *Royal Academy of Jurisprudence and Legislation*, Madrid, December 10, 1894 (available at the National Library of Spain).

market regulations such as limits on working hours or restrictions on child labor as well as on the extent of social insurance mechanisms such as accident compensation and insurance against unemployment, sickness, and old age (Huberman and Lewchuk, 2003). Spain, as shown in Figure 1.3, lagged behind not only the most advanced European countries of the day but also the median European country. Despite some measures taken in Spain in the latter part of the period, such as prohibiting night labor for children (in 1900) and women (in 1909) and the introduction of factory inspections (in 1907), Spain remained towards the bottom. By 1913 it was 15th out of 17 European countries in terms of the protection for workers of its labor compact. At the same time, Figure 1.3 also clearly shows that, like the rest of Europe, Spain saw significant transformations in the early twentieth century.

The statements by Canalejas about the potential for violence would turn out to be ill omens. Both Cánovas and Canalejas would be assassinated by anarchists while holding the presidency of the government, in 1897 and 1912, respectively. These magnicides, like other instances of violence, had consequences. After the assassination of Cánovas, the renewal of the leadership would prove problematic, giving rise to infighting between rival factions (Moreno-Luzón, 2018, p. 61). New cross-country empirical evidence suggests, in fact, that assassinations of leaders tend to enflame low-scale conflicts (Jones and Olken, 2009).

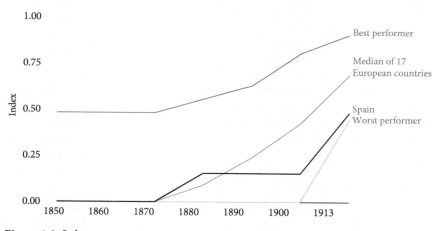

Figure 1.3 Labor compact in comparative perspective

Note: The index takes higher values the more protections are in place. By 'best' performing I denote the country with the highest degree of protection for workers. While excessive labor market protection can have negative consequences for welfare, given the low levels of employment protection during the period it seems less controversial to equate greater protection with better performance. The 17 countries are Austria, Belgium, Bulgaria, Denmark, Finland, France, Germany, Hungary, Italy, Netherlands, Norway, Portugal, Russia, Spain, Sweden, Switzerland, and the United Kingdom.

Source: Huberman and Lewchuk (2003).

Political assassinations were just one manifestation of a new type of violence that originated from social groups that were excluded from the political process. A mix of anticlericalism, nationalism, republicanism, anarchism, and socialism would make for a turbulent beginning of the twentieth century. It took many forms, from national strikes to violent uprisings—as in the so-called *Tragic Week* in Barcelona in 1909. Anarchists, which had initially been particularly successful among the landless peasants in Andalucía, spread widely into urban centers and were eventually responsible for numerous high-profile episodes of political violence.

Another way in which violence added to political instability was through external wars, particularly in Cuba and Morocco. They are also manifestations of a conflict between the citizenry and a state over the extent to which the polity is open. The case of Cuba is significant. From 1868 until 1898 there were three wars in Cuba on account of demands by locals for a greater say in the running of the island. These demands were only partially met. Cuba was first turned into a province of Spain in 1869 and later granted autonomy in 1897, through an arrangement similar to that of Canada and the UK in 1867. But it was too little too late. With the support of the United States, which declared war on Spain in 1898 after the US Navy ship *Maine* was sunk in the Havana port in disputed circumstances, the Cuban independentists prevailed. These events had an outsized influence in Spanish political life over the following decades.

Why does Cuba matter for the political development of Spain? The Spanish military was simply crushed by that of the US, leading to the loss of the Spanish colonies of Puerto Rico, the Philippines, as well as Cuba. The events in 1898 came to be known in the country quite simply as "The Disaster" and proved to be a psychological watershed for Spanish society. At the turn of the twentieth century, the change from an absolutist to a liberal order was not only incomplete but it had been associated with the country going from great empire to minor European power. It also polarized the political landscape. Military officers complained about a "stab in the back" by the government—a viewpoint in which the blame for the defeat belonged exclusively to an incompetent civilian government which had undermined and impeded the Spanish military. This argument, not dissimilar to the one that the German military elite espoused in the aftermath of World War I, would dominate the thinking of the Spanish military officer corps for decades to come, further strengthening the antiliberal bent of the military.

The unraveling of the "peaceful turn" proceeded gradually but surely. The growing dissatisfaction of the working classes in urban areas, coupled with the introduction of the universal male suffrage in 1890, led to an increasing number of left-wing parties being represented in parliament. As the Liberal and Conservative parties became weaker, the local elites increasingly saw the opportunity to put forward their own candidates for parliament, disregarding directions from the center. As a result, the share of members of parliament not affiliated with either the Liberal or Conservative party increased. After 1916, neither the Liberal nor Conservative party would be able to reach a simple majority in parliament, a sharp contrast with the situation in earlier decades, when each party alternated in power with majorities of around two-thirds of seats in parliament.

The shifts in the balance of power had wide-ranging consequences. The allocation of public spending also changed (Curto-Grau et al., 2012). As noted above, in earlier years districts that elected official candidates had been rewarded. In contrast, as independent deputies played an increasingly bigger role, it would be the provinces that elected independent candidates that would receive more public funds in later years. Cracks in the political system kept widening, and after the assassination of Canalejas in 1912, the leader of the Conservative party, Antonio Maura, refused to alternate in power with the Liberal party. This led to sharp divisions within the parties. But this did not mean that access to political power had become more open: At the end of the regime in 1923 there were 144 congressmen that had a relative also in Congress, and the prime minister counted nine family members among the congressmen.[20]

World War I added to the momentum for transformation. Spain remained neutral throughout the war and benefited from rising international prices, posting rare trade surpluses as imports plummeted. Economic activity increased but not without tensions. While wages increased, they did not keep up with inflation for large segments of society. Bread riots broke out in cities and the first general strike in Spanish history took place in 1916. After the war, the working class would step up its activism and outright challenged the political order.[21]

Social violence took many forms, including strikes, bombings, and acts of sabotage. In response, the authorities suspended the constitutional guarantees with increasing frequency. Social violence reached "revolutionary dimensions" (Linz et al., 2005, p. 1045). The army, charged with maintaining public order and with the support of the upper classes, became increasingly ruthless in the suppression of workers' movements. The army also drifted towards being increasingly involved in political disputes, all with the implicit support of the monarch. In 1923, in a return to the era of the *pronunciamientos*, general Miguel Primo de Rivera revolted against the civilian government. In response, King Alfonso XIII appointed Primo de Rivera as his prime minister, who immediately created a military directorate, and dissolved parliament.

The dictatorship of Primo de Rivera, as well as the Republic that would succeed it in 1931, would each have very different features. The dictatorship was characterized by efforts at modernizing the nation within a regime that promised to ensure law and order as its number one priority. In contrast, the Republic would be a remarkably ambitious effort to expand access to both political and economic

---

[20] Tusell (1991). Parliamentary data from Linz et al. (2005).
[21] For a synthesis of the period 1914–23 see Townson (2018), pp. 63–75.

power. For example, female universal suffrage was introduced, public education was widely expanded, full religious freedom was granted for the first time in Spain's history, and a whole host of institutional changes were put in place affecting labor markets, including in rural areas. Why do we then lump these regimes together and take 1875–1950 as a single period?

The reason to consider these distinct regimes as part of a longer period is because none of these regimes managed to sustainably control violence. Without a firm control of violence, they could not guarantee political stability.[22] Political crises would keep reoccurring and episodes of economic shrinking would thus continue to be frequent. The dictatorship of Primo de Rivera, even if it restored order for a while, increased the chances of more political violence if only because it became living proof that regime change through violence remained a viable and legitimate option. In fact, conspiracies by disaffected elements would occur in 1926 and 1929. As such, even if Primo de Rivera presided over an unprecedented program of nation-building, he brought back the country to the nineteenth century in so far as legitimizing the role of political violence. As the great Hispanist Sir Raymond Carr put it, Primo de Rivera thought he was giving the deathblow to a dying entity (the liberal regime) when he was in fact "strangling a new birth" (a parliamentary regime).[23]

Political violence would also mark the republican project that would follow Primo de Rivera. Social mobilization in the 1930s was unprecedented. Unrest spread widely, including a substantial rise in rural conflict, spurred by sweeping institutional changes in labor markets that drastically increased the viability of collective action (Domènech, 2013). Conflict was perhaps spurred by the ambitiousness of the reforms undertaken. As one historian put it, the early republican governments "took on more tasks than even the most powerful and efficient regimes could hope to fulfill by peaceful, parliamentary means" (Malefakis, 2015, p. 117).

Finally, it is worth extending our period through the Civil War (1936–9) and the early years of the Franco regime also for the same reason: Violence control remained in question until around 1950. While in retrospect we know that the Franco regime would go on to last for almost 40 years, this obviously could not have been known at the time. As we will discuss in detail in the next two chapters, threats to the survival of the Franco regime were much dampened after 1950. While political regimes, and certainly the economy, saw profound changes in the century and a half before 1950, the tensions that those changes gave rise to were

---

[22] Another common dynamic was that, throughout this period, the country would still remain involved in colonial wars (three in Cuba and later in Morocco) that would contribute to increased political instability.

[23] Townson (2018), p. 71. The manifesto by Primo de Rivera at the time of his coup itself fails to convincingly tackle the issue of legitimacy, noting that "although we are born from what is formally an indiscipline, we represent the true discipline" (September 12, 1923).

often not solved peacefully. Before we move on to discuss that in detail, let us conclude the discussion of the historical backdrop to Spain's unexpected prosperity by discussing how violence undermined long-run economic development in the long period of history that preceded Spain's takeoff.

How violence undermined development

Even a high-level overview of historical events as the one provided above makes it clear that the century and a half before 1950 was not only eventful but also saw very significant change. At this point we may face a seeming paradox: How do we reconcile the fact that history proved to be so volatile with the emphasis that we have placed on what appears to be a static explanation like the role of violence? How do we explain that throughout the historical record there were episodes of relatively fast growth? Given the deep transformations of the society in the century or so before Spain's economic takeoff, it is important to address these questions before proceeding with the argument. To answer these questions, it is useful to provide a schematic of how violence undermined development throughout this volatile but evolving period (see Figure 1.4).

Let us take first the situation where political violence was not under control—the top line on Figure 1.4. The argument here is that the ensuing fragility and political instability contributed to low accumulation of capital as well as to an inefficient use of resources as economic agents worried about the enforcement of contracts, who to trust, and spent a considerable amount of time and resources on transaction costs. In this context where violence is not controlled—and therefore policy continuity and enforcement are barely credible—we encounter the familiar pattern that institutional reforms that aim to guarantee property rights do not prove to be particularly effective. For example, in 1829 the first Commercial Code in Spanish history was introduced, replacing norms that had been in place since the fourteenth century. But in a context of continued volatility, the pace at which new enterprises were formed in Spain did not budge and would remain stagnant for another century—only taking off in the 1960s (as discussed in later chapters). A similar pattern can be used to describe efforts to build human capital. The law requiring universal schooling of 6- to 9-year-olds, which also made it

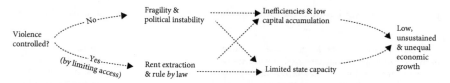

Figure 1.4 The economic impact of political violence under a limited access order
Source: Author's elaboration.

free of charge for those who could not afford it, was in the books since 1857 but made little difference for decades after its enactment—as we saw above.

But this was not the only way in which fragility and instability contributed to poor economic outcomes. As shown in recent empirical literature, civil wars are particularly detrimental for state formation. This is one of the main reasons why the economics profession, while belatedly, has been paying increasing attention to civil conflict and why it "ought to be central in the study of international development" (Blattman and Miguel, 2010). In contrast to interstate wars and wars of territorial conquest, which played a positive role in the development of the state throughout European history, civil wars typically have a negative impact on the development of state capacity. The reason is that external and internal wars correspond to two very different situations. The threat of external conflict can enhance common interests against the external enemy. Agreements between otherwise competing groups may be reached for the sake of survival of the society. In contrast, the logic of internal conflict is one of extreme struggle between domestic groups (Besley and Persson, 2011).

Frequent political violence undermined state capacity first and foremost by diverting fiscal resources to paying for the debts incurred during wars. The persistent political violence was at the root of a fiscal sustainability problem, as debt to finance the repeated wars ballooned in a classic debt spiral. Refinancing debts for a de facto bankrupt Treasury—which had also repudiated debt entered into by some of the constitutional governments—proved prohibitively expensive. Foreign creditors, which by the middle of the nineteenth century accounted for around 40 percent of all public debt, demanded that new bonds be issued at very high discounts (Comín, 2016). The result was a debt overhang that would limit significantly the potential scope of state action.

The nineteenth-century Austrian statesman Metternich captured the wider implications of the poor finances for state-building when he referred to the Spanish administration as being sustained by an army "accustomed to not receiving its pay," civil servants that were "almost certain of not being rewarded for their services," and by contractors who profited not based on getting paid for services "but on embezzlements."[24] Consequences also extended over time. Even though violence was greatly reduced after 1875, the high public debt would take decades to work itself out. By 1900, Spain still had a public debt to GDP that was much higher than in most countries—as shown in Figure 1.5. Servicing this debt would prove to be a significant constraint on state action given how small the state was.

---

[24] Letter, April 21, 1844. Metternich is often quoted for his bafflement about Spain's affairs: "I have been following Spanish affairs closely for thirty-five years and the only conclusion I have reached in respect of them is that the action most in keeping with reason is that one that is the least likely to happen." Having observed the back and forth of the first half of the nineteenth century, it is not surprising that Metternich believed that Spain will always swing between being "either frankly monarchical or emphatically radical." All reproduced in Bertier de Sauvigny (1962).

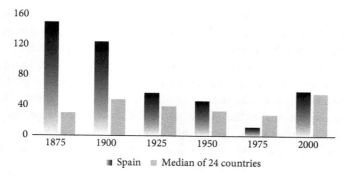

Figure 1.5 Public debt over the long run in a comparative perspective as percentage of GDP

Note: The 24 countries with comparable data as of 1900 are Argentina, Australia, Austria, Belgium, Brazil, Canada, Chile, Denmark, France, Germany, Greece, Italy, Japan, the Netherlands, New Zealand, Norway, Peru, Portugal, Russia, Spain, Sweden, Switzerland, the United Kingdom, and the United States.

Source: International Monetary Fund's *Public Finances in Modern History Database* (see Mauro et al. 2013).

On the eve of the twentieth century, public spending in Spain stood at around 7 percent of GDP or less than half of what it was in Britain, France, or Germany. Perhaps even more importantly, 31 percent of all public expenditure went to service the debt (Comín and Díaz, 2005).

With a relatively weak state, efforts to promote economic development often fared poorly. For example, in 1832 the Ministry of Development (*Ministerio de Fomento*) was created with overarching responsibilities ranging from education and the promotion of public welfare to statistics, military conscription, and enforcing law and order. In practice little was accomplished. Outlays remained minimal and, given its institutional weakness, its functioning was effectively controlled by members of the elites (the court, the Church, and the army) who saw it as a potential threat to their privileges (Alonso, 2018, p. 29).

Let us then return to the bottom half of Figure 1.4, which denotes the situation when violence is controlled through a limited access order, which we argued can be said to characterize the period 1875–1950. As discussed above, rent extraction was an integral part of the system, and corruption was commonplace under the Restoration (Muñoz Jofre, 2016). While the country saw the beginning of economic and social transformations, there was a great deal of continuity in terms of elites, typically from landowning families and dynasties of elite administrators and professionals—most with roots in the nobility. Political order was held together by a "powerful minority" that exercised power "by means of corrupt electoral practices" (Cruz, 2000, p. 35).

Those in power benefited from the application of the rule *by* law, so that the rigors of formal law were applied only to non-elites.[25] Perhaps the most illustrative example of how the rule *by* law operated is in taxes. Fraud was rampant across all taxes and industries. Tellingly, property owners blocked efforts to undertake a cadastre and empowered the local authorities to decide how the property tax burden would be shared. The result was that individual tax contributions were "inversely proportional to the degree of political influence of taxpayers" (Comín, 2018, p. 488). Besides taxes, the rule *by* law logic applied widely to public spending, to how exemptions from the military service were handled, and to public employment.

The control of violence helped improve economic performance, and there were even bursts of fast economic growth during this period. But ultimately, rent extraction and rule *by* law impose limits on how sustained and inclusive economic prosperity can be. The type of tax fraud and lobbying we have just described limited the resources available to the state and thus constrained the building of state capacity for any type of developmental activity. In addition, and besides the deadweight loss for society from the lower than optimal level of output produced by monopolies, all rent-seeking activity carries significant welfare losses as agents allocate resources to nonproductive uses (Tullock, 1967). Thus, even though violence may be controlled, the fact that it is so under a limited access order contributes eventually to inefficiency and low capital accumulation (see Figure 1.4). This helps to explain why, as we saw in the Introduction, the frequency of economic *shrinking* in Spain does not abate before 1950. It also helps explain why gross capital formation was held back throughout the nineteenth century, even during periods of relative stability, and would have to wait until after 1950 to be sustained above 20 percent of GDP (Figure 1.6).

Let us conclude here the argument on the economic impact of political violence under a limited access order. A summary of the discussion is illustrated schematically in Figure 1.4. This is of course a simplification subject to numerous caveats. There are certainly other factors that can be thought of as having an impact on the economic outcomes of interest. And the direction of causality could be said to be even more complicated than the arrows drawn in the figure suggest. Our argument has focused on the indirect effects of political violence and conflict. These indirect economic effects tend to be orders of magnitude higher than the direct losses to life and treasure (World Bank, 2011). Despite all its simplifying assumptions, the argument made here leads us to conclude that both the limited control of violence and the reliance on a limited access order to do so were contributing factors to economic growth being relatively low, unsustained, and unequal in the long period that preceded 1950.

---

[25] In contrast, the rule *of* law occurs only when elites accept the application of laws to themselves. This distinction is from World Bank (2017).

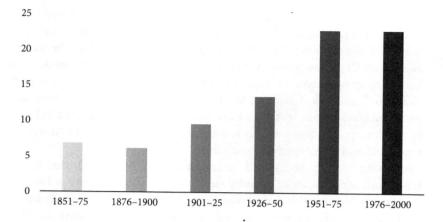

Figure 1.6 Gross capital formation, 1850–2000, as percentage of GDP
Source: Carreras et al. (2005).

Conclusions

What would be a good model to explain Spain's unexpected prosperity? A good model would be one that helps us answer the three traits that characterized growth after 1950: Why was growth fast? Why was it sustained? And why was growth more inclusive? A good model would also help us explain why before 1950 none of those things happened. Before 1950, episodes of fast economic growth were not sustained over the long run, in fact there was much economic shrinking. And while the living conditions of the population certainly improved over the long run, society was characterized by sharp inequality of opportunities.

In this chapter we have addressed the questions relating to the period before 1950. We have done so by explicitly using the framework of Douglass North and coauthors as a guide to our analysis over the period that preceded Spain's unexpected prosperity. Any framework that can encompass such a broad historical process is bound to be a general one.[26] Some would see this as a shortcoming. While the cost of such a general model is often its triviality, in our case the framework is useful because it helps us explain seemingly contradictory developments before 1950: Why were there episodes of fast economic growth? Why did the frequency of economic shrinking not abate despite significant economic transformation? Why did inequality of opportunity proved to be so persistent, even during periods of stability?[27]

---

[26] This is why I refer to it as a framework more than a model. As economic historians have noted, predictions from formal growth models are often at odds with recorded economic history (Mokyr and Voth, 2010).

[27] As Spanish economic historians Prados de la Escosura and Sánchez-Alonso (2019) have argued: "The absence of debate on long-run Spanish economic performance during the twentieth century is striking. [. . .] A convincing explanation of why the historical determinants of Spain's economic backwardness weakened or faded away from the 1960s onwards is still lacking" (p. 26).

Economic growth can happen even in limited access orders and even in fragile settings. Elite factions that benefit from rents have in fact the incentives to grow the source of such rents, if it is not at the expense of their control. But we should avoid mistaking an economy that is growing for one that is transforming from a limited to an open access order. This important insight from the framework by North and coauthors—referred to as "our framework" for short hereafter—is particularly relevant for the analysis of Spanish economic history. In its light it is not at all surprising that we observe varying rates of economic growth across the nineteenth and early twentieth centuries.

In so far as economic growth is concerned, the main prediction from our framework is not about its quantity but about its quality. Growth is likely to be less sustainable over the long run in limited access orders, especially in fragile ones that succumb to bouts of violence. This is precisely what we observe throughout this period in Spain, with the frequent economic contractions described above in the Introduction. At the same time, the precise reasons for why growth may be higher or lower in a given decade may stem from a multitude of factors, and we should refrain from using our framework to "over-fit" the ups and downs of economic growth.

In addition, while our framework provides a useful compass to navigate the broad contours of Spain's economic development, it does not mean that other factors, like policy, geography, globalization, or technology diffusion played no role. The control of violence is a necessary but not a sufficient condition for growth. Falling transport prices, technological change, large demographic movements, and the emergence of world markets for certain commodities and products were all hallmarks of the first wave of globalization in the late nineteenth century. All these had an undeniable impact on the trajectory of the Spanish economy. But those impacts were mediated by the type of institutions and policies in place.

What explains the high frequency of economic shrinking up to 1950? Here our framework helps again. Just as it explains why there are no deterministic links between the type of order and economic growth, it also helps to explain why regimes regress. When elites in a limited access order disagree about how relative power may have shifted, they may end up in various forms of disorder. The unraveling of the political settlement in the late nineteenth century and early twentieth century, and the ensuing violent period, fit particularly well with the predictions of our framework. The fact that the economic takeoff has much to do with fewer shrinking episodes gives us some clues—even if not definitive—that the cessation of the political backtracking played a role in the change of fortunes. One hypothesis is that it was the transition from a limited access order to an open access order that underpinned this improved economic performance. We will explore this transition in subsequent chapters in which we discuss the role of increasing contestability in markets, ideas, and politics.

A final implication of our framework is that economic growth is also likely to be less inclusive in limited access orders. So, what do we know about the evolution of inequality in this period? Although there is no household survey data before the late twentieth century, researchers have been able to paint a relatively detailed picture of the evolution of income inequality since 1850. Income inequality increased throughout the nineteenth and early twentieth centuries, reaching a peak in 1918 and then in 1953 (Prados de la Escosura, 2008). And while income per capita was increasing during the early phases of modern economic growth in Spain, other indicators such as mortality rates, life expectancy, or heights showed stagnation or even a deterioration up to 1880, especially among the bottom of the income distribution (Beltrán Tapia, 2015). This is all fully consistent with the predictions of our framework.

Overall, the conceptual framework used here helps us by prompting us to focus on the relevance of political violence and, on the question of economic growth, by putting emphasis not only on its speed, but mainly on its sustainability and distributional aspects. Our framework provides only the contours of the long-run narrative. In fact, one of the advantages of our framework is that it preserves a key role for policy at any given moment. The precise role of policy will be one of the key focus of most of our attention as our story unfolds.

2

A Critical Juncture

The news reached Washington, D.C., around 10 p.m. on June 24, 1950. It was a Saturday and John Hickerson, an Assistant Secretary of State, was urgently called into the office for an unspecified purpose. As he drove through Rock Creek Park on his way to the State Department, Hickerson wondered what the matter could be. It had been the officer watching over the Far East who had called, and he had sounded particularly urgent on the phone, so Hickerson thought it most likely that Communist China had attempted to invade Taiwan. When he finally reached his office, he learnt that North Korea had launched a massive assault on the South, an attack that had caught everyone in Washington by surprise.[1] What Hickerson could not have known at the time is that the events set in motion over that weekend would be of great consequence to Spain's economic future.

Early reports indicated the disarray of the South Korean forces, which were easily overrun by the better equipped Northern rivals. President Harry S. Truman, who was spending the weekend in his home state of Missouri, was quickly informed and convened a meeting with key officials for Sunday evening. Truman had time to think on the three-hour plane ride back to Washington. The memories of prior occasions where the strong had attacked the weak—Manchuria, Ethiopia, and Austria in his own generation—and how the failure of democracies to act had emboldened aggressors dominated his thinking. The aggression in Korea, he concluded, was "the test of all the talk" about collective security.[2]

The White House was undergoing renovations, so the Sunday evening meeting took place across the street at Blair House. The gathering was marked by what Truman would describe as a complete, almost unspoken, acceptance by everyone that "whatever had to be done to meet this aggression had to be done." Unable to see the North Koreans as anything but a Soviet puppet, the US could simply not accept the conquest of a territory in their defensive perimeter without resistance. One by one, each of the 12 men gathered by Truman spoke in favor of taking military action to counter the North Korean attack. Not doing so would be appeasement, as summed up by General Omar Bradley, who was attending the meeting as Chairman of the Joint Chiefs of Staff.

---

[1] Third Oral History Interview with John D. Hickerson, Washington, D.C., June 5, 1973, by Richard D. McKinzie, Harry S. Truman Library (https://www.trumanlibrary.gov/library/oral-histories/hickrson#oh2, accessed March 18, 2019).

[2] Truman's own thinking and quote are from *Memoirs of Harry S. Truman. Volume II: Years of Trial and Hope, 1946–1952* (1955), pp. 334–5.

Unexpected Prosperity: How Spain Escaped the Middle Income Trap. Oscar Calvo-Gonzalez, Oxford University Press.
© Oscar Calvo-Gonzalez 2021. DOI: 10.1093/oso/9780198853978.003.0003

The surprise in Washington had not been *that* a crisis had broken out but *where* it had. Berlin, Turkey, Greece, or Iran were all hotspots where the Soviets were at a greater advantage. Korea was too close to American bases in Japan and too far from Soviet ones to offer a tempting target. This was yet another reason why the hostilities in the Korean peninsula would be interpreted by Washington as a litmus test of American determination to defend its sphere of influence. Communist aggression could not go unchecked. As Truman would tell Hickerson, it was "time to call their bluff."[3]

The Korean War and what it meant for American strategy in the Cold War would have significant consequences for American policy towards Spain. In short order, the Franco regime would go from being a pariah state, banned from the United Nations and left out of the Marshall Plan, to becoming a military partner of the US in the defense of the West. The shift was felt just weeks after the outbreak of the Korean War, when in August 1950 the US Congress voted to grant a small loan to Spain, eventually followed by more substantive sums of aid over the next decade and a half. But why would any of this matter to explain Spain's path to prosperity?

Stumbling on stability

With the benefit of hindsight, we know that the Franco regime would prove to be remarkably stable, lasting almost four decades, and would be characterized by an effective control of political violence. But none of this would have been taken for granted in the 1940s. Throughout the century and a half before 1950, the Spanish polity had been largely unable to maintain an enduring stability. By the time Franco assumed the position of head of government in 1938, there had been 145 heads of government in the century since the position of President of the Council of Ministers was created in 1834. The average stint of a head of Spanish government was therefore around a year. Franco would go on to be the head of government for 35 years. The history of violent *pronunciamientos*, which had helped elevate Franco himself to power, made such a long tenure most unlikely.

A long-lasting Franco regime was also unlikely from the vantage point of the international balance of power in 1945. The acceptance of an unreformed Franco regime into the community of Western nations in the 1950s is remarkable given the political nature of Franco's Spain. To begin with, the Franco regime owed its very existence to the military support it received from Hitler and Mussolini during the Spanish Civil War. With the end of World War II, one could have

---

[3] Truman (1955), p. 334. Bradley's account in his autobiography (Bradley and Blair, 1983, p. 535). Acheson's quote in his *Present at the Creation. My Years in the State Department* (1969), p. 405. Truman's statement to Hickerson in the latter's Oral History interview quoted above.

expected that Franco would have to pay for his Nazi sympathies and the fascist origins of his regime.[4] Far from such an outcome, the end Franco's Spain would end up as a solid military partner of the US and increasingly tolerated among the West liberal democracies. Two high-level meetings serve as bookends of this unlikely turnaround. On October 23, 1940, Franco had traveled to the French railway station of Hendaye, near the Spanish border, to confer with Hitler and offer him his support. The following decade would end with Franco receiving the embrace of President Dwight Eisenhower during a visit to Madrid on December 21, 1959.

As much as Hitler and Eisenhower provide a study in contrasts, so does the Spanish economy of 1940 and 1959. The early 1950s constitute a critical juncture for Spain's long-term development. Econometric tests show that economic growth experienced a significant acceleration around 1951 (Prados de la Escosura, 2007). The economy not only grew faster but also spent much less time *shrinking* after 1950 (recall Figure 0.5 in the Introduction). Many other economic variables also show a break around the early 1950s. For example, the transformation of the economy away from agriculture, which had almost ground to a halt in the two decades before 1950, resumed at an increased pace and capital formation in real terms took off (see Figure 2.1). Gross capital formation increased significantly also as a share of aggregate demand: from an average of 11 percent of GDP in the first half of the twentieth century, it would more than double to 23 percent of GDP in the quarter century after 1950. As a result, not only economic growth

Figure 2.1 Structural change in Spain before and after 1950
Source: Own elaboration with data from Carreras et al. (2005).

[4] The characterization of the Franco regime remains a controversial issue. Even during its first phase, the regime was never fully fascistic. The Franco regime lacked a well-defined ideology and evolved over its long existence. An enduring characteristic of the regime was being an eclectic authoritarian coalition, drawing support from diverse groups such as the military, conservatives, traditionalists, fascists, and the Church. The dictatorial regime allowed some limited pluralism within some boundaries and is therefore better seen as an authoritarian than a totalitarian regime, using the seminal distinction of Juan J. Linz (1964).

accelerated but also its determinants changed. After 1950, efficiency gains played a much greater role than factor accumulation. Indeed, the contribution of total factor productivity to economic growth shot up from a mere 0.3 percent annually in 1850–1950 to 3.7 percent in 1951–1974.[5]

The improved economic performance of Spain in the 1950s is a puzzle given that it took place in a relatively unfavorable regulatory and economic policy environment. Most economic policies remained a burden and would not be significantly improved until the late 1950s, as we will see in the next chapter. The literature has therefore concluded that economic growth spurted not because of but *in spite of* economic policies put in place by the Franco regime. Yet this only makes the Spanish economic takeoff more of a mystery.[6] The interpretation of Spanish economic history advanced here, by focusing on how the control of violence and the ensuing political stability underpins the process of economic development, helps us solve this fundamental puzzle.

But where did political stability spring from? Franco had already been in charge for over a decade by the time the 1940s ended. Yet, there was a lingering uncertainty about the long-term viability of his regime. In turn, this political uncertainty had negative economic consequences, on which contemporary observers of Spanish affairs frequently reflected. The flat line on capital formation shown in Figure 2.1 was in part the consequence of a shyness among the capitalist class to invest when they lacked confidence in the capacity of the Franco regime both to survive and for basic economic management. The American *chargé d'affaires* in Madrid summed it up crisply when, just before the Korean War, he concluded that one of the problems afflicting Spain was that men of ability "do not want to associate themselves with the Regime." In Culbertson's analysis there was a link between the political fragility of the regime and the choice of inward-looking economic policies which were damaging economic confidence. As he put it, "Spain today, that is the business world of Spain, has no confidence in the conduct of the economy of Spain."[7]

A political regime can prove to be long-lasting *ex post* yet be experienced contemporaneously as unstable by those living within it. This was the predicament of Spain in the late 1940s. It affected economic activity through lower confidence and private investment, as we saw above. The poor economic performance of the

---

[5] As Prados de la Escosura and Rosés (2009, p. 1082) sum it up: "The early 1950s represent a divide between a hundred years of moderate growth dominated by factor accumulation, and half a century of fast growth led by total factor productivity, with 70 percent of the more rapid GDP growth after 1950 coming from efficiency gains."

[6] As aptly pointed out by historian Fernando Guirao, given the growth in the 1950s despite burdening policies, we "should be looking for those elements that could explain this evidence rather than limiting themselves to hammer again and again at the mass of obstructionist measures then in place" (1998, pp. 204–5).

[7] Culbertson to Acheson, Madrid, June 20, 1950, *FRUS*, vol. 3, document 685.

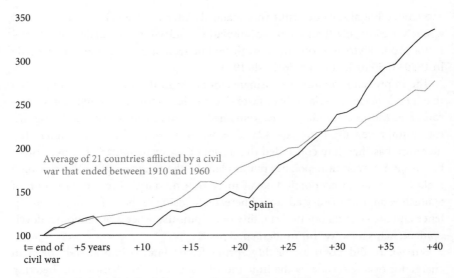

Figure 2.2 Comparing Spain's economic performance with other countries afflicted by civil war

Note: To compare Spain's performance with countries that suffered a civil war in a broadly similar period only civil wars that ended during the half a century between 1910 and 1960 were considered – this is roughly a quarter century before or after the Spanish Civil War. There were a total of 41 such civil wars affecting a total of 29 countries, as some countries suffered multiple civil wars (in those cases the country is only included once with the year in which the first civil war in data set as the baseline). Limitations on economic data brought down the set of comparators to 21 countries as follows (in parenthesis the years in which the respective civil war ended): Argentina (1955), Bolivia (1952), Brazil (1932), Bulgaria (1923), China (1911), Colombia (1958), Costa Rica (1948), Cuba (1959), El Salvador (1932), Finland (1918), Greece (1945), Honduras (1925), Hungary (1920), Indonesia (1953), Iraq (1953), Lao (1962), Lebanon (1958), Mexico (1920), Myanmar (1960), Peru (1932), and the Philippines (1954).

Source: Maddison project for real per capita (as cited above) and Sarkees and Wayman (2010) as part of the *Correlates of War Project* for civil wars.

1940s resulted in Spain not being able to regain its pre–Civil War level of GDP per capita until 1951, 15 years after the start of the Civil War.

Spain's economic performance after the Civil War was particularly poor even if we compare it with that of countries that also went through a civil war during roughly the same historical period. Ten years after the war ended, the economic recovery was on a much slower path than for the average of countries that also experienced a civil war at an equivalent point of time (ten years after the end of their respective civil war), as shown in Figure 2.2. After around 1950 the catching up begins and does so in earnest after 1960 (around 20 years after the Civil War ended). Putting Franco's Spain in a comparative perspective, this time focusing only on civil war–afflicted countries, again makes the contrasting performance between the 1950s and the 1940s stand out. The nonlinear path of Spain also suggests that something in addition to the passage of time may have been at play.

If length of tenure in office was not the decisive factor in bringing about political stability, how was it achieved? This chapter argues, in short, that the climate created by the worsening of the Cold War would prove decisive for a change in military bilateral relations between the US and Spain. This shift would crystallize in reaching an agreement in 1953 under which the US located four major military bases in Spain, including a large naval station for the Sixth Fleet of the US Navy. This was a large and not easily reversible commitment of the US to Spain. Once American military bases were established, the interests of the US became aligned with those of Franco in ensuring the political stability of the regime. The agreements between the US and Spain, combined with domestic factors that had helped reduce and fragment the domestic opposition to the Franco regime, will be interpreted by economic agents as confirmation that the Franco regime was there to stay. This, in turn, had a significant positive impact on business confidence, private investment, and ultimately economic performance (Calvo-Gonzalez, 2007a).

To sum up, given the regime's origins, the international postwar order, and the history of political violence over the previous century in Spain, the stability that the country eventually achieved was an unlikely event from the vantage point of 1945 or 1950. Yet a mere few years later, the Franco regime was solidly entrenched. The influential historian and liberal thinker, Salvador de Madariaga, conveyed the extraordinary nature of the turnaround for the Franco regime when he starkly compared its prospects in the mid-1950s with what they had been just ten years earlier:

At the end of the Second World War, General Franco was in Spain the head of all that which lay dead on the ground; and outside of Spain, a pariah. Ten years later, he was in Spain the head of a strong regime (how really strong, it was difficult to say), and an ally and "favorite son" of the United States.[8]

In other words, somewhat unexpectedly the Franco regime stumbled on stability. Following Madariaga, we will separate the internal and external aspects to this happy accident. We will deal in this chapter with the external factors, and in particular how the evolving American policy contributed to political stability in Spain.[9] The turnaround in prospects for the regime was not only unlikely but also consequential. Our main interest is not to explain how Franco pulled a Houdini-like

---

[8] Importantly, Madariaga was writing in the mid-1950s (1958, p. 593).
[9] Our treatment will be limited to key developments and their consequences. Those interested in a more thorough treatment of the American rapprochement to Spain, see Viñas (1981 and 2003), Jarque (1998), and, in English, Liedtke (1998).

escapist stunt but, as we will discuss in the final section of the chapter, to explore its consequences for Spain's path to prosperity. The next chapter will then consider the domestic aspects of this accidental making of a stable polity.

From *pariah* to partner

In the early days of World War II, Franco took steps that closely aligned him with the Axis. In June 1940, eight days after the evacuation of Dunkirk and when German victory seemed imminent, Franco declared Spain to be nonbelligerent, a move that Mussolini's Italy had also taken a few months before entering the war on the German side. Later that year, at their meeting in Hendaye, Franco went as far as offering to join Hitler provided he would get control over French Morocco in exchange. Hitler was visibly irritated with Franco's ask and his overall fastidiousness—which is sometimes construed as evidence of Franco's deft handling of Hitler—but ultimately the Führer achieved what he set out to do: Franco agreed to a secret protocol by which Spain would join the Axis at a date to be decided jointly upon completion of military preparations. In the end Spain would not enter the war, a fact that some see as evidence of Franco's skill in resisting foreign pressures. The evidence, however, suggests otherwise.[10]

The Germans ultimately considered that Spain's offer was not worth much and her entry into the war did not warrant paying the political price that Franco had asked. This basic calculus would remain unchanged for most of the war. Hitler would come to regard Franco as unrealistic and an opportunist. He intimated to Mussolini on the eve of the attack on the Soviet Union that Spain would take sides "only when the outcome of the war is decided."[11] When Franco sent an 18,000-strong volunteer division to fight alongside the Nazis against the Soviet Union, it still did little to carry Germany's favor, while it effectively put the decision of Spain's entry into war at the discretion of Stalin, who could have easily declared war on Spain as a result of this action.

Just as Germany had thought of Spain as inconsequential in the early stages of the war, in later stages of the war US military planners would not consider that occupying Spain was worth the effort. As a result, American policy was geared towards preserving Spain's neutrality, and Allied policy towards Spain was mostly delegated to the British. Fortunately for Franco, among the Allies, the government of Prime Minister Winston Churchill was the most understanding towards

---

[10] One area where the regime's policies were truly neutral was in its treatment of refugees. Some 40,000 Jews received safe passage through Spain (Avni, 1982).

[11] As quoted in Preston, 1994, p. 437. See also Leitz (1999), p. 137. For an account in English of the so-called Spanish "Blue Division" that fought alongside the Wehrmacht see Moreno (2015).

Spain.[12] Britain had maintained a policy of economic cooperation, allowing trade with Spain during the world war. British authorities were concerned that a potential entry of Spain into the war would immediately threaten Britain's possession of Gibraltar. In the early stages of the conflict, efforts of the British to dissuade Spain from entering the war went as far as paying generous sums of money to high-level Spanish military officials, spending the large sum of $20 million at the time in such bribes, channeled with the help of financier Juan March (Viñas, 2016). Although it's unclear what impact these sweeteners may have had, recipients included the brother of Franco and around a half-dozen of the top generals of the military.[13]

A potential entry of Spain into the war had been less of a concern for the US, except in the run-up to the landing of Allied forces in North Africa in November 1942. In preparation of the so-called Operation Torch, the US cautiously insisted that one of the landing sites be on the Atlantic coast of Morocco to limit the risk of having the entire expeditionary force sail through the Strait of Gibraltar in what could easily turn into a hostile environment if Spain decided to enter the war. At that time, the US also conveyed directly to Franco that Spain had nothing to fear from the Allies if it remained neutral.[14]

By then, most Spaniards needed little convincing not to jump on the Nazi bandwagon. After the successful landing of the US in North Africa, which had brought the war closer to Spain than at any time before, most of the Spanish generals favored a true neutral stance. This included the Anglophile General Francisco Gómez-Jordana, Foreign Minister from September 1942 until his death in August 1944, and the Carlist General José Varela, Army Minister from August 1939 until September 1942. Other key generals, like Antonio Aranda, head of the army school and who was with Varela among the recipients of British payments, also advocated for a neutralist stance.

In May 1943, the top brass of the Spanish army concluded that Germany would most likely lose the war. But the Franco regime, which was effectively a coalition of very diverse political families, also included elements that remained staunchly pro-Axis. Ultimately, it was the position of Franco—as arbiter among the factions of the regime—that mattered. As late as 1944, Franco appears to have believed that the Axis would end up winning the war, or at least that a stalemate would be

---

[12] Churchill would later be the strongest advocate for not interfering in the internal affairs of Spain at the Potsdam Conference in the summer of 1945. At that time, Truman agreed with Churchill that while "he would be happy to recognize another government in Spain" he thought "Spain itself must settle that question." (Truman, *Memoirs of Harry S. Truman. Volume I: Year of Decisions, 1945*, 1955, pp. 357–8).

[13] Bribery was not the exclusive tool of the British. The Germans, whose embassy in Madrid was by 1941 their largest in the world, had over 400 Spaniards on their payroll (Payne, 2000, p. 299).

[14] To ensure Spain did not spring a surprise, monthly burglaries on the Spanish embassy in Washington allowed the Americans to keep up with the secret code of Spanish diplomatic communications and check that no war preparations were under discussion (Smyth, 1999, p. 203).

reached thanks to the new weapons being developed by the Nazis (Preston, 1994, p. 517). Far from proving his skillful handling of world politics, Franco missed an opportunity to demonstrate a true neutral stance when the Allies could have valued it in the aftermath of the attack on Pearl Harbor. On the contrary, Spain's nonbelligerence remained in effect until October 1943, when it returned to a strict neutrality and announced the withdrawal of the division that had been fighting with the Nazis in the Soviet front for over two years.

Ostracism

As prospects for the Axis continued to deteriorate in 1944, Franco feared that the Allies were getting ready to land in Spain to open another front against Germany before landing in France. While no such plans materialized, the US hardened its negotiating position and was able to gain some concessions from Spain. The Franco regime had played a hard bargain vis-à-vis the US during most of the war, leveraging in particular the role of Spanish shipments of wolfram to Germany as a bargaining chip.[15] Spain repeatedly threatened to increase its sales of wolfram to Germany unless the US shipped more oil to Spain. In 1944, as Franco's negotiating position weakened, the US announced a suspension of oil shipments to Spain, which were only resumed after an agreement was reached to stop all Spanish shipments of wolfram to Germany.

The alleged "skilled prudence" of the Franco regime during World War II had not fooled the Allies. The views of Dean Acheson, who had great familiarity with Spain because he oversaw American policy regarding neutrals during the war, are symptomatic of the opinion of many in the West. Acheson regarded Franco as outright hostile and a Nazi ally of Hitler. In Acheson's mind, Spain was the last of the neutral countries in understanding that the war was unfolding in favor of the Allies. In April 1944, Acheson would tell the British ambassador in Washington, Lord Halifax, that the US would have little sympathy for hostile neutrals. The Spanish government, Acheson warned, would do well to think that over.[16] As the US shifted its thinking towards a postwar world, the disapproval of the Franco regime in Western circles became more consequential for American policy-setting. President Roosevelt's instructions to his ambassador in Madrid in March 1945 stressed how the regime had been "helped to power" by Fascist Italy and Nazi Germany, that the US could not forget Spain's "assistance to our Axis

---

[15] Wolfram, or tungsten ore, is one of the hardest metals and was used in armor-piercing shells. After the loss of access to Asian sources of wolfram, the Germans increasingly depended on shipments of wolfram from the Iberian peninsula. The US put in place a program to purchase wolfram from Spain to force the Germans to pay more for and consume less tungsten (Caruana and Rockoff, 2003).

[16] For Acheson's views on Spain see Acheson (1969), pp. 48, 53–4, and 59.

enemies," and ultimately, that he saw no place in the community of nations for "governments founded on fascist principles."[17]

The way the world war was ending posed a threat to the survival of Franco. Thus, in July 1945 the US, Britain, and the Soviet Union agreed at Potsdam that Spain could not be a member of the UN—a decision that was later endorsed in the first session of the General Assembly of the UN held in February 1946. Regime change was the remedy in mind. To this end, the General Assembly explicitly reaffirmed that, for countries with regimes that had benefited from support of the Axis, membership in the UN was out of the question "so long as these regimes are in power."[18] The UN would take the Spanish question up again in April and December 1946, when the General Assembly passed a Resolution recommending that all UN member states recall their ambassadors from Madrid. The ostracism in the UN was not only symbolic: France's border with Spain was closed indefinitely. As 1946 was coming to an end, Spain was isolated and plagued by material shortages and hunger. The Franco regime seemed an unlikely candidate to become the guarantor of long-term political stability.

Receding tide

Against most prognostications, however, Franco would survive a period that would be the riskiest for his rule. He did so by being ruthlessly violent against the remnants of the Republican opposition, playing his lukewarm supporters against each other, and, above all, by patiently waiting for a change in world politics that would end up favoring him. As early as January 1947, when many close to Franco worried about the future of the regime, Franco intimated to close collaborators his conviction that the growing Soviet–American antagonism guaranteed that "he would soon be courted by Washington."[19]

Franco would start to be proven right just a few weeks after this pronouncement. Following the decision of the British to withdraw support to the democratic forces in the Greek civil war, the US took decisive action against the Greek communists, believed to be pawns of the Soviets. Speaking before Congress on March 12, 1947, Truman laid out a new orientation of American foreign policy, considering the deterioration of relations with the Soviet Union. The new Truman Doctrine, as it was quickly referred to, called for American economic and military

[17] Memorandum from President Franklin D. Roosevelt to Ambassador Norman Armour, March 10, 1945, *Foreign Relations of the United States*, 5:667.

[18] The Declaration of the General Assembly on Spain noted that the Franco regime, "having been founded with the support of the Axis powers, in view of its origins, nature, its record and its close association with the aggressor States, does not possess the necessary qualifications to justify its admission." Full text available through the Official Document System of the United Nations at https://documents.un.org/prod/ods.nsf/home.xsp (accessed June 20, 2019).

[19] As quoted in Preston (1994), p. 565.

support to free nations under threat. It stated that the policy of the United States was to support "free peoples who are resisting attempted subjugation by armed minorities or by outside pressures." Truman spoke about the choice that every nation must make was between two distinct worlds. In one corner countries distinguished by free institutions, representative government, free elections, guarantees of individual liberty, freedom of speech and religion, and freedom from political oppression. In the opposite corner were the countries where government is based upon the will of a minority forcibly imposed upon the majority and relying "upon terror and oppression, a controlled press and radio; fixed elections, and the suppression of personal freedoms."[20]

The Franco regime was a perfect fit under the heading describing regimes that the Truman Doctrine meant to combat. Therein lies the first of two paradoxes that would mark the *rapprochement* of the US to Spain. On the one hand, the nature of the Franco regime was reprehensible to Truman and many of his close associates. On the other hand, Spain was increasingly attractive from a military standpoint. It was an excellent location for naval bases, close to the Strait of Gibraltar. Spain was also an ideal place for American air bases. With the new B-52 bomber still in development, the US Air Force still depended in the mid-1950s on mid-range bombers like the B-29. Air bases near the Spanish cities of Madrid and Zaragoza, which are around two thousand miles from Moscow, would just about allow existing planes like the B-29 to reach Moscow and return to base. Moreover, bases in Spain were close enough to quickly reach the main theater of operations in Western Europe in the event of a Soviet invasion, yet far enough that air bases would not be easily captured by an invading Soviet army. Distance was also helped by the physical barrier of the Pyrenees mountain range, which American military planners considered one of the strongest defensive assets of Spain.

The Truman administration would need to come to terms with the contradiction of embracing an oppressive regime such as Franco's for the purpose of combating oppressive regimes such as the Communist ones. While supporting right-wing dictators was not a totally new course of action for an American administration, the practice was particularly at odds with the goals and policies of the early Truman administration (Schmitz, 1999). As the Cold War intensified, the American government would increasingly face this ambiguity, to which it did not always respond consistently. From the vantage point of 1947, it was not a foregone conclusion how President Truman would ultimately come down on the Franco regime. It resulted in a lack of consistency of the Truman administration in dealing with Spain (Portero, 1989).

---

[20] President Harry S. Truman's address to the US Congress, March 12, 1947. Available at the Truman Library (https://www.trumanlibrary.gov/library/online-collections/truman-doctrine) which includes earlier drafts and reactions to the speech.

Because of the ambivalence o the Truman administration towards Franco, the increased American military interest in Spain could have led not to the strengthening but to the ousting of Franco. This is the second paradox about the *rapprochement* of the US to Spain, one that is not always fully appreciated—perhaps not even by Franco himself, as he was apparently relieved by Truman's speech to Congress in March 1947 (Portero, 1989, p. 224). Emboldened by what he seemed to have interpreted as unambiguously good news, Franco set out to apply a veneer of legitimacy to his rule: a law of succession that installed Franco as Head of State indefinitely and left it up to him to propose his successor. The chosen successor would carry the title of King, so Spain was now to be considered a monarchy under the law. Franco would even engineer a popular referendum in July 1947, which predictably approved the Law of Succession with 90 percent of votes cast.

The dubious establishment of a "monarchy" with Franco as a lifelong dictator fooled no one. In the spring of 1947, weeks after the Truman Doctrine was enunciated, the US explored with the UK the prospects for removing Franco. Acheson, at the time Acting Secretary of State, was among the most vocal American officials in his opposition to Franco. He transmitted instructions to the American ambassador in Britain to discuss with the authorities in London what "positive" action could be taken to remove Franco, who "must go." As Acheson concluded in his instructions, "we hope it will be possible" for the British government "to concert with us in achieving our common end, namely the restoration of a democratic Spain."[21]

On the same day that Acheson was instructing his ambassador in London, the pretender to the Spanish throne, Don Juan, issued a public manifesto denouncing Franco's efforts at deriving legitimacy from declaring Spain a monarchy without a king. From his exile in Estoril, Don Juan was spot on in his diagnosis. One of the key flaws of the Law of Succession was, Don Juan wrote, that it did not consider "the pressing need of stable institutions in Spain." Don Juan perceptively stressed that the way forward proposed by Franco "left the door open to internal infighting" and therefore could not be counted on as a source of stability.

That a hereditary monarchy, as opposed to an elective one, was a source of political stability was a powerful argument that had been made in Spain as early as the School of Salamanca in the late sixteenth century.[22] It matters for our argument because it goes to the core of the question of how political stability was actually achieved in Spain. We will return to the domestic aspects of political

---

[21] Acheson to ambassador in the UK, Washington, April 7, 1947, *FRUS*, vol. 3, document 716.

[22] As Juan de Mariana put it in *De rege et regis institutione* (1599): "Certainly to ensure domestic stability there is nothing more appropriate than a law that designates the successor, thus removing the opportunity of infighting among people with ambition to be prince; this is why I judge it more convenient to establish the monarchy on the basis of the hereditary principle." Own translation based on the 1845 Spanish translation *Del Rey y de la dignidad real*.

stability throughout the book, including about the end of the Franco regime, but let us for now continue to focus on the external factors that facilitated the conditions for political stability to arise.

A military effort to remove Franco would not come from Britain or the US. But American policy towards Spain would shift back and forth and remain uncertain over the next several years. At times the geostrategic considerations advanced by the US military seemed to reign supreme. They were endorsed by the newly created Policy Planning Staff at the Department of State, headed by one of the intellectual architects of the policy of containment, George F. Kennan. In December 1947, the National Security Council (NSC) issued its "Report on U.S. Policy toward Spain" (known as document NSC 3). The objective of NSC 3 was, as Undersecretary of State Robert Lovett put it when it was brought up for discussion, "to quit kidding ourselves as to our interest in Spain and to reorient our policy in relation thereto."[23]

At other times, and notwithstanding the formal adoption of NSC 3 as the policy of the American administration, the military interests were not enough to overcome the political objections against working with Franco. In fact, Spain would be left out of the two key instruments of US foreign policy in the early Cold War years: the Marshall Plan and the North Atlantic Treaty Organization. This was so despite efforts by a considerable lobby sympathetic to the Franco regime.[24]

The White House seemed genuinely conflicted over the next couple of years in navigating the contradictions between their distaste for Franco and their military interests in Spain. The result was that the official adoption of NSC 3 in January 1948 did not result in significant changes in actual policy actions. A string of American legislators advocated for Spain but had limited impact. In fact, over the next couple of years the White House would end up flexing its muscle on more than one occasion to oppose moves that could have facilitated Spain's inclusion in the West. Most notably in the spring of 1948, when the Marshall Plan was being discussed in Congress, Representative Alvin O'Konski of Wisconsin introduced an amendment that would have allowed Spain to become a participant of the Marshall Plan. The amendment was later dropped because of White House intervention. Additional efforts to secure funding for Spain led by Senator Pat

---

[23] Minutes of the 4th meeting of the National Security Council (NSC), 17th December 1947, reproduced in D. Merrill (ed.), *Documentary History of the Truman Presidency*, vol. 23 (Bethesda, Md.: University Publications of America, 1998), p. 248.

[24] Spain had been cultivating, at great financial expense, a number of American politicians like Senator Pat McCarran. But there is little evidence that such efforts had any impact on the change of policy of the American administration. There is limited evidence on the impact of this "Spanish lobby." The timing of the change, coinciding with the Korean War, and the fact that it was driven by officials from the Department of Defense, suggests that the "Spanish lobby" had little effect. At the same time, it is true that the first US assistance to Spain was led by the Congress, where lobbying efforts had been focused.

McCarran of Nevada, chairman of the Senate Appropriations Committee and a frequent visitor to Franco in the late 1940s, also failed to overcome the veto of the White House.

Yet by early 1950, there was a growing recognition even among the most anti-Franco American officials that the isolation of Spain had failed in its intended purpose to bring about regime change. Dean Acheson, who had been elevated to Secretary of State in 1949, concluded that Franco benefited from the support of many who, although they might prefer a different government, "fear that chaos and civil strife would follow a move to overthrow the Government."[25] Yet even this growing frustration among US officials did not lead immediately to a change but to a further impasse in American foreign policy towards Spain. US policymakers were wary that any US–Spanish military cooperation outside the framework of NATO raised concerns among the French and the British. The French worried that the American interest in bases in Spain was an implicit recognition that the US would not defend Germany and France and instead retreat behind the Pyrenees in the event of a Soviet invasion of Western Europe. The British also worried that after bases were secured in Spain the US would prioritize the Mediterranean over the Middle East (Edwards, 1999). British and French concerns were important considerations for US policymakers. As late as April 1950, the view within the State Department was that not only should Spain not be invited into NATO, but given the negative implications for the relationship with Britain and France, the US should not entertain a bilateral military cooperation with Spain.[26]

Korea

Things had been moving in the direction hoped for by Franco, but prior to the Korean War the shift in policy toward Spain had not crystalized. We know this because of the detailed back and forth in Washington circles in the spring of 1950. The State Department's review of policy on Spain in April 1950 left policy unchanged.[27] In response, the Chairman of the Joint Chiefs of Staff, General Omar Bradley, complained that "insufficient weight" was being given to the "more important" security and strategic interests of the US in Spain. The key military argument was that Spain may indeed become the last foothold in Continental

---

[25] Acheson to Senator Tom Connally, Chairman of the Foreign Relations Committee of the US Senate, Washington, January 18, 1950, *FRUS*, vol. 3, document 679.

[26] Acting Assistant Secretary of State for European Affairs (Thompson) to the Secretary of State, April 21, 1950, *FRUS*, vol. 3, document 682.

[27] Acting Assistant Secretary of State for European Affairs (Thompson) to the Secretary of State, Washington, April 21, 1950, *FRUS*, vol. 3, document 682.

Europe and that, in Bradley's view, if the US did not retain a European Continental foothold, the possibility of re-entry into Europe was much in doubt. The Joint Chiefs of Staff "strongly" recommended action without delay to obtain military cooperation with Spain. Not convinced by the State Department view that such a move would alienate Britain and France, the Joint Chiefs of Staff felt strongly that some way should be found to overcome their political objections.[28]

We thus reach June 1950 with a clear contrast of opinions of what to do about Spain within the US administration. It is not hard to imagine a scenario in which the ambivalent policy of the US towards Spain would have continued over a prolonged period. For all the intensification of the Cold War from 1947 to mid-1950, American policy towards Spain had seen little change in practice. Officials inside the administration noted that even if the military was keen to secure the cooperation of Spain, there remained even more powerful voices against it, including President Truman's. Less than two weeks before the start of the Korean War, President Truman would write to the Secretary of State complaining that the National Security Council report on US policy toward Spain was "decidedly militaristic and in my opinion not realistic with present conditions."[29]

These concerns would be much alleviated after the outbreak of the Korean War. It made a difference not just in American policy toward Spain but in the overall stance of the US administration regarding the Cold War. Against the background of the Soviets' acquiring the atomic bomb and the fall of China to the communists in 1949, the National Security Council had prepared in April 1950 its policy paper on objectives and programs for national security, better known as NSC 68, and which would become one of the most influential documents to guide US policy during the Cold War. NSC 68 advocated a substantial increase in US military spending and a "rapid" buildup of the "military strength of the free world."

President Truman, who had initially rejected the conclusions of NSC 68 since he had felt that a massive buildup of the military was not called for, would change his mind after Korea. The Truman administration would go on to undertake one of the fastest increases in military spending, increasing it from 5 to over 14 percent of GDP from 1950 to 1953. Discussions about Spain are characteristic of the broader considerations within the Truman administration about the appropriate posture in the evolving Cold War climate. In short, what Korea meant was an acceleration in the evolution of a policy towards Spain which had already been drifting in favor of Franco. It was as if the Cold War had dealt Franco a "winning hand," to use the phrase of the great historian Paul Preston.

---

[28] Bradley to Johnson (Secretary of Defense). Washington, May 3, 1950, *FRUS*, vol. 3, document 683.

[29] Truman to Acheson, Washington, June 16, 1950, *FRUS*, vol. 3, document 684.

The Pact

Given the new climate after Korea, one could have expected swift action from the US to secure military bases in Spain. Such agreements would be eventually reached, but only in September 1953. The Pact of Madrid, as the agreements would be known, covered defense, economic cooperation, and technical assistance, and committed the Americans to provide economic and military aid in return for the use of four military bases in Spanish territory. The US agreed that the conditions of use of the bases were relegated to secret clauses so that the Spaniards could publicly claim these "joint" bases to be under the sovereignty of Spain while the US secretly obtained the right to unilaterally decide how to use them even during war (Viñas, 1981).

In retrospect it is tempting to see the Pact of Madrid as inevitable. But this was not at all obvious to those present in discussions at the time. Once negotiations began, the complexity of dealing with the Spaniards became apparent to the Americans. The Franco regime not only opposed any demands for political change but also refused any demands for reforms to its economic policies as a condition for the granting of aid. The Spaniards insisted on avoiding the impression of a loss of national sovereignty or of a "price tag" in exchange for the military bases. For them it was of the utmost importance that the agreements were seen as a true "pact," a long-term commitment on the side of the US. The fact that the US was not prepared to agree outright to most of the Spanish requests is further evidence that the ultimate outcome of negotiations remained uncertain. It took time for the Americans to come to terms with the *sine qua non* conditions put forward by Spain (Calvo-Gonzalez, 2002, pp. 112–23).

Time, in this case, was not running in favor of Franco. The US was also exploring the possibility of securing bases in French Morocco. Technological advances were also working against the strategic importance of bases in Spain. The B-52 bomber, with its much greater range that would allow reaching the Soviet Union from bases in the US, had its maiden flight in April 1952. Truly intercontinental bombers limited the essential nature of air bases in places like Spain. Moreover, President Truman remained steadfast in his contempt for Franco. And even the arrival of Eisenhower to the White House did not speed things significantly. As late as June 1953, the incoming Deputy Director of the economic mission in Madrid was briefed in Washington that if Spain overreached, the US would simply "walk away from the table."[30]

Herein lies another apparent paradox: The change in American policy toward Spain and the eventual agreements were not the result of the vast military

---

[30] Rubottom and Murphy (1984, p. 27). On Truman's dislike of Franco, Acheson gives it as the only example in an otherwise out of context description of Truman's strong beliefs: "Mr. Truman held deep-seated convictions on many subjects, among them, for instance, a dislike of Franco and Catholic obscurantism in Spain." (Acheson, 1969, p. 169).

importance of Spain but the fact that Spain was a relatively marginal question on which the US administration could have ended up on either side of the issue. One could argue that Franco did not have a winning hand; he had a weak hand but was lucky that the opposing player simply folded, more preoccupied with events elsewhere. This is an important point because it shows that a different course of action was clearly possible. Franco may have been right in predicting that the US would court him, but it seems that he did not understand that the interest of the US in Spain was relatively marginal. It is precisely because Spain was not an issue of critical importance for the Americans that the US was able to shift its position (Tusell, 1989a).

Spain was indeed a relatively minor issue for US policy when compared to Britain or France, as Acheson pointed out in early 1950 when he wrote to the Chairman of the Senate Foreign Relations Committee, Senator Connally, to explain the policy on Spain. At the outset, one can read Acheson's frustration that the Spanish question was being paid an attention "which is disproportionate to its intrinsic importance," and blaming lobbying efforts for it.[31] This was not just cheap talk from Acheson. For example, Spain took almost no space on Acheson's agenda as Secretary of State. This is so especially when compared with other peripheral European countries like Yugoslavia.[32]

The fact that the ambiguity of the American position stemmed from an assessment of the marginal importance of Spain would prove critical in explaining why it took three long years for the military agreements between the US and Spain to materialize. The fact that it took a relatively long time to finalize the agreements is a reminder that a different outcome was clearly possible. Yet, the outcome that materialized, with the long-term commitment of the Americans to Spain, was indeed most crucial for Spaniards. This outcome would come to play a significant role in Spain's fortunes over the next decades: It helped to reduce political uncertainty about the future of the Franco regime.

Economic consequences

With the benefit of hindsight, historians have come to stress how the American support to Spain contributed to the definitive consolidation of the Franco regime. Importantly, that was an assessment widely shared by contemporary observers— both supporters and critics of the regime—as events unfolded. Among the

---

[31] Acheson to Connally, Washington, January 18, 1950, *FRUS*, vol. 3, document 679.
[32] This explains why Spain is barely discussed in most overviews of the Cold War: Melvyn Leffler (1992) includes only one reference to Spain or Franco in over 600 pages dedicated to national security, the Truman administration, and the Cold War; John Lewis Gaddis (1997) includes four references to Spain compared to 14 to Yugoslavia and 19 to Turkey.

critics, *The New York Times* lamented that American support "will be helping to perpetuate Franco in power." What were the economic consequences of the American-supported consolidation of the Franco regime?[33]

A short few months after the agreements between the US and Spain had been signed, a staffer from the Bank of England visited Spain to take the pulse of the economy, as it was customary for staff in the Overseas Division of that central bank. The visitor noted an increase in what he referred to as "confidence in the future" and ventured some explanations as to the reasons for this positive turn of events. His crisp analysis is worth quoting at length:

> [...] one important factor underlying the confidence in the future is the psychological reaction to the U.S. agreement. I say "psychological" because it is the potential effects of the Agreement which has made the impact rather than the assistance itself (for this, although welcome, is a mere "drop in the ocean" in the light of Spain's requirements), i.e., the very fact that an agreement of any sort has been concluded with the U.S.A. as representing an end to Spain's isolation and an indication of U.S. Government confidence in the future stability of the country.[34]

Given the official censorship that crippled the domestic press, the accounts of external observers are particularly helpful to interpret the reaction of Spanish economic agents of the time. Still, domestic sources also provide some window into the domestic perception of the expected impact of the reaffirmed American support to Spain. A week after the agreements had been signed, the editorial of the weekly *Economía* wrote about the economic aid that Spain was about to start receiving as a result of the agreements as follows: "[Its] volume is not in our view the most important [consequence], but the influence that it could have on the normal development of our economy."[35]

The mechanism by which this influence would materialize was widely understood to hinge on the new interests that the US would now have. By setting up military bases in Spain, the US now had a stake in the political and economic stability of the country. In the spring of 1954, the influential newspaper *The Economist* would comment on the American support to Spain with its usual clarity: "Now that the Americans have an interest in the country, it is reasonable to assume that they will help it get out of the most serious economic difficulties."[36]

Behind closed doors, American officials discussed matters in very similar terms. When thinking about how much aid should the US be prepared to furnish Spain, the National Security Council settled internally on the following principle

---

[33] Fusi (1995, p. 146). *The New York Times* quote is from August 30, 1953. A longer treatment of this question can be found in Calvo-Gonzalez (2001, 2002, and 2007a) on which this section draws.

[34] Excerpt from report on Spain by G. J. MacGilivray, May 21, 1954, Bank of England Archive, OV61/5.

[35] *Economía*, September 30, 1953.   [36] *The Economist*, April 17, 1954.

to guide the actions of the American administration: "to provide the minimum additional aid that would guarantee internal stability in Spain so that the use of our bases is not jeopardized by civil disorders." Before a Senate hearing, the Director of the Mutual Security Agency, Harold Stassen, simply noted that "you cannot defend the U.S. air bases without defending Spain." The interpretation of defending Spain included defending the Franco government, as years later Senator J. William Fulbright would find out on a visit to Spain. Fulbright was appalled to learn that the type of joint military maneuvers undertaken by American and Spanish armed forces included a scenario of "a domestic insurrection in which the American military intervened to save the Spanish government."[37]

Observers' assessments of what this American commitment implied for the Spanish economy are particularly insightful, but we do not need to restrict ourselves to qualitative sources to assess the impact of the American support on economic confidence inside Spain. Financial markets also showed a positive reaction to news of American support, as I explored in an earlier contribution (see Calvo-Gonzalez, 2007a for details of the following findings). The reaction can be seen across many asset classes. As with most currencies in the world, the fixed exchange rate regimes that were widespread at the time resulted in black markets appearing in key trading cities over the world, notably in New York and in the North African city of Tangiers. We will return to exchange rate policy later in the book, but for now it is useful to note how both the level and the volatility of the peseta exchange rate in New York changed in the early 1950s. In 1950, as it had been during most of the 1940s, the peseta traded in New York around 60 percent below the rate that would be justified by the purchasing parity condition to hold. This spread, which can be thought of as a measure of the risk of holding pesetas, would drop to less than 10 percent by 1953 and stay at that low level. The volatility of the peseta exchange rate also declined significantly from the early 1950s onwards. Similarly, the spread between the US dollar price of gold in Madrid's black market and the US dollar price of gold in Zurich also dropped and stabilized around the early 1950s.

The signing of the agreements provides us with a unique opportunity to test the impact of the American support to the Franco regime because it was a distinct episode in what was an otherwise long and protracted process. It is therefore as close to a natural experiment as we can have to observe and isolate the impact of positive news related to the American rapprochement. Drawing on an event study methodology, I have shown elsewhere (Calvo-Gonzalez, 2007a) that the Madrid stock market posted a statistically significant positive response after the announcement of the signature of the agreements. Finally, and equally important,

---

[37] Memorandum of the 248th meeting of the NSC, Washington, May 12, 1955, *FRUS, 1955–1957*, vol. XXVII, p. 539. Stassen's statement as quoted in Durá (1985) p. 344. Fulbright's reaction in Woods (1995), p. 511.

I also found in my earlier work that these measures of increased economic confidence—such as the volatility of the peseta exchange rate—contributed to an increase in capital formation (in a Granger-causality sense). This suggests that the increased economic confidence that resulted from the American backing of the Franco regime helps to explain the increase in investment that we saw in Figure 2.1 above.

Before we move on, let us return to the Bank of England staffer that had traveled to Spain in early 1954. In his assessment he had pointed out two channels for the increased confidence in Spain. One was the commitment of the US to Spain's future stability. The second was the expectation that the agreements would bring about an end to economic isolation. The latter would eventually come—as we will see in later chapters—but with a relatively long lag. Over time, Spain would be allowed to join the United Nations in 1955, as well as in 1958 the Organisation for European Economic Cooperation (OEEC), the International Monetary Fund (IMF), and the World Bank. All this would prove consequential, as membership in the multilateral system would strengthen the position of those within the Franco regime that wanted to shift economic policies in the direction that the Bretton Woods institutions were advocating.

Calibrating the actual importance of economic policy changes is something to which we will return in later chapters, but it is important to stress that the economic policy changes endorsed by the international financial institutions cannot be the primary reason for the acceleration of growth in the early 1950s. The economic takeoff simply preceded them. This is not to say that the only cause for the improved business sentiment or economic performance throughout the 1950s was the American support. Other factors, including some changes in economic policy that we will explore later, contributed positively to improved economic outcomes. Still, American support, especially after the critical juncture of the Korean War, tipped the scales.

Conclusions

"I have now won the Civil War," Franco told his cousin and confidant on the evening of September 23, 1953.[38] Such a gushing statement was out of character for the usually restrained Franco. The dictator was utterly thrilled with the signature, earlier that day, of the agreements by which the US would set up four military bases on Spanish territory and Spain would get an unspecified military and economic cooperation. More importantly, the agreements helped secure Franco in power and removed any lingering doubts that his regime was not firmly established. The stability of the Franco regime would mark a most significant

[38] Hills (1967, p. 416).

departure from the volatility that had dominated Spanish politics since the beginning of the nineteenth century.

How did the Franco regime become a stable polity? This is the first piece of the puzzle that any explanation about Spain's path to prosperity needs to address. It can indeed seem mystifying that a regime as flawed as Franco's would become the guarantor of stability and ultimately an enabler of economic prosperity. Both external and internal dynamics helped the regime achieve the political stability that had escaped countless previous Spanish regimes. In this chapter we have dealt with the external factors that created the critical juncture that facilitated the emergence of political stability in Spain.

The achievement of political stability in Spain was unlikely, fast, and externally facilitated. Unlikely because of the origins and nature of the Franco regime. The alignment by Franco with the Axis was clear and well understood by all parties. The main reason why the Franco regime survived without getting entangled in the hostilities was the limited value that first German and then American war planners saw in Spain. At the end of the world war, Spain was an ostracized anomaly. Franco's was a rare leftover regime of fascist origins in a world that had moved on by 1945. Such a regime seemed in no position to ensure the long-term political stability that had eluded Spain during the previous century and a half. The Cold War would unexpectedly provide a critical juncture that would change the course of Spanish history. In the increasingly global world of the Cold War, the interests of the American military in securing bases in Spain would carry an increasing weight in American foreign policy, especially after the outbreak of war in the Korean peninsula.

One of the underappreciated paradoxes of this time is that, even as the tide was turning in Franco's favor, it did not immediately lift uncertainty about the political viability of the Franco regime. The tide may have turned, but in doing so, instead of reinforcing Franco in power, it could have swept him away. Just because history unfolded in one way, it could not have easily done so differently. Franco would eventually be proven right that the rising tensions between the Soviet Union and the US would lead the latter to embrace his regime. But, paradoxically, the increased interest of the US in Spain also increased initially the risk of an American-backed toppling of his regime. This helps to explain the continuation of uncertainty about the viability of the Franco regime until at least the outbreak of the Korean War. The conclusion of economic and military agreements between the US and Spain in 1953 lifted all remaining clouds about the long-term prospects of the Franco regime.

The stability of the Franco regime would come to underpin the process of economic development. In 1947, Salvador de Madariaga would perceptively tell John Hickerson, whom we met at the beginning of this chapter racing back to the State Department on the evening of the first day of hostilities in Korea, that "from the point of view of the Spanish people only, the longer Franco continued in power, the better."[39] But Madariaga's assessment was only half prophetic. Somewhat cynically, his argument to Hickerson was that the Spanish people had so often resorted to civil war during the past century "that they ought to learn the hard way the evils of that practice." The long-lasting nature of Franco's hold on power carried indeed a heavy price in the loss of political freedoms for multiple generations of Spaniards. At the same time, in economic terms the political stability that the regime had achieved by the 1950s would prove a foundation for economic prosperity.

The Cold War may have been a critical juncture, but American support for the Franco regime could not have been, by itself, a sufficient condition for securing political stability. It is easy to think of scenarios in which the Americans could have secured the military bases without having this necessarily eliminated political instability in the country. Elsewhere in Southern Europe, left-wing movements posed an increasing threat to the stability of governments that also had the backing of the US. And from the perspective of Spanish political history, it was not at all obvious why the history of *pronunciamientos* would end with Franco's. American support can best be seen as the final act that removed any lingering uncertainty about the likelihood that the Franco regime would last. The making of such stability had domestic origins. In fact, American policy toward Spain was based on what Acheson thought that by 1950 were the two essential facts of Spanish politics: "there is no sign of an alternative" to Franco and that "the internal position of the present regime is strong."[40] How was such domestic political strength achieved? We now turn to address this question.

---

[39] Memorandum of Conversation, by the Acting Director of the Office of European Affairs (Hickerson), Washington, March 10, 1947, *FRUS*, vol. 3, document 714.

[40] Acheson to Senator Tom Connally, Chairman of the Foreign Relations Committee of the US Senate, Washington, January 18, 1950, *FRUS*, vol. 3, document 679.

3

Political Stability

When Franco's head of propaganda, Dionisio Ridruejo, was fired from his post in 1941, he went on a soul-searching journey that would take him to unlikely truth-teller and eventually to exile. After spending a year in the Russian front fighting for the Nazis, Ridruejo had a change of heart and sent a candid letter to Franco in which he described what he now could see was the reality of the regime. Besides noting the widespread hunger and the overall failure of the government's economic plan, Ridruejo offered the following political assessment. Spain in the early 1940s was characterized by a weak state which relied on the army as the active watchdog of political life; the threat of political violence was looming, something which, Ridruejo lamented, was very much in keeping with a recent history marked by a century of civil wars.[1]

The consequence of the country not having yet overcome the predicament of frequent violence to resolve political disputes, Ridruejo went on, was the inherent instability of the Franco regime. The unlikely critic of the regime did not stop his analysis there. He went on to highlight the "arbitrariness" in the administration of justice and how the confusion between public and private interests not only led to resentment among much of the population but was also associated with what he saw as an even bigger problem: an "incessant conspiracy" and intrigue "by those who defend privilege" (Ridruejo, 1976, pp. 236–40). This diagnosis of Spain could have served as the inspiration for the framework of North, Wallis, and Weingast (2009) on violence and social orders. Franco's Spain in the 1940s was not only a closed access order, filled with privileges and arbitrary justice, but also one plagued by instability, intrigues and conspiracies, and ultimately the threat of political violence. None of this bode well for the future.

How come such a precarious regime could become the guarantor of stability? This is a question that is relevant not only for understanding Spain's path to prosperity but one that also speaks to a broader literature on fragility. It is easy to forget that all states were once fragile and that, while there is no single path out of fragility, the experience of currently developed countries may be informative for today's fragile countries that are trying to get out of the vicious circle of violence

---

[1] Ridruejo's position was head of propaganda of the official and only party of the regime, headed by Franco himself. He had been fired for having been the ghostwriter of an article in the *Falangist* newspaper, *Arriba*, deriding the appointment of a military man, Colonel Valentín Galarza, as Minister of the Interior, a post that *Falangists* thought should go to one of their own. See Payne (2000, p. 287).

Unexpected Prosperity: How Spain Escaped the Middle Income Trap. Oscar Calvo-Gonzalez, Oxford University Press.
© Oscar Calvo-Gonzalez 2021. DOI: 10.1093/oso/9780198853978.003.0004

and instability in which they may be stuck. It can help us build a collection of case studies of not only failures but what one could think of as "how nations succeed." In the case of Spain, the evolving external environment, with the intensification of the Cold War after the outbreak of war in Korea, helped create the conditions to align the interests of the US with those of Franco. This helped solidify Franco in power, as argued in the previous chapter. Yet, by itself, this would not have been enough to usher in an era of political stability in Spain.

Conceptually, it is easy to see why the alignment of American interests with those of Franco cannot be a sufficient condition to guarantee political stability. Imagine another military leader replacing Franco through a violent coup and then offering the same terms of access to military bases to the Americans. Why would the US refuse to deal with the new leader? *Ex post* the US would want to maintain good relations with the new strongman that had gained power. Because of this fundamental time inconsistency, the US could not be the sole guarantor of political stability in the country.

The Americans might prefer to avoid a change in government, and with it the risk that it could bring about instability that could jeopardize its continued use of the military bases. But it is not in the interests of the US to sacrifice more than needed to maintain access to the military bases. After all, the American interest in the country was relatively narrow. The US may have had a strong incentive to ensure that no revolutionary regime would replace Franco, but it could not have been a credible deterrent for other right-wing aspiring dictators inside Spain. It follows that the external support cannot by itself explain fully the achievement of political stability in Spain.

If political stability also had domestic roots, what were those? In this chapter we explore how Franco was able to secure a monopoly on the use of violence for political purposes. In short, he did so by a brutal repression against the left and by co-opting and playing against each other the members of the coalition that had risen against the Republic. While Franco continued to demonstrate his willingness to use violence to remain in power, the appetite of those against him to risk their lives in the pursuit of his removal from office would shrink over time. This was due to both external factors—examined in the previous chapter—and domestic developments which we now turn to examine.

A defining event

The fact that we refer to the regime that emerged victorious from the Civil War as Francoism and that the dictatorship was so closely identified with the person of Franco is worth stressing. How this became the case is highly significant to understand the political economy of Spain thereafter. Francoism did not exist before the Civil War. It was the outcome of a war that proved to be the defining event of Spain in the twentieth century, much like civil wars today are central to many countries' development around the world. To understand Spain's path to prosperity it will therefore be necessary to briefly discuss key aspects of the conflict and its consequences. The war had arguably started out as an old-fashioned military *pronunciamiento* that most participants thought would be over in a matter of days or weeks. As it turned out, the coup failed to overthrow the government, unleashing much violence.[2] The failed coup gave rise to a vicious war that would last for almost three years, which in turn paved the way to a dictatorship that would be in place for over three decades.

So, what type of regime was Franco's? At the outset, the rebels seemed to be united only in their opposition to the Republic, which they perceived as revolutionary and anti-Church. But there was little agreement as to what they espoused. At first, the rebels had no leader, no consistent ideology, or even agreed on the desired form of government for Spain. They did not even have a name—the label "Nationalist" to refer to the rebels emerged as a catch-all term in the weeks after the military uprising. The leader of the *pronunciamiento* was supposed to be General José Sanjurjo, who had been exiled to Lisbon after he had attempted a coup in 1932 which had quickly failed. But Sanjurjo died in an airplane crash on his way to Spain in July 1936, leaving the rebels without a nominal figure head. Franco would then become the leader of the rebels two months into the war, when the military commanders of the rebel forces convened to discuss the need for a unified command to win the war.

The selection of a *Generalísimo* would come to be decided by the nine generals that had risen against the Republic. The choice of Franco was not necessarily the most obvious one. There were a couple of other rebel generals with greater seniority. And General Emilio Mola had been much more instrumental in organizing the rebellion and led the army of the North that had successfully controlled most of Castile and León. But Franco had three advantages over them. First, he commanded the colonial army of Morocco, and thus had the most battle-hardened troops. Second, he had personally secured the material support of Germany and Italy, having engaged in contacts with those countries and spoken as the de facto leader of the rebels from the outset. Third, Franco was perceived to be the most pro-monarchist among the rebel generals, which played a role in Franco garnering a critical support to be elevated to the supreme leadership.

How Franco came to lead the rebels is relevant for understanding how the future threats to his hold on power will evolve. Crucially, many of those who supported Franco did so under the belief that he would be the supreme military

---

[2] A spiral of reprisals quickly escalated. It also led to much chaos. To give but one example, the Republican intellectual Salvador de Madariaga—from whom we took the story about Narváez having eliminated all his enemies—was detained by an anarchist militia on July 18, 1936 and about to be executed when the militiamen realized they had confused him with a right-wing congressman with the same surname.

leader only for the duration of the war. But Franco had other plans. He would not relinquish any of the extraordinary powers that he accumulated in his persona as chief of state, head of government, supreme commander of the army, and head of the only legal political party. Some of those who had helped select Franco as leader would come to resent his refusal to step down after the end of the Civil War and to hold on to power. These disgruntled military men would prove an enduring source of intrigues about attempts to remove Franco from power throughout the 1940s.

Classifying the Franco dictatorship is a complicated exercise that has attracted extensive attention in both the literature and the public debate. The difficulty of cataloging the regime stems in part from its longevity, as it evolved significantly over time. At the outset, Franco's regime had totalitarian aspirations, even if it still had within it supporters from a broad range of ideologically different factions, including traditionalists, monarchists, and others that were not necessarily fascistic. As the eventual fate of Mussolini and Hitler became increasingly clear, the Franco regime moved away from its totalitarianism and settle into what became an authoritarian regime, as categorized by the great twentieth-century sociologist and political scientist Juan Linz.[3] While there is still an academic debate about the precise labeling and phases of Francoism, a key aspect on which there is virtual unanimity among historians of all persuasions is that, from the outset, Franco's overriding objective was to remain in power until his death. This is an element that would have the most enduring and significant consequences. Perhaps paradoxically, as we will see below, this would first contribute to undermine political stability yet come to be one of its foundations.

An authoritarian regime, as defined by Linz, permits a limited pluralism within it. Indeed, ideologically the Franco regime contained a variety of forces that would in principle be hard to reconcile. At the start of the Civil War the *Falange*—a Fascist-inspired party—supported the rebels, but it was far from constituting a plurality among them. Most monarchists were also drawn to the rebel side, even the Nationalist uprising was not initially identified with a form of government. In fact, it was only several weeks after the coup that the rebels stopped using the Republican flag and replaced it with the old monarchist flag. Many among the rebels, included those who were instrumental in elevating Franco to the role of sole leader, had done so with the implicit understanding that, among the rebel generals, it was Franco who provided the best hopes for a speedy restoration of the monarchy after an eventual victory of the rebels. Monarchists were themselves

---

[3] It is worth quoting from Linz's original, and arguably unsurpassed, taxonomy of totalitarianism and authoritarianism: "Authoritarian regimes are political systems with limited, not responsible, pluralism: without elaborate and guiding ideology (but with distinctive mentalities); without intensive or extensive political mobilization (except at some points in their development); and in which a leader (or occasionally a small group) exercises power within formally ill-defined limits but actually quite predictable ones." (Linz, 1964).

divided in two distinct groups, on one side supporters of the pretender Don Juan, son of the late Alfonso XIII, and on the other side the traditionalist faction that originated with the Carlists of the nineteenth century and which on the eve of the Civil War had a militia of around ten thousand armed men that fought on the Nationalist side.

The fact that such diverse ideological groups could be unified under the Nationalist banner speaks to how divisive the Civil War was. These politically diverse factions were at first united, above all, in their disgust for what the Republic had become. Paradoxically, after the initial coup failed in cities like Madrid or Barcelona, it spurred those on the left to undertake the type of revolutionary acts that the rebels had risen to thwart. The spiral of violence that ensued also helps to explain how very different ideologies could coexist under the Nationalist tent, joined only in their opposition to what they saw as a revolutionary and anti-clerical left dominated by foreign and unnatural influences such as Marxism. And we now know that the Soviet Union took advantage of the conflict as an opportunity to meddle in Spanish affairs, seeking to take over the Spanish economy, government, and armed forces (Radosh et al., 2011).

In another example of how the Nationalist movement amalgamated seemingly incompatible forces, the fascist *Falange* and the traditionalists were unified into a single party by dictate of Franco during the civil war. This is not to say that there would be no tensions between these factions, sometimes even violent clashes occurred, but by and large these seemingly incompatible groups stuck together given their common opposition to the Republic.

The consequences of sectarian violence

The Civil War stands out for the dehumanization of the enemy that took place. The rebel General Emilio Mola said shortly after the insurrection that if "I see my father in the enemy lines, I execute him."[4] By volunteering such a shocking statement, Mola was conveying in no uncertain terms that being a loyalist to the Republic amounted to such a violation of human values that was inexcusable under any circumstance. Basic morals, like respect for one's father, not only did not apply but were superseded by a duty to get rid of an enemy thus stripped of any humanity. This is what social psychologists refer to as moral disengagement (Bandura, 2016). Moral disengagement allows the wrongdoer to harm others because, in his mind, the victims are deserving of maltreatment. It provides a way to selectively circumvent one's moral standards, thus resolving the paradox of

---

[4] See Álvarez (2007, p. 83) for this and other statements of similar nature by rebel leaders. Mola also called for "extreme violence" in his instructions to rebels ahead of the coup.

how one can violate certain moral principles—filial duty in Mola's pointed example—without the loss of self-respect while doing so.

This type of dehumanization illustrated by Mola's statement was in fact widespread. The rebel General Gonzalo Queipo de Llano became known for his nightly and gruesome radio broadcasts in which he called for the extermination of loyalists to the Republic. Queipo de Llano would repeatedly ask his supporters to kill "like a dog" anyone who opposed them.[5] Early in the war Franco himself stated in an interview with the Chicago Tribune that he would be prepared to kill half of Spain if that was required to rid it of communism. During the early stages of the war, the rebels did not take prisoners and extolled rape as a weapon. Executions were routine and justified for anyone who had not defected and joined the rebels. Mola would not get to shoot his father, but Franco got close to it: He did not oppose the execution of his cousin, who had remained loyal to the Republic and was one of Franco's closest childhood friends; Franco feared that a pardon would be regarded as a sign of weakness on his part.[6]

Our main interest here is to explore how this profound trauma influenced the later socioeconomic development of Spain. While the terror that we sparingly described above is horrifying, it is not unique. Social psychologists have found that the type of dehumanization and delegitimization that we saw in Spain during the Civil War often plays a key role in intense, vicious, and prolonged intergroup conflicts (Bar-Tal and Hammack, 2012). Importantly, social psychologists have studied the consequences that such delegitimization of the enemy has. This can help us better understand the future course of the Franco regime and even the post-Francoism transition.

There are several detrimental effects that typically arise from the delegitimization of the enemy, according to the social psychology literature. From a cognitive perspective, the most significant consequence is that it tends to frame the conflict as immutable. This is because the conflict is connected to a naturalized status quo: With this type of rival it is impossible to make peace because of its inherently unworthy characteristics. A related consequence is that groups that feel threatened externally tend to be particularly averse to tolerating internal dissent, an issue to which we will return when we discuss the factors that help to explain the economic policy reform process.

Spain was no exception to suffering the detrimental long-term consequences of extensive delegitimization during intergroup conflict. The intense delegitimization

---

[5] Queipo de Llano stressed to his supporters that in killing such inhuman enemy, "you will be free of all blame." Preston (2012, p. 149).

[6] Preston (1994, p. 151). The exercise of authority required, in Franco's interpretation, a very discretionary use of clemency. Often, pleas for mercy were disregarded even—or possibly because—they originated in high places. For example, despite the pleas of Queipo de Llano, General Domingo Batet was executed for having failed to join the rebels. Queipo de Llano had previously ignored Franco's plea to spare the life of his friend General Miguel Campins during the early weeks of the rebellion when Franco had not yet been elevated to the supreme leadership.

that went on during the Civil War helps to explain—not justify—why there was no pursuit of reconciliation in its aftermath. Having demonized the Republican side and framed the Civil War as a "crusade" against evil there was no room for forgiveness in the aftermath of the war. An amnesty would have been against the very logic to "purge" and "purify" Spain (Richards, 1998, pp. 26–8). Thus, the framing of the conflict as an existential fight between a "true" Spain and an unnatural "Red" foreign enemy predictably had long-lasting effects. As we will see in the next chapter, it also affected the realm of economic policymaking. It is also not surprising that, decades later, as we will see in due time, episodes such as the legalization of the Communist Party—which had been framed as subhuman during the Civil War—would be one of the most critical moments of the political transition.

Nothing that happened in Spain in the decades after the Civil War can be properly understood without it. It was the Civil War that decisively split the country in two, giving rise to a discourse about the existence of "two Spains."[7] This narrative would play a significant role first in uniting forces around the "Nationalist" Spain under Franco and then, much later, in eliciting a consensus on the need to move beyond the two Spains. While the war gave rise to a narrative of a divided country, it was also one that ended with a conclusive victory of one side. The decisiveness of the victory of the Nationalist side is what makes the Spanish Civil War "the" central event of Spanish history of the twentieth century, as the winners went on to impose a ruthless repression meant to complete the extermination of the enemy that had started during the war.

Repression

The brutal repression of those suspected of sympathies for the Republican side stands out as one of the defining characteristics of the early Franco regime. Indeed, the new administration sought and achieved its hold on power through violence and the recurrent threat of it. Fear of reprisals was so acute that many families that had lost members because of their Republican sympathies would simply hide their mourning and not dare to mention their lost ones even in private. It was truly, and would be for decades, a time of silence (Richards, 1998). The fear was understandable given the track record of the new regime.

The extent and cruelty of the repression is hard to overstate. During the war, around 200,000 people were killed away from the military frontlines. Mass graves became ordinary. Extrajudicial killings, corpses of the executed left in the streets to instill fear, or women and children being targeted are just some examples of the brutality that the population endured far from the battlefront. As has been shown

---

[7] It was not, as it is often argued, that the existence of "two Spains" had led to the Civil War (Juliá, 2010, p. 123).

by political scientist Laia Balcells (2017), the politics of violence against civilians during the Civil War was not random. Rather, it responded to a logic, whereas the harshest repression occurred in areas where political rivalry had been most intense in the past. Revenge emotions made it more likely that previous violence would be met with stronger violence.

Violence continued after the war was over, when tens of thousands of suspected loyalists were executed. The war had been framed not as a fight for control of the government, or even for a particular form of government, as the *pronunciamientos* of the past. Rather, the Civil War was couched as an existential fight against an unnatural and anti-Spanish "Red" menace. This delegitimization of the enemy, the social psychology literature tells us, calls for violence to go on until the adversary is eliminated.

Thus, after the war finished, the repression continued. It was as if the war "had not ended in 1939" (Fontana, 2003). The extent and inhumanity of the repression, after decades of silence, has become the subject of extensive documentation in recent years.[8] The imprisonment of those suspected of disloyalty was widespread. While the precise number of political prisoners is probably unknowable, it is estimated that after the war, the prison population reached at least a quarter million in a country of 25 million people. This was coupled with a systematic use of torture and concentration camps, where psychiatric experiments on prisoners were also performed. Summary proceedings with few if any legal guarantees were also characteristic of a postwar politics of revenge that instead of reconciliation sought the extermination of the losing side. Around twenty thousand people were executed after the war ended.[9]

A comparative perspective helps to put the severity of punishment in postwar Spain in context. The rates of incarceration are an order of magnitude or two above what has been recorded in other countries after internal conflict. Spain's prison rate after its civil war was twelve times higher than that recorded in the US in the years after its own civil war. As for the extent of malnutrition, which stemmed largely from the application of autarkic policies that promoted stockholding and a misallocation of resources, as we will see in the next chapter, it far exceeded what was to be seen anywhere else in Europe even under the worst of the Nazi occupation, such as during the Dutch "Hunger Winter" of 1944–5.[10]

---

[8] Among the many books documenting the memories of the victims, see the riveting Serrano and Serrano (2016).

[9] Preston (2012) and Alvarez (2007) for details of the atrocities. *The Politics of Revenge* is the title of an important early contribution on this topic by Paul Preston (1990). There were also extrajudicial killings and other deplorable acts of violence on the Republican side. However, given the victory of the Nationalist side, it is of greater interest to understand the Nationalist violence as it laid the foundation for the postwar society.

[10] Cahalan (1986, p. 28) for the US prison rate after the American Civil War and Cazorla-Sánchez (2010) for famine rates in postwar Europe. Angel Viñas has also shown that executions of Nazi collaborators in liberated France were much smaller than in Spain (see http://www.angelvinas.es/?p=1790, June 11, 2019).

The control of the population was extensive. It not only applied to political activity but also aimed to control labor relations by creating single "vertical" syndicates. Working conditions, wages, and prices were all regulated. Few public spaces were unaffected, with prior censorship for all mass media. Religious worship and the use of national languages were limited. The autarkic economic policies also contributed to social control. Food rationing, introduced a month after the end of the Civil War, was so poorly managed that it led to widespread hunger and malnutrition. It also meant in practice the criminalization of most of the population, which could not live on the meager rations and had to turn to the black market to survive, thus engaging in illicit activities.

The subsequent arbitrary enforcement of the law provided an opportunity to further victimize those on the losing side of the civil war. The authorities turned a blind eye to those close to the regime that benefited from diverting food to the black market, while targeting others. The leniency against most black marketeers contrasts with the intensity of the policing of rural communities by the increasingly militarized Civil Guard.[11] The widespread repression and social control kept risks to the regime from the left to the minimum.

The first source of threat to the Franco regime came from Republican fighters who had crossed in the thousands into France at the end of the Civil War. After the outbreak of World War II, these fighters had mostly joined the French Resistance and operated as part of the *maquis* in a guerrilla war against the Germans. During World War II, many Republican exiles hoped that the impending victory of the Allies would lead to an international effort to remove Franco from power. In late 1944, as the Germans retreated from France, several hundred *maquis* crossed the Pyrenees to encourage a popular uprising inside Spain. The operation failed, in part because Franco's intelligence services had prior knowledge of the plans. Many fighters, however, were able to elude Franco's security forces and joined other *maquis* operating within Spain.

The Allies, although they toyed with the idea, in the end never moved on a military intervention against Franco, as we saw in the previous chapter. The main hope of the Republican exiles thus faded over time. Nevertheless, the threat of violence from internal guerrillas persisted throughout the 1940s, although, without external support, it could never seriously challenge the authority of the central state. From 1943 to 1952, the official security forces arrested or killed 25,000

---

[11] Some of the earliest memories of my mother, Aurora, as a child in the 1940s were not only of the pains of hunger but also the fear she felt during the frequent searches of her home by the Civil Guard, allegedly looking for agricultural produce being diverted to the black market. My grandparents were landless sharecroppers, so it is hard to imagine this intense policing as driven by anything other than a show of force. On the Civil Guard in this period see García Carrero (2019).

people said to be involved in the guerrilla war against the Franco regime.[12] By the early 1950s, this threat virtually disappeared.

Overall, the continued repression against the left was effective in achieving its goal of eliminating the opposition from formerly Republican sympathizers. As a result, by the end of the 1940s there was a very low probability of a successful left-wing uprising against the regime. Achieved at an extraordinarily high human cost, this was also to be the first foundation of political stability under the Franco regime. For the remainder of the life of the dictator, there would be no real threat to his hold on power originating from the left of the ideological spectrum.

As the economy developed in later decades, there would be, nevertheless, a growing student and trade union movement. There would also be a new generation of clergymen that, inspired by the Second Vatican Council, distanced itself from the regime and embraced grassroots activist groups. Strikes and other forms of civic protest became more common and eventually a true opposition to the Franco regime emerged. But this was much later. For years, fear of reprisals made many opponents to Franco weary and reluctant to participate in demonstrations and strikes. The eventual emergence of an opposition to the regime would neither threaten the dictatorship's hold on power nor, by and large, resort to violence. Exceptions to the non-use of violence were the Basque nationalist terrorist ETA as well as a couple of much smaller left-wing terrorist groups. Between 1968, the date of ETA's first assassination, and 1975 the combined death toll of terrorist groups in Spain stood at fewer than 50 people, mostly at the hands of ETA, which was also responsible for the assassination of the President of the Government, Admiral Luis Carrero Blanco, in 1973.

Even though the left-wing revolutionary threat had virtually disappeared by the late 1940s, the Franco regime would continue to derive great benefit from the rhetorical use of the "Red menace" for years to come. One of Franco's personal triumphs was his ability to frame the narrative about the political future of Spain as one in which the only two options were either his regime or civil war. Many stakeholders and observers from all political persuasions fell for this false dichotomy, as we will see further below. Franco's frequent references to the threat of a Judeo-Masonic conspiracy and the Communist International are often interpreted as evidence of Franco's own personal obsessions and paranoia (González Duro, 1992). But these obsessions also helped him to cast the debate, both publicly and privately, in ways that would benefit Franco's own prospects.

Ultimately, however, it was Franco's skilled manipulation of the different political families within its regime which, as we will see next, became the true foundation of political stability. By the 1950s, the different factions of that uneasy rebel

---

[12] Figures, however, vary according to different sources and authors. See Bardavío and Sinova (2000), pp. 334–7.

coalition that had initially been united only in their opposition to the Republic now also shared in their support of Franco as leader. Each group came to think that they were better off with Franco than without him. This required a significant effort at co-opting a variety of elites.

Co-opting elites

The second and even more critical pillar of political stability was the balancing of power within the Francoist coalition. It was achieved mainly by co-opting the elites of the different factions that supported the regime. Students of the Franco regime identify at least six distinct political families that would be represented, in varying degrees, in governments throughout more than three decades of the Franco regime: military, monarchists, Catholics, traditionalists, *Falangists*, and technocrats (De Miguel, 1975). Each of these groups would hold some share of power through the end of the regime. Their precise share of power would be adjusted along the way to reflect imperfectly but visibly trends in the true balance of forces among them. Franco would prove adept at handling each of these families, deploying a variety of divisive and manipulating tactics that ultimately had in common the co-opting of these elites into the exercise of power under the ultimate control of Franco himself.

What is most relevant from our perspective is how this co-opting of various elites will ultimately result in an equilibrium of political stability. As we saw in Chapter 1, after 1939 there would be a period of over 40 years without a military coup attempt. In fact, the regime installed in 1939 would be the last one that achieved power through violence. Besides the move away from violence as a means to gain power, the period would be characterized by other markers of stability. While most cabinets had lasted no more than a year during the nineteenth and early twentieth century, governments under the new regime would prove much more lasting. In the 30 years before the Civil War, there were 50 different cabinets; in contrast, in the 30 years after 1945, there would be only 8 different cabinets.

Political stability is far from being fully captured by a simple metric like the turnover of governments, but one advantage of analyzing this indicator is that it allows us to have a long time series and move away from imposing an a priori periodization. As economic historians Leandro Prados de la Escosura and Blanca Sánchez-Alonso (2019) have noted, the Civil War has marked "a dividing line in research" that prevents a global vision of the twentieth century, resulting in what the authors consider a striking absence of debate on long-run economic performance during that century.

A long-run approach is indeed needed to look for explanations as to why the determinants of Spain's economic backwardness gave way in the second half of

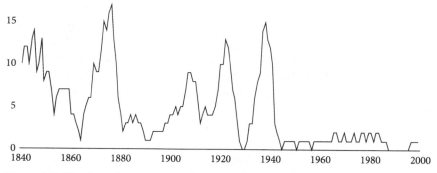

Figure 3.1 Number of government changes in Spain over previous five years, 1840–2000

Note: From 1840 to 1937 only changes in the Prime Minister are considered changes of government. Given that Franco held the Prime Minister job for three decades during the Franco regime we consider government changes the major cabinet reshuffles, as in Urquijo (2008) and many others.

Source: Own elaboration with data from Urquijo (2008).

the twentieth century. While this is obviously a general argument, a concrete example of the benefits from this long-run approach is seen in Figure 3.1. The long-run data allow us to conclusively establish that the increased stability of governments in the second half of the twentieth century, unlike in the past, became entrenched. This created the conditions for a potential continuity in policy and a greater chance of having a long-term horizon for policymaking, an issue to which we will return in subsequent chapters.

Achieving such stability took time. In fact, and seemingly paradoxically, the very same tactics that would eventually underpin political stability under the Franco regime were the source of uncertainty and instability in its early years. As the case of Spain shows, there were many factors both external and internal in the early years of the 1940s that militated against political stability even if governments were now lasting longer. Moreover, as has often been argued here, we must put ourselves in the shoes of those living through the events in real time. For them, the type of break that we see in Figure 3.1 could only have been detected, and trusted that it would not be undone, with a lag.

Because of the difficulty of all humans to change our beliefs, we should not assume that a change in the perception of political stability would be automatic or fast. Confirmation bias, change blindness, and other psychological processes militate against it. Some momentous occasions, however, can help people craft a new narrative, with significant impacts on expectations and economic outcomes, as Nobel Prize winner Robert Shiller has emphasized (2019). Shiller points out that the type of narratives more likely to have an impact are those that are oversimplified and easily transmitted. This is another reason why the *show* of support by the Americans discussed in the previous chapter made a difference. A certainly oversimplified story of American support became a powerful narrative in Spain in the early 1950s: One of the most popular and influential films in Spain in 1952 was the comedy titled "Welcome! Mr. Marshall" which would be followed by other films that exploit the theme of the increased contact and cooperation between Americans and Spaniards (Treglown, 2013; Sojo, 2011). Thus, the impact of the American rapprochement to Spain can also be detected in having helped spread a new narrative.

Unite and rule

Franco would prove adept at forcing rivals to operate together, which often resulted that such rivals neutralized each other and diminished their power. One of the best examples was the merger of the fascist party, *Falange*, and the traditionalist party that was heir to the Carlists in the midst of the Civil War. The two parties stood for sharply contrasting ideologies. One was monarchist, the other not. One had a long history and longed for a return to the institutions of the past, while the other wanted to create a new state. Even though up until the spring of 1936, the *Falange* had not been a particularly large player—it received less than one percent of the vote in the general elections held in February 1936—the war had resulted in the swelling of members who volunteered to fight for the Nationalist cause. The merger between the two would be lopsided and had the predictable effect of splitting the Carlists between those who collaborated with the regime and those who opposed such collaboration (Canal, 2003).

By merging the *Falange* with the Carlist traditionalist party and becoming the head of the now single official party, Franco achieved numerous goals at once. By becoming the leader of the single party, Franco ensured no challenger could emerge from within the ranks of the party. Outside of the military, the strongest challenger to Franco would have been the charismatic José Antonio Primo de Rivera, founder of the *Falange* party and son of the former dictator Miguel Primo de Rivera. But he was already imprisoned by the time of the rebellion and the Republican authorities had executed him in late 1936. With Primo de Rivera dead, Franco could safely foster a cult of personality to the founder of the *Falange* in parallel to his own, without fearing that it would undermine his power.

While tensions between the Carlists and the old-time *Falangists* would continue, Franco would prove adept at making the most of this conflict to strengthen his own position. Perhaps the best example of such handling is the crisis created in August 1942, when *Falangists* threw a couple of hand grenades at the crowd that had participated in a Carlist ceremony in Bilbao's Basilica of Begoña—a sixteenth-century church of great symbolic importance for its prominence during the Carlist wars. There were numerous injuries, though no fatalities. Most importantly, the ceremony had been attended by the Minister of War, General José

Varela, who quickly interpreted the attack as an attempt on his life and set out to take political advantage of it. Franco, in what would become his characteristic way of handling such crises, used the opportunity to remove not only key *Falangists* from the government but also Varela. Franco was sending a strong signal that he would not tolerate attempts at gaining notoriety at his expense. In addition, Franco showed his characteristic firmness by executing one of the *Falangists* who participated in the attack.

By turning the *Falange* into the official party, the power of *Falangist* old-timers was diluted in a much bigger organization. The membership would eventually swell to the millions, and the organization became even less of a cohesive programmatic party. Emerging splinter groups within the *Falange* that longed for a more authentic fascist party were also dealt with harshly. For example, in 1941 a *Falangist*, J. Pérez de Cabo, was executed for selling wheat in the black market—a crime that for most carried an administrative penalty—to finance a clandestine group of the *Falange* (Cazorla Sánchez, 2000, p. 87).

Once the defeat of the Axis became a near certainty, Franco ditched much of the regalia associated with the *Falange* which he had adopted in the early years—including the Nazi salute. But Falangists would maintain a share of power for decades, including ministerial and many other lower ranking appointments. This way, Franco secured the loyalty of the *Falange* for the remainder of the regime. In fact, after the defeat of Germany, many of the pro-Nazi *Falangists* became among the most fervent Franco supporters, since Franco became their best bet not only for retaining some share of power but also for their survival.

Monarchists

Conspiracies against Franco would become common among the monarchist supporters of Don Juan, son of King Alfonso XIII, who had inherited the rights to the Crown from his father when the latter passed away in exile in February 1941. Don Juan had initially volunteered to fight in Franco's army during the Civil War, although he was turned away. Rumors of pro-monarchist conspiracies would become frequent during World War II. As time passed by and Franco's unwillingness to give up power became evident, Don Juan and his supporters grew impatient. The monarchists crafted a strategy to gain the throne that had three distinct phases, to be implemented in sequence if efforts failed under the previous one: "With Franco. Without Franco. Against Franco."

By mid-1945, both Hitler and Mussolini were dead, and for many, it was hard to see how Franco would be able to continue to rule Spain. This turn of events could only encourage the monarchists. They no longer believed that the restoration could happen with Franco. Anticipating the end of the world war, Don Juan issued a manifesto in March 1945 declaring the Franco regime incompatible with the emerging world order and asking Franco to leave office and give way to the restoration of the monarchy.[13] A month later, Don Juan asked supporters of the monarchy working within the Franco administration to resign their posts. It was meant to be the beginning of the "against Franco" phase of the monarchist's plan.

Yet, Don Juan's strategy would prove to be a losing proposition. The face-off between Franco and Don Juan was highly mismatched. Franco had the advantage of an extensive security apparatus who collected much intelligence about anything connected with the monarchists, to which he paid great attention, as evidenced by the copious underlining and annotations he made on such reports (Fernández-Miranda and García Calero, 2018). He was thus always able to be a step ahead. Franco also punished those who engaged in monarchist organizations, levying hefty fines, imposing exile, and sometimes imprisoning for mere propagandistic activities. Particularly harsh financial penalties, and some prison time, were imposed on a daring young woman, the Duchess Luisa de Narváez, heiress of the noble title given to Ramón María Narváez, the nineteenth-century general who could not forgive his enemies because he had had them all shot and whom we met in Chapter 1. While the Duchess was particularly active in spreading monarchist propaganda—and paid a hefty price for it—not even she resorted to the type of violence to which her ancestor confessed.

There were too few monarchists prepared to turn to violence and risk everything to get rid of Franco. Having supported and been part of the Franco regime in its early years, few were prepared to completely break with Franco. In contrast, the *Caudillo* was determined not to leave office and was prepared to put his life on the line to hold on to power. In private he made displays of his appreciation of the heroics of martyrdom. After Mussolini's death, he even showed his brother a photograph of the dead body of Mussolini, noting that if things went bad, he would end up like that because he would always refuse to live in exile.[14] By being prepared to die in office, Franco left only one avenue to the opposition, the use of violence to remove him.

The risks for the country, let alone the individuals involved, of a violent uprising against Franco were regarded as too great for many supporters of the restoration of the monarchy. An exchange of letters in July 1945 between Don Alfonso de Orleans, the representative of Don Juan in Spain, and Eduardo González Gallarza—both Air Force Generals—illustrates the dilemma that the monarchists faced. Don Alfonso de Orleans lays out the contrast between the positions held by

---

[13] The manifesto was allegedly agreed with Allen Dulles, Director of the Office of Strategic Services. At the time Dulles was, like Don Juan, based in Switzerland (Anson, 1994, p. 223).

[14] This was in keeping with Franco's character. For example, when General Sanjurjo failed in his *pronunciamiento* in 1932, Franco was asked to defend Sanjurjo. Franco refused, noting that when a military man rises in a *pronunciamiento* and fails, he has "earned" the right to die. As quoted in Preston (1994), p. 92.

Don Juan and Franco, criticizing what he saw as totalitarian ways of the latter. Eduardo González Gallarza, who had served as personal aide to king Alfonso XIII and was considered a reliable monarchist, responded promptly and in no uncertain terms about his disagreement with the representative of Don Juan.

For González Gallarza, the options were not Franco or the monarchy. Rather, he saw the choice as being between supporting Franco unconditionally and a catastrophic revolutionary regime. Avoiding the latter "trumps my desires for a restoration." González Gallarza went on to say that his wish was for a monarchical restoration "done by Franco." He also volunteered a theory as to why the two airmen did not see eye to eye: His understanding of the perils of an alternative regime to Franco's stemmed from having lived through the first ten months of the war in Madrid under the Reds, a predicament which "fortunately His Highness did not have to endure."[15]

In addition, for those monarchists prepared to work with Franco, the personal rewards for keeping within the fold of the regime could be substantial. González Gallarza's response that we quoted above was written just one day before he would be appointed as Minister for the Air Force, a position he would hold for the following 12 years. The regime rewarded handsomely those at the top, many of whom benefited privately not only from perks and opportunities such as company board appointments but also from multiple corrupt practices.

The concern about the alternative to Franco was a legitimate one. Even those few individuals who personally sacrificed their careers by directly calling on Franco to step down were unsure about the calculus. The views of General Alfredo Kindelán, who after having been instrumental in elevating Franco to the leadership of the nationalists had become a staunch critic, are indicative of this concern. Kindelán privately recognized that given the reluctance of Franco to move aside, a decision of the military to act could have unintended consequences, not least it "could lead to a new civil war." He was not alone in having this apprehension.[16]

It was this concern that also eventually tilted the Allies against any intervention in Spain. World War II could have easily led to the toppling of the Franco regime. Both the Allies and the Germans considered the possibility of invading Spain, which would have likely led to the end of the regime, as well as supporting coups to overthrow Franco. For example, in February 1945 Allen Dulles was in touch

---

[15] The letters are reproduced in Kindelán (1981), pp. 239–42. González Gallarza's claim that his experience during the war gave him greater insight about the stakes at play probably added insult to injury. Alfonso de Orleans may not have lived in Republican territory during the Civil War, but he had directly felt the war: His own son, aged 24, had died in battle fighting for the Nationalist forces.

[16] Kindelán (1981), p. 227. Ridruejo also conceded the point that, as he put it in a bizarre face-to-face meeting with Franco in early 1947, "if your Excellency were to suddenly resign as Head of State without a clear succession, it would lead to anarchy and civil war, likely concluding in the victory of the communists" (1976, p. 283). Ridruejo was nevertheless arguing for the regime to drop the *Falange*, convene a government of technical administrators, and open a constitutional period.

with Don Juan about a plan to replace Franco. Spanish guerrilla fighters who had joined the French Resistance during the world war would launch a series of attacks in the North of Spain. Considering the increased tensions, the plan went on, the Allies would intervene to keep the peace, remove Franco, and call in on Don Juan as king to organize free elections (Anson, 1994, p. 219). Neither this nor any other plan to intervene in Spain was brought to implementation because the Allies ultimately shared the concern about the future stability of Spain after Franco. But all the rumors gave a false hope to monarchists that the overthrow of Franco by the Allies was simply a matter of time.

By mid-1948, Don Juan had come to terms with the fact that the Allied powers had moved on and were unlikely to help oust Franco. Don Juan also changed tactics. A meeting in person between Franco and Don Juan took place in August 1948 at which it was agreed that Don Juan's ten-year-old son and heir, Prince Juan Carlos, would move to Spain in the fall to study. With Don Juan's son under his protection in Madrid, Franco both neutralized Don Juan and could show the world that his 1947 Law of Succession, which had declared Spain a kingdom and granted Franco the right to appoint the king at any moment, was in fact being implemented. The Law had set the minimum age to be king at 30 years of age, which gave Franco at least another 20 years in power before Prince Juan Carlos could be made king.[17]

The dog that didn't bark

The military was both the undisputable basis of power of the regime as well as the source of conspiracies with the greatest potential to oust Franco. During the first decade of Franco's rule there was no shortage of rumors about imminent *pronunciamientos*. To give just one example, in mid-1943 General Orgaz claimed to have agreed with General Aranda and others to be ready to rise with 100,000 men to restore the monarchy as long as the Allies recognized the new regime (Preston, 1994, p. 496). But none of these plans materialized. For the rest of Franco's life, no other military man staged a rebellion against the established regime. Given the history of the previous century and a half, this is noteworthy. Why did military *pronunciamientos* cease after 1939?

To begin to address this question, we need to note that the coup in 1936 had split the armed forces roughly in half between Republican loyalists and rebels, but

---

[17] In November 1948, the 10-year-old Prince made the life-changing train ride from Lisbon to Madrid, alone and worried about being away from home and about his accented Spanish, as he was born in Rome and had never before lived in Spain. A few weeks earlier, a very different but also life-changing train ride took my then 8-year-old mother, also alone and worried, from the poverty of her Andalusian home to Madrid to attend a boarding school for poor girls, one of the many operated by the *Falange*.

the majority of the top command remained loyal to the Republic. The result was that there were few senior generals among the rebels that could challenge Franco. At the outset of the Civil War, Franco was only twenty-third in seniority among the top 24 division generals in existence in 1936, but he was one of only five of them that rebelled. Most loyalist generals that were caught in rebel territory were executed. Conversely, many generals caught in Republican territory that were deemed to be sympathetic to the Nationalists were also executed, some by militias. In addition, two of the generals that rebelled failed in their effort to secure the cities of Madrid and Barcelona and were executed. All of this reduced the number of generals that could potentially upstage Franco.

Franco also demonstrated to be a master manipulator in the handling of his fellow generals and most likely competitors (Preston, 2008). He pitted them against each other, for example sending both Yagüe (*Falangist*) and Orgaz (Anglophile) to the North African city of Melilla, effectively to cancel each other. He changed generals' assignments frequently to keep them from establishing a strong base of support in a given post. Doubting the loyalty of another top general, Aranda, he appointed him director of the war college in 1940, thus relieving him of command of troops—and he would later do the same to Kindelán. All the above-mentioned, plus others, were in fact actively engaged in conspiracies throughout the early years of the regime, but Franco had the upper hand in terms of intelligence services.

Franco spent significant amounts of time and resources tracking all these intrigues. His *modus operandi* when handling his fellow generals typically involved compiling voluminous information against a given individual, confronting him with that information, and then imposing a penalty that could be thought of as lenient given the activities involved. Even rehabilitation was possible, especially if it served the purpose of keeping the balance of forces among the different factions. This contrasts with the harshness of the repression against the left. For example, General Yagüe was fired as Minister of the Air Force and confined for 29 months in his hometown for his role in a *Falangist* plot to replace Franco.[18] But Yagüe would be brought back to a position of power when he was sent, as noted above, to Africa in part as a check on fellow general Orgaz. He would be later promoted to Lieutenant-General and put in charge of the troops battling the *maquis* that entered into Spain from the Pyrenees.

Paradoxically, World War II helped Franco stay in power not only because of the absence of an external intervention but also by creating a polarization within the military that made collective action against Franco more difficult. There were generals that were pro-Axis, like Asensio or the *Falangists* Yagüe and

---

[18] The extensive memo prepared by Franco before he met Yagüe to inform him of his removal as Minister provides a rare glimpse of the amount of intelligence information that Franco had at his disposal (Fernández Santander, 1985, p. 32).

Muñoz-Grandes. There were generals that favored a strict neutralist position, like the Carlist Varela, and some with sympathies for the Allies, like the monarchists Aranda, Gómez-Jordana, and Orgaz.[19] This intricate ideological tapestry was in addition to the already diverse views of those that composed the "Nationalist" side and made a move against Franco all the more difficult to orchestrate.

The only such joint effort to push Franco aside came in September 1943, when eight of the top 12 generals wrote a letter to Franco asking him to resign and restore the monarchy. Written in polite language, the letter was nevertheless stark. It reminded Franco that the signatories of the letter were the same comrades in arms that had "placed in your hands seven years ago . . . the supreme powers of military command and of the state" (Payne, 2000, p. 329). Although not an ultimatum, the letter could be interpreted as a threat, and General Varela is said to have rushed into Franco's office unannounced and with his riding whip in his hand to hand over the letter. In characteristic fashion, Franco chose not to respond to the letter and dealt with the signatories one-on-one. As it turned out, Franco persuaded some that, while he agreed that the eventual goal was the restoration of the monarchy, it was not the right time. Both the tactic of dealing with each general individually and the request for patience would become hallmarks of Franco's handling of his generals over the years.

With his fellow "comrades in arms," Franco proved adept at using not just the stick but especially the carrot. Despite having been a signatory of the 1943 letter, General Dávila would be given responsibilities as Minister of the Army as well as a noble title in 1949.[20] Queipo de Llano and Saliquet, the only two rebel generals that had more seniority than Franco at the outset of the Civil War, were also made marquises in 1950. In addition, many generals enjoyed lucrative board memberships in companies that sought influence with the regime. Franco, always well informed of potential *kompromat*, stood ready to use this information as needed. Thus, when a delegation of generals visited Franco in January 1947 and Saliquet took the floor to express concern about the international isolation of Spain, Franco is said to have replied: "there's no need to worry. What's the matter? Isn't your soap factory doing well?"[21]

We should not overlook the possibility that the stability of Franco at the top of the regime may have been in part the result of chance events. General Mola, who next to Franco had the strongest claim to being named *Generalísimo*, died in June

[19] The precise leaning of individual high-ranking officials is not without debate. Gómez-Jordana is often seen as favoring the Allies. In practice, Gómez-Jordana "always spoke for Franco" (Beaulac, 1986, p. 134). While this made him a reliable counterpart, it is hard to think of him as pro-Allied.

[20] Franco assumed the royal prerogative of conferring titles of nobility, granting 39 titles over 25 years. As Paul Preston (1994) points out, Franco's bestowing of nobility titles was a poignant act for monarchist generals such as Kindelán, who would be made a marquis in 1961, since accepting the title could be seen as reneging their recognition of Don Juan as king.

[21] Garriga (1971, p. 472).

1937 in an airplane accident. Mola was said to be on his way to meet with Franco precisely to raise the issue of leadership. The fact that none of the conspiracies materialized is sometimes given as evidence of the robustness of the Franco regime from the outset. But the fact that there were multiple intrigues can also be interpreted as evidence of precisely the opposite view: Many thought the regime was so weak that it was worth considering plans to overthrow it.

Finally, Franco had an age advantage over his competitors. Having been promoted to the rank of Division General at the relatively young age of 41, Franco would go on to outlive the vast majority of generals that were sufficiently senior to challenge him. Of the eight lieutenant generals that had signed the 1943 letter asking Franco to step aside, none were younger than Franco and four had already died by 1953. In fact, most of the generals who played a key role during the Civil War and later dissented with Franco died in the late 1940s and early 1950s: Orgaz in 1946; Queipo de Llano and Varela in 1951; Yagüe, Monasterio, and Ponte in 1952; and Solchaga in 1953. Miguel Cabanellas, the only general who opposed Franco's initial appointment as *Generalísimo*, had already died during the war in 1938. Overall, Franco combined the rare characteristics of being relatively young and simultaneously having significant seniority among the rebels.

And why were there no younger military men ready to rise? It is commonly argued that military rebellions often involve lower-level officers, such as colonels. Franco had an advantage in this regard having been the leader of the army during the formative years of the younger generation officers. It was Franco's army that they had risen through the ranks. Many had been "provisional" officers that were supposed to be so only for the duration of the war. Franco, instead of reducing the cadre of officers after the war, simply went on to confirm them in their positions, thus doubling the officer ranks. The swelled ranks of officers would characterize the army for decades to come, as shown in Figure 3.2, panel (a). It also made the former provisional officers a particularly diehard group of Franco loyalists. On a per capita basis, the Spain of the 1960s and 1970s had as many army officers as it had a century earlier. Compulsory military service meant that the army remained large and, given the pro-Franco stance of the middle ranks, an instrument of indoctrination.

Military budgets also swelled. In the 1940s, defense took an astonishing 38 percent of all public expenditures, as shown in Figure 3.2, panel (b). Both the peak and the steep decline after 1950 are of interest. The peak in expenditures throughout the 1940s does not appear to be driven by an anticipation of entering World War II: In the four years after the end of the world war, the military still accounted for around 36 percent of all expenditures. Rather, it seems more plausible that it shows that the regime itself believed that it was still not secure in power. Before the agreements with the US, the expenditure of defense had been at least around one-third of all public expenditures in every year since the Civil War. In the

(a) Army officer corps, thousands

(b) Share of military in total public
expenditures, percent

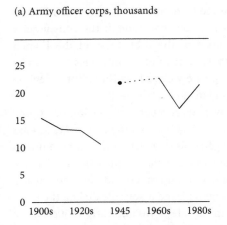
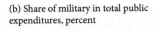
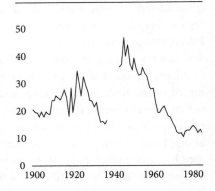

Figure 3.2 The rise and fall of the military

Source: Jordana and Ramió (2005) and Puell (2009) for panel (a). Comín and Díaz (2005) for panel (b).

following two decades, it would drop steadily and precipitously to stability at around 12 percent of all public expenditure by the 1970s, a decline of at least 20 percentage points in the relative share of defense in total public expenditures.

In line with its relative decline in expenditures, and on par with a professionalization of its management structures, the participation of the military in political affairs would decline over the following decades. The decline in the political influence of the military is evidenced by a decline in top-level positions outside the military hierarchy such as ministerial appointments that were held by military officers (Olmeda, 1988). There was also a relative decline in numbers of military personnel. Between 1955 and 1975, salaried military personnel declined from 24 to 19 percent of all public central administration employees (Jordana and Ramió, 2005). The civilian bureaucracy gained strength, and as it did so, it no longer left an unoccupied space for the military. The ensuing retreat of the military could be some vindication of the long-held view among conservative Spanish thinkers that it was the weakness of civilian institutions that had prompted the army's repeated involvement in political affairs.[22] But the military would remain a key source of political power and legitimacy of the regime till its end. The military

---

[22] Already in the mid-nineteenth century, the Catholic Catalan writer Jaime Balmes had argued that "We do not believe that civilian power is weak because of the strength of the military; on the contrary, military power is strong because of the weakness of civilian power." See "La preponderancia militar" (March 18, 1846 issue of the journal *El Pensamiento de la Nación*). Available in the digitized National Library of Spain: http://hemerotecadigital.bne.es/issue.vm?id=0004031795 (accessed August 3, 2019).

did not relinquish power, it was simply that Franco monopolized it on behalf of all of the military.

Conclusions

Does the state control political violence? For all the shortcomings of the political regime installed in Spain in 1939, it will be the last that took power through violence. This is perhaps the single most significant political milestone in contemporary Spanish history. It is one that would also have profound consequences for the country's rise to prosperity. In the decades after 1950, there will be no credible threat to the power of the central government. Political stability came to be expected. The control of violence has featured prominently in political thinking, old and new. Put crisply, "authority has to exist before it can be limited" (Huntington, 1968, p. 8). This insight also plays a key role in the framework of open and closed access societies of North et al. (2009), which we have adopted in previous chapters, as societies can only sustainably transition from closed to open if political violence is in check. A common thread among these thinkers is the existence of stages in the development of polities.

How was the monopoly of violence achieved? It was far from a linear process. The Civil War had a profound effect on Spanish society, and the regime that emerged from it cannot be understood without it. The choices of the winners of the war in the exercise of their newly gained power first undermined stability but later underpinned a period largely free of political violence over the following decades. The Civil War stood out for the dehumanization of the enemy. As social psychologists tell us, this was bound to have longer-term consequences. It had the predictable—but never excusable—effect of prolonging violence against the enemy after the war was over. Franco and his associates indeed undertook a brutal repression that extended into the 1940s. As the left was repeatedly crushed and opponents of the right proved unwilling to risk their lives to unseat Franco, the regime would eventually become a source of political stability.

Initially, the regime fueled instability. The many ideologically diverse groups that had won the Civil War were joined only in their enmity against the Republic. Intrigues among them were rife and a sense of instability dominated. When Dionisio Ridruejo, the head of propaganda turned critic, wrote his scathing letter to Franco in 1942, he stressed how insiders of the regime did not feel responsibility for the decisions of the regime "because they all think that this is a provisional thing."[23] With the benefit of the historical record, it is easy to see the consolidation of the regime as inevitable and many of the conspiracies, for

---

[23] Ridruejo (1976, p. 238).

example the monarchist attempts at displacing Franco, as destined to fail. But we must resist this hindsight bias and instead try to see how those living through the events perceived them. The actions of the government, which continued to spend over a third of the budget on the military through the end of the 1940s, suggest that the regime itself did not feel that it had secured the monopoly of political violence by the end of that decade. None of this bode well for the future of the country.

Franco coopted large swathes of the political spectrum under his Nationalist government. He put himself at the helm of every organization with violence potential that operated within the regime. By unifying the pro-Nazi *Falangists* and the traditionalist Carlists into a single party, he diluted the power of both. Benefiting from the state's intelligence apparatus, Franco had an informational advantage over his competitors and used it to his personal benefit. He dealt with his fellow generals individually, finding the right combination of sticks and carrots. He tolerated and encouraged corruption at high levels and even granted nobility titles. The result of this combination of actions was a military leadership that had much more to lose without Franco than with him.

By the early 1950s, the strategy was paying off for Franco. His old comrades in arms had either died or grown comfortable within the regime. Disgruntled members like Dionisio Ridruejo were unprepared to mobilize a violent opposition. While the Nationalist coalition was united at first only in their opposition to the Republic, in later stages it would become united in their subordination to the leadership of Franco himself. This is what justifies the labeling of the regime as Francoism (and would later expose the vulnerability of how Francoism could not exist without Franco), even more so than the cult of personality that Franco fostered.

It was also an accidental making of a monopoly on violence. For all the skills in manipulation demonstrated by Franco, it is hard to escape the conclusion that the changing external environment proved critical in securing his regime in power. Initially, Republican exiles and others pinned their hopes on the Allies. The Franco regime was so intrinsically connected with the defeated Axis powers that it was hard to imagine that it would be tolerated in the postwar period. But such external intervention did not materialize. During World War II, events unfolded in such a way that the invasion of Spain did not prove necessary. After the world war, the winning powers, much as they disliked Franco, soon came to fear what type of regime would replace his. Eventually, the intensification of the Cold War would prove to be a critical juncture that turned the attention of the Americans towards the geostrategic importance of Spain. The American rapprochement to Franco's Spain made a significant difference, as we saw in the previous chapter, in shaping the expectations about the future stability of the country.

Above all, Franco demonstrated that he was bent on being dictator for life, thus forcing the use of violence if anyone wanted to oust him. The domestic opposition was ultimately unprepared to use force against Franco, out of fear of reprisal or because they feared that it could bring the country into yet another Civil War. In sharp contrast, the dictator sought to stay in power, no matter what, and was prepared to kill and die for it. It was ultimately this asymmetry that helps to explain why the long history of *pronunciamientos* was altered.[24] If Francoism was the unintended consequence of the rebel uprising, stability was the unintended consequence of Francoism.

Over time, the improvement in economic outcomes will further reduce the willingness of moderate groups to stage a coup or use force against Franco. But it would be wrong to conclude that the economic recovery was the primary cause of the unwillingness to use violence by opposing forces to Franco. In fact, the reluctance to use force preceded the economic upswing. By 1950, the economy remained mired in problems, with living standards still below those achieved before the Civil War. Yet few were prepared to risk life in opposing Franco.

Civil wars are unfortunately not a thing of the past. As Blattman and Miguel (2010) remind us, during the past half century about a third of all countries in the world have experienced a civil war, defined as an intra-state conflict with at least one thousand battle deaths. Given the limited consensus that exists in the literature about how to avert conflicts or promote postwar recovery, the Spanish Civil War provides an unusual example of a conflict with an extremely thorough historiography yet seldom referred to in the growing economics literature on civil wars.

The apparent paradox is that an era of political stability was ushered in Spain under a regime that had gained power through force and that violently repressed those who opposed it. Statements like this can create a dissonance, amplified by the relative recency of the Civil War and the Franco dictatorship and the prominence that they still carry in Spanish society. As the British literary critic Jeremy Treglown (2013) reminds us, pointing out developments that occurred during the dictatorship and are regarded as positive is often misinterpreted as a justification for the dictatorship. There is still a "halo effect" when discussing the Franco dictatorship that is unhelpful for social science inquiry. We are better off guiding our research by frameworks such as the one of North et al. (2009), which can help us explore these paradoxes and make sense of the role played by violence and its control. Or, if moral proverbs are preferred to models, we can draw insight from the words of a Sephardi thinker of the Middle Ages, Santob de Carrión: "Hardly a thing can be acquired in this world, whether ugly or beautiful, except through its opposite . . . Peace is achieved only through warfare."[25]

Yet peace is far from a guarantee to achieve prosperity. Many stable governments get stuck in low-level equilibria. How did Spain escape them? The rest of the book turns to this question.

---

[24] An argument already made by historian Javier Tusell, see his prologue to Portero (1989), though not often emphasized enough in the subsequent literature.
[25] Santob de Carrión (1345). Also known for his Jewish name Shem Tov. See Perry (1987, pp. 23–4).

PART II
TAKEOFF

4

More Than Macro Stability

We have so far shown that by the 1950s the state gained control over the monopoly of violence and political stability was achieved. But the links between political stability and economic growth are not straightforward. Although political stability is associated with higher economic growth in some cases, a vast literature shows that this is far from being universally so. For example, changes in political regimes have been found to be significant predictors of growth *accelerations* (Hausmann et al., 2005). Indeed, growth accelerations are on average less likely to happen the longer a political regime has been in place (Jong-A-Pin and De Haan, 2011). And political persistence has even been found to negatively impact growth in countries with high levels of red tape, perhaps because it facilitates rent-seeking (Belletini et al., 2013). As put by Samuel Huntington, "some forms of political stability may encourage economic growth; other forms may discourage it" (1968, p. 6). The explanation for Spain's economic takeoff still lies ahead of us.

The findings from the cross-country literature highlight how unusual Spain's case was. It is rare that a regime that had initially tanked the economy, as the Franco regime did in the 1940s, would also lead it into a sustained episode of high growth. How can we make sense of this puzzle? We have seen that the intensification of the Cold War in the early 1950s proved to be a critical juncture that decisively shifted American policy towards Spain. As a result, it helped solidify expectations that the Franco regime was more secure after a decade and a half already in power. Same regime, much greater political stability. Crucially, this was widely believed to be the case by private economic agents.

But why would this increased political stability result in an improved economic performance? One of the potential channels of transmission is that political stability can lead to more secure property rights, which in turn contribute to higher investment (Svensson, 1998). In this theory of change, the *perception* of a stable political arrangement directly contributes to increased economic activity as it reduces the risk that preexisting property rights would not be enforced. Any regime needs to resolve the paradox that a government strong enough to enforce property rights is also strong enough to confiscate from its citizens, which may discourage investment (Weingast, 1995).[1] But for a regime which is not perceived to be secure in power, the promise to enforce property rights is less credible: The

---

[1] Almost two thousand years ago, Tacitus intimated a similar argument: "There can never be complete confidence in a power which is excessive" (*Histories, II*).

Unexpected Prosperity: How Spain Escaped the Middle Income Trap. Oscar Calvo-Gonzalez, Oxford University Press.
© Oscar Calvo-Gonzalez 2021. DOI: 10.1093/oso/9780198853978.003.0005

government itself may be replaced by another that does not feel bound to respect the commitments of the previous one. For governments facing this credibility gap, an increase in the regime's hold on power helps to address this situation.[2]

A second mechanism that links political stability and economic growth is, indirectly, through macroeconomic policies that are more conducive for growth. The relationship between specific macroeconomic policies and economic growth is the subject of many controversies, but there is a broad consensus in the literature that macroeconomic instability is harmful for growth (Spence, 2008). Maintaining price stability and fiscal responsibility supports growth by reducing uncertainty over the risks and returns faced by private investors. If political stability were to enhance macroeconomic stability, that would create a second impetus to economic growth *beyond* the security of property rights channel that we have discussed above. Crucially, and distinct with the property rights channel, for this second pathway to growth to materialize requires that macroeconomic policies change.

The two pathways from political stability to economic growth reinforce each other. It is easy to see why when we consider the situation in the absence of political stability. When political instability is the norm, economic policy reforms often do not have the expected impact because the private sector remains skeptical about the long-term institutional setting or policy stance. Political stability and sound economic policies can be thought of as mutually necessary conditions for there to be a vigorous supply-side response. In cases where one of the two are absent, growth suffers. When both are present, they help boost growth. In conclusion, a credible commitment to both secure property rights and pro-growth policies are an essential foundation for policies to be effective policies and thus contribute to sustained development (World Bank, 2017).

Enough of the theoretical argument. Let us then see what happened in Spain. Both mechanisms linking political stability and economic growth imply that there would be a supply response in the wake of increased political stability. In the case at hand, we observe indeed that investment rates increased from 16 percent of GDP in the second half of the 1940s to 23 percent of GDP in the same period a decade later, stabilizing around 25 percent of GDP in the corresponding period of the 1960s. This fast and sustained acceleration in investment rates over a short period of a couple of decades in the late 1950s and throughout the 1960s was unlike anything observed before, even though capital formation had seen a long-term upward trend since the late nineteenth century (see Figure 4.1, panel (a)).

Importantly, this was not a public sector–driven phenomenon. The increase in investment was driven by both public and private sources. The growth of new private businesses saw something of a sustained spurt. The rate at which new

---

[2] As I have elsewhere argued for the case of Franco's Spain (Calvo-Gonzalez, 2001, 2002).

(a) Gross fixed capital formation, percentage of GDP

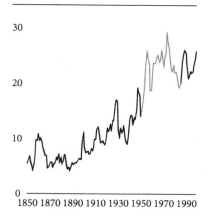

(b) New business entry density, firms created per 1,000 population

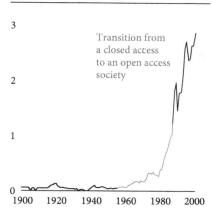

Figure 4.1 The supply response in the transition from a closed to an open access society

Source: Carreras et al. (2005) for panel (a) and Tafunell (2005) for panel (b).

firms were created, which had averaged around 1,400 new firms in a given year during the first half of the twentieth century, tripled to 4,500 per year in the 1960s—or, if we account for population growth, more than doubled from six new firms per 100,000 population to 14 in the same periods (new business entry density is shown in panel (b) of Figure 4.1). Many of today's successful businesses have their origins in this period, as documented by a growing business history literature to which we will return in later chapters.

Business entry is one way through which greater contestability became an increasing hallmark of the Spanish economy and a source of the unexpected prosperity—which is one of our main claims in the overarching narrative of the book. When we introduced the framework of closed and open access societies earlier in the book, we argued that in Spain the transition between the two likely took place during the period 1950–85. This is indeed the period during which we see the acceleration in business entry. In line with what the open access framework would predict, much higher rates of business entry became the norm once Spain became an open access society. In fact, latest data for 2016 from the World Bank shows Spain in the top third of countries worldwide in terms of business entry density. This process of increasing entrepreneurial activity continued well after the 1950s, but the much higher rates of new business creation observed since the 1980s should not overshadow the significance of the earlier transition period. The structural transformation of the Spanish economy may have manifested itself with greatest intensity in the decades after 1980, but it had its foundations in earlier periods.

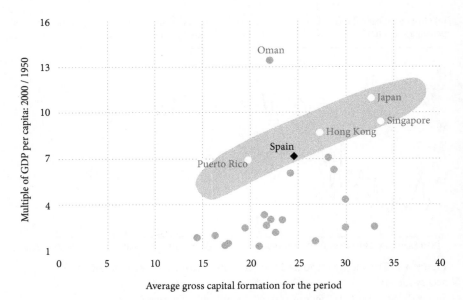

Figure 4.2 At the "efficiency frontier" of gross capital formation

Note: Of the 28 economies with a comparable GDP per capita to Spain in 1950, as identified in the Introduction, only Djibouti and Trinidad and Tobago lacked the data on gross capital formation and dropped out of the comparison here. The average gross capital formation is calculated for the longest period available, since 1960 for most countries.

Source: Own elaboration with data from World Development Indicators and Maddison Project Database.

In any case, what stands out from a comparative perspective is not so much Spain's capital accumulation but its efficiency in generating economic growth. To illustrate this, let us go back to the 28 economies which in 1950 had a similar level of output per capita as Spain, as we identified in the Introduction. At that time, we saw that Spain outperformed all but five of those economies over the following half-century. We can now also see that Spain achieved this growth performance with a relatively efficient use of the capital that it accumulated. In fact, Spain was at the frontier in terms of growth achieved given a certain investment rate, as shown in the shaded area in Figure 4.2, where each dot represents one of the economies that had a comparable per capita output to Spain in 1950. The few economies that grew faster, except for oil-rich Oman, did so with higher investment rates. And Spain's growth rate outpaced all other comparable economies that had similar investment rates.

The main conclusion from this analysis is the importance not only to explain how macroeconomic policies helped drive investment rates up, but also to examine what made it possible to achieve a comparatively efficient use of that capital. This is far from the standard question that the Spanish historiography tends to pose to the record, and one which will require us to dig deeper into the type of growth that occurred and the policies that were put in place to support it. We will do so in the next two chapters but, to anticipate some of their main themes, increased openness and greater contestability will feature prominently in our argument.

Yet if we were to put ourselves back in 1950, as we have done on several occasions in this book so far, none of this investment and growth would have been taken for granted. The country had adopted an autarkic economic policy in the 1940s that was the opposite of increased openness and greater contestability. This brings us to three critical questions: What impact did economic reforms have? Which reforms were most impactful? And, why were reforms adopted in the first place?

To be able to answer these questions we need to start by briefly reviewing the autarkic policies put in place at the end of the Civil War and the reforms that were subsequently adopted. We will then proceed to assess the impact on economic growth of reforms. In the next chapter we will explore the political economy of reform in Spain, a most discussed topic in the development literature. For now, let us get on with the core facts of our case: how the macroeconomic framework changed over time and what impact it had on economic performance.

Autarky

If you were a worker in Spain in 1950, your wages were set by the state. Prices were also fixed by the state. But you would not be able to find most goods at the official prices so, if you could afford it, you would have to rely on the black market for necessities from basic foodstuffs to life-saving drugs.[3] In most cases you would have to do without. Your standard of living was lower than it had been since the Civil War: Average real wages in 1950 were indeed below what they had been in 1940. If you were an agricultural producer you were to hand over your crops to the state, which would pay you a fraction of its free market price. If you were in business, you would need a license not only to operate but also if you wanted to import any inputs or machinery. Holding foreign exchange had been illegal since 1938. If you were an exporter, your foreign exchange revenues would be exchanged for pesetas at one of the multiple fixed rates that the state established for different types of transactions.

What was distinctive about this type of widespread controls, common in many other countries in the aftermath of World War II, was that in Spain it responded to a deliberate policy of autarky. Policymakers sought self-sufficiency for Spain and thought state intervention was the instrument to make it happen. The ideological

---

[3] For an account of the black market for penicillin see Santesmases (2018, chapter 4).

foundation for autarky had fascistic origins and was advocated by some of those linked to the *Falange*, the sole legal and official party under the Franco regime.[4] While the military and the *Falange* did not always see eye to eye, the autarkic ideas were well received among military men, many of whom saw economic matters in a simplistic way, as if orchestrating the national economy was equivalent to managing an army regiment in barracks. This did not mean, however, that there were no disagreements about the way to pursue these objectives.

Intervention extended into all aspects of economic life, agriculture, industry, foreign trade and investment, prices and monetary issues, etc. To compensate for what was seen as a lack of initiative by the private sector, and inspired by Mussolini's Institute for Industrial Reconstruction, the government established in 1941 a National Institute of Industry (INI for *Instituto Nacional de Industria*). It would go on to play a key role in basic industrial sectors such as petrochemicals, electricity, steel, shipbuilding, and mining. While there has been a vigorous debate about the extent to which INI crowded out private initiative, there is no denying that it played a central role in the industrialization of the country. Besides INI, the many interventionist policies of this period have been amply documented in the Spanish economic literature, which has passed a justifiably harsh judgement on the consequences of the autarkic policies.[5] These were self-inflicted wounds. The Franco regime would later disingenuously claim that the isolation that Spain endured after World War II was the reason for the autarkic policies, but it is worth stressing that these policies were never "forced" on Spain—rather they were chosen at the outset of the Franco regime. Also, during the days of international isolation, Spain could have ended it unilaterally had it chosen to reform politically. This never happened, as for the Franco regime economic policy would always be subordinated to political goals.

Of all state controls, the ones on food and agriculture probably had the most immediate consequences for public welfare, if only because food still accounted for 60 percent of households' expenditure in 1939 and would go down only slightly to 55 percent by 1958, when the first household budgets survey was conducted. Food rationing was common during wars and in many postwar settings, but it was particularly long-lasting in Spain. Even in countries such as Britain, which kept some controls longer than most after World War II, bread rationing was lifted in 1948, three years after the end of the war. In France, food rationing

---

[4] For example, by Higinio Paris Eguilaz, a physician by training who became the Secretary of the National Economic Council and a close advisor to Franco on economic issues. His fascist fervor was such that, upon volunteering to join the Blue Division within the Wehrmacht, he stated that his being denied going to the Soviet front was "the worst time of my life" (Bowen, 2000, p. 109).

[5] Clavera et al. (1973), Viñas (1984), Martín Aceña and Comín (1991), San Román (1999), Gómez-Mendoza (2000), and a thorough synthesis on the impact of autarky in Barciela (2003).

was lifted in 1949. In Spain, food rationing would last until 1952, 13 years after the end of the Civil War.

The drop in agricultural production was particularly acute. The decline was across the board, affecting the main foodstuffs of the diet. Wheat output in the 1940s was almost a quarter lower than it had been in the decade before the Civil War. For years, the literature explained the contraction in output as driven by the misguided price system that was put in place. The low fixed prices paid to producers had the consequence, the argument went, to disincentivize production. Predictably, a black market also appeared. In fact, it blossomed. Uneven and politically influenced enforcement of rules did little to stop illegal activities. More than half of the wheat produced in the 1940s was sold on the black market. But the very size of the unofficial market puts in question the argument that the price-fixing system drove production down. In most cases, the relevant price for producers' decision-making would have been that of the black market, as insightfully shown by Christiansen (2012). The same author also highlights how lack of fertilizers and draft animals were a significant contributor to the decline in production in the 1940s.

Corruption and mismanagement combined to intensify the shortages. The cause of the decline in production may have been other policies, just not the price-fixing mechanism. The interventionist policies introduced distortions even in markets for commodities, where initially there was no imbalance between supply and demand. For example, prices were fixed before the growing season. As a result, in the case of bad harvests, producers had even more of an incentive to divert their output to the black market. In addition, the massive undertaking of purchasing and distributing the entire wheat crop was put at the hands of newly created organizations which relied on a network of delegates at the local and provincial levels. This provided ample opportunities for rent-seeking. Widespread corruption helped solidify support for Franco, although there are few studies of the links between autarky and corruption based on documentary evidence. In addition to graft, there were also inefficiencies which resulted in large losses, partly because of incompetence in the task of managing the entire food supply. In 1940 in Malaga, a total of 50,000 tons of rice was reportedly thrown out to sea as it had rotted away (del Arco, 2006, p. 248).

Waste and corruption happened amid widespread hunger. Rations were insufficient to meet the caloric and nutritional needs of the population. In 1941 the daily bread ration, when available, was a meager 80 gr per person per day. A nutritional survey conducted by the Rockefeller Foundation in a village near Madrid showed the average caloric intake at just 1,600 calories/day per adult male, less than two-thirds of what is normally considered adequate. While there is much more to nutrition than mere calory intake, this gives an idea of the extent of food scarcity. The extent and the duration of this deprivation are striking.

Nine years after the end of the Civil War, in 1948, a follow-up survey in a relatively affluent neighborhood of Madrid showed the average caloric intake in 1948 still at 2,080 calories/day per adult male. In Italy, which had also seen a significant impact of World War II on nutrition, the available caloric intake was back to pre-war levels at 2,500 calories/day by 1947, two years after the war ended.[6] Shortages led to desperate efforts by the population to feed off of whatever they could find, including animal feed such as acorns or vetches inadequate for human consumption, which contributed to widespread neurological diseases (del Cura and Huertas, 2007, pp. 75, 125, 134).

Even if we leave aside human development dimensions and concentrate only on the macroeconomic picture, the performance of Spain in the 1940s can only be characterized as a failure. Over the decade, the government was consistently running an annual fiscal deficit that averaged over 3 percent of GDP. The lack of discipline and the fiscal dominance over monetary policy resulted in a persistently high rate of inflation, which averaged over 12 percent annually. The autarkic policies limited exchanges with the outside world, resulting in a degree of openness, as measured by the sum of exports and exports to GDP, of only 5 percent. The lack of confidence in the economic management of Spain was evident in a black market premium for the exchange rate of the peseta that, on average, exceeded 100 percent for the decade. The result was an annual rate of growth of real per capita GDP of only 0.8 percent during the 1940s.[7] In sum, from the vantage point of 1950, the macroeconomic framework did not bode well for the future.

A turnaround

It would have been hard to predict in 1950 that merely a decade later the economic policy framework would be significantly different. In the 1960s, the government fiscal balance would post on average a slight surplus, inflation would average less than 6 percent annually, the economy would open significantly to foreign trade, more than tripling the rate of openness seen in the 1940s, and the black market premium on the exchange rate would virtually disappear (see Table 4.1). All of this had a clear reflection in growth. Real per capita GDP in the 1960s would grow at 6.7 percent annually, more than eight times what it had grown in the 1940s.

Of all the changes in economic policy, the most salient was the 1959 Stabilization Plan. Few events in the standard narrative of modern Spanish economic history

---

[6] Daniele and Ghezzi (2017). While data on caloric intake in this period is not fully comparable across countries, it is still informative to put Spain's experience in context.

[7] This rate of growth is even more disappointing given the opportunities that World War II afforded neutral countries to grow (Catalan, 1995).

Table 4.1 Economic performance in the mid-twentieth century, decade averages

Variable	1940s	1950s	1960s	1970s
Real per capita GDP growth *Percent*	0.8	3.9	6.7	3.9
Government budget balance *Percentage of GDP*	−3.3	0.4	0.3	−0.3
Inflation *Percent*	12.5	6.2	5.8	14.5
Black market premium *Unofficial exchange rate (pesetas per US$) minus* *official rate, as percentage of official exchange rate*	108	44	1	3
Trade openness *Exports plus imports as percentage of GDP*	5	12	17	22

Source: Own calculations using Carreras and Tafunell (2005).

play as leading a role in spurring growth as the Stabilization Plan of 1959. The Plan has since been hailed as a "Copernican turnaround" in the direction of economic policies (Viñas, 2003, p. 279) and the history of the Francoist economy is thus divided into two periods, with 1959 as the clear watershed between an economy of autarkic features and a liberal one (Tortella, 1994, p. 385). Other prominent economic historians suggest that the Plan "laid the basis for the long-run development of the Spanish economy" (Martín Aceña and Martínez Ruiz, 2007, p. 36). To this day, there is a broad consensus on the outsized importance of the Plan, as well as on the view that the adoption of the Plan was due to a survival instinct among the Spanish authorities that in the face of a foreign exchange crisis saw no other way out than undertaking drastic measures (Sánchez Lissen and Sanz Díaz, 2015). A conference held in late 2019 by the Bank of Spain to commemorate the sixtieth anniversary of the Plan still emphasized the familiar themes of, first, the transformational nature of the policy changes undertaken in 1959, and second, the critical and unsustainable economic situation that prompted the adoption of reforms (Banco de España, 2019). Unsurprisingly, political and other historians have taken their cues from their economic historian colleagues.[8]

Yet, while the 1959 Plan was undoubtedly a milestone, economic policy change was not so abrupt. As Table 4.1 makes clear, the decade of the 1950s appears as distinct from the 1940s. In fact, most of the variables shown in the table, and

---

[8] The Plan thus became framed as a "drastic remedy" that was taken "from the recipe book of orthodox capitalism [to] cure the economy of its inherited impurities so that it would function as a modern, 'neo-capitalist' economy" (Carr, 1980, pp. 156–7). The "choice of a neo-capitalist liberalisation of the Spanish economy" was "precisely the type of model which had been anathema to the Francoist authorities" (Fusi, 1995[1985], p. 168). Perhaps inevitably, praise for the 1959 Plan is most eloquent in the autobiographical works of those involved in it. "[The Plan] remains the most thoughtful and best structured economic-political action of the twentieth century" (Estapé, 2000, p. 192).

especially those that can be thought of as more directly driven by policy decisions like fiscal deficits or the overvaluation of the exchange rate as viewed from the black market, show the 1950s to be more like the 1960s than the 1940s. The reality that one policy measure, the 1959 Stabilization Plan, was more important than all others has led to the literature putting too much stock in 1960 as a sharp discontinuity, as Prados de la Escosura and Sánchez-Alonso (2019) argue. For our purposes, it is important to disentangle this issue if we are to get to the bottom of what drove the unexpected, fast, and sustained economic performance after 1950.

Early reforms

Most of the early policy moves were often too unorthodox for us to think of them as shifts towards a market economy. For example, a package of measures in 1948 aimed at curbing inflation and reducing external imbalances included a much-needed devaluation of the peseta. At the same time, it introduced a complex system of multiple exchange rates that can hardly be thought of as a move towards a market economy. But it is undeniable that these moves achieved greater macro-economic stability in the 1950s compared to the 1940s. Inflation, which had reached 31 percent in 1946 and 18 percent in 1947, was brought down to below 6 percent in 1949. Throughout the 1950s, inflation would be much less volatile; for example, the standard deviation of inflation more than halved compared to the previous decade. Even the cumbersome system of multiple exchange rates, far from a move towards free markets, was nevertheless used in part to engineer a stealth devaluation of the peseta in 1949–51. Although these policy changes did not fully correct the overvaluation of the real exchange rate, they brought it closer to equilibrium.

Perhaps the most significant changes were those regulating the agricultural sector, which in 1950 still accounted for half of all employment in the country. A partial deregulation of the wheat market started in 1948, when it was allowed that wheat growth on so-called "improved land" could be sold legally at free prices to some industries and types of buyers. In 1950, this parallel market was extended significantly, leading to benefits for producers and consumers alike as the partial liberalization helped reduce the black market and contributed to a supply response that contributed to an increase in output (Christiansen, 2012, p. 111). Finally, this led to the end of bread rationing in April 1952. This was a significant milestone given both the symbolic and quantitative importance of bread for the diet of the average Spaniard. As late as 1958, the year in which the first household budget survey was conducted, bread and other cereals accounted for over 10 percent of total household consumption.

Other shifts in the policy environment were almost imperceptible, partly because they were a series of adjustments at the margin—as in the case of the fiscal accounts—or because they manifested themselves not in legal changes but in a less restrictive stance in the implementation of existing policies. This is the case of the treatment of foreign direct investment. In pursuit of the stated autarkic goal of a "large and prosperous Spanish industry free of foreign dependency," a 1939 law had set out that foreigners could own at most 25 percent of any company in Spain. Exceptions were possible, but the fact that they were expected to be far and few between is underscored by the process for granting such exceptions: The Council of Ministers would need to consider requests for such exceptions. Although cumbersome, this escape clause still allowed for a de facto relaxation of the policy over time.

While initially kept to a minimum, the number of exceptions granted in favor foreign investors increased throughout the 1950s. The trend towards increased liberalization was clear by the mid-1950s. Among the favorable decisions to allow greater foreign investments was a high-profile case in 1956 allowing Citroën to own 45 percent of a new automobile-producing company that would compete with the state-owned champion—an issue to which we will return later in our story. By April 1958 the Economist Intelligence Unit, which had been tracking the issue closely as part of its quarterly report on Spain, was unambiguously reporting that restrictions on foreign ownership of businesses had been "partially relaxed."[9]

As one would expect in a political system which lacked transparency, the direction of reforms was not always easily scrutable. For a brief period of about a year in 1956 the then Minister for the National Movement was bent on a process to institutionalize the regime that would have given much power to the fascist party, *Falange*. The effort is now widely regarded as doomed to fail, and the minister in charge was demoted in a February 1957 cabinet reshuffle which brought two more so-called technocrats as Ministers for Finance and Commerce.

Undoubtedly, the new economic team faced a challenging situation. As economic growth had picked up in the mid-1950s there were signs of overheating, with inflation rising and strong demand for imports putting further pressure on scarce foreign exchange reserves. While ultimately the source of inflation was the fiscal deficit, the control of inflationary episodes was made more difficult by the fact that banks, which held large amounts of public debt, could turn over government bonds to the Bank of Spain for liquidity. This practice had been in place since 1917 and effectively left the control of monetary aggregates at the hands of

---

[9] The treatment of foreign direct investment was presumably of particular interest to the readership of the Economist Intelligence Unit quarterly reports on Spain. I have analyzed elsewhere these reports, available since 1952, and their discussion of foreign direct investment (Calvo-Gonzalez, 2008).

private banks (Pueyo, 2006). On the fiscal front, an early effort in 1957 to revamp the tax system was quickly watered down, amid wrangling within the reformist camp, due to heavy opposition of many in parliament with a strong private interest to defend the status quo (Comín and Vallejo, 2012). The infighting among the technocrats underlines the fact that they were far from a homogeneous group with a fully formed government program. Yet, they would come to play a critical role in policymaking for years to come, including their most notable contribution, the stabilization program in 1959.

The 1959 Stabilization Plan

In the summer of 1959, the Spanish government devalued the peseta, declared convertibility, introduced a cap on public expenditure, and relaxed constraints on foreign investment and state intervention in the economy. From July 17 to August 5, it issued a total of ten decrees aimed at overhauling fiscal, monetary, exchange rate, trade, and competition policy. The measures followed the contents of an Economic Memorandum addressed on June 30, 1959 by the Spanish authorities to the IMF and the OEEC which, in turn, was the basis for the financial support of those organizations to the Stabilization Plan.[10] The goal was to decrease the current account deficit, contain inflation, eliminate public sector deficits, and reduce the interventions and regulations of the domestic market. One useful way to think about the 1959 Plan is as both a classic stabilization program combined and a liberalization effort (see measures taken in Table 4.2).

Among the stabilization measures, the main ones were on the monetary and exchange rate front. In this respect it was largely a classic stabilization program, much like others that the IMF was supporting at the time, including in France in 1958 and in Iceland in 1960, as well as in many Latin American countries. The measures aimed to bring about external balance through a 25 percent devaluation of the peseta against the US dollar, which brought the official rate in full alignment with the black market rate. In addition, Spain declared convertibility of the peseta vis-à-vis the major currencies. Domestically, interest rates were raised and, importantly, the practice by which government bonds could be turned over to the Bank of Spain for liquidity was discontinued. As noted above, this had effectively left the control of monetary aggregates at the hands of the holders of public debt. To further ensure monetary conditions were under control, a quantitative limit on credit by banks was imposed—a rather unorthodox measure given the general tone of the program but one which was put in place to absolutely ensure that

---

[10] While there is no single document that can be considered "the Stabilization Plan," the cornerstone was the decree-law 10, of July 21, 1959. Details of how the measures were translated in law are provided by Clavera et al. (1973, pp. 281–4).

Table 4.2 Policy reforms in the 1959 Stabilization Plan

Policy area	Measures
Fiscal	• Set general government spending ceilings • Increased taxes (excise on petrol)
Monetary	• Imposed a quantitative limit on credit to the private sector • Ceased to issue public debt that could be automatically pledged at the Bank of Spain • Increased interest rates (rediscount rate from 4 to 5 percent)
Exchange rate	• Peseta becomes convertible with major currencies • Unified the existing multiple exchange rate system • Devalued the peseta from 48 to 60 pesetas per US dollar
Foreign trade	• Removed import license system, replaced with a new customs tariff • Replaced bilateral clearing agreements with multilateral one • Imposed advance deposit of 25 percent of value of goods to be imported
Competition	• Relaxed restrictions on foreign direct investment • Announced the intention to close an unspecified number of regulatory bodies following a review of their effectiveness

Source: Own compilation based on Sardá (1970), Clavera et al. (1973), and González (1979).

inflation would be under control. There were also stabilization measures on the fiscal front, though they were relatively less stringent than the monetary and exchange rate policy ones: A cap on public expenditure for the next budget was introduced, and some taxes, especially on petrol and tobacco, as well as prices on publicly provided utilities like telephone and transport were raised.

But the Plan went beyond that, seeking to liberalize the economy. The authorities liberalized 50 percent of its trade. They also relaxed restrictions on foreign investment, increasing from 25 to 50 percent the share of a company's capital that could be foreign owned. From a comparative perspective, Spain's Plan was in this respect more ambitious than most IMF-sponsored adjustment programs of the time, which typically did not include provisions affecting foreign investment. In addition, the Plan sought to liberalize the domestic economy, laying out a process to review and ultimately reduce the large number of regulatory bodies. Overall, while the impact of the 1959 Plan on the Spanish economy is almost a given in the literature, it is worth discussing the extent to which economic growth and policy reforms were linked, the question to which we now turn.

Good policies or good luck?

One of the difficulties of assessing the impact of any reforms on the growth performance of European countries in the second half of the twentieth century is the fact that so many positive factors combined to support growth. As World Bank economists Indermit Gill and Martin Raiser put it, Europe's growth model in recent decades became such a "convergence machine" that European countries seemed destined to catch up with little effort (Gill and Raiser, 2012). Growth in this period may have been overdetermined. The demographic transition, shifting gender norms, increased openness to trade and investment, and a process of structural transformation were all positive forces for growth. In fact, cross-country studies find growth accelerations in the 1950s or 1960s to be roughly twice as likely as in the following two decades (Jong-A-Pin and De Haan, 2011). In such light we may wonder not only whether Spain's growth performance is remarkable at all, but also whether any growth dividend can be attributed to economic policies or was simply driven by the happy coincidence of Spain's geographical location and the time period. We addressed the first question at length in the Introduction, in which we answered it in the positive. We will now tackle the second question.

The growth dividend of reforms

To assess the impact of economic policy reforms in the path of Spain towards economic prosperity we need to tackle the key question of the counterfactual: What would economic growth have been in the absence of reforms? Surprisingly, given the voluminous discussion of the 1959 Plan in Spanish economic history, this critical question is often overlooked or discussed in largely qualitative terms, sometimes relying on simple before-and-after exercises. To the best of my knowledge, there has been only one attempt at quantifying the growth impact of the economic reforms in the 1950s (Prados de la Escosura et al., 2011). The largely qualitative discussion of the impact of reforms leads to a traditional interpretation that suffers from two main conceptual shortcomings.

The first problem is the most fundamental. The implicit counterfactual in the standard account of the impact of the 1959 Plan is an implausible collapse of the economy. It is very common to read in the literature that prior to 1959 the economic model had become "exhausted" and that growth would have been "blocked" in the absence of the Plan.[11] This line of argument rightly suggests that the true measure of the economic impact of the 1959 Stabilization Plan cannot be gauged by comparing growth performance before and after the Plan. In the

---

[11] See one of many examples that could be provided: "By the mid-1950s it was obvious that the growth model adopted at the end of the Civil War (1936–39) had become exhausted. Pressing disequilibria, such as strong inflationary pressure, an appalling public deficit, and a serious balance of payments' problem, threatened to block the Spanish economy's hitherto timid advance" (Martín Aceña and Martínez Ruiz, 2007, pp. 34–5).

absence of the Plan, economic performance may have deteriorated. However, it does not follow that one can readily assume that economic stagnation is the appropriate counterfactual with which to measure the impact of the 1959 reforms.

The literature on growth empirics has profusely pointed out that economic growth can in fact happen in far from perfect economic policy settings. For all the distortions that characterized the business environment in Spain before 1959, economic growth had already accelerated during the 1950s, as we saw in Table 4.1 above. In fact, econometric analyses point to a structural break in economic growth around 1950, highlighting that the growth acceleration takes place well ahead of the 1959 Stabilization Plan (Prados de la Escosura, 2003, p. 146 and 2007). This does not necessarily mean that the reforms undertaken in 1959 were unimportant but highlights the need for a rigorous analysis of the growth impact of the Plan, particularly because the literature is typically unable to separate the impact of what we have referred to above as "early reforms" and of the 1959 Plan.

Indeed, the only model-based approach in the literature (Prados de la Escosura et al., 2011), stands out for being able to separate the impact of the Plan from earlier reforms. Significantly, these authors find that compared to the actual per capita GDP growth rate of 5.6 percent from 1959 to 1975, had policy determinants returned to their 1940s levels, growth would have only been 1.7 percent. If they had stayed at their 1950s levels, growth would have been 3.2 percent. While this can be seen as evidence that growth would have slowed down in the absence of the Plan, it is hard to think of an estimate of per capita GDP growth of 3.2 percent as evidence of an "exhausted" model.

The second conceptual problem is that, without an explicit model, the literature often lumps all the economic measures of the 1959 Stabilization Plan as the source of its success. This is unavoidable given the qualitative nature of their argument and leaves unanswered the question of whether some policy reforms mattered more than others.

What emerges from the above discussion is the importance of being explicit about the counterfactual when discussing the impact of reforms. Yet, with the exception of the work by Prados de la Escosura et al. (2011) already discussed and that of Pablo Martín Aceña (2004), the literature does not provide such an explicit counterfactual. To complement those contributions, I will provide next my own assessment of the impact of reforms that, in addition to being able to disentangle the effect of earlier reforms and of the 1959 Plan, has two additional advantages. First, it is built with a comparative perspective in mind, as it draws on an existing cross-country empirical model of economic performance in the second half of the twentieth century. Second, it allows for unpacking which reforms had the most importance in explaining the improved economic performance. Because the method that I will use to estimate the impact of reforms is different than that of Prados de la Escosura et al. (2011), it can be thought of as a robustness check on the latter.

A counterfactual: Spain without reforms

To estimate the impact of reforms on economic growth in Spain we need two things. First, we need to link changes in policy variables to changes in output. Second, we need to determine what would have been those policy variables in the absence of reforms. To capture the long-run growth effects of macroeconomic policies I will use the empirical model in Bill Easterly's contribution to the *Handbook of Economic Growth* (Aghion and Durlauf, 2005). Easterly's is a reduced-form model estimated on cross-country growth regressions using five-year averages for the period 1960–2000. The cross-country coverage has the main advantage that coefficients that link policy variables to growth are calibrated on a much broader dataset, with much greater intertemporal variation in policies to obtain significant coefficients than if we were to undertake single-country regression analysis. This is one of the main reasons why this simple but informative model has been used to undertake simulations on the impact of policy choices by development practitioners like Shanta Devarajan and Delfin Go (2003).

Easterly's empirical model is particularly relevant for our purposes for several reasons. It is also a parsimonious model that covers a broad set of variables commonly thought of as being determinants of economic growth, including policy determinants, shocks, and initial conditions.[12] Those variables can be mapped with relative ease to the actual policy measures undertaken by Spain, allowing us to have a proxy for the relative importance of the different policy changes on monetary and exchange rate policy, fiscal policy, financial sector regulation, and trade policy.[13] Easterly's model is also estimated for a time span that covers our period of interest, so that concerns about temporal effects such as terms of trade shocks are thus alleviated. Finally, and crucially, because the model is estimated on cross-country experience, the underlying data would help put Spain's experience in a comparative perspective.

Some caveats are, nevertheless, in order. This exercise assumes that the empirical cross-country model applies to Spain. It is also based on a stylized model that cannot account for all the indirect impacts that the Plan may have had. Like any model, its insights are constrained by what it focuses on, which in turn is heavily influenced by the data requirements to estimate it across a large sample of countries. One such area that is highly relevant for the case of Spain but is only

---

[12] The full list of variables in Easterly's model are as follows: Policy determinants: black market premium, M2/GDP, inflation, real exchange rate, secondary education enrollment, and telephone lines/1,000 population; Shocks: terms of trade as percentage of GDP, interest on external debt as percentage of GDP, and OECD trading partner growth; as well as initial income and an intercept.

[13] While the data requirements of the model are limited, it is worth noting that because of the multiple exchange rate system introduced in 1948, a weighted average exchange rate for all transactions in the basic balance, as calculated by Martínez (2003), is used. On the fiscal front, the main difficulty is the lack of a broad general government balance that includes autonomous government agencies.

captured at a high level of aggregation in this model is trade policy reform. While there is an emerging body of literature that suggests that trade liberalization is beneficial for economic growth (Wacziarg and Welch, 2008; Irwin, 2019), the model that we will use only captures trade intensity (exports plus imports over GDP), which is influenced by factors other than trade reforms and provides thus for an imperfect way to assess the impact of trade reforms on growth. All said, the rigor and insights that can be derived from a model like the one that we will use compensate for its shortcomings.

A crucial finding from Easterly's work is the importance of correcting large macroeconomic imbalances. As he himself puts it, extremely bad policy can "destroy any chance of growth" (Easterly, 2005, p. 1017). But he also calls for curbing one's enthusiasm about the potential for good macroeconomic alone to generate high growth. He estimates that a change of one standard deviation in each of the six macroeconomic variables in his model combine for a growth effect of 3 percentage points per year (see Table 4.3). While this seems to be a large effect, Easterly warns us that a one standard deviation change in the policy variables is often very large, requiring, for example, a 5-percentage-point improvement in the budget balance as a ratio to GDP or a 25-percentage-point increase in the M2/GDP ratio. The reason for Easterly's results is that the underlying distribution of most policy variables have long tails of extreme bad policies, which drive much of the correlation between bad policies and poor growth. This highlights the importance of avoiding big policy mistakes, as also argued from a more qualitative perspective by the Growth Commission (Spence, 2008). It is also a finding that fits particularly well with the literature that we reviewed in the Introduction that stressed how the key to sustained convergence lay not so much in increases in economic growth but in reductions of economic shrinking (Broadberry and Wallis, 2017).

But if avoiding bad mistakes is the top priority for macroeconomic management, how does this insight affect our understanding of the role of the 1959 Stabilization Plan and other earlier reforms in spurring economic growth in Spain? To begin with, we know from Table 4.1 above that some macroeconomic policy variables were significantly out of balance in the 1940s, and to a lesser extent in the 1950s. If the positive impact of reforms may not lie as much in how close to an ideal policy scenario one gets but in staying away from truly bad policies, a reinterpretation of reforms in the early 1950s may come to see them in a better light. To quantitatively answer these questions, we now combine the data on Spanish economic policy variables with the estimates of Easterly (2005) to obtain the impact of reforms. The results are shown in Table 4.3.

It is worth explaining Table 4.3 in some detail. Column (a) lists the six macroeconomic variables used in Easterly's model. Columns (b) and (c) provide the extent to which those policy variables changed in the 1950s (compared to their

Table 4.3 Impact of policy reforms on growth

(a)	(b)	(c)	(d)	(e)	(f)
	Actual improvement in Spain's policy variables		Impact on growth from one standard deviation shift in policy variable (Easterly, 2005)	Impact on annual real per capita GDP growth	
	1950s vs. 1940s	1960s vs. 1950s		Early reforms (1950–58)	1959 Plan
Policy determinants	(in standard deviations for each policy variable)		(percentage points)	(percentage points)	
Inflation, Log(1+inflation rate)	0.8	0.1	0.6	0.5	0.0
Government budget balance/GDP, ratio	0.6	0.0	0.5	0.3	0.0
M2/GDP, ratio	−0.1	0.4	0.3	0.0	0.1
Real exchange rate, Log(RER index/100)	0.8	0.2	0.5	0.4	0.1
Black market premium, Log(1+bmp)	0.7	2.4	0.7	0.5	1.7
Trade, (X+M)/GDP ratio	0.2	0.1	0.5	0.1	0.1
Combined impact (percentage points per year)			*3.0*	*1.7*	*2.0*

Source: Own compilation based on Easterly (2005) and data for Spain from Carreras and Tafunell (2005).

1940s values) and in the 1960s (compared to their 1950s values). This data, combined with the policy-growth elasticities uncovered by Easterly shown in column (d) will be the basis for our estimate of the growth impact of reforms. Note that the data about the shift in policy variables is expressed as standard deviations, in which the entire cross-country dataset is used to calculate those units. Finally, columns (e) and (f) show the impact on growth of the reforms undertaken in the 1950s and 1960s. The impact of the early reforms in 1950–8 is estimated to be 1.7 percentage points per year (shown in column (e), which is the result of multiplying columns (b) and (d)). The final column (f) provides the estimate of the impact on growth of the 1959 Plan alone, which is calculated by multiplying columns (c) and (d). At 2 percentage points per year, this is a large impact that lends support to the view on the importance of the Plan.

My approximation on the impact of economic reforms on growth conforms broadly with that of Prados de la Escosura et al. (2011) but differs in two significant ways. First, my estimates are higher. For the 1959 Plan alone, Prados de la Escosura et al. (2011) obtain an estimate of around 1.5 percentage points of added annual growth, while I obtain 2.0 percentage points. My estimate of the impact of earlier reforms is, moreover, further apart (0.8 percentage points compared to 1.7 percentage points in my case). This likely reflects the importance that correcting bad policy mistakes has in Easterly's empirical results. Overall, given the very different methodologies used, it is nevertheless reassuring that the effects found are of not too different magnitudes, especially in the case of the 1959 Plan.

We can now derive a counterfactual level of real per capita GDP in 1975. We do so by reducing the actual growth rate observed by the estimated percentages of the growth effect of the 1950s reforms and of the 1959 Plan. If we apply these in two steps, we can differentiate what portion of the counterfactual output is the result of the early reforms and what share is due to the 1959 Plan reforms. This counterfactual exercise is shown in Figure 4.3.

As informative as the headline number is, the disaggregated analysis can shed additional light on which policy change was particularly important and when. If we focus on the growth effect of the 1959 Plan first, what stands out from column (f) in Table 4.3, is that the impact on growth does not come from a correction of fiscal balances or inflation. This finding contradicts, at least in part, much of what has been written about the impact of the 1959 Plan. For example, in his synthesis on Spanish economic history, Gabriel Tortella (1994, p. 387) notes that the explanation for the success of the Plan was, on one hand the devaluation of the peseta and the elimination of the multiple exchange rates, and on the other hand the reduction in the fiscal deficit which helped reduce inflation. Regarding both inflation and fiscal deficits, our analysis suggests that the growth impact from correcting those imbalances already happened in the early reforms of 1950–8, as shown in column (e) of Table 4.3. This should come as no surprise, given that, as we

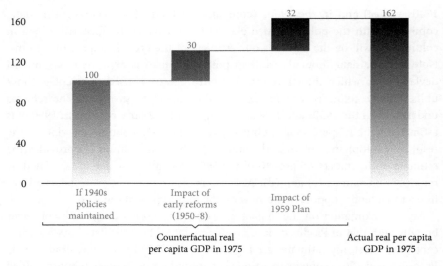

Figure 4.3 Counterfactual without economic policy reforms, 1960–75
Source: Own elaboration.

already saw, over the 1950s both inflation and fiscal deficits were on average much reduced compared to the 1940s.

It is true, however, that inflation in 1957 and 1958 had increased. An argument could be made that, had the 1959 Plan not been implemented, the correct counterfactual scenario would be for inflation to remain at its 1958 level. This is unlikely given that inflation in the years 1957 and 1958 years originated in part from a rare one-off wage increase. But even if we were to assume that inflation would have remained at its 1958 level in the absence of the Plan, this would still not mean that the growth impact of the 1959 Plan from correcting inflation would have been substantial. To see why, we need to show the evolution of inflation in Spain as well as how it stacks in a comparative perspective (Figure 4.4).

Figure 4.4 makes it clear that the inflationary episodes of the 1950s were much less severe than those in the previous decade. No wonder that the growth dividend from correcting inflationary imbalances had already been largely reaped in the early reforms that preceded the 1959 Plan. By the 1950s, the inflation rate in Spain was relatively low in comparative perspective, as shown in panel (b) of Figure 4.4. The growth econometric literature has also shown that such inflation rates as those recorded by Spain anytime in the 1950s can hardly be considered an insurmountable obstacle for economic growth. In fact, the literature suggests that it is high inflation crises, with inflation much higher than the 13 percent observed in Spain in 1958, that are associated with sharp growth reductions (Bruno and Easterly, 1998).

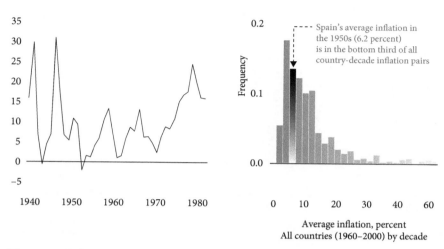

Figure 4.4 Inflation in comparative perspective
Source: Carreras et al. (2005) for panel (a) and own elaboration based on *Global Financial Statistics* for panel (b).

Our analysis also casts doubt on the view that the 1959 Plan contributed to growth through the correction of fiscal imbalances. The lesson from the empirical growth literature suggests that it is governments that produce "extreme deficits" that are detrimental to an economy (Sala-i-Martin, 2002, p. 11). This was far from the case in the Spain of the 1950s. The broadest measure of the general government budget balance in Spain showed a relatively modest deficit of less than 3 percent of GDP in 1958, and the central government balance was in fact in surplus for most of the period. Again, it is the early fiscal reforms in the 1950s before the Plan that carried more punch in terms of their effect of growth. This is because the imbalances had been much greater in the 1940s. Public debt as a share of national income had come down from 72 percent in 1935 to 40 percent in 1955 (Comín and Díaz, 2005, p. 877).

In contrast, our calculations suggest that the strongest contribution of the 1959 Plan to the acceleration of economic growth stems from the changes in policies that regulate trade with the external world. In particular, the Plan helped to correct the misalignment of the real exchange rate overvaluation that had resulted in a large black market premium. It is easy to see why the 1959 reforms had a significant impact through the external channel given that the imbalances on the exchange rate front remained large up until 1959, especially as shown in Figure 4.5 in a comparative perspective. In contrast with what we saw in the case of inflation or the fiscal

(a) Black market premium in Spain, percent

(b)Histogram of country-decade black market premium averages, percent (all countries, 1960–2000)

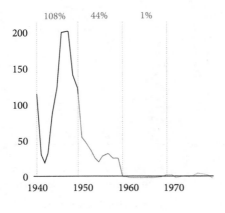

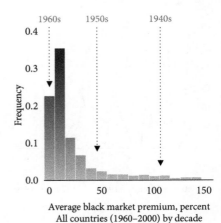

Average black market premium, percent
All countries (1960–2000) by decade

Figure 4.5 The exchange rate black market premium in comparative perspective

Source: Data for the 1940s and 1950s for Spain is taken from Martínez (2003), which provides a weighted average exchange rate for the basic balance, and Tena (2005) for the black market rate. All data from 1960 onwards is taken from *Global Financial Statistics* (Levine and Renelt, 1992; World's Currency Yearbook; and Wood, 1988).

position, here Spain's experience in the 1940s and even the 1950s is squarely in the tail end of the distribution of this policy determinant across countries.[14]

While the 1959 Plan was an impressive package of reforms, some were more substantial than others—if only because many of the truly bad policies and macroeconomic imbalances had already been partially addressed during the 1950s. This is a point that is often overlooked in the existing literature, which tends to note the overall strength of the 1959 reform program but typically does not identify which reforms may have tackled more binding constraints.

---

[14] Note that, while the reduction of the black market premium was greater in the 1950s than as a result of the 1959 Plan, the growth effect was greater after the 1959 reforms because of the way in which this variable enters Easterly's model, i.e., Log(1+black market premium). This functional form puts a penalty on large reductions of the black market premium that are still far from zero. The intuition is that dialing down disastrous policies into very bad ones, even if they require a large policy shift, is not as effective for growth as correcting bad policies and bringing them close to good ones.

Conclusion

We started this chapter with the useful reminder that political stability would not by itself generate fast economic growth. Spain was no exception to this rule. Growth took off after political stability was achieved, but it also required significant economic policy reforms. What was exceptional about Spain was the drastic turnaround in economic policymaking, from an autarkic and statist orientation to a more open and market-friendly one. We devoted most of the chapter to first document those reforms and then to perform a counterfactual exercise to help us gauge the impact of economic reforms. Our analysis makes clear two important conclusions.

First and foremost, the growth dividend from improving economic policies in Spain was large. And by improving policies what we mean is largely to remove excesses that were causing harm. My estimates suggest that in the decade and a half after 1960, the improved economic policies accounted for much of the increase in per capita growth: Two full percentage points are accounted for by the reforms in the 1959 Stabilization Plan and 1.7 percentage points by the reforms in the 1950s prior to the Plan. Spain proves the case that there can be high returns from getting policies right, or more precisely, from correcting bad policy mistakes. Removing acute distortions in the fiscal and monetary policy arenas, as well as getting the external price of the peseta right, were essential prerequisites for growth to take off. Macroeconomic management became much more predictable, without the wild swings in fiscal accounts or inflation that characterized the 1940s. In addition, there were movements towards greater contestability in markets, in part through the greater inflows of foreign direct investment (FDI) and through trade openness, which stood at only 5 percent of GDP in the 1940s and which had more than tripled, to around 17 percent of GDP, by the 1960s. Increased contestability is an element which will also feature prominently in later chapters.

The second conclusion is that this improved performance was the result of a decade-long reform process. Drawing on an empirical model that links policy determinants to economic growth (Easterly, 2005), we performed a counterfactual analysis that allows us to distinguish between the impact on growth from the early reforms and from the 1959 Plan. The results from this exercise suggest that the early reforms undertaken before 1959 played almost as much of a role as the 1959 Plan did in stoking growth. This finding is in contrast with most of the literature which, with few exceptions (Prados de la Escosura et al., 2011), has focused perhaps too much on the importance of the 1959 Stabilization Plan. While this is not a common finding in the Spanish economic historiography, on closer inspection it comes as no surprise, since some of the major imbalances in the economy, like high fiscal deficits or inflationary crises, had been largely corrected by the

1950s. It is also a finding that is fully in sync with the emerging growth literature that suggests that avoiding bad policy mistakes is probably the most important contribution of macroeconomic policies to growth. In short, do no harm.

Our results do not question the importance of the 1959 Stabilization Plan, which not only added its own boost to growth but also enshrined some of the earlier reforms so that macroeconomic prudence became much more entrenched. Our findings simply put the 1959 Plan in a broader context. But, by doing so, they raise important questions not only about the relative importance of reforms for spurring growth but even more so about the standard political economy narrative that helps explain the reason why reforms were undertaken. Until now, the emphasis on the 1959 Plan as the epitome of reforms had gone hand in hand with a view that highlighted the crisis-led nature of reforms. In short, it was commonly argued that a desperate situation had prompted the adoption of the 1959 Plan. But, if we now see that meaningful reforms were much longer in the making, how does that affect our view of why were reforms adopted? We turn to this question in the next chapter.

5
Why Reform?

Given that policy choices played such a significant role in spurring economic growth, a critical line of inquiry into explaining the Spanish ascent to prosperity is what prompted those reforms. This is a question particularly relevant for the broader debate on development, which has spent considerable effort in trying to model and better understand the political economy of reform.[1] As it turns out, to draw insights from Spain will require that we first question much of the conventional wisdom that we have received on the political economy of the period, which has suffered from both conceptual flaws and limited supporting evidence.

The fundamental shortcoming of the abundant literature on the economic stabilization in Spain is that it assumes that economic reforms had mainly *economic* origins rather than *political* ones. In particular, the significant economic reforms that Spain adopted in 1959 are widely interpreted as the result of a balance of payments crisis that in the view of most authors pushed the government into sweeping reforms. In contrast, I will argue that this is an unhelpful framing of events. In a departure from most of the existing historiography, I will maintain that the adoption of economic reforms in Spain can be better understood not as the result of economic *instability* but of political *stability*.

The focus on interpreting reforms as prompted by a crisis is not exclusive to the Spanish literature. Economic crises often feature in a protagonist role in narratives of policy reforms. It is part of a "new conventional wisdom on reform" (Tommasi and Velasco, 1996, p. 197). But, as in these authors' delightful fable of an imaginary country, conventional wisdom often goes unchallenged even in cases where it should. The role of the economic crisis remains today the predominant account of the explanation for the adoption of reforms in Spain.

The standard account of reforms

Perhaps there is no one better than the head of research of the Bank of Spain and intellectual engine behind the reforms, the economist Joan Sardá, to provide us

---

[1] For a review of the very broad literature on the political economy of reform see Khemani (2020). A particularly useful insight from this review is the growing importance in political economy work given to examining norms of behavior and preferences.

Unexpected Prosperity: How Spain Escaped the Middle Income Trap. Oscar Calvo-Gonzalez, Oxford University Press.
© Oscar Calvo-Gonzalez 2021. DOI: 10.1093/oso/9780198853978.003.0006

with the canonical view of the making of the 1959 Plan. There are three key elements in this standard view. First, the economic situation before the Plan was one of crisis. Thus, according to Sardá, economic development in Spain in the 1950s was "neutralized" by a "collapse" of the economy created by poor policies.

The second element in the standard account of reforms in Franco's Spain is that it was the severity of the situation that forced policy changes. The crisis, Sardá went on, made it impossible to continue with the status quo and the Spanish government was "forced, undoubtedly by the difficult situation" to undertake a "radical change in the orientation of economic policy." Finally, the third common element is that the ideas and the momentum for change were in large part driven by the international financial institutions as conditions for their support to the operation. Sardá left no doubt that this was an "acceptance" of "ideas proposed by the international organizations."[2]

These three elements—severity of the crisis, dramatic change in policies, and foreign influence—reinforce each other in the standard narrative. The more one stresses the severity of the crisis, the more it seems logical that radical measures were needed. The more one sees reforms as sharply different from previous policies, the more it makes sense to think that they were not voluntarily adopted but imposed by circumstance or external forces. As we will see below, new evidence suggests otherwise, with important consequences for the lessons from Spain's turnaround in economic policies, for example for our view on aid conditionality.

The dominant explanation of the political economy of reforms during the Franco regime, heavily influenced by the work of Manuel-Jesús González (1979) takes the above narrative one step further to its logical conclusion: As the crisis subsided, the appetite for reform must have faded too. The intellectual appeal of this interpretation is obvious. It provides a parsimonious account of not only the adoption of reforms in 1959 but of the entire political economy of the Franco regime: When autarky proved disastrous and failed, the regime had no alternative but to implement market reforms; when the economy turned around, the appetite for market discipline faded, giving way to a resumed rent-seeking behavior which manifested itself in the indicative planning of the 1960s.[3] While its appeal owes much to its impeccable logic, González's contribution was largely a hypothesis with limited supporting evidence.

In contrast to the interest provoked among economists, the political economy of reforms during the Franco regime has attracted limited attention among

---

[2] Sardá is widely regarded as the main technical architect of the Plan. Quotes are from Sardá (1973), pp. 12–13.

[3] Which was indeed the title of González's book. The subtitle, "Dirigisme, Market, and Planning" fit neatly the interpretative model.

professional historians. The result is a limited use of primary evidence and a heavy reliance on the accounts of the Plan written by many of its participants, which predictably paint the Plan in a very positive light.[4] The Finance Minister at the time, Mariano Navarro Rubio, summed it up in an autobiographical account in which he stressed his role in persuading Franco to go ahead with the reforms on the argument that otherwise the country would be "heading for bankruptcy" (Navarro Rubio, 1976, p. 198). The Finance Minister's account is worth quoting at length to portray the sense of drama:

> The Cabinet meeting was certainly difficult for proponents of the stabilization. The Ministers of Finance and Commerce defended it firmly but the Minister of Commerce, as usual, would not volunteer data about the situation of the Foreign Exchange Institute . . . the Minister of Commerce, with everybody's attention, uncovered in moments of true suspense, that our situation was certainly critical. The Minister of Commerce had to listen to the reproaches of some ministers for not having kept them informed of the situation. He replied, with dignity, that he had wanted to bear the burden on his own. And in this atmosphere, close to desperate, the government finally approved the Stabilization Plan.
>
> (Navarro Rubio, 1976, p. 202)

Some authors have rightly questioned Mariano Navarro Rubio's memoirs as self-serving, pointing to their lack of reliability on some details.[5] But ultimately, Navarro Rubio's narrative looms large in the historiography of the period when it comes to the critical aspects of the decision-making regarding the Plan. In short, most of the literature stresses that without the threat of economic collapse there would have been no Stabilization Plan (Preston, 2008, pp. 19–20). In the standard account, Franco "reluctantly conceded defeat," which led to his "grudging acceptance of the 1959 operation" (Viñas, 1999). The 1959 Stabilization Plan was thus "accepted as inevitable by Franco but unenthusiastically" (Tusell, 1989b, p. 168).

However, with the benefit of archival sources we will modify some of these interpretations, which otherwise would lead us to deriving the wrong conclusions about Spain's change of course in economic policies. To tap into those insights, we need first to peel some layers off the existing narrative of the political economy of reform in Spain in this period.

---

[4] There is no shortage of first-hand accounts of the Plan (Sardá, 1970; Navarro Rubio, 1976; Fuentes Quintana, 1984; Varela Parache, 1989; Ullastres, 1994; and Estapé, 2000).
[5] Viñas et al. (1979).

Limitations of the standard view of the political economy of reforms

There are five major shortcomings with the standard account of the causes of economic reform in Franco's Spain.[6] First, if the economic crisis was the key driver of reform, one needs to answer why reforms were not adopted earlier, when there were more acute crises. Second, the crisis that, in the traditional view, explains the adoption of reforms was not a full-blown economic collapse but rather limited to a foreign exchange crisis: Why would such a relatively narrow crisis lead to a broad-ranging reform program? Third, since reforms started long before the foreign exchange crisis materialized, what explains the push for early reforms? Fourth, if economic crisis provided the main impetus for change, reforms would have stalled after the 1959 Plan. This is indeed the logical argument provided in the literature, but as we will document, many reforms were continued and even strengthened after 1959. Finally, the standard account puts too much emphasis on the role played by international organizations, which are often seen as imposing policy conditions in exchange for their financial support to the reform program. Let us briefly take each of these shortcomings in turn.

Crisis, what crisis?

The view that it was the depth of the economic crisis in Spain that explains the adoption of reforms remains widely held. But for this to be a convincing explanation of reforms, we cannot simply overlook previous crises that did not lead to reforms (Rodrik, 1996). This concern is particularly important in our case. This is because previous economic crises in earlier years of the Franco regime were worse than the situation in 1959, yet they did not lead to the adoption of broad-ranging reforms.

Autarkic economic policies had demonstrated its disastrous consequences already by the 1940s, when shortages led to malnutrition being so widespread that the country underwent famine conditions that historians estimate caused an additional 200,000 deaths (Cazorla-Sanchez, 2010). Even if we limit ourselves to macroeconomic variables only, the mid- to late 1950s compares favorably with the late 1940s. Inflation, for example, peaked at 13 percent in 1958, much less than the 30 percent that it reached on more than one occasion in the late 1940s (recall Figure 4.4 in Chapter 4). Similarly, the fiscal position had been much

[6] Most of the archival research on which this section draws was made possible by financial support by the Irwin Studentship of the University of London, which is here gratefully acknowledged, and previously featured in Chapter 7 of my unpublished PhD dissertation (Calvo-Gonzalez, 2002).

worse in the 1940s than at any point in time in the 1950s. Fiscal discipline had been reinforced by a fiscal reform in December 1957 which, among other elements, terminated funds from the budget to INI. Revenues increased and debt issued to finance the deficit decreased sharply from 30 percent of total budget expenditures in 1956 to 16 percent in 1957 and 1 percent in 1958. I am not the first to note that, at least on the fiscal front, the Stabilization Plan came to solve "problems that were already partly overcome."[7] Somehow, however, the literature has paid little attention to it.

There is an additional question that is often overlooked: Why would Franco entrust the reforms to the same economic team that was responsible for the alleged crisis? In fact, this would be out of Franco's character, who was not shy of dismissing ministers seen as responsible for specific failures, to assign blame. We have seen examples of this in earlier chapters, as when Franco dismissed Serrano Suñer and Varela for the fights between *Falangists* and Carlists. Ministers of the regime often enjoyed long tenures, but Franco was not beyond getting his ministers to take the fall for specific events, a pattern that continued over the years.[8]

An exchange rate crisis, not an economic collapse

The situation that prompted the adoption of the 1959 Stabilization Plan was far from a full-blown collapse of the Spanish economy. Rather, it was a relatively mild balance of payments crisis under a fixed exchange rate regime that authorities could have tried to tackle with action on the official exchange rate. To show that the crisis was relatively mild, we need to look no further than to the size of the current account deficit. Although it widened in the mid-1950s, the current account deficit peaked at a relatively modest 2.3 percent of GDP in 1957. If we take a comparative perspective, this value would be right in the fiftieth percentile of all country-year pairs of current account balances during the last four decades of the twentieth century—hardly an early warning (see Figure 5.1).

It is nevertheless the case that the current account deficit had increased, and foreign reserves sharply dropped. But we need to understand why the current account deficit widened before concluding that this was a sign of an economy on the verge of collapse. Economic theory tells us that whether a current account deficit is good or bad depends on the factors giving rise to that deficit. A current account deficit driven by sluggish exports may be indicative of competitiveness problems, but if it is driven by an increase in investment it could equally be

---

[7] Rubio (1968, p. 29). This contribution has received insufficient attention in the literature.

[8] The technocrat ministers entered the cabinet shortly after the Minister of Education had been removed on account of failing to suppress student demonstrations in 1956, and in early 1957 the Minister of the National Movement had been removed after only one year in his position.

(a) Current account balance of Spain, 1940–58, percentage of GDP

(b) Worldwide distribution of current account balances

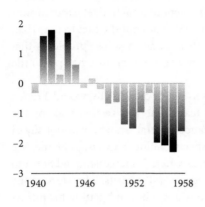

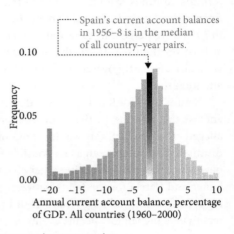

Annual current account balance, percentage of GDP. All countries (1960–2000)

Figure 5.1 Current account balances in comparative perspective

Source: Own elaboration based on based on Martínez (2003) and Carreras et al. (2005) and own elaboration based on World Development Indicators for panel (b).

pointing to a growing economy. On this basis, the assessment for 1950s Spain is mixed at best. Exports had picked up in the early 1950s but declined after 1956, perhaps evidence of the erosion of Spanish competitiveness on account of the persistent overvaluation of the exchange rate. At the same time, the widening of the current account deficit reflected a balanced growth of both consumption and investment, with the latter showing in fact a slightly more dynamic evolution in the 1950s, as seen in Figure 5.2.

But what about the depletion of official foreign reserves, is not that a sign of a serious economic crisis? Interestingly, this is the go-to argument of the standard account in the literature today, just as it was for pro-reformers at the time. Importantly, this depletion of official foreign reserves reflected both a real trend as well as a data-reporting issue that muddles the interpretation about the underlying strength of the economic situation. The data issue stems from the ease with which official channels were bypassed. For example, the number of foreign tourists to Spain increased by 50 percent from 1956 to 1958, from 1.6 to 2.4 million. Yet, official statistics reflected that the dollar earnings from these visitors dropped by more than a quarter in the same period, from $97 to $72 million.

In addition, and even more substantial, was the common practices of under-invoicing of exports and capital flight. The staff of the American Embassy in Madrid estimated that only about three-quarters of all foreign exchange earnings were processed through the official channels, while Bank of England staff estimated

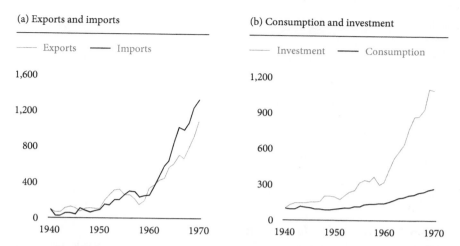

Figure 5.2 How severe was the external crisis in 1959?
Source: Own elaboration based on Carreras et al. (2005).

the ratio to be only two-thirds.[9] Moreover, observers at the time noted that the practice of under-invoicing and the retention of export proceeds abroad intensified in early 1959, "evidently in the expectation of a devaluation of the peseta." IMF staff estimated that Spaniards held around $300 million abroad by June 1959.[10] These are not small numbers when compared to the size of the current account deficit, which peaked at $281 million in 1957. That same year the errors and omissions of the balance of payment soared to $203 million, offsetting almost three-quarters of the current account deficit. In 1958 the errors would again be large, offsetting around two thirds of the current account deficit.[11]

This is not to say that there was no exchange rate crisis or an overvaluation of the peseta in the late 1950s. This had been an enduring problem for Spain since the 1940s, when there was in fact a much greater exchange rate misalignment, as shown in Figure 5.3. Other authors have also confirmed, through an analysis of exchange market pressure indices, that the exchange rate crisis in 1959 had a fore-runner earlier in the decade, in 1950–1 (Martínez-Ruiz and Nogues-Marco, 2014). The crisis in 1951 was addressed by making changes within the multiple exchange

[9] The OEEC had similarly asked if "some explanation could be given" to the fall in net earnings from travel in 1957 despite it having "been a good tourist year." See Calvo-Gonzalez (2002, pp. 256–7).
[10] See Calvo-Gonzalez (2002, pp. 256–7).
[11] Under-invoicing of exports would not directly result in errors and omissions unless the illegitimate payments were then channeled back to Spain in an irregular fashion. The large positive errors and omissions in this period suggest such irregular inflows were happening and that they were large. The data on the balance of payments is available thanks to the painstaking reconstruction by Martínez (2003).

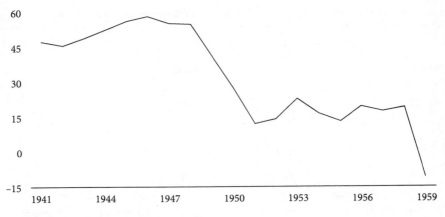

Figure 5.3 Overvaluation of the peseta

Note: Variable shows the deviation of the official exchange rate from the one that satisfied the purchasing power parity condition, percent (positive values indicate overvaluation of the official exchange rate).

Source: Own elaboration based on Aixalá (1999).

rate regime which amounted to a stealth devaluation of the peseta that brought down the black market premium from over 100 percent in the late 1940s to around 50 percent in the first years of the 1950s—as we saw in Chapter 4.

Overall, the overvaluation of the peseta and loss of reserves would have required a policy response. But the authorities could have adopted a narrower set of policies like a devaluation, as the regime had done repeatedly in earlier years, including as recently as in 1957, without taking additional measures. Speaking a few months after the 1959 Plan had been launched, the American ambassador captured this skeptical view on the crisis-induced reform narrative when he praised the authorities for undertaking reforms despite the fact that the "Spanish economy had not reached a phase of crisis, and despite external and internal debt was much lower than that of many other countries."[12] While the ambassador's framing of the discussion failed to gain traction in the literature, it points to the question that the standard account of the political reform of the period needs to address: Why would such a relatively limited crisis lead to a major overhaul of economic policies?

Long in the making

Decisions that started to move the economy away from autarkic principles long preceded the exchange rate crisis of the late 1950s. A cabinet reshuffle in 1951 led to significant changes in personnel at the top. Perhaps the most important was the

---

[12] John Davis Lodge, before the American Club in Madrid on 15th October 1959. General Archive of the Administration [henceforth AGA], box 36624.

inclusion of Luis Carrero Blanco, with ministerial rank, in charge of coordinating the entire cabinet. Carrero, who was not affiliated with any of the traditional families but rather a pure Franco loyalist, would come to play a critical role in both policy and personnel selection (Tusell, 1993). There were changes in numerous ministries, including Finance, Agriculture, and Education. One of those relieved from their posts was the Minister of Industry and Commerce, which from 1945 to 1951 had been Juan Antonio Suanzes, simultaneously head of INI and thus in charge of the state-led efforts at industrialization. Suanzes, a childhood friend of Franco's, would retain the chairmanship of INI but his influence in pushing for a strategy of import substitution industrialization would diminish throughout the 1950s. The Ministry of Industry and Commerce was split in two and a trained economist who was in favor of a cautious trade liberalization was appointed as Minister of Commerce.

The 1951 cabinet reshuffle took place simultaneously with a visit to Spain by US Admiral Forrest Sherman, Chief of Naval Operations.[13] Because of this coincidence, the literature has sometimes seen a connection between the two. While there is no evidence of a direct link, the government changes in 1951 are to be interpreted in a context where Franco saw the turn of international events as favorable to him, as an opportunity to present the regime as modern and socially just (Brydan, 2019). The logic behind the change of government in 1951 appears to be the same as previous ones, in which the dictator sought to balance the power of the different political families. Once cabinet appointments were made to reflect the relative balance of power, Ministers were left significant discretion in the implementation of policies provided they did not challenge the ultimate authority of the dictator or put the regime at risk. This logic had important consequences for policy formulation. It increased the stakes of personnel decisions, an issue that is often not discussed in standard accounts of economic development but which would prove particularly relevant in the case of Spain.

One of the features of high-level appointments in the 1950s is the increasing power given to technical experts. The technocrats, as they would later become known, did not coalesce around a single policy blueprint but shared the overall goal of modernizing the economy. Most immediately in their sights was the reform of the public administration. At the heart of this task would be Laureano López Rodó, a law professor with the ambition to modernize the state while preserving the nature of the regime. López Rodó became in 1956 the Undersecretary of the Presidency and would come to play a decisive role in government for the next two decades as the right-hand man of Carrero Blanco.[14]

---

[13] Sherman had been one of the 12 men in the room with Truman to discuss how to respond to the North Korean attack, the momentous decision with which we started the last chapter.

[14] The rise of the technocracy, to which we will return in later chapters, has attracted the attention of scholars in recent years (Cañellas, 2016).

The liberal approach to economic policymaking would be strengthened in February 1957, when two reform-minded technocrats, Mariano Navarro Rubio and Alberto Ullastres Calvo, were appointed as ministers of Finance and Commerce respectively. Minister Ullastres stands out for his technical credentials and convictions, which will prove critical for the evolution of policymaking. But Ullastres was far from being alone. At the Bank of Spain, in a move that preceded the ministerial reshuffling, the job of Head of Research was given in 1956 to Joan Sardá, a strong advocate of reform. With control over the ministries of Finance and Commerce, and the central bank, the reformist camp was in a position of strength.[15]

Since taking office in February 1957, the new cabinet was in fact able to show action on a relatively broad range of economic policy issues. In his second cabinet meeting, Ullastres got through a devaluation of the exchange rate from 25.5 to 42 pesetas per US dollar, close to the rate at which the peseta was trading in the parallel markets. It was also an effort to unify the exchange rate, though it proved short-lived as a range of exceptions was introduced by the end of 1957 that effectively brought back the system of multiple exchange rates. The central bank's rediscount rate was increased in July 1957 and, most importantly, fiscal consolidation was launched with a tax reform in December 1957 aimed at broadening the tax base as well as raising additional revenues. Spain also joined the IMF and the World Bank in July 1958, passed a new law on long-term credit aimed at curbing financing of the holding of state-owned enterprises, and set out to improve the coordination of economic policies by setting up two bodies, a technical office for coordination and programming and a delegate committee on economic affairs which, since March 1957, was tasked with preparing all cabinet decisions on economic policy issues.[16]

Limited backtracking of reforms

If the push for reforms was a desperate situation that forced the hand of the regime, it follows that one would expect that reforms would stall once the emergency is over. The clearest exposition of this view comes from the influential economist and policymaker Enrique Fuentes Quintana (1984), who coined a phrase for posterity: "foreign exchange reserves kill the will to reform." This is a powerful narrative that has come to dominate the literature. The liberalizing period is seen as an "anomalous parenthesis" (Ros Hombravella, 1979, p. 57) and "brief, from 1959 to around 1964" (García Delgado, 1989, p. 180). Yet, digging

---

[15] Yet, an enduring part of the narrative about the 1959 Stabilization Plan is that it was accomplished by a "liberal commando" (González, 1979, p. 33).

[16] Muns (1986) and Varela (1994) on Spain joining the international financial institutions. For a monograph focused on the pre-stabilization measures from 1957 to 1959 see Zaratiegui (2018a).

behind the rhetoric, we find mixed evidence at best of a backtracking of reforms, especially in some of the most critical and pro-growth elements of the reform like trade liberalization and openness to FDI.

Before 1959, all imports were subject to import restrictions in the form of licensing requirements or bilateral quotas.[17] The measures undertaken at that time committed Spain to liberalize 50 percent of its trade. Although this target was met with some initial delays, Spain continued to make progress in subsequent years, liberalizing higher shares of its trade as shown in Figure 5.4. In 1963, Spain joined the General Agreement on Tariffs and Trade. As late as October 1964, a full five years after the launch of the Stabilization Plan, the Economist Intelligence Unit noted that "the process of creeping liberalization continues."[18] The literature has made much of the fact that after 1967 the share of liberalized trade plateaus. This may be interpreted as evidence indeed that the liberalization efforts waned. At the same time, tariffs, which had been raised initially when they replaced quantitative restrictions as the main protectionist mechanism after 1959, saw a clear decline from 1967 onwards (Figure 5.4). One may have wished liberalization to go even further and faster, but overall the continued trade liberalization, either through eliminating quantitative restrictions or later lowering tariffs, is inconsistent with the standard narrative of a reversal of reforms in the 1960s.

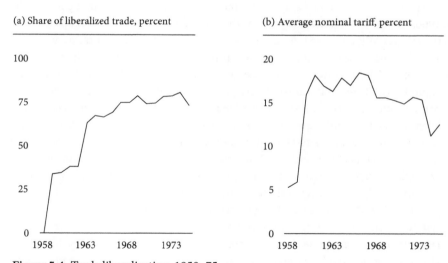

Figure 5.4 Trade liberalization, 1958–75
Source: Viñas et al. (1979), González (1979), and Tena (2005).

[17] The only exception were watches, which had always been free to import subject to the prevailing tariff. For a detailed description of the trade practices of the time, see the monumental Viñas et al. (1979).
[18] Economic Review of Spain, no. 51 (October 1964), by the Economist Intelligence Unit.

The trend towards greater liberalization is even stronger in the case of openness to FDI. As discussed in Chapter 4, the main measure in 1959 had been the increase from 25 to 50 percent in the share of capital that could be foreign owned. Over the years after 1959, the authorities had the opportunity to tighten conditions for FDI, yet at every opportunity they took steps that either preserved or enhanced the freedom of foreign investors. The result was an increasingly liberal legal regime for FDI.[19]

Half a year after the initial liberalizing measures were adopted, the authorities expanded the modalities of foreign investment that were covered by the freer regime, equalizing the treatment of monetary contributions, physical capital, technical assistance, patents, and licenses. In January 1960, an annual repatriation of dividends of up to 6 percent of invested capital is allowed. In early 1962, the treatment of portfolio investments is given the same treatment as that of FDI. And in 1963, foreign ownership in excess of 50 percent was allowed for firms operating in many economic activities. In those sectors, foreigners could now own from 50 to 100 percent of the firm subject to a prior authorization system—a system which introduced some confusion, but which ultimately did not prove to be a particularly binding constraint. A 1971 report by the OECD on Spain's capital markets noted that over 90 percent of requests to increase foreign ownership above 50 percent had been granted (OECD, 1971, p. 103).

From a comparative perspective, the legal regime of FDI in Spain in the 1960s could be considered as one of the most favorable for the foreign investor (Garrigues-Walker, 1965). It is also worth noting that the measures approved in 1959 left the door open for a relatively restricted interpretation of the liberalization of FDI by mentioning that the goal of maximizing the impact of foreign capital would be guaranteed if foreign capital inflows fit within investment prioritization criteria yet to be determined. Such prioritization criteria could have been invoked to limit capital inflows. Yet that door remained open. At least until October 1973, when criteria such as size, exporting capacity, technology to be used, financial backing, and location were introduced to help determine whether an application for foreign ownership in excess of 50 percent would be approved.

Importantly, the timing of these restrictive measures is all wrong if it is to support the view that foreign exchange reserves kill the will to reform. These newly restrictive measures were introduced a full decade and a half after the initial reforms. Moreover, these measures coincide with the first oil shock to hit the global economy. And, perhaps even more importantly, the new conditions to allow foreign ownership in excess of 50 percent needs to be put in the context of the industrial policies that were common in Western Europe in the 1970s—an issue to which we will return in Chapter 7.

---

[19] As documented by Martínez González-Tablas (1979, p. 74). This literature, however, did not connect this with the discussion on the political economy of reforms, see my earlier contribution (Calvo-Gonzalez, 2008).

Reforms were not imposed as conditions for external aid

Another key element in the standard account of the political economy of reforms in the period is the presumed leverage of the international organizations in pushing for reform.[20] Implicitly, the leverage by the international financial institutions stemmed from the desperate foreign exchange position that Spain suffered and the need for aid to bridge that gap.

New evidence, however, suggests that the international financial institutions played no role in demanding certain types of reforms against the will of reluctant national authorities. The underutilized archives of the IMF and the World Bank are particularly helpful to shed light on this issue.[21] In short, the role of the international financial institutions was much different from the alleged pressure which they put on the Spanish authorities to reform. IMF staff and management were keenly aware of divisions within the Franco government. Fund management would typically take the side of their reform-minded counterparts, with whom Fund staffers saw eye to eye. But this did not materialize in tough conditionality. On the contrary, Fund management agreed on several occasions with the assessment of pro-reformers that their hand would be weakened if tough conditionality was applied. If policies came to be regarded as impositions by the Fund, reformers would be accused of not putting the interests of the country first, a particularly high crime in such a Nationalist regime.[22]

The willingness of the IMF to be flexible on account of this argument included matters of the greatest importance like the parity to be set for the peseta. While the IMF mission chief had suggested a rate of 62 pesetas per US dollar, the IMF Managing Director, Per Jacobsson, thought it unnecessary to fight the Spanish proposal of 60 pesetas per US dollar because, as he recorded in his diary on June 23, 1959, that way "nobody can now say that it is the Fund that has forced Spain to devalue—it's their own proposal that has been accepted." Other concessions by the Fund are worth noting.

Importers were asked to deposit in the central bank in advance 25 percent of the value of goods to be imported.[23] In addition, specific taxes on the export of oranges were put in place. Finance Minister Navarro Rubio also pleaded that the program gave him enough flexibility on the monetary front. He resisted, in particular, a firm limit on the amount of commercial paper that banks could

---

[20] Many praise the positive consequences of the "policy conditionality attached to the aid" by the international organizations (Fuentes Quintana, 1984, p. 30). In English, see De la Dehesa (1993, p. 124), who considers that "pressure from the OEEC and the IMF to introduce a stabilization plan" was key to the reform process.

[21] Per Jacobsson, Managing Director of the IMF at the time, also kept a diary throughout his life. During his term of office at the IMF, Jacobsson filled three to five pages daily with his thoughts.

[22] For a detail discussion of these issues, see my earlier work, Calvo-Gonzalez (2007b).

[23] See Table 4.2 in Chapter 4. It was removed in January 1960 once the fear of a sharp rise in imports did not materialize.

rediscount at the central bank. Navarro Rubio argued that "the whole stabilization program will be accepted more readily if I am left in a position to give assurance that [the program has] sufficient flexibility." All of the above were seen by the IMF team as regrettable and not ideal. But the Fund agreed to the unorthodox measures and was also satisfied with entering into a gentleman's agreement with Navarro Rubio so that, instead of formal limits publicly announced, Navarro Rubio's intentions to limit the rediscount of commercial paper and to implement a further increase in the discount rate could be made in private letters.[24]

This did not mean that Fund management bet on the pro-reform ministers at face value or without regard to their authorizing environment. The Fund team could rely on the broad range of reforms that the Ministers of Finance and Commerce had undertaken already in the two years since being in office. And the IMF would continue to probe the degree of ownership of the reforms. At the level of ministers, the Fund was concerned that, while there was agreement over the substance of the policies, personal differences and struggles for administrative power between the Ministers of Finance and Commerce could jeopardize the success of the program. The Fund mission chief deliberately avoided topics that could spark a turf battle between Navarro Rubio and Ullastres.[25]

More importantly, the question of whether Franco himself supported the program or not was on everyone's mind. By mid-May there were reports that cabinet was "fully behind the stabilization program" and that "Franco has made it plain to the Council that any Minister who fails to co-operate will be replaced."[26] Ullastres had also assured the Americans that Franco had stated his firm support for the stabilization plan at a cabinet meeting in early May. Around that time, the Deputy Secretary General of the OEEC concluded that there was "real support" for the program within the Spanish Government, and "felt that this attitude might also extend to Franco himself."[27] In any case, the Fund mission continued to worry about the possibility that Franco could withdraw his support for the program at any time.

As the negotiations were about to conclude, the IMF Managing Director, Per Jacobsson, traveled to Madrid. His main purpose was to get a sense of the extent to which Franco was behind the program. Jacobsson pressed Franco at their

[24] Navarro Rubio to Jacobsson, Madrid, June 25, 1959, in General Archive of the Spanish Administration, box 36624.

[25] For example: "As you know, one of the main deficiencies of the Spanish administrative structure lies in the extreme weakness of the Bank of Spain. The question is now being discussed in Madrid, but it unfortunately causes conflict between the two Ministers who are working hardest for stabilization, the Minister of Finance and the Minister of Commerce. I am afraid that any effort on our part to bring about an early change in the system would only destroy the existing unity between the two Ministers." Ferras to Jacobsson, May 29, 1959, in AIMF C/Spain/420 Stabilization Program (oversize file).

[26] "Report of British Embassy in Spain on IMF-OEEC Negotiations," by Milton Barall, Madrid, May 20, 1959, in Spain, Madrid Emb., CGR 1953–63, FSPF, RG84 (entry 3167B, box 11), NACP.

[27] Memorandum of conversation between OEEC and U.S. officials, April 22, 1959, in "OEEC, 1959–1961," Spain, Madrid Emb., CGR 1953–63, FSPF, RG84 (entry 3167B, box 11), NACP.

meeting in the palace of El Pardo on June 25, 1959. As he put in his diary, Jacobsson stressed that he had seen "many technically good programs failing because the political backing was insufficient." Franco assured Jacobsson that he was "fully behind the program—that he would see to it that it was carried out—that he considered it in the interest of Spain." Most reassuring to Jacobsson, judging from his diary entry, was the fact that although Franco did not speak technicalities, "it was clear he knew a lot about the program."

Per Jacobsson is recognized for having been the first to articulate the concept of the country's ownership of reforms for the success of Fund-supported programs. Jacobsson's thinking crystallized precisely as he was trying to determine the extent to which the Spanish authorities supported the program. It was in Madrid, in a TV interview, that Jacobsson publicly articulated that Fund programs "can only succeed" if countries "themselves freely have come to the conclusion that the measures they arrange to take—even when they are sometimes harsh—are in the best interests of their own countries" (as quoted in James, 1996, p. 109).

A reinterpretation

In May 1959, as discussions between Spain and the international organizations continued on a Stabilization Plan, Minister Ullastres happily confided in one of his American counterparts that the situation in the balance of payments was "much better than had been anticipated and there is almost no trade deficit so far this year."[28] Ullastres did not see this as a reason to slow down on the preparations for the Stabilization Plan. On the contrary, he seemed pleased with the possibility that the Stabilization Plan may be given credit for an outcome already on its way. In fact, he wanted to make sure that the negotiations ended soon so that the Plan could begin to be implemented by the end of June, "which is a good time because of seasonality in the foreign exchange," and pleaded with his counterparts for an American credit line not because he anticipated any drawings on it but he thought it would be "extremely important in building up Spanish support for the measures agreed to."[29] Contrast that with the gripping accounts about the role of the foreign exchange crisis in convincing the cabinet that we read above.

Politicians having a sharply different discourse depending on their interlocutor should surprise nobody. But this has an important implication for our explanation of why reforms were undertaken. Recall that the standard interpretation of the

---

[28] "Views of the Minister of Commerce on OEEC membership and economic stabilization," by Milton Barall, Madrid, May 14, 1959, in Spain, Madrid Emb., CGR 1953–63, FSPF, RG84 (entry 3167B, box 11), NACP.

[29] "Views of the Minister of Commerce on OEEC membership and economic stabilization," by Milton Barall, Madrid, May 14, 1959, in Spain, Madrid Emb., CGR 1953–63, FSPF, RG84 (entry 3167B, box 11), NACP.

adoption of the Plan is one in which "the dramatic situation of foreign payments did not allow waiting much longer" (Viñas et al., 1979, p. 1060). This may have been how the Plan was sold to those reluctant to support it, perhaps including Franco himself in some moments of doubt, but it is clear from the accounts of private conversations that have survived in archives that Ullastres exaggerated the situation to be more persuasive.

More indirect evidence of the doublespeak of reformers within the Spanish government comes from the way in which the amounts of aid were discussed with the international organizations. The OEEC noticed, and appreciated, that the Spanish authorities did not use their presentations to plead their case for aid but rather to convey their policy priorities. Similarly, in negotiations with the IMF and the US, the amount of aid to be received was not discussed in terms of the foreign exchange gap that needed to be filled but because of its "utmost psychological importance."[30] This may suggest that Ullastres and his team did not have the foreign exchange gap at their top of mind when thinking about the reforms. Aware that support for the reforms was far from sure among the full cabinet, pro-reformers seemed eager to use any talking point that could help sell the policy. This included finding ways that could save face for the government. This group welcomed the French franc devaluation and the declaration of convertibility of many European currencies at the end of 1958 because they thought it provided a unique opportunity for the Spanish government to "reorient itself economically without admitting that it has made errors in the past."[31]

Importantly, the group of technocrats controlled the menu of policy options to tackle the external crisis. And they chose to put forward only one option. Herein lies the most important role that the technocrats played. In setting the agenda, they could have presented a range of policy responses and not just the Stabilization Plan as the only possible solution to the exchange rate crisis. Ullastres may now be known for his technical credentials, but what he truly stood out for was his political skill. Most of the literature has since bought into this framing about the broad reform package as the only way out of the exchange rate crisis. As one of the most influential early discussions of the period put it, the Plan was inevitable "because by then it was the only possible remedy" (Viñas et al., 1979, p. 1055). This view on the inevitability of the Plan has endured in the literature. To give just one example: "the plans which [the technocrats] carried out were very much the only way out of the crisis" (Crespo MacLennan, 2000, p. 22).

---

[30] "Views of the Minister of Commerce on OEEC membership and economic stabilization," by Milton Barall, Madrid, May 14, 1959, in Spain, Madrid Emb., CGR 1953–63, FSPF, RG84 (entry 3167B, box 11), National Archives at College Park.

[31] Memorandum of conversation Barall, A. Garrigues [lawyer and frequent intermediary between US Embassy and Ullastres], E. Garrigues, Rovira, Count of Mieres, J. Beltrán, and J. Tejero, Madrid, January 23, 1959, in Spain, Madrid Emb., CGR 1953–1963, FSPF, RG84 (entry 3167B, box 11), National Archives at College Park.

This view on the "inevitability" of the reforms takes the rhetoric of pro-reformers too much at face value. There are always different policy alternatives. For example, the approach in 1959 could have been to adopt similar measures as those taken to tackle the exchange rate overvaluation of the late 1940s. Many of the measures included in the broad-ranging Stabilization Plan, such as the reduction in the number of regulatory bodies, the increase in limits to foreign ownership of Spanish firms, and even the liberalization of trade, were not essential to regain a sustainable current account position. A rare exception in the literature for being explicit about the fact that there is always more than one policy option is provided by economic historians Albert Carreras and Xavier Tafunell (2021). They note that that there were two alternatives: either to drastically reduce the volume of imports to match the actual exports, or undertake the trade liberalization, opening to FDI, and full integration in international organizations (Carreras and Tafunell, 2021, p. 165).

This framing of the policy choice still bundles together elements that were not, strictly speaking, an essential part of a stabilization program, like the opening to FDI. In fact, this was not part of the standard recipe for stabilization. We can tell because most other IMF-supported stabilization programs at the time did not include an easing of foreign investment among their policy reforms. In fact, of all the stabilization programs adopted around the time, such as Bolivia and Chile in 1956, Paraguay in 1957, and Argentina and France in 1958, only in the case of Chile did the stabilization program include a liberalization of foreign investment. This illustrates not also the broad-ranging nature of the reform program but also the fact that reforms had in fact a domestic origin. If foreign pressure had been the driving force behind such a measure, one would expect similar requirements in other stabilization programs endorsed by the IMF at the time.

More importantly, Carreras and Tafunell (2021, p. 165) provide us with a hypothesis as to why, between the two alternatives of import restrictions and full-blown liberalization, the regime chose the latter. And by regime we ultimately mean Franco because in a regime where the dictator was the ultimate decision maker, the question of why reforms were adopted overlaps fully with an interpretation of Franco's actions—a most difficult task to properly assess and document. These authors suggest that faced with the prospect of deprivations on one hand, and liberalization on the other hand, Franco reluctantly gave in and agreed with the liberalization option because he likely feared the political consequences if he were to impose on the population a return to the deprivations and restrictions of the 1940s. More recently, historian Paul Preston suggests that the appointment of the technocrats in 1957 was a pragmatic response, though he still argues that the situation faced by the regime at the time was one of "political and economic bankruptcy" (Preston, 2019, p. 448).

But why would Franco, who had earlier opted for economic restrictions and control, now choose liberalization? The assumption in Carreras and Tafunell's account is that the source of legitimacy had shifted and that by the late 1950s the Spanish population would not have tolerated a stagnant economy. In this view, it was ultimately Franco's fear of the consequences of inaction that forced his hand. In what follows I will modify this argument, introducing one important change. I will argue that a more consistent explanation for the adoption of reforms is not *fear* but, for lack of a better word, *greed*. It was not the economic instability that explains the reforms but rather the political stability of the regime, who was so secure in power that it was prepared to take risks and make changes in the economic policy sphere.

Back to politics

Our reinterpretation of the political economy of reform in Franco's Spain starts with the crucial role that the control of violence plays in societies, which we have also used in earlier chapters. In a situation that is not secure for those in power, economic policy—and everything else—would be subordinated to the larger objective of securing the hold on power. This starting point is not in question in the historiography of the early Franco regime. Most authors note when discussing the autarkic period that economic policies were subordinated to political objectives.

Early on, Viñas (1980) pointed out that autarky was not an end in itself. Rather, what was clearly an objective for Franco was the subordination of economic policies to the political goal. Autarky was in part a punishment of the defeated. Put simply, there was a "political function of self-sufficiency" (Richards, 1998, p. 26). Let us take this to its logical conclusion. If, from the perspective of weakening a social class, the autarkic policies were a "total success" (Del Arco (2006), it follows that the "usefulness" of autarky would be greatly diminished when the regime had achieved greater political stability. The progressive abandonment of autarky would not be the result of its economic failures but due to its political success.

Much has been made in the standard interpretation that Franco seemed to only reluctantly accept the Plan. Franco is even seen as hopeful that economic policy could eventually return to autarkic principles (Preston, 1994, p. 678). Yet the evidence for this is largely second or third hand and typically from later accounts of unreliable raconteurs like Navarro Rubio. To piece together the decision-making of a single person, and one characterized as hermetic and inscrutable as Franco was, is one of the most difficult challenges for any historian. This is a particularly slippery slope in which we all risk inferring too much about Franco's mindset and decision-making from truly sparse data.[32]

---

[32] "It is amazing how dull history books are, given how much of what's in them must be invented," once quipped Amos Tversky. As the great psychologist warns us, explaining the actions of a single individual is a tall order in any case, but if we are to answer the critical question of why reforms were adopted, we must nevertheless undertake some hypothesizing. And we should be prepared to test these hypotheses against a rather messy evidence.

But we can also say that the literature has not put enough emphasis on a verifiable fact about Franco's exchanges regarding the 1959 Plan: He too was telling different things to different people. We know this not only because of the account of his conversation with the IMF Managing Director that has survived in the Fund's Archives. Franco's cousin and confidante for decades also kept a diary, which includes one particularly revealing entry about the economic reforms just adopted. On July 16, 1959, Franco's cousin entered in his diary that when he transmitted a congratulatory message from a financier about the measures taken, Franco responded that he was "not overly optimistic, as there are many challenges to overcome. This plan—he said—should have been carried out earlier, but my Ministers of Finance had not clearly seen the issue, they were technicians that did not want to look overseas" (Franco Salgado-Araujo, 2005, p. 352). This is a remarkable self-justification by Franco, blaming his ministers without taking any responsibility.

But, even if he was self-justifying, it is important to stress that the story Franco is telling his cousin is that reforms were risky not because they were seeking to increase the outward orientation of the economy. On the contrary, he is concerned that they were too late in doing so. Franco appears to be self-handicapping.[33] Worried that the reforms may not succeed, he has already found reasons to exculpate himself. But this is not the same as reluctance to go ahead with the Plan. The unhappiness and "deeply suspicious" mood with which Franco is said to have accepted the Plan, as Carrero would tell his close associates like López Rodó, may very well have been manifestations of this type of self-handicapping. We know that by late October, Franco was in private more optimistic about the Plan—as he would tell his cousin—but he would remain relatively silent about it in public. In his New Year's Eve speech, he referred to a "well-thought-out stabilization plan" but would only be more vocal about his endorsement of the goal of stabilization in speeches in the spring and summer of 1960. It fits Franco's well-established pattern of hedging and laying the groundwork for a plausible denial should things not turn out well.[34]

Additional interpretative models can help shed light on the turnaround in economic policies over the first two decades of the Franco regime. A first model focuses on the interplay between incentives and political stability. The incentives faced by an autocratic government depend on how long it expects to hold on to power. A long-lived autocrat does not have the same temptations for looting as does a short-lived or unstable one (McGuire and Olson, 1996). With his

---

[33] Self-handicapping is defined in the psychological literature as any action "that enhances the opportunity to externalize (or excuse) failure and to internalize (reasonably accept credit for) success" (Jones and Berglas, 1978). For a more general discussion on how the person and the situation interact in helping to explain behavior see Ross and Nisbett (2011) and Gilovich and Ross (2016).

[34] Preston (1994) provides ample examples of this hedging behavior, starting with Franco's role in the 1936 coup. See also Fusi (1995, p. 169) and López Rodó (1990, p. 184) for the discussion of events in 1959 and 1960 mentioned in this paragraph.

characteristically compelling imagery, Olson (2000) notes that a roving bandit will act differently from a stationary one. Of course, not all stationary bandits will seek to maximize output, but the stationary bandit at least faces incentives that do not necessarily push him into the sheer disregard for the future that characterizes the roving bandit.

Olson's is not the only possible model to interpret these developments. In fact, a very different interpretive framework, based on Kahneman and Tversky's prospect theory, could also be of help here. A key insight from prospect theory is that people react differently between potential losses and potential gains. And, critically, it notes that what is a loss and gain depend on the reference point against which one assesses oneself.[35] Recall how, in the Conclusions to Chapter 2 we noted that Franco had been as close to euphoric as he ever was when securing the agreements with the US. "I have now won the Civil War," Franco told his cousin. If this accurately captures Franco's reference point, we could think of the pre-1953 as a "loss frame" in which Franco still felt insecure and his regime under external threat.

A related way to look at this is through the idea that decision makers can become locked into a costly course of action—what in gambling is known as "chasing a loss." The escalation of commitment to a predetermined action has long been studied by social psychologists. One finding that is relevant here is that individuals are more prone to double down on a course of action when they believe that an earlier setback was driven by an exogenous force outside of their control (Staw, 1981). The ostracism which the Franco regime endured through the late 1940s, and which was endlessly mentioned by official sources as the source of all problems at the time, was just the type of situation that would make staying the course more probable.

External pressure is also likely to result in *less* willingness to change. This issue has also been examined at length in the social psychology literature. As an early theorist on the function of social conflict put it, groups "engaged in continued struggle with the outside . . . are unlikely to tolerate more than limited departures from the group unit."[36] In such a context one can imagine that it would be difficult for different opinions to surface in, for example, cabinet discussions. By implication, once the Franco regime felt relieved from the intense external pressure, and even validated as the Cold War intensified, it would be more open to revisit its decision-making.

After 1953 or thereabouts, Franco may have felt either the prospect of having a longer time horizon in power (Olsonian view) or no longer under external threats (social conflict view) or no longer in a loss frame (prospect theory view). Either

---

[35] Prospect theory places a crucial emphasis on the importance of the situation, the perception of loss in calculations of value, and the critical nature of value trade-offs (McDermott, 2004).

[36] Coser (1956), as cited in Bar-Tal and Hammack (2012).

way, these three different interpretative frames result in similar conclusions. One would expect Franco to be more prepared to trade short-term costs for long-term gain (Olsonian view), to be increasingly more open to alternatives (social conflict view), and to be more likely to stop doubling down on autarky (prospect theory view).

Just like the increased political stability extended the time horizons of private sector agents, as we saw in Chapter 2, it is likely that policymakers' time horizons were also extended into the future. This would have had consequences for how policymakers considered trade-offs between rents now and in the future. For example, it would have made policymakers more amenable to put up with the short-term costs of an economic reform program. They would be more confident that the government would be able to withstand any short-term negative consequences and also that the regime would benefit from whatever long-term gains may accrue from the reforms. Since many economic reforms often incur short-term costs to obtain long-term benefits, it follows that political stability may make it more likely that economic reforms be adopted.

But this increased long-termism of public policy does not necessarily happen in all instances of political stability. When it happens, as I argue was the case in Spain, it is useful to explore how it happened. One way it manifests itself is through a bureaucratization of policy arenas. Indeed, one of the promises of bureaucratization was precisely to increase the time horizons of public policy. The themes of politicians behaving like bureaucrats, and of bureaucrats becoming policymakers, will be picked up again later in the book when we discuss the role that planning and increasing contestability had in sustaining the growth acceleration in Spain.

Another way to look at the question of why reforms were adopted is by focusing on personnel selection. If the rise of the technocrats is crucial to explain the adoption of reforms then, why were these technocrats put in power? Most authors agree that Franco interpreted his role as arbiter among different factions. In this spirit, his cabinet reshuffles aimed to reflect the evolving balance of power while preserving the representation in some form of the core constituencies of his regime. If this view is correct, it must mean that the weight of technocrats in Spanish society and politics had already increased by the time they were brought into the cabinet—a premise that is consistent with the idea that as political stability was secured other goods, like economic prosperity, gained in value for the regime.

Moreover, since the selection of these ministers was the result of a deliberate decision-making process which often took months of vetting, it is hard to believe that their beliefs about the appropriate course of economic policy were a complete surprise to Franco and his right-hand man Carrero. The fact that Ullastres pushed for a devaluation of the peseta within weeks of taking office seems to confirm that, while there was no master plan, further changes in the direction of economic policymaking were expected of the new economic team. What the ministerial appointments of 1957 show was a renewed emphasis on technical expertise (Payne, 2000, p. 450). This prominence reflected, as a number of authors have argued, that by the mid-1950s the regime had adopted economic progress as a major argument to justify its legitimacy (Guirao, 1998, p. 205).

The shift in the source of legitimacy underpinning the Franco regime was likely a gradual one. This is important for our explanation of reforms. If the evolving source of legitimacy underpinning the Franco regime was indeed a key explanation behind the adoption of reforms, we would also expect policy changes to be somewhat gradual. This is fully consistent with the picture that we observed in Chapter 4 where there were, for sure, moments of greater reform intensity like the 1959 Plan but set against a broader context of earlier and gradual reforms since the beginning of the 1950s. But can we test the hypothesis that economic concerns were an increasing priority of the Franco regime?

The evolution of policy priorities under the Franco regime

Every New Year's Eve since 1946, Franco gave a speech to the nation that was much like a State of the Union address. In these speeches Franco provided to the nation his take on both developments and priorities for the future. Under the assumption that what Franco talked about in these speeches was what he wanted to draw attention to, they can help us shed light on what Franco thought was relevant to the population and what were the priorities of the regime. The analysis of speeches has long been essential in the historiography, but tackling the analysis of these speeches in a systematic way has been greatly facilitated by recent advances in computing.

With the benefit of new topic modeling techniques, we can mine text as data to rigorously examine the content of those speeches and their evolution over time. To this end, we digitized all the speeches and applied a machine learning algorithm, the Latent Dirichlet Allocation model, that extracts the main themes in collections of documents (Blei, 2012). A key advantage of these algorithms is the fact that they do not require the researcher to arbitrarily specify topics. Instead, topic models independently "discover" a set of topics based on the co-occurrence of words and simultaneously assign documents to those topics.[37]

The application of this algorithm gives us seven distinct topics in which, with different proportions over time, all of Franco's New Year's Eve speeches fall. Based

---

[37] Topic models have been used for a wide range of purposes, including to analyze the content of two centuries of State of the Union addresses by American presidents (Wang and McCallum, 2006).

Table 5.1 Topics in Franco's speeches

Topic label	Social progress	Development	Economy	Patriotism
Most common words	economy*	law	economy*	Spain*
	development	principles	nation	nation
	progress	future	situation	world
	future	development	order	politics
	social	permanent	system	life

Topic label	War	Communism	Religion
Most common words	war	communism	hour
	wealth	action	land
	gold	front	faith
	revolution	possibility	rebirth
	creation	war	Catholic

Note: * indicates that items were stemmed. So, for example, economy, economic, and other words with the same stem were included as one.

Source: Own elaboration with Axel Eizmendi.

on the most frequent words for each topic, which is in fact the output of the algorithm, I have labeled these seven topics as: social progress, development, economy, patriotism, war, communism, and religion.[38] Franco, of course, spoke about other things in these speeches, but what the algorithm is telling us is that those other issues were not distinct or common enough to emerge as a separate topic. Table 5.1 shows the five most frequent words for each topic, as generated by the algorithm. Note that some words appear in more than one topic. This is because a topic, in these models, is nothing more than a probability distribution over the entire lexicon. The algorithm maximizes the distance between those distributions, but it is possible, as in our case, that the same word is highly used in more than one topic. What is important is whether we can interpret the topics as sufficiently distinct from each other.

Based on the keywords above, we see that the topics, as uncovered independently by the algorithm, reflect reasonably different sets of issues. This is particularly the case when we compare the three topics of an economic nature (the three to the left in Table 5.1) with the other four. We are now able to also show the evolution of these topics over time, shown in Figure 5.5. This figure deserves some additional introduction as it is not a frequent chart. What the figure shows is the evolution over time of the different topics in which Franco's speeches have

---

[38] Labels are only provided as helpful shortcuts to synthesize the content of the topic, but they are of course subjective—indeed they are the only arbitrary choice of the researcher. Should the reader find any of the labels objectionable, simply replace the labels with numbers (topic 1, etc.); the conclusions of the analysis would be unaffected.

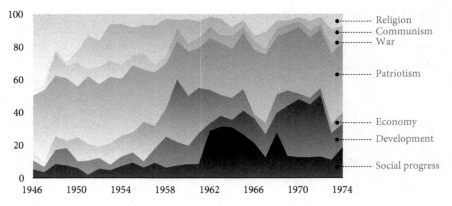

Figure 5.5 Evolution of topics in Franco's speeches

Note: Topics are identified by using the LDA algorithm on the set of New Year's Eve speeches made by Franco. See main text for discussion of the labels for each topic.

Source: Own elaboration with Axel Eizmendi.

been categorized by the algorithm used. For a given year, it shows how the speech for that year was divided into the different topics. For example, in 1946 the three topics that have been identified as related to economic issues combined account for around 16 percent of the speech that year.

This analysis of speeches shows that the share of the speeches devoted to economic topics rose indeed from the early 1950s. By 1956, over a third of the speech was devoted to economic topics, either social progress, development, or the economy. The upward trend continues until 1959 and thereafter the share of these topics remains relatively steady at around 40 percent. Under the assumption that what Franco talked about in these annual speeches was what he wanted to draw attention to, it is unmistakable that the shift towards a greater focus on economic development issues was both gradual and started before 1959.

This is fully consistent with the hypothesis of a shift in the underlying legitimacy of the Franco regime. It also shows that such a shift occurred gradually, although of course some moments were more distinct than others. As noted in the literature, one of the characteristics of the Franco regime was its capacity to change, particularly striking given the fact that it was a personal dictatorship (Townson, 2007, p. 24). The advantages of this quantitative method of analyzing text as data to speak to this issue of shifting priorities are significant. It provides a synthetic measure over a very long span of time. It is also a fully replicable analysis that minimizes subjective interpretations by the researcher. It also lends itself to potential comparisons with other countries. Together with colleagues Axel Eizmendi and Germán Reyes, we performed a similar analysis as the one shown above using 953 speeches from ten Latin American countries and Spain over the

1940–2010 period.[39] When reviewing the individual countries' evolution of speech topics, one of the things that struck us was the relatively frequent and sudden changes in policy priorities that we observe in many other countries. This was in sharp contrast with what we saw for Spain.

Conclusions

What drives economic policy reform? This is one of the most fundamental questions in the political economy of reform. One of the contributions of this chapter is to discuss the economic policy reforms in Spain in connection with the newly prevailing political stability. In contrast with most of the literature, I argue that economic reforms in Spain can be better understood not as the result of economic instability but of political stability. In short, my argument goes as follows. Autarkic economic policies were adopted in the 1940s largely for political reasons, and they were progressively abandoned in the 1950s also because of a change in the political environment. The main difference between the two decades was that the regime had become much more secure in power in the 1950s. The increase in stability extended the time horizons of policymakers, as well as reduced the perception of external threats. With security concerns minimized, one would expect the regime to be ready to trade off short-term costs for long-term gain, as in an Olsonian model, and to be less likely to resist change if we see this issue from the perspective of the literature on social conflict.

The result was a gradual shift of policies because the underlying political realities also changed gradually. As the political environment changed and the regime achieved greater stability, it paid increasing attention to economic issues. We saw, for example through the analysis of Franco's speeches, that this was also a gradual process. There were, of course, moments of greater reform intensity. The adoption of the 1959 Stabilization Plan was one of them. But too much of a focus on the 1959 Plan risks drawing the wrong conclusions about the reform process. Much of the earlier literature has indeed focused excessively on the reforms in 1959, providing a standard account of the political economy of reform that can be summarized as crisis-induced.

As we have shown in this chapter, this standard, crisis-led interpretation of reforms has several shortcomings. First, the disastrous economic effects of autarkic policies manifested themselves well before the adoption of the 1959 Stabilization Plan. If economic instability had driven reforms, we would have

---

[39] In the case of Spain, we use Franco's New Year's Eve speeches from 1946 to 1974, the speeches of incoming prime ministers (*investidura*) for 1979–82, and either the speeches of incoming prime ministers or the debates about the state of the nation after 1983.

expected to see them earlier. Second, the crisis that allegedly pushed the authorities to adopt the 1959 Plan was a relatively limited exchange rate crisis; it could have been addressed with measures that were far less broad-ranging than the liberalization ones actually adopted, especially in terms of opening to FDI. Fourth, there was no backtracking of reforms after the 1959 Plan on critical areas such as openness to FDI or, to some extent, trade liberalization. On close inspection, the maxim that "foreign reserves kill the will to reform" does not explain well the decade after 1959.

Our reinterpretation of reforms as a gradual shift driven by more favorable political conditions fits better these stylized facts. A comparative perspective on macroeconomic variables in the run-up to the adoption of the 1959 Plan shows just how average many of the macroeconomic conditions in Spain were at the time. Archival evidence demonstrates that, far from exercising strict conditionality and imposing policy changes, the international financial institutions played only a supporting role. The fact that reforms were long in the making, and that they were not substantially reversed, is fully consistent with the new policies being adopted because of a gradual shift in the political environment. The foreign exchange crisis may have helped to explain the precise timing of the adoption of reforms by providing the final argument that overcame the conservative resistance to any change of Franco himself. But to zero in on the foreign exchange situation alone would be misleading. As in a pointillist painting, we can make more sense of the political economy of reform in Spain by taking a step back and looking at a longer time horizon and in a comparative perspective.

Revisiting these questions is not only relevant for a fuller understanding of the Spanish case, but also because it affects lessons that may be drawn from it. The traditional narrative puts too heavy an emphasis on the role of external aid conditionality. It also misleads us about the role of technocracy. The standard interpretation suggests that the technocrats were trusted with the 1959 reform operation out of desperation and disappointment with the previous economic results. It seems more consistent with the evidence that the technocrats were relied upon because political stability made it possible to take chances on economic matters and because the economic successes of the 1950s had contributed to build their collective reputation. It may have been true, as Joan Sardá put it, that "it became possible to get accepted the ideas of a minority which were not fully understood by the majority" (1970, p. 244). Sardá was speaking about the role of the OEEC as an advisor, but the comment seems even more fitting about the rise of technocracy in Spain. The technocrats, however, did not rise to power on the strength of their own technical capacity alone, but on the back of a political process.

6

Openness

One of the key contributions of economic history to our understanding of development revolves around the role of economic backwardness. It was Alexander Gerschenkron who, in the 1950s, pointed out the consequences of the fact that most nations start their path to prosperity lagging behind other more advanced economies. He argued that this necessarily implied a diversity of potential trajectories towards becoming a developed economy. That there be no single path to success struck a personal chord with Gerschenkron, a Russian *emigré* who escaped prosecution twice, from the Bolshevik revolution first and then from the Nazis, and who had several careers before becoming a professor.[1]

Gerschenkron's crucial insight is that different initial conditions call for different policy responses. Since such policies are therefore country-specific, there is no predetermined path or stages towards growth—in contrast to the model of Walt Rostow, with whom he frequently clashed. Gerschenkron (1962) suggested that the very fact of relative backwardness created both a tension and an opportunity. Nations that lacked what Rostow called the preconditions for growth, would fall behind more successful ones. In turn, the desire to catch up would play up in the political sphere and create the impetus for institutional innovations. Many, and perhaps most, of these institutional variations would prove unhelpful or even harmful to growth. But when countries successfully catch up, the argument goes, the reason for their success may not be despite of but rather *because of* countries' adaptation of institutional forms to their conditions. Gerschenkron's is a call to pay attention to the detail of how countries adapt to their circumstances to develop and a caution not to draw overly general lessons from individual cases. In other words, dismiss institutional adaptations at your own risk.

In what follows, I will argue that at the core of Spain's unexpected rise to prosperity lie several of these Gerschenkronian adaptations in the way the economy was exposed to greater openness and contestability. The policies adopted in these two domains were not necessarily the first best prescription that economic theory would espouse. In fact, those adaptations left much to be desired when benchmarked against the theoretical optimal. The shortcomings of the policies and regulatory frameworks have been duly documented in the Spanish historiography of the period. But the literature has missed the bigger point that those policy

---

[1] See the delightful biography on Gerschenkron by his grandson (Dawidoff, 2002).

Unexpected Prosperity: How Spain Escaped the Middle Income Trap. Oscar Calvo-Gonzalez, Oxford University Press.
© Oscar Calvo-Gonzalez 2021. DOI: 10.1093/oso/9780198853978.003.0007

choices were successful in shifting the economy towards greater openness and contestability.

While the two issues of openness and contestability are closely connected, for clarity we will devote this chapter to the rising openness and the next one to the role of contestability. In this chapter we will first document how an opening up characterized several economic policy spheres, including not only trade but also foreign investment, migration, and tourism. We will then assess the impact that this increased openness had on economic performance. Finally, we will ask how the idea of openness came to play such a prominent role in actual policymaking.

Opening up, three ways

Does trade cause economic growth? From a theoretical perspective there are reasons to think so. Trade reforms can help expand the size of the market and allows for economies of scale and scope. It is also a way to benefit from cutting-edge technology or know-how that would result in productivity gains. If so, policy reforms that result in greater openness can be a contributing factor to long-run growth. However, this is ultimately an empirical question and one that has proven difficult to settle decisively due to significant methodological challenges. In fact, the positive view on the impact of trade reform for the long-run prospects of an economy has had some notable sceptics (see, for example, Rodríguez and Rodrik, 2001).

There is, nevertheless, an emerging corpus of consistent empirical findings. A comprehensive review of different strands of the literature, from cross-country growth regressions to case studies, suggests that trade reforms tend to have on average positive effects on growth, although with heterogeneity across countries (Irwin, 2019). One of the reasons why findings of trade reforms across countries differ is because the details of specific policies matter. For example, tariff reductions on consumption goods cannot be expected to increase long-run growth, in contrast to tariff reductions on capital goods (Estevadeordal and Taylor, 2013).

More generally, there is more to openness than barriers to trade. A truly open economy enjoys not only free flows of goods and services but also free movement of the factors of production, capital, and labor.[2] At times, there can be a complex relationship between these flows. For example, barriers to trade in goods may discourage imports, but they can also create incentives for attracting foreign direct

---

[2] Openness of an economy is sometimes interpreted narrowly as the ability to trade goods and services with the external world. The most common indicator used, the share of exports plus imports over GDP, is in fact often referred to as the openness ratio. This is critically important for economic performance, but it is not the full measure of how an economy interacts with the world.

investment. As it happened, increased flows in all three—trade, capital, and labor—would play a critical part in explaining Spain's path to prosperity.

Trade of goods *and* services

As in other European countries, the extent to which the Spanish economy traded with other economies has been far from steady over time. The late nineteenth century had seen an increase in the degree of openness of the economy. Spain's exports had grown at a similar annual rate as world's export in the four decades before World War I. But this was severely curtailed in the interwar period, when Spain did even worse than its neighbors. The openness ratio slid down from 24 percent in 1900 to less than 10 percent on the eve of the Spanish Civil War. This was low but not that dissimilar from that of France, Germany, or Italy throughout the 1930s, a period of rampant isolationism. A large gap with its neighbors, however, would emerge in the immediate postwar period. By 1950, the openness ratio in Spain stood at only 7 percent of GDP, less than half of what it was in Italy and a third of France's ratio.[3]

Spain's openness ratio would nevertheless start recovering in the 1950s. In short order, its openness ratio doubled to 15 percent of GDP by 1960. The trend would continue. By 1970 the openness ratio had further increased to 22 percent of GDP, a remarkable increase given the large expansion of the economy, which in real terms had increased by more than three and half times in the two decades since 1950. This increase is particularly significant because larger economies tend to have smaller openness ratios (Alesina and Wacziarg, 1998).

Trade openness is typically measured as the ratio of total trade to GDP. But this is a particularly difficult indicator for benchmarking purposes because larger and richer economies tend to have lower trade openness ratios. Fortunately, the literature on trade has made significant advances in computing the welfare cost of autarky and the benefits from freer trade. Of interest to us is a new measure of trade openness, the trade potential index, that factors in the size and income level of countries (Waugh and Ravikumar, 2016). This makes it particularly suitable for the type of comparative perspective that is of particular interest to us here.

The evolution of the trade potential index, which maps countries between autarky and the frictionless trade equilibrium, shows a remarkable process of relatively steady opening up of Spain (see Figure 6.1). Starting from much lower levels of openness, Spain not only caught up with comparator European countries but surpassed them since the mid-1960s. Importantly, the faster pace of opening up in Spain continued after it had caught up with its European comparators—as

---

[3] The comparison with Italy, France, and Germany is from Tena (2005, p. 578), which provides a most interesting long-term comparison between Spain and those countries.

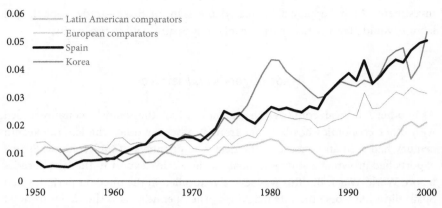

Figure 6.1   Opening to trade over half a century

Note: Figure shows the trade potential index (higher values indicate freer trade; 0 denotes autarky). The trade potential index developed by Waugh and Ravikumar (2016) measures the distance of an economy from a situation of frictionless trade taking into account the size of the economy and parameters estimated from the gravity literature like the elasticity of trade to income. Comparators are the group of 27 countries identified in the Introduction as having a similar per capita GDP to Spain in 1950; since trade openness patterns within that group are very different by region, we show here separately two regional sub-sets of those comparators.

Source: Own elaboration using Penn World Table 9.1 data (Feenstra et al, 2015).

shown by the steeper slope of its time series of the trade potential index shown in Figure 6.1. This suggests that Spain's opening up was not driven exclusively by continental trends during the Golden Age of growth. The sustained trend increase in openness suggests that this was more than a bounceback after bottoming out in the 1950s. Openness had its ups and downs, but such fluctuations appear to be common across countries. Overall, Spain's rapid and relatively steady opening up can only be compared with some of the East Asian countries like Korea.

Importantly, the comparative perspective shown here underestimates the extent to which Spain opened up to the benefits of international trade. This is because, to be able to benchmark Spain's performance since 1950 and against a broad set of comparators, the analysis uses data for merchandise exports only. For Spain, exports of services, and in particular tourism, would play a critical role. As the 1960s unfolded, tourism revenues would become an increasingly important source of foreign exchange. The number of visitors skyrocketed, from less than half a million in 1950 to over 20 million a year by 1970. And this was not just because tourism was booming as an activity among Western European societies. Spain was able to increase its share in the global market of tourism from less than 2 percent to over 12 percent during those two decades (see Figure 6.2).

How did this happen? Spain had the good fortune of its geography to take advantage of the fast growth of tourism. But to capture that economic potential required the regime to overcome its initial suspiciousness of foreign visitors,

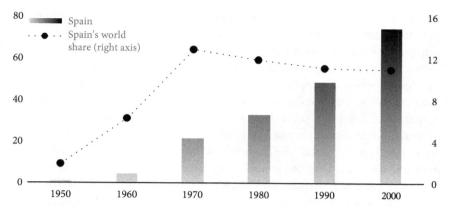

Figure 6.2 Tourist visitors to Spain (millions) and percentage share in world's tourism
Source: Tena (2005).

which in earlier years it had seen as potential agitators. When tourism was raised to a ministerial rank in 1951, it was as part of the Ministry of Information and Tourism, signaling that the growth of that industry could not come at the expense of a diminished control on society. As the 1950s progressed, with a regime increasingly secure in power, the regime became much less worried about possible risks from increased tourism and eased controls and visa requirements.

Tourism grew as a lightly regulated and largely private sector-led activity. Hotel builders received no special tax incentives that could have distorted price signals, nor was tourism the subject of particularly onerous taxation. The assessment of the development of the Spanish economy prepared for World Bank President Robert S. McNamara ahead of a visit by the Spanish Minister of Finance in 1969 had the following take on tourism:

> The boom that Spain has experienced in tourism since 1960 was largely a spontaneous one resulting from private initiative, and government policy has played only a limited role. The tourist sector did not receive any preferential fiscal treatment and the contribution of official credit for hotel construction appears to have been marginal. Direct public investment has been very small and public investment in infrastructure has fallen behind.[4]

The government lagged behind the private sector in part because officials were not convinced that tourism would prove a sure bet. In March 1958, when annual

---

[4] Memo Spain—Your Meeting with the Minister of Finance, July 16, 1969, Contacts with member countries: Spain—Correspondence 01, Folder 1771181, Records of the Office of the President, World Bank Archive.

tourist visitors already surpassed two million, Minister Ullastres was still of the view that tourism revenues were "too inconstant for us to trust" that they would help preserve the stability of the economy (Pack, 2006, p. 84).

Eventually, the government caught up to the reality of a booming tourist sector. In a limited effort to support its growth it opened an official tourism school in 1963. The same year it included tourism among the industries in which foreign capital could flow freely on account of the industry being considered of national interest. This declaration notwithstanding, the government continued to leave the sector largely unregulated. The ease of doing business was often noted. A French industry commentator noted in 1968 that "one needs a maximum of one month to get a construction permit, or 48 hours if one has connections."[5] The statement by the French observer clearly suggested the existence of corruption and implied the lack of a level playing field. The downside for this imperfect and light governance framework would not be too little growth but rather a disregard for environmental harm.

Benidorm, which for better or worse has come to be a symbol of lowbrow mass tourism, provides a good illustration of this process. It went from being a fishing village with a couple of thousand inhabitants in the 1940s to boasting the largest concentration of hotel beds in Europe outside of London and Paris thanks to a frenzied building of skyscrapers that makes Benidorm's skyline not unlike that of Hong Kong. Both the idea and the realization of Benidorm as a tourist resort were local initiatives championed by a charismatic mayor who rallied the existing small hoteliers behind his ambitious dreams.[6] Much emphasis has been given to the fact that an urban plan from 1956, as adapted in 1964, remains the blueprint for the growth of the city to this day, but the reality is that there was little in the form of actual planning in the sense of anticipating bottlenecks.

The approach that characterized the growth of tourism was more akin to test, learn, and adapt than to strategic planning. To stay with the case of Benidorm, as it grew further and faster than its entrepreneurial mayor had dreamed of, it faced unanticipated challenges. For example, serious water shortages emerged, a challenge that would return with some regularity over time. The central government's actions were also lagging, including in the provision of transport infrastructure. The local airport, publicly built, would only be constructed in the late 1960s— once a steady flow of hundreds of thousands of tourists flowed in and out of Benidorm every year. The pattern was repeated elsewhere. While this can be construed as suboptimal, it allowed for a saving of resources, limited investments in

---

[5] As quoted in Sánchez Sánchez (2006, p. 286).

[6] Pedro Zaragoza, famous for his vision and knack for marketing, would earn an obituary from *The Economist* (April 17, 2008) and, more recently, a delightful documentary film that explores the myths surrounding the man: "*El hombre que embotelló el sol*" by Oscar Bernàcer (2016).

white elephant projects, and supported a greater reliance on market signals, as we will see in the next chapter.

Foreign direct investment

Foreign investors were increasingly eyeing the opportunity to enter Spain, a large market that was increasingly seen as politically stable and with increasing prospects for developing an emerging consumer class. The relaxation of constraints in the 1950s had already prompted many investors to consider operations in Spain, but it would be in the 1960s that the floodgates would open. The best available estimates suggest that inflows of long-term capital averaged around 2.4 percent of GDP in the 1960s, with an increasing trend over time. Although comparable data across countries is limited for the 1960s, this was likely an outlier (Carreras and Tafunell, 2004, p. 341). Between 1959 and 1973, over 20 percent of the industrial investment in Spain came from abroad. From a different perspective, over seven thousand Spanish firms, more than one in ten registered companies, would receive foreign capital (Martínez Serrano, 1982, p. 202).

Why were foreign investors attracted to Spain? This question has been addressed both qualitatively in the business history literature as well as econometrically. Numerous histories of the decision-making of foreign firms in the period emphasize how multinational enterprises crafted entry strategies that, heavily influenced by the institutional constraints of protectionist policies, sought to establish a lasting presence in the local Spanish market (Puig and Alvaro, 2018). The protection against imports was in contrast with the relaxation of constraints on capital flows which, as we saw in previous chapters, had already started in the 1950s.

The importance of the size of the domestic market to attract foreign investors has also been shown econometrically (Bajo-Rubio and Sosvilla-Rivero, 1994). These authors also confirm that FDI was not correlated with domestic unit labor costs, suggesting that the search for low wages was not a key factor in the decision-making of foreign investors. In addition, the econometric results also confirm that that trade barriers were found to be positively linked with FDI during the period of 1964–88. This suggests that foreign investors were attracted to investing in the Spanish economy to overcome relatively high trade barriers.

Automobiles, for example, had traditionally been the subject of extremely high rates of tariff protection. This was largely because of the need to raise revenues for the state not to protect the market for domestic producers. On top of tariffs, the exchange rate used to import cars was the least favorable for importers, and there were quantitative restrictions on how many cars could be imported. The resulting licensing scheme gave rise to widespread corruption, or at least the perception of such.[7] But it also prompted the interest of foreign firms to establish themselves in Spain to produce cars. Although this interest was not reciprocated at first by the Spanish authorities, it would eventually help drive the creation of a vibrant car industry, as we will see in the next chapter.

These findings call into question the view that a greater liberalization of trade would have led to faster economic growth during the 1960s. It is possible that in the absence of tariff protections for certain imports, foreign investors would have simply preferred to export the goods to Spain than to set up production in the country. But, importantly, these findings do not imply that openness was not at the core of the growth spurt.

Migration

Another way in which Spain became more interconnected with the external world was through the movement of people. Outmigration, especially to Latin America, had been common in the early twentieth century (Sánchez-Alonso, 2000). But, as in the case of other countries, the effects of wars and the Great Depression dampened significantly the magnitude of the outflows. From the 1950s onwards, however, a new dynamic would characterize Spanish migration patterns. The main destination would shift from Latin America to Europe, and the tradition of seasonal migration of agricultural workers would be complemented with long-term migratory flows.

In the 1960s, over two million migrants left Spain for Europe. This was significant given that in 1960 Spain's total population was around 30 million. This was part of a dedicated policy effort. In 1956, Spain created an official institute for migration and negotiated a first agreement with Belgium. In 1960, a new law on emigration envisaged that programs to support outmigration were particularly appropriate for situations of involuntary unemployment. Migration worked as the makeshift social safety net that was intended to be. Without outmigration, unemployment in Spain would have been significantly higher than it was, perhaps around 5 percent in the late-1960s as opposed the almost full employment that was officially reported at the time (Babiano and Fernández Asperilla, 2003).

From a comparative perspective, Spain's experience does not stand out among other Southern European countries, which typically had a greater share of its population overseas—as shown in Table 6.1. But when we compare Spain with the broader set of 28 comparator countries which we identified in the Introduction as having had a similar level of per capita income as Spain in 1950, we can see how unusual it was to have such a large outmigration at the time. It provided an

---

[7] The Minister of Commerce in the early 1950s, Manuel Arburúa, received the nickname "*Gracias Manolo*" for his role in selectively granting permits for importing cars.

Table 6.1 Stock of migrants abroad as a share of population Percent

	1960	1970	1980	1990
Cyprus	16	20	27	36
Greece	12	14	14	13
Portugal	11	14	21	20
Italy	9	11	9	8
Spain	6	8	6	5
28 comparators' median	2	3	8	13

Source: Global Bilateral Migration Database (Özden et al., 2011).

outlet for the unemployed or underemployed that was far from common among other countries. And the benefits of migration included also large remittances sent home by migrants.

Throughout the 1960s, private remittances as a share of GDP peaked at 1.8 percent of GDP in 1967. This was not only sizable but particularly timely. Like receipts from tourism, remittances jumped upwards sharply in the early 1960s at a time when exports of goods were yet to show a significant upward trend. Thanks to a combination of policy decisions, geographical assets, and economic trends and policies in neighboring countries, Spain was able to roughly double its imports-to-GDP ratio, from around 6 to 12 percent of GDP, in five short years in the early 1960s.

From a comparative perspective, however, the patter shown in Figure 6.3 is unusual but not all that uncommon. In the 1960s there were 18 economies world-wide that saw an increase in the imports-to-GDP ratio that was greater than the one experienced by Spain. And far from all those economies were able to sustain high rates of economic growth.

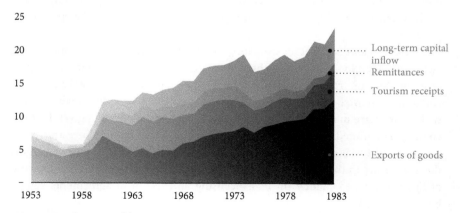

Figure 6.3 Sources of foreign exchange
Source: Own elaboration based on Tena (2005) and Carreras et al. (2005).

Impact of opening up

To what extent did openness drive the growth spurt? At some level, we have already started to answer this question with the help of the empirical model of Bill Easterly presented in Chapter 4. Changes in the variables related to the opening up of the economy in Easterly's model, namely the real exchange rate, black market premium of the peseta, and the openness ratio itself, account for over three-quarters of the boost in economic growth observed after 1960 (to be precise, 2.9 percentage points of the total 3.7 percentage points in additional annual real GDP had policies prevalent in 1950 been maintained, see Table 4.3 on the impacts of policy reforms on growth).

The simultaneous boost to tourism receipts, remittances, and capital inflows resulted in a significant increase in the capacity to import in the early 1960s. But, as noted above, a sudden increase in imports does not necessarily lead to a boost in economic growth. In the case of Spain, what we observe is that not only imports increased significantly but also that their composition changed substantially. In 1959, around 19 percent of total imports were of equipment goods. By 1967, the corresponding share had increased to 26 percent and to 31 percent in 1973 (Tena, 2005).

Imported equipment and machinery contributed to an acceleration in the growth of capital stock, posting its fastest growth ever recorded in Spanish economic history from 1959 to 1974 at an annual average of 7 percent. In addition, the quality of capital also increased, by around 0.4 percent annually during the same period (Prados de la Escosura and Rosés, 2009, p. 158). But growth-accounting exercises suggest that those factors can only partially explain the growth spurt. In fact, the combined effect of the deepening and quality upgrading of capital only accounts for around one-fifth of the growth in per capita output observed from 1959 to 1974. Increases in human capital also explain only a relatively small share of the growth. The reasons behind most of the growth lie elsewhere.

Efficiency gains account for two-thirds of the growth in output per capita. Total factor productivity grew during the Golden Age of 1951–74 at a rate of 3.7 percent annually, up from an average of only 0.3 percent annually over the previous century, as we first discussed in the Introduction. But how could Spain achieve such an increase in efficiency? The question is even more puzzling given that the country had limited human capital and research and development investment. As economic historians Mar Cebrián and Santiago López (2005) persuasively argue, the answer lies in the role played by the transfer of technology, which in the case of Spain happened mainly through licensing and technical agreements signed between companies.

Foreign enterprises provided high levels of technical assistance. Nearly all the technology transfer contracts entered in by Spanish firms provided for onsite training by foreign personnel. The importance of the licensing and technical agreements as learning-by-doing mechanisms can be gauged quantitatively through balance of payments statistics. The ratio of payments to revenues from copyrights and patent royalties shot up in the 1960s.

The impact of FDI on the transfer of management practices was strengthened by the form in which foreign investors established themselves in the country. Before World War II, the most common form of entry of American firms into Spain was through wholly owned subsidiaries. After the war, however, things would change. The protected domestic market attracted foreign investors, but heavy regulation cautioned them against entering the Spanish market without local knowledge and connections. Foreign investors in Spain sought partnerships with local businesses to deal with the complex regulatory framework (Guillén, 2001). This phenomenon, which was already in place throughout the 1950s, became particularly widespread (Álvaro, 2011).

Spain also had a growing crop of engineering and consultancy enterprises ready to take on the challenge of absorbing the foreign technology. Engineering schools had a long tradition in Spain. But the role in society of prominent engineers had suffered, like that of any other of the educated elites, from the ups and downs of violence that characterized much of the century and a half before 1950. In the wake of conflict, many prominent engineers had chosen or were forced to exit. And this was a recurrent problem over a long time. In the early nineteenth century, the founder of Spain's engineering school of roads, Agustín de Betancourt, who had traveled to Britain and France and was inspired by the French *École nationale des ponts et chaussées*, would end his days far from Spain as a highly decorated official at the service of the Russian Tsar Alexander I. Over a century later, hundreds of Spain's engineers would leave the country as exiles following the defeat of the Republic in the Civil War.[8]

Despite the loss of human capital provoked by the Civil War, engineering firms in the 1960s and 1970s were able to draw on a substantial pool of newly trained professionals. Foreign firms, which were allowed to enter the market with limited constraints, also found an adequate supply of local engineers.[9] Recognizing that these firms were fertile ground for the successful transfer of technology, the authorities regulated them to ensure a high degree of local expertise was developed (Cebrián and López, 2005). Thus, in 1968 a decree gave preference in public procurement contracts to firms with a majority national ownership and where at least 80 percent of employees with university degrees were Spanish nationals.

---

[8] Around 200 engineers moved to Mexico alone, as documented by the late engineer Gonzalo López de Haro. Interest in Betancourt's contributions grew among Spanish engineers in the 1960s, as evidenced by the biographical accounts commissioned or written by the school of road engineers that he had founded (see García Ormaechea, 1965; Rumeu de Armas, 1968).

[9] Early notable entrants included the American firm Foster Wheeler, which will be involved in the construction of refineries in Spain, Procon, Lummus, and McKee (Puig, 2005, p. 196).

It is, however, unclear whether these constraints had any impact on the behavior of these engineering firms at least in so far as staffing goes.[10] In any case, the largest Spanish engineering firms were able to assimilate imported knowledge and build new capabilities increasingly approaching those of firms in advanced economies (Álvaro, 2014). Over time, these engineering and consultancy firms would turn to the world to export their services, becoming one of the success stories of the internationalization of Spanish businesses.

The pieces of the puzzle start to fit more tightly. Traditionally, the Spanish economic historiography had regarded the role of foreign investment as particularly negative for Spain's economic development, pointing out the lack or irrelevance of economic spillovers. Foreign investment had been seen as reinforcing Spain's backwardness (Nadal, 1975). But the new evidence that has been uncovered in recent years on the interactions between foreign investors and local entrepreneurs suggests that "the time is ripe for comprehensive re-assessments of the long-term impact of foreign multinational enterprises and the role of Spain in the global economy" (Puig and Alvaro, 2016).

Importantly, the contribution of these increased interactions with the external world went far beyond the upgrading of technology embodied in machines. There were also discernible impacts on managerial approaches and skills. The first American-style business school was launched in 1955 with the financial support of the American aid program. One of its goals was to help liberalize the economy and stem the rise of any anticapitalism in Spanish society (Guillén, 1994). Five more business schools would follow within the next decade. Founded outside the higher education system, these schools sought to enable entrepreneurs and managers to adapt and apply foreign ideas and techniques to their situations and proved remarkably successful at doing so (Puig, 2008).

The increased outward orientation was also supported by efforts in the 1950s to connect Spanish industry with management. A National Commission of Productivity in Industry was set up as part of the American aid program. In time, it would finance so-called productivity missions through which Spanish businesses would come into contact with new techniques and, increasingly, new markets for their products. A well-documented case is that of the Spanish shoe industry (Miranda Encarnación, 2004). Early participation in trade fairs in the US, financed by the productivity commission, led to no sales but contributed to a growing recognition among Spanish businessmen of the need to upgrade the quality of their product and to modernize their designs if they were to compete in the American market. In short order, producers adapted and succeed in exporting. Sales of footwear to the US, which had been almost nonexistent in the 1950s,

---

[10] My own father, Domiciano, who trained as an engineer in Spain and Britain and had already worked at Procon in the late 1950s, recalls that when he joined Foster Wheeler in 1972 to work on refinery projects, the engineering staff was composed exclusively of Spanish nationals.

increased rapidly, from $6 million in 1965 to $73 million in 1970. Exports would continue to grow, reaching yet another tenfold increase in the value of exports by the early 1980s as well as a more diversified set of markets.

We have seen that, in cases as diverse as engineering firms and shoe manufacturers, the increased connectedness with foreigners led not only to the diffusion and adaption of technology but also to an increased outward orientation. This is one of the underappreciated aspects of Spain's path to prosperity. The revenues from tourism and migrants may have helped finance imports but by themselves do not help to explain the shift towards greater outward orientation. Neither does the arrival of foreign capital guarantee such a turn to export markets. Numerous examples, both from other countries and even from Spain's own past, testify to this. One of the defining traits of Spain's experience in the second half of the twentieth century was the quick succession from the adoption and adaptation of foreign ideas to seeking out exporting opportunities.

It is hard to escape the conclusion that local businesses and entrepreneurs played a critical role in this process of turning contact with the external world into more outward-oriented businesses. The patent for the modern variant of the mop was obtained by a Spanish Air Force engineer, Manuel Jalón, who was inspired by how hangers were cleaned at an American Air Force training facility in Illinois. He had traveled there in the 1950s only because of the increased contact between the Spanish and American air forces resulting from agreements signed between the two countries in 1953. Jalón's company exported his invention to over 40 countries and over time was able to successfully diversify its product range. Building on the capabilities that his firm had developed in working with plastics, he would produce a more hermetic type of food container that competed with Tupperware and which was also exported to dozens of countries. He later obtained in the 1970s yet another patent for a type of disposable syringe that would also be exported widely. It was the ability to produce the plastic components of the syringe with much greater precision that gave Jalón's factory a competitive edge, making this seemingly simple common-use product a high-technology export for decades.[11]

The evidence of export diversification is more than anecdotal. Thanks to an overall measure of export diversification recently constructed by the IMF, we can even perform cross-country comparisons dating back to 1962. This is illustrated in Figure 6.4, which compares Spain to the six countries that were most similar to Spain in terms of export diversification at the beginning of the period. This new evidence shows that Spain experienced an unusually sharp increase in the diversification of exports for about a decade and a half after 1962. Without the benefit of a comparative dataset such as the one produced by the IMF, this remarkable

---

[11] Jalón passed away in 2011. A particularly rich talk on innovation that he gave just months before his death is available online at https://youtu.be/7fgtft0nBLM (accessed February 2, 2020).

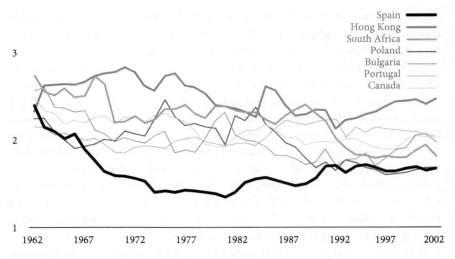

Figure 6.4   Export diversification in comparative perspective
Note: Index, lower values indicate greater diversification.
Source: International Monetary Fund (2014).

outperformance had until now gone largely unnoticed in the literature. This is an important finding because diversification in production, exports, and trading partners has been recently found to play an important role in accompanying growth, especially in low- and middle-income stages of development (IMF, 2014).

Similar findings emerge using other indicators that have mined the extremely rich country-product export data available internationally since the 1960s. The economist Ricardo Hausmann and colleagues have synthesized the data on trade in goods in a summary measure, the Economic Complexity Index, which takes account of both the diversity of products that a country exports and what they refer to as the ubiquity of those products or how common it is that countries export a particular product. The latter aspect is included in the calculation because more complex products require broader competencies to be produced and as a result are exported by fewer countries. While, due to data limitations, the index relies only on export data and does not cover services, it is a useful proxy for the ability of economies to produce more sophisticated bundles of goods (Hausmann et al., 2013).

The story that surfaces from an analysis of the Economic Complexity Index is also one of a remarkable rise of Spain in the rankings from the 1960s to the early 1980s. Spain ranked as the twenty-fourth economy in the world in terms of the complexity of its exports in 1964. It maintained or improved its ranking over the next two decades, peaking as the fourteenth economy in the world in 1984. This may not appear to be such a remarkable achievement until we realize how much persistence there is at the top of this classification: In the period that Spain climbed from twenty-fourth to fourteenth in the world, there were no changes in the group of countries that occupied the top dozen spots in the list.

What role did policy play in all of this? The differential tariff protection of consumer, intermediate, and equipment goods has been well documented in the Spanish historiography (Viñas et al., 1979). Imports of high-tech machinery needed to produce intermediate goods were subject to low tariffs. This imbalance benefited the growth of some industries more than others. In addition, the government offered the reimbursement of internal taxes levied on the production of exported goods. The argument is that reimbursements exceeded actual tax payments, thus resulting in a subsidy to export (Carreras and Tafunell, 2010, p. 352). Tax refunds were not insignificant, amounting to over 13 percent of the total value of exports in 1973, although the evidence on the extent of over-repayment, and thus subsidization, is rather limited. More importantly, exporters also benefited from access to credit on subsidized terms. But the role of these policy instruments should not be overstated. Subsidized credit was largely channeled through the Industrial Credit Bank into a few selected sectors. Much was spent to promote shipbuilding, which temporarily saw an increase in exports but would eventually decline. Through agreements between the state and private enterprises, the so-called "concerted actions," the authorities agreed to channel subsidized credit in exchange for private agents reaching certain productivity growth targets or starting certain industrial activities. In practice, these agreements were largely ineffective, although the secrecy of these agreements has made it difficult to carefully document. The good news is that the amounts spent on this type of policy were relatively small, around $100 million a year the World Bank estimated in the early 1970s, so even though ineffective, they did not bankrupt the state.

Nevertheless, the influence of state actions went beyond tariffs and financial incentives. The example of shoe exports is instructive. The official support provided to shoemakers was extremely limited, barely covering the financing of a few trips and some short-term advisors. Yet it may have been instrumental in setting the industry on the path to export by clearly identifying the upgrades in quality and design needed. Like the shoe producers, it was also thanks to the Spanish-American agreements that Manuel Jalón also traveled to the US, where he observed the product that would set him on the path to his first patent. Even small official interventions can at times have large unintended consequences, in this case positive ones.

The idea that the benefits of openness go beyond the adoption of new technology embodied in imports of capital goods has been given greater attention in recent years. Economic growth may have deep institutional roots, but, as economists Enrico Spolaore and Romain Wacziarg suggest, those roots are far from destiny. Societies can achieve significant catching up in income by fostering cross-cultural exchanges and reducing the barriers to adapting technological and institutional innovations. Policies that help reduce those barriers are to be fostered (Spolaore and Wacziarg, 2009 and 2013). Migration, cross-cultural exchanges, and technical assistance programs can play a positive role in this regard, as they did in Spain.

Where did the idea of openness come from?

Besides the influence of the ideas espoused by defunct economists, as Keynes famously put it, several prominent economists would also come to hold positions of power. Among them, Minister Alberto Ullastres stood out for both the high-level position he reached and for his technical competence. A professor of economic history, Ullastres had completed his PhD dissertation on the monetary ideas of Juan de Mariana—a seventeenth-century thinker heir to the School of Salamanca.[12] Prior to entering government service, Ullastres had been on the editorial board of the leading economics journal in Spain and closely followed international debates and developments in economics. He had also been the translator of Earl J. Hamilton, known for his account of the price revolution in the sixteenth century, and of Heinrich von Stackelberg, who had moved to Spain during World War II and was instrumental in the spread of the marginal revolution in Spain.[13]

And Ullastres was not alone. At the Bank of Spain, the Director of Research was the like-minded Joan Sardà, widely recognized for his sheer intellectual capacity and brilliance but entrusted with a position of less authority. Ullastres and the other new ministers that joined the cabinet in 1957 brought with them a cadre of technical staff, mostly professional academic economists. New technical secretary-generals were appointed at the Ministries of Commerce and Finance. The latter, Juan Antonio Ortiz Gracia, had just returned to Spain in May 1957 from a stint at the World Bank, and he quickly put the idea of a Stabilization Plan in Navarro Rubio's mind. As for Ullastres, he would later comment that it had been the reading of a 1936 essay by fellow Spanish economist Romà Perpinyà, included as an annex in the Spanish translation of Gottfried Haberler's *Theory of International Trade*, that had persuaded him of the need to open the economy (Velarde Fuertes, 2019).

---

[12] Over two hundred years before Adam Smith, the School of Salamanca emphasized the importance of clearing markets for allocating resources, considering a price to be just if determined by the forces of supply and demand. Juan de Mariana was also an influential voice on political economy debates, as noted in Chapter 3.
[13] As part of a growing but still limited fraternity of economists in the country, Ullastres also hosted many of the frequent lecturers invited to Spain, including Walter Eucken and Friedrich von Hayek. On Ullastres see Zaratiegui (2018a), who has also researched Ullastres' personal archive. The indirect role of Stackelberg in influencing policy reforms in Spain is discussed by Velarde (1999). For a broader overview on the development of ideas about economic development among professional economists see Gallego and Trincado (2020), who point to an evolution already noticeable in the 1950s.

The reference to Perpinyà is important for several reasons. Perpinyà was writing in 1935. His indictment is not of Franco's autarkic policies but of what he saw as a "nationalist way" that had dominated Spanish economic policy since the Restoration in the late nineteenth century.[14] Perpinyà was a true pioneer in favor of integrating into the European markets to catch up with their most advanced standards of living. The autarkic policies of the Franco regime were but an extreme version of the policies that Perpinyà had discredited. This makes the changes to open up the economy all the more significant. It was not just a matter of freeing the economy from a decade and a half of particularly bad policies under Franco. The policy change was a departure from a way of life that had underpinned the closed access society that had characterized Spain since 1875.

Haberler and the Austrian school of economics were not the only European influences of Perpinyà. Born at the turn of the twentieth century in a Catalan family of merchants which produced and exported both galena and Priorat wine to London, Perpinyà was to travel to Belgium to study when World War I broke out. He would later study in Frankfurt, Berlin, and Kiel and become fluent in seven languages. Perpinyà helped Catalan politician Francesc Cambó prepare for a League of Nations' International Economic Conference held in Geneva in 1927, where like-minded internationalists emphatically concluded that "any strictly nationalistic policy is harmful not only to the nation which practices it, but also to the others, and therefore defeats its own."[15] Perpinyà will not waver from this idea regardless of the fashion of the day. Besides Haberler, he would later include Jacob Viner and Bertil Ohlin as his greatest influences and would remain steadfast on the idea that the growth of the Spanish economy was critically tied to its capacity to connect with the external world.

Yet, opening up the economy was the precise opposite of what the intellectual classes of Spain had advocated in the first decades of the twentieth century. In Spain, this period was dominated by the reaction to the loss of the colonies of Cuba, Puerto Rico, and the Philippines (Balfour, 1997). The so-called Disaster of 1898 was a truly traumatic event for Spanish society. It prompted much self-reflection and a political project that was predicated on a simple diagnosis and remedy: Spain was the problem; Europe was the solution. And those looking at Europe in the 1920s and 1930s were often captivated by the rise of Nazism and

---

[14] Perpiñá Grau (1936) argued that "Spanish economic policy has had only one concern: production; one means: turn it all national; and one big mistake: believing that domestic consumption was unlimited and of similar purchasing power across regions; in other others, worrying only about production without taking markets into account," as reproduced in Navarrete Fernández (2005), who stresses also the continuity of economic policies from 1875 to the 1950s.

[15] The nature, and limitations, of this Conference are unwittingly summed up by the rapporteur for the Royal Economic Society: "Almost the only occupation which was comparatively unrepresented was the professional politician, and there can be little doubt that the non-political quality of the Conference was to a large degree responsible for its success in dealing with economic problems" (Runciman, 1927, p. 466).

fascism, the rejection of liberal democracy, and—in economic policy—nationalism. Opening the economy to external trade was not yet a dominant position elsewhere in Europe and would not be so in the Spain of the first half of the twentieth century. But the view of *Europe as the solution* became firmly ingrained among many of the intellectual elites of Spain.

When the political and intellectual landscape in Europe was transformed after the war, looking at Europe for solutions now meant endorsing the process of European economic integration. Ullastres would later point out the importance of the Treaty of Rome that created the European Economic Community in persuading the public of the need for a new economic policy. "The big headlines in the Spanish press about the entry into force of the Treaty of Rome," Ullastres would argue, "contributed to sensitize the country of the need to get closer to the rest of Europe, and to begin accepting our ideas about a Stabilization Plan."[16] The devaluations and declarations of convertibility of several currencies in 1958 also drew attention to the possibility of doing the same in Spain.

The appeal of Europe was indeed a common point of reference shared by both Franco loyalists and by opponents to the regime known for their liberal democrat views, like the famed Europeanist Salvador de Madariaga. And within Europe, the influence of developments in France was particularly strong. The memoirs of Franco's technocratic ministers contain numerous references to European post-war leaders and especially French figures like Jean Monnet or Charles de Gaulle. Contemporaneous sources also reveal the special attention paid to France; in the 1960s, photographs of officials like Navarro Rubio or López Rodó with visitors like French Finance Minister Valéry Giscard d'Estaing were proudly included in official publications.

On occasion, French leaders provided more than just a distant inspiration. Jacques Rueff, economic advisor to French President Charles de Gaulle and main author of the stabilization plan adopted in France in 1958, visited Madrid on April 18, 1959. His talk had not been arranged by any of the economic ministries or the central bank but, somewhat surprisingly, by the National Delegation of Syndicates, a body that had been subsumed within the *Falange* party. Regardless of who invited Rueff to Madrid, his message on the need for decisive action against inflation was most welcome by proponents of the stabilization (Navarro Rubio, 1991, p. 152).

But why were the economic technocrats appointed in the first place? The rise of technocracy is in fact one of the most notable developments of the period. As we started to discuss in Chapter 5, the available evidence suggests that the key to the appointments of Ullastres, Navarro Rubio, and López Rodó was their technical

---

[16] This interview, one of the rare times in which Ullastres spoke about his role in the Stabilization Plan, was first published in 1985 and has since been made available in Varela (1994) and Perdices de Blas and Baumert (2010).

expertise. They were sought out for their professional knowledge and for their relatively low political profile. They were conservative, religious, and of upper middle-class backgrounds—Ullastres had studied in the prestigious *El Pilar* school in Madrid. Crucially, they did not enter the government as representatives of any of the factions that have risen against the Republic in 1936. Ullastres, born in 1914, was the youngest minister in the 1957 cabinet. Like Navarro Rubio, born in 1913, they were too young to have played a prominent role in politics before the Civil War, which they spent, also on account of their age, on the frontlines. Having literally fought and killed for Franco, like the military men of their age, their allegiance to Franco would never be in question. The technocrats would become the closest to a pure Francoist party, loyalists only to the regime.

To be clear, ministerial appointments were the sole discretion of Franco. They were clouded in secrecy and as such we may never know the true motivations for selecting one or another minister. But we know something about the process by which candidates were considered in the ministerial shortlists. Navarro Rubio, for example, was first contacted by Carrero Blanco in early 1956 and asked to provide a note summarizing his views on public finance issues—which he delivered in the form of a letter in March 1956. With time, Navarro Rubio would conclude that he had been put through some sort of test before being considered for the position of Minister of Finance. Both the timing and the content of the letter are of interest here. Navarro Rubio would not be appointed until a year after he was first contacted. And Navarro Rubio's program was one of reform of both the expenditure and revenue side, including a renewed effort to put in place an effective income tax (Navarro Rubio would eventually fail in this regard). He also envisaged a much greater coordination between ministries with Finance clearly in charge, what he considered to be a French-type of Ministry of Finance. Among other things, it was telling that Navarro Rubio concluded that "if we are to do things right, we will have to use economists" (Navarro Rubio, 1991, p. 73).

The rise in the role of economists in government has often been interpreted as a complete outsourcing of policymaking and capitulation by Franco. This view is well summarized by the great historian Paul Preston who, discussing the adoption of the 1959 Plan, dates this as the moment "in which Franco retires" as the chief executive and he "cedes the political and economic power to technicians" (Preston, 2008, p. 20). While certainly true that technocrats gained in power, neither they received a carte blanche nor was the economic program implemented behind Franco's back.

Ahead of the launch of the 1959 Plan, Franco gave some interviews in which he articulated many aspects of the new economic thinking. Asked about why the importance of wages keeping up with inflation, Franco stresses that the state "cannot intervene in everything," and that price stability is achieved through competition "which limits [profit] margins." Even more significant was a subsequent statement in the same interview that "the aspiration of rising wages without a parallel increase in productivity is a chimera" (*ABC* newspaper, May 1, 1959). Franco was perhaps simply regurgitating talking points given to him, but it is a good example that he at least lent his voice to the new economic program.

Crucially, this interview was not an isolated example. It was in fact a precursor of things to come, as the way Franco discussed economic issues would shift significantly after 1960. We can show this by performing a keyword-in-context analysis using the annual end-of-year speeches on which we already drew in the previous chapter. In this additional analysis of the speeches, we first isolate the 40 words, excluding stop-words such as prepositions or determinants, that surround any mention in these speeches of the word "economy" or any of its derivative words like "economic," etc. Within that subset of the speech, we then run the same topic model algorithm that we did before. To detect a shift from an "old" to a "new" way of discussing economic issues, we set the parameters of the algorithm so that it uncovers two topics. What we observe is a rather striking difference between the excerpts of speeches that discuss the economy before and after 1960 (Figure 6.5). Before 1960, the economy is discussed mostly in terms of words like nation, problems, and war. In contrast, after 1960, the topic that captures most of the discussion of the economy is associated with terms that include the words social, world, development, and peace. The new way of discussing the economy was clearly more outward-oriented.

The relatively sharp change in the way that Franco discussed economic issues help us understand also why the 1959 Plan is often seen as a dividing line when analyzing the economy of the time. Franco's speeches were prepared by others, but it is undeniable that the way the regime discussed the economy had a before and after 1960. How does this fit with our earlier arguments that policies displayed a significant degree of continuity? And how does it square with the finding, from the topic analysis of the entire text of Franco's speeches, that concern with social and economic development objectives grew gradually over time in the 1950s? What our analyses surface is the following interpretation: The type of issues that were of concern to the regime changes starting in the early 1950s. We document a growing interest in economic issues, which I argue stemmed from the fact that the regime felt increasingly secure politically. Economic policies are gradually changed accordingly, due to political stability rather than economic instability, but the public rhetoric around the economy only changed after those policies start to show positive results.[17]

As for the alleged retirement by Franco from economic policymaking after 1959, the evidence is mixed at best. Franco would continue to chair the bimonthly

---

[17] Tellingly, the discussion of the economy in Franco's speech on December 31, 1959, half a year after the Stabilization Plan was launched and when the economy was still mired in a recession following the contractionary measures of the Plan, was very much in the "old" language, according to our topic modeling algorithm.

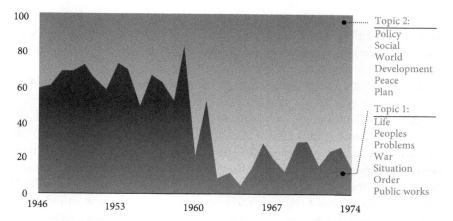

Figure 6.5 Out with the old, in with the new: discussions of the economy in Franco's end-of-year speeches

Notes: Share of each topic in speech excerpts that discuss economic issues (in percent). Text boxes indicate the most frequent words that are distinct for each topic. Topics are identified using the LDA algorithm discussed in Chapter 5 on excerpts of Franco's end-of-year speeches that discuss the economy. The most frequent words for each of the two topics are, in order, as follows. Topic 1: nation, Spain*, economy*, life, peoples, problems, war, situation, order, and public works. Topic 2: economy*, Spain*, policy, social, world, development, nation, peace, and plan.

Although the words economy, Spain, and nation appear in both lists, it is relevant that nation is the most frequent word in topic 1 while it is only the seventh-most frequent word in topic 2.

Asterisks indicate that the word is stemmed to include all derivate forms.

Source: Own elaboration with Axel Eizmendi.

meetings of the Delegate Commission for Economic Affairs, created in 1957 to improve the coordination of economic policies, and there were no changes in his schedule until several years later when his aging became noticeable. Much like the IMF's Per Jacobsson had found Franco to be well informed of the details of the economic plans in 1959, so would the staff and management of the World Bank as it developed a program in the country. Given the concentration of power held by Franco, the World Bank would remain wary over the years of a possible change of heart of Franco's economic policies and as such paid close attention to Franco's views and any interaction with him.

World Bank staff found Franco long-winded and hard to read, but never poorly informed or lacking in attention to details. One particularly relevant interaction can serve as an example. Franco himself reached out to meet the leader of the World Bank mission tasked with writing an assessment of Spain's economy in 1961, Sir Hugh Ellis-Rees. The meeting was scheduled as a protocol visit of a quarter of an hour but would last about three-quarters of an hour, in part because, as Ellis-Rees put it in his report back to Washington, "General Franco then gave me a dissertation on the origins of the Spanish economic problems." But Ellis-Rees was also positively surprised that it had been Franco himself who in the meeting "mentioned the shortcomings of Spanish bureaucracy and the lack of coordination." Franco also impressed upon Ellis-Rees the view that the Stabilization Plan had only been "the first action" and that he was "anxious to bring about" the next phase.[18]

Importantly, the rise of technocracy should not be equated with just the rise of economists. In 1962, new entrants in the cabinet included a chemistry professor as Minister of Education, a naval engineer as Minister of Industry, and a law professor as the minister in charge of the Economic and Social Development Plan. We cannot be sure what was behind all these ministerial appointments, and there were no programmatic declarations that explain the rise of technocracy. However, there was no shortage of authors that aimed to provide an intellectual rationale for the developmentalist stage of Francoism. Among those, the most influential was a book entitled *The Crepuscule of Ideologies*, although this was largely *ex post* rationalization of events, as the book came out in 1965, well after the rise of technocracy started.[19]

Economists were not the only group endorsing and benefiting from the rise of technocracy. Entrepreneurs, engineers, and other professional elites were equally supportive. Engineers and agricultural scientists were also well prepared for a modernization push and became active participants within a Franco regime that welcomed their modernizing agendas (Camprubí, 2014). A particularly noteworthy modernizing project was that of dam-building for the purposes of massive irrigation and hydroelectric production. It led to the construction of over 600 dams, small and large, during the Franco regime. It resulted in Spain becoming the country with the largest number of dams in the world per population. Not a drop of water in the Southern water basins would be left unproductive. Although this dam-building is often presented as an obsession of Franco himself, it reflected as much the modernizing push of the professional elites (Swyngedouw, 2015).

Conclusions

Much of the growth dividend from reforms stemmed from increased openness. But this increased openness to the world economy did not equate with a unilateral and across-the-board reduction of tariff protection. On the contrary, tariffs remained broadly unchanged and tilted against some consumer goods. But foreign

---

[18] Ellis-Rees also noted that it was "difficult to draw conclusions" from his conversation because Franco, "though he listens intently, and reputedly takes in every point, he does not often give way to any expression of approval or dissent." Ellis-Rees to Cope, March 29, 1961 (the meeting took place on March 22), World Bank Archive Folder 1740805 (Spain. General Survey. Mission I).

[19] Its author, Gonzalo Fernández de la Mora, became Minister of Public Works in 1970 and would end his days, paradoxically, as one of the members of the regime most ideologically opposed to any political reform.

businesses were attracted to invest in Spain in part precisely because of its protected and relatively large domestic market. The inflows of foreign capital, along with with revenues from tourism and migrant's remittances, combined to make possible a sharp rise in imports of equipment and machinery that embodied more updated technology.

Even more importantly, technology transfer took place through licensing, technical cooperation contracts and programs, and through onsite learning-by-doing and demonstrations. A well-trained cadre of local professionals and entre-preneurs was ready to adopt and adapt the new technology to the realities of Spain. Greater focus on management led to the creation of new business schools inspired by practices overseas. Productivity committees and missions were pur-sued. All of this helps to explain that, from a growth-accounting perspective, the most critical element in the economic takeoff of Spain was the growth of total factor productivity.

The increased interactions with the external world led not merely to techno-logical adoption and catch-up but also to an increased outward orientation. Spanish businesses, from shoemakers to engineering firms, were able to build on their contacts with the international market to explore opportunities and achieve exporting success. From a comparative perspective, the economy experienced a fast and substantial diversification of exports, a remarkable development that had until recently been somewhat hidden due to the lack of comparable data across countries.

It is equally notable that this increased openness happened at all, certainly with regard to foreign capital. Those in favor of greater openness had been a small minority of the body politic in the first half of the twentieth century in Spain. In fact, the predominant view that had carried the day in the wake of the Disaster of 1898, in which Spain lost the colonies of Cuba, Puerto Rico, and the Philippines, was the need to double down on nationalist policies. But, simultaneously, a supra-consensus emerged on the desirability of Spain becoming more like Europe.

While in the 1920s and 1930s, looking at Europe meant copying fascistic ideas, the intellectual and political climate in Western Europe since the 1950s was decidedly integrationist. The Treaty of Rome provided ultimate proof. Economists would prove increasingly influential within the Franco regime, just like other pro-fessional elites like engineers or agricultural scientists that had their own mod-ernizing projects, like the extensive dam-building and irrigation which came to characterize the regime. Economists, just like other technocrats, were elevated to power on account of their technical expertise and their low political profile. They did not represent any of the previous political families and were thus pure Franco loyalists in political terms.

If the general rise of technocracy helps to explain the increasing influence of economists in economic policymaking, the specific policies pursued owe much to the clarity of thinking and intellectual influences of the policymakers involved.

Minister of Commerce Alberto Ullastres, in particular, had a clear vision of what he wanted to accomplish. Openness became easier to defend as time passed by and the boom in tourism and remittances vindicated earlier decisions, but, at the outset, it required much perseverance and advocacy—as we saw with regard to the adoption of the 1959 Stabilization Plan in the previous chapter. The policy of greater openness to capital resulted in greater interactions between professional groups, technology transfer through technical assistance and licensing, and advisory services—all examples of what economists Enrico Spolaore and Romain Wacziarg refer to as policies that reduce the barriers to the adoption and adaptation of the technological and institutional innovations that drive growth.

The way in which this opening up contributed to its long-run growth prospects was specific to Spain. It was made possible by policy choices such as the correction of the exchange rate misalignment and the loosening of controls on foreign capital influences. But it was also heavily influenced by the size of the economy, its otherwise protectionist trade policies, the stability of the regime, and the strength of entrepreneurs, engineers, and other professionals that did the learning-by-doing and contributed to a remarkable spurt in efficiency gains. In short, Spain traveled its own distinct path to prosperity, just like Gerschenkron emphasized any backward country would.

7

Contestability

The richest man in Spain during the mid-twentieth century was Juan March. At the peak of his fortune, he was amongst the half-dozen or so richest men on the planet. He had amassed his wealth through all sorts of dubious means. He bribed Spanish politicians to secure the monopoly of tobacco in Spanish North Africa, from where he would then smuggle cigarettes into the mainland, paying off customs officers as needed. A financier of the Nationalist rebels in 1936, he would later be instrumental in the British scheme to pay generals close to Franco to keep Spain out of World War II. Throughout his life, Juan March's source of wealth was the dark intersection between politics and business. In the 1950s, he engineered the takeover of the Barcelona Traction, a foreign-owned utility which was forced into bankruptcy to his benefit. A portrait of Juan March in *The New Yorker* referred to him as a privateer. Perhaps more aptly, one of the biographies written about him was subtitled "Mister Monopoly."[1]

Compare that with the story of the richest man in Spain in the early twenty-first century, Amancio Ortega. Born in 1936 in a modest family and working in the garment industry since the age of 14, Ortega set up his own business in the early 1970s. Instead of monopoly rents, the success of Ortega's business was based on a process innovation. In an extremely competitive landscape, Ortega's firm *Zara* thrived by developing a supply chain that turned a new line of clothing in a matter of weeks when others took months. Amancio Ortega's involvement in national politics was virtually nonexistent. His success did not depend on protections by the state. On the contrary, his business sought competition. The source of most of his income was in fact outside of Spain.

The stark difference between Juan March and Amancio Ortega illustrates the change experienced by Spanish society which this book seeks to explain. When and how did this happen? And how is it connected with Spain's path to prosperity?

Growth within a closed access society

The stories of Juan March and Amancio Ortega are both quintessential success stories, only of two very different types of societies. The success of Juan March in

---

[1] See Brooks (1980) and Dixon (1985). For a more recent biography of Juan March see Mercedes Cabrera (2011).

Unexpected Prosperity: How Spain Escaped the Middle Income Trap. Oscar Calvo-Gonzalez, Oxford University Press.
© Oscar Calvo-Gonzalez 2021. DOI: 10.1093/oso/9780198853978.003.0008

seeking rents is characteristic of closed access societies. Smuggling and monopoly rents are two sides of the same coin of limiting competition in economic activities. In contrast, Ortega's success story could not have been possible in a society where economic opportunities were fully monopolized by elites and without access to national, European, and global markets.

The transformation of Spain into an open access society is usually seen as having taken place largely after 1978, when the country regained a democratic constitution, and completed in the aftermath of 1986, when the country finally joined the European Economic Community. Politically speaking, there is no doubt about the importance of those milestones in transitioning the country towards a modern democracy. It is therefore understandable that a similar view is often held about economic matters, with the source of prosperity in contemporary Spain commonly thought of as being founded upon the successful consolidation of an open access society in the early- to mid-1980s. To simplify somewhat, the process is typically seen as largely sequential: The political and economic success of the country follow as the consequence of adopting political and economic institutions that characterize open access societies.

But the economic development path followed by Spain defies such a simple interpretation. Economic growth took off well before this transition into an open access society—both from a political as well as an economic angle—was complete. In fact, the most intense economic catching up happened before 1986. This can be illustrated if we compare a key measure of economic performance such as labor productivity across countries. As shown in Figure 7.1, the period of true convergence precedes the adoption of unambiguously open institutions. When we compare Spain against the sample of economies for which output per hour worked is available since 1950, the period of most intense catching up was in the two decades after 1960, when Spain improved its rank among all economies for which labor productivity data is available from approximately the 40th percentile the 80th percentile by 1980.

The fact that the economic takeoff took place before the transformation from the Spain of Juan March to that of Amancio Ortega has not typically been considered a puzzle by Spanish economic historians. The explanation usually given in the literature for this phenomenon is that economic growth occurred "in spite of" its economic policies and practices (Carreras and Tafunell, 2010, p. 360). This is of course accurate but not particularly informative about the nature of the observed growth. After all, growth in a closed access society could take two very different forms. In its first variety, growth could simply reproduce the existing patterns of ownership and distribution of rents, just at higher levels of income due to the accumulation of capital. In a second variety, growth could be leading to changes in the allocation of rents. In both cases, growth could be characterized as happening *despite bad institutions*, but this would miss an important distinction.

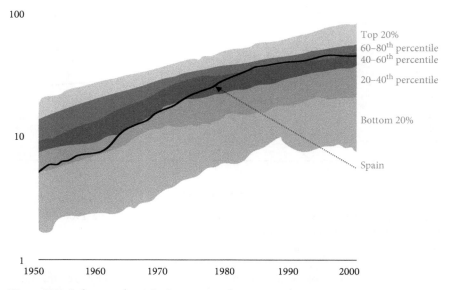

Figure 7.1   Labor productivity in comparative perspective

Note: Output per hour worked, in real terms (log scale) for 31 countries for which data is available since 1950.

Source: Total Economy Database.

In the case of Spain, the literature has explicitly or implicitly put forward the view that up until the mid-1980s, growth resembled the first variety described above. For example, the planning instruments of the 1960s are often seen as nothing more than the mechanism through which rents were extracted and shared (González, 1999, p. 711). Some authors have taken the argument to its logical conclusion, suggesting that growth could have been faster in the absence of those policies.[2] A comparative perspective, however, lends little support to this view.

That growth could hardly have been faster is clear when we look at productivity trends. Compared to all countries for which information is available in the Penn World Table, Spain stands out not only for its fast pace of economic growth in the years after 1960 but also for having had a particularly fast rate of growth of total factor productivity (TFP). Whatever shortcomings the Spanish institutional setup had, they proved to be at the very least compatible with a fast rate of growth of both output and productivity. In fact, as shown in Figure 7.2, during the decade and a half or so of most intense convergence Spain was an outlier in both high economic growth and high TFP growth.

[2] De la Torre and García-Zúñiga (2009) provide an insightful dissection of the criticisms of planning.

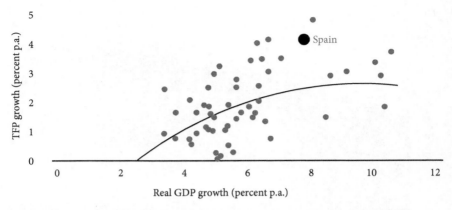

Figure 7.2   Growth of real GDP and TFP in comparative perspective, 1960–73
Note: Sample of 57 countries for which data is available.
Source: Penn World Table (see Feenstra et al., 2015).

Bad policies and poor institutions would typically depress TFP growth. But at 4.2 percent, Spain's average annual growth rate of TFP from 1960 to 1973 was among the top three highest across countries for which we have data; it was also higher than seven economies that had achieved faster overall output growth. The fact that TFP played such a big role in Spain's transformation calls for a deeper look. A high rate of TFP growth is often interpreted as having an element of technological catching up, an issue which played a significant role in Spain, as we discussed in the last chapter and we will further discuss below. Of course, the interpretation of TFP trends is more complicated than that.[3] But, even if technological catch-up explains the lion's share of the acceleration of TFP growth in Spain, we are still left with the puzzle of why technology adoption would see a boost despite bad policies. What is missing in the traditional explanation?

Recent evidence compiled by the Spanish economic historian Leandro Prados de la Escosura on a historical index of economic liberty can help us shed light on this question. In an effort to expand the coverage of indices of economic freedom that have become mainstream for contemporary economies, Prados de la Escosura (2016) provides a summary measure of economic liberty over the long run. The resulting indicator draws on different dimensions affecting economic freedom, including the legal structure and security of property rights, the extent and type of economic regulation, the freedom to trade internationally, and the threats to the value of money. This is particularly relevant to our argument because these

---

[3] Strictly speaking, TFP is quite simply a measure of output growth that is not explained by input growth. As the economist Moses Abramovitz put it, the derivation of TFP as a residual implies that it amounts to being "some sort of measure of ignorance" (1993, p. 218).

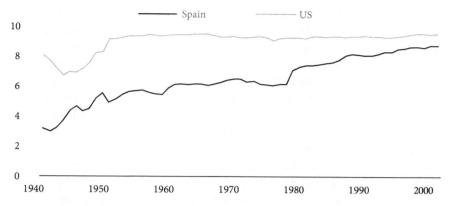

Figure 7.3 Evolution of economic freedom, 1940–2000
Note: Index; higher numbers indicate greater economic freedom.
Source: Own elaboration based on Prados de la Escosura (2016).

dimensions are closely related to what we have been referring to as open access societies. The picture that emerges confirms that it was only in the 1980s that Spain came close to countries like the United States that have traditionally enjoyed greater economic liberty (Figure 7.3). But this data also shows that, driven in large part by improvements in the freedom to trade internationally but also in the security of property rights, there were improvements in the overall index of economic liberty in Spain in the decades prior to the 1980s. In the language of open access societies, there is some evidence of increasing openness in access to economic opportunities, while political access remained tightly closed until the 1980s. A first implication from this evidence is the importance to distinguish between the openness of political and economic institutions.

Much of the literature has focused on the fact that Spain's economic institutions fell short from those in what we have been calling here open access societies. It is as if, looking at a figure like the one for economic liberty, the attention was overly concentrated on the large gap between Spain and the US. That gap is of course very real. But we ought to look also at the evolution of those institutions over time. Therefore, the question to interrogate the historical record is no longer whether Spain grew despite its poor economic institutions. Rather, a more interesting line of inquiry is whether incremental institutional changes—of the type picked up in the slow but steady rise in economic liberty—contributed to the takeoff in growth.

What if Spain's takeoff happened not *despite* bad institutions but *because of* relatively minor but successive policy reforms? The idea that economies can grow even in the absence of inclusive institutions changes fundamentally the frame through which to look at Spain's path to prosperity. It is an idea that is at the core of the conceptual framework of access orders by Douglass North and coauthors (2009) which we have used throughout this book. In fact, as these authors remind us, the principal problem of development is making improvements within the limited access order framework (North et al., 2013, p. 346). How those improvements materialize is a fundamental question to explain economic convergence or divergence across countries. It is precisely the experience of growth with closed but opening institutions that makes Spain a noteworthy case.

Among the institutional adaptations that were taking place in Spain, in this chapter we will focus on the increase in contestability. Greater competition is a hallmark of open access orders. It helps achieve better outcomes in open access orders because it encourages innovative solutions to societal problems, both in the political and economic spheres. It follows that tracking whether and how competition increases may be particularly fruitful to understand the path of a developing economy.

What's on a label?

The focus on contestability may surprise readers familiar with discussions of Spain's recent past as well as its present. Much has been written about the lack of competition as one of the secular characteristics of the Spanish economy. Certainly, the rhetoric against competition has always been in abundant supply and had a sympathetic audience in Spain (Fraile, 1998). Many notable authors argue that an increase in competition remains today one of the priority areas for Spain to escape from the rent-seeking and extractive institutions that are seen as characterizing the country's society.[4] The argument advanced here does not dispute those points of view but simply notes that we should not ignore institutional changes which, even if slow or sometimes seemingly minor, contributed to achieving more contestable markets. Importantly, the result of greater contestability was often unexpected and unplanned. To borrow from the well-known language of the theory of the second best, if one of the optimal equilibrium conditions cannot be met, the next best outcome may require moving away from some other optimality conditions. In other words, the path towards a second best may be winding and cannot be judged ahead of time.

When I use the term contestability I do so to capture two distinct phenomena. The first is more strictly linked to the existence of a market test. As used in the

---

[4] In particular, César Molinas (2013) and Luis Garicano (2014) argue that, since the turn of the twenty-first century, the quality of institutions in Spain has deteriorated, turning into more extractive. This book is not concerned with this latter time period but ends its coverage roughly after the accession of Spain to the EU.

pioneering work by economist William Baumol (1982) on contestable markets, the term draws attention to the importance of the threat of competition, and not necessarily competition itself, in securing competitive outcomes from markets. One of the assumptions in Baumol's framework is that access to the same technology is critical for contestability to take hold. Even if there are only a few players in a given market, if others have access to the same technology and there are no other barriers to entry, a contestable market may be achieved. Everything else constant, an increase in access to more advanced technology would increase contestability. This latter point is particularly relevant for the case of Spain. As we saw in the last chapter, there was in fact a much improved access to foreign technology in the decades after 1950. This is one of the ways in which the topics of openness—discussed in the last chapter—and contestability are intertwined.

Second, I use contestability also in the sense that it has come to be used in the governance literature, to capture the extent to which different actors can exercise influence in the policy arena. This may seem surprising, since for a good part of the period that concerns this chapter, Spain was a dictatorship. Contestability, which can be thought of as who is included and who is excluded from the policy arena, would thus seem at first to be an unhelpful frame for our discussion of Spain during the period.

So, why do I think this concept of contestability is useful to understand Spain's trajectory? To begin with, there was a limited but important expansion of those involved in the policy arena, notably the rise of the technocrats as a new group that participates in the decision-making process—as discussed in the last two chapters. But, more importantly, enhancing the contestability of the policy arena has both *ex ante* and *ex post* elements. Contestability can be increased *ex ante* through more inclusive lawmaking. Contestability can also be increased *ex post*, through the extent to which the law is applied consistently and fairly (World Bank, 2017, p. 13). When the law is applied in the same way to every person, including those in power, we typically refer to such a situation as the rule of law.

Contestability is thus a good shorthand for two phenomena that are not usually discussed together, economic competition and the rule of law. In both senses, contestability implies the presence of a check, which can be either a market or legal test. For it to increase contestability, this check needs to be external to the organization or actor in question, and there needs to be a credible enforcement of the provisions of that external check. As we will see, some of the institutional developments of the period in Spain fit under this rubric. To be clear, I am not characterizing the period of the economic takeoff in Spain as one of a fully competitive economy or of a strong rule of law. Rather, what I seek to explore is how the emergence, even if imperfect, of greater economic competition and a stronger rule of law contributed to Spain's economic development. Compared to the transition to democracy, the transition to the rule of law in Spain is a much less analyzed question—as it is indeed across the world (Fukuyama, 2010).

An unplanned success

When then Spanish Prime Minister José María Aznar visited US President George W. Bush at his ranch in Texas he had the following exchange with one of Bush's close advisors while waiting to meet with President Bush: "What is the main export of Spain?" asked the American, to which Aznar replied "Cars." "No, I am asking about the number one product that Spain exports," explained the American interlocutor, believing that Aznar had misunderstood the question. "Cars," replied again Aznar. "No, no, what I want to know is which Spanish product sells most successfully abroad," went on the American, to which Aznar simply said, "Yes, cars, cars." The story, crisply told by William Chislett, a correspondent of *The Times* in Spain during the democratic transition, illustrates well how little-known Spain's economy really is (Chislett, 2013, p. 3). It is also a reminder of how an unlikely success is the Spanish car industry. As of the time of writing, annual exports of cars and other vehicles, including parts, amounted to more than $54 billion, or almost 12 percent of all Spanish exports. When the entire sector is taken as a whole, including many exporters of sophisticated parts, it employs almost one in ten workers in Spain (ANFAC, 2019). And, crucially, this success began during a period of extraordinarily high regulation of the sector. As will be clear by the end of the chapter, this makes it a most enlightening case study in our search for the keys to Spain's rise to prosperity.

Before digging into the factors behind this success it is important to stress how unexpected it was. When World Bank President Robert McNamara visited Spain in April 1971, his main message to his hosts was the importance of developing new exports, as it was thought at the time that the growth of tourism seen in the 1960s could not possibly be sustained. McNamara's pitch was effectively a version of what has since been captured in the phrase "what got you here won't get you there." Not only were the prognostications about tourism completely off mark, but McNamara's briefing book contained no references to the car industry as holding any potential for export. McNamara and the Bank staff were not alone in ignoring the export potential of the car industry. When McNamara asked private sector representatives about their views on what exports of manufactures were poised to grow, Spanish private entrepreneurs pointed out to a range of products—shipbuilding, chemicals, metal transformation, machine tools, food canned products, and electronic components—but not to cars.[5]

---

[5] "The point of departure for all discussions was Mr. McNamara's presentation of the Bank's diagnosis that the 'economic miracle' of the 1960s could not be duplicated in the 1970s, in particular because the growth in tourism could not be expected to be as rapid, therefore the need would be to stimulate exports, particularly exports of manufactures. What, under these conditions, were the sectors and factors which would determine future growth?" in "Summary of discussions," Mr McNamara's visit to Spain, April 27–May 1, 1971, World Bank Archive File 1771181.

At the time of McNamara's visit, Spain was actually on the eve of a boom in car exports. Eighteen months after McNamara's trip, Spain had already become the eleventh car-exporting country in the world, with a total of over 170,000 vehicles exported in 1973. Throughout the 1970s, the value of car exports would double roughly every two years, so that by 1980 exports would be around 30 times what they had been in 1970. This led to rapid convergence with other major car-exporting countries, like Italy or France, as shown in Figure 7.4. The pace of growth of car exports from Spain was in fact similar to Korea's, a much better-known case of rapid rise as a car-exporting power.

Yet the Spanish car industry had the most inauspicious beginnings. In 1950 it was dominated by a state-owned company, SEAT. Not only was the industry, like all others, subject to licensing, but the authorities in charge were eager to avoid new entrants and often denied requests such as the ones that local truck manufacturer Eduardo Barreiros made to enter the car segment (Thomas, 2009). Throughout the 1950s, there would be only two new entrants in the market, Renault in 1951 and Citroen in 1957. Renault would go into business in Spain with a group of prominent local businessmen which included Franco's brother. Citroen would partner with, among others, a former minister that had served with Franco in the early days of the regime. A 90 percent tariff on imported cars, coupled with quantitative restrictions on imports and very low levels of cars per inhabitants to begin with, led to an excess demand for domestically produced cars. Prices were set by the government.

This was as far as one can think of from an open access industry: Dominance by a state-owned firm, discretionary decisions regarding market entry, politically connected players among the few private competitors, publicly set prices, exorbitant rates of protection, and quantitative restrictions make for an almost perfect

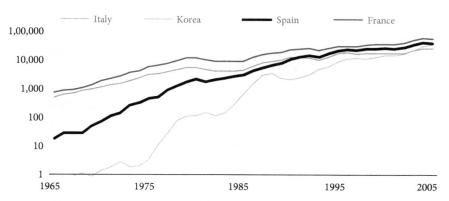

Figure 7.4 Exports of vehicles in comparative perspective, 1965–2005
Note: Millions of US dollars; logarithmic scale.
Source: Own elaboration with UN COMTRADE data for SITC rev.1 code 732 (road motor vehicles).

setting for rent-seeking. One where lack of dynamism and underperformance would be expected to be the norm. Unsurprisingly, an estimate of the domestic resource cost, which compares the domestic cost of producing a good with its value added in the international market, confirms the manufacturing of automobiles in Spain as of 1958 as inefficient (Martínez Ruiz, 2008). But despite this troubled beginning, the industry would set off on a path to achieving greater competitiveness. How did this unlikely success materialize?

The way the new entrants, Renault and Citroen, were set up contributed to the development of local suppliers. Citroen sought to establish a factory where up to 70 percent of parts would not be produced in-house but made by local suppliers. This was a strategy to limit the capital investment needed to set up a factory in Spain. It had a positive unintended consequence, helping to grow a network of local suppliers. Over time, the car parts industry would become another successful exporting sector. This is no small feat, since components manufacturing requires different organizational arrangements to succeed in what has become a relatively knowledge-intensive activity that requires much flexibility (Guillén, 2001, chapter 6). To illustrate this point, while Spain succeeded in exporting both cars and components, Korea achieved high growth only in exports of cars.

The evolution of industrial policy of the sector also played a critical role. Earlier, I noted that it was only through a former Francoist minister, Pedro González-Bueno, that Citroen was able to secure its license. Exactly how Citroen got its license to establish a factory is revealing of the workings of industrial policy in the 1950s. After a contact with the French firm, González-Bueno went to visit with the Minister of Industry. Access to decision-makers was valuable—and a clear indication of the type of closed access society that Spain was. But the minister ruled out giving Citroen the license and González-Bueno, who was "frankly worried" about how firm the minister's views were, used his ability to secure a meeting with Franco to plead his case directly with the dictator. Franco, however, simply referred him back to the Minister of Industry, "who is the one that runs industrial policy."[6]

Herein lies one of the most Machiavellian features of the Franco regime. On one hand, the regime can be characterized as one in which a "single elector" had final say over all issues. And one where corruption was widespread, as many authors have emphasized. Franco was a typical dictator who came to power by force, violated human rights, and enriched himself, especially during the Civil War.[7]

[6] All quotes in this and the next two paragraphs are from the memoirs of González-Bueno (2006, pp. 270–86). See also Carmona (2018, pp. 248–9) for a description of the process by which Citroen got its license.

[7] Franco acquired wealth in many corrupt ways, from dubious real estate deals, "gifts" from supporters, stipends from state-owned enterprises, and, until 1957, even private laws issued for his benefit but not publicly disclosed (Viñas, 2015). However, unlike dictators of the time like Rafael Trujillo of the Dominican Republic, Franco did not own monopolistic firms across a range of industries.

Regime insiders constituted a privileged elite. Former ministers, for example, were typically given lucrative jobs in state-owned companies and, as the case of the former minister lobbying for Citroen illustrates, they retained privileged access to decision-makers.

On the other hand, the way Franco exercised his power—seeking to maximize his time in office—allowed and even encouraged a contest of policy ideas so long as the fundamental basis of his power was never questioned. In the case of Citroen, after the initial noncommittal response by Franco, the former minister on Citroen's payroll mounted a year-long lobbying campaign to show that the new plant would not cannibalize the sales or suppliers of the state-owned SEAT. When the licensing request went to the cabinet, the Minister of Industry advised against it and threatened to resign if it was approved. Franco, who used the cabinet meetings as a mini-parliament, asked the opinion of others around the table, and the Minister of Agriculture voiced his support for granting the license. The cabinet ruled against granting the manufacturing license, although as consolation it gave the lobbying former minister the lucrative right to import 2,000 Citroen cars.

The defeat of Citroen would nevertheless prove to be short-lived. A few months later, SEAT was on track with its new and highly successful 600 model, and the Minister of Industry reconsidered his position. Exactly why is hard to know. He simply stated that it was now an "opportune moment" to go ahead with the new factory proposed by Citroen. The French investors were allowed by the cabinet to own 45 percent of the capital and Citroen was incorporated in Spain in July 1957. A year later it started production, having set up its factory in the special economic zone of Vigo, Galicia.[8] A decade later, it reached 40,000 cars produced annually and it started exporting.

Pitting insiders against insiders, as Franco did in the case of Citroen's licensing and many others, does not necessarily result in an environment more conducive to economic development. It can result in great instability. What stands out after 1950 is the way in which insiders were pitted against each other. It was done mainly within the confines of the law. In the case of the car industry, this increase in the rule of law was most notable in the application of local content rules which specified a minimum amount of domestically produced inputs in the manufacturing of cars. When Renault set up shop in 1951, it was given a grace period of four years before it had to use only locally produced parts. Such an ambitious goal would prove impossible to reach, but Renault would still be "forced to gradually decrease the proportion of imported foreign parts" (Catalan, 2010, p. 211). Similar targets were required of Citroen.

---

[8] The special economic zone of Vigo was created in 1947 and was the third such zone in Spain after Barcelona (1916) and Cádiz (1933). But the status by itself did little. It was completely empty until Citroen established its factory there. See López Ortiz and Melgarejo (2018).

Crucially, local content rules were not only established but broadly enforced. And local content rules, which had been initially decided on a case-by-case basis for specific investments, became generalized in 1964 in another example of the move towards rules-based policymaking. The policies in place during the late 1950s and early 1960s started to yield results. By 1965, the local content of Spanish car manufacturing was between 90 and 100 percent. And Spain also enjoyed significantly lower unit costs than other countries that had set out to boost their domestic production such as Argentina, Mexico, Brazil, or India. Argentina, for example, had unit costs twice as high as those of Spain while achieving a lower local content of around 70 to 90 percent.[9]

Still, from 1950 to the mid-1960s, the Spanish car industry was viable only because of the high degree of protection it enjoyed. With only 140,000 cars manufactured per year, the unit costs of the Spanish car manufacturers were still around 30 percent higher than in mature markets, where runs of 200,000 per model/year were becoming the minimum to be economically competitive. The impressive growth of Spain's car production, over 20 percent annually between 1958 and 1972, would not result in a sustainable industry if efficiency could not be improved. Because car producers had set up production in a way that relied significantly on local suppliers, it was most critical to increasing the efficiency of independent suppliers of car parts, which by 1967 amounted to around 1,500 businesses that employed around fifty thousand employees in supplying parts to car manufacturers.

Foreign investment proved to be crucial for increasing the productivity of those suppliers. The first-ever equity investment of the International Finance Corporation, the private sector arm of the World Bank Group, was the purchase in 1962 of a 13 percent stake in Spain's FEMSA, a leading manufacturer of automotive electrical components. A decade and a half later, FEMSA would be bought by the Bosch Group of Germany, which had started its acquisitions of Spanish car parts suppliers in 1967. Besides Bosch, the list of foreign investors that entered the automotive parts sector in Spain since the 1960s was extraordinarily large.[10] The extensive foreign presence not only brought technology and dynamism but also helped ensure a degree of competition in the marketplace. The increased competition was in fact an explicit goal of measures like the decision in 1967 to attract Italian suppliers to the industrial district of Zaragoza, in a deliberate effort to boost productivity by increasing competition to local suppliers (García Ruiz, 2003, p. 44). There were also other indications that increasing competition was

---

[9] García Ruiz (2003 and 2018) and Catalan (2010) are the sources for all data in this paragraph.

[10] It included Allied Signal-Bendix, Behr, Bekaert, Chausson, Cibié, Dunlop, Eaton, Ferodo, Mahle, Mann & Hummel, Michelin, Motoren Werke Mannheim, Philips, Saint Gobain, SKF, and Tenneco (García Ruiz, 2003, p. 45).

in the minds of policymakers. In 1966, prices of cars ceased to be administratively set, though they would remain regulated.

Over time, and almost imperceptibly at first, the policy goal became to turn the car industry into an exporting one. Starting in the mid-1960s, a series of public pronouncements by government officials stressed the need for the car industry to export as a way to ensure a degree of competition and competitiveness (García Ruiz, 2003, p. 47). This increased attention to the external market was a response to the poor prospects for increasing efficiency based on the domestic market alone. Large runs of a single car model were considered to be the only way to achieve efficiency. Unfortunately, not only was the national market limited but it was also clear that domestic car producers could not merge because they each depended on different foreign manufacturers for patents and technology. Exporting was a good theoretical solution to this problem. But from the perspective of 1970, when car exports amounted to barely $74 million, it was also an unlikely one to materialize.

In another example to move away from purely discretionary to more rules-based mechanisms, a 1965 policy set a minimum threshold of production for any new entrant in the market. But at 250,000 cars per year, this threshold was so high, roughly equivalent to the total sales in the domestic market in the mid-1960s, that it implicitly required any newcomer to do so with the intention of exporting a very large share of its output. The policy failed to attract new entrants. In fact, it was widely interpreted as having had both the intent and the effect of further protecting existing producers from additional competition. As early as 1966, market analysts dissatisfied with the existing rules were explicitly proposing that, instead of setting a minimum production target, "why not set a minimum of exports and allow car manufacturers to set up freely?" (García Ruiz, 2003, p. 47). Although no policy changes took place, some government officials became convinced of the need to change the rules if the car industry was to succeed. Among those that became convinced of the need for change was José María López de Letona, an engineer who had been involved in the national development plans and who was appointed as Minister of Industry in 1969.

Then in early 1970, the ongoing negotiations between Spain and the European Economic Community for a preferential trade agreement reached a satisfactory conclusion. The prospect of producing cars in Spain for exporting to the rest of Europe was now much more realistic. The agreement not only increased certainty about the regulatory framework, but it also provided tariffs to decrease significantly to 3.3 percent for car exports from Spain to the EEC by 1974. López de Letona thought the timing was opportune to offer foreign car manufacturers the possibility of reducing local content rules in exchange for them setting up a large factory that would be aimed mainly at exporting.

Ford, which had been looking to expand its production in Europe, was interested.[11] Negotiations started in earnest in early 1972, and by the end of that year the Spanish government had already passed the new legislation that would set in motion the greenfield investment of Ford in Spain. The new rules, which became popularly known as the "Ford Decrees," reduced the requirement of local content from 90 to 50 percent for new investments that met both a minimum amount of investment and that would export at least two-thirds of their new output. In exchange for the lower national content requirement, these new producers would only be allowed to collectively sell domestically the equivalent of 10 percent of the units sold in national market the previous year. In early 1973, Ford acquired a site in Valencia, and by 1976 the factory was in production. Two years later, it was producing over a quarter million cars, of which more than three-quarters was exported.

The new regulatory framework has typically been criticized as being overly favorable to Ford. The fact that the local content requirements were lowered, together with generous support in terms for land purchases and other entice-ments to attract Ford, have often been judged as unnecessarily advantageous to the multinational company. Some critics go as far as arguing that the Spanish gov-ernment "gave up on all its industrial policy and regional development objectives which could have attained" (Pérez Sancho, 2003, p. 161). This seems to miss the mark in terms of the achievements of the new policy. The 1972 so-called Ford Decrees were in fact a boost to contestability and productivity growth. They could hardly be considered a first-best policy, but if a legitimate role for industrial pol-icy is to speed up the process of structural transformation, then it is hard to see them as anything but successful. Exports of cars would more than quadruple from 1975 to 1980, exceeding $2.2 billion in the latter year (see Figure 7.4 above).

The Ford Decrees stand out for how incentive-compatible they proved to be. They had four strengths. First, the requirement for two-thirds of exports was time consistent because the domestic market would not be able to absorb the entire production of the new factory. The minimum requirement of new investment, equivalent to over $150 million, implied that the new factory could only be viable by serving the export market. And once Ford made a large investment in the fac-tory, it would have something to lose if it were to renege on its production plans. Second, they helped drive productivity increases among local parts producers because the exported cars still had to incorporate at least 50 percent of local con-tent. Lack of competitive suppliers would drag down the ability of the cars to profitably sell in the foreign markets.

A third strength of the Ford Decrees was the existence of a built-in incentive to nudge foreign investors into committing to the project because the cap at 10 percent

---

[11] Perhaps inevitably, both Ford and López de Letona would later claim that the first contact came from their side (García Ruiz, 2018, pp. 38–9).

of the market that collectively the new producers could sell domestically created a first mover advantage. The first factory could snap up to a 10 percent market share of the Spanish market, competing simply against the existing producers. The economics would be very different for a second firm that would have to compete for a share of that 10 percent of the market. Minister López de Letona knew this, and perhaps to keep up the pace of the negotiations with Ford, he let it be known publicly that other manufacturers were interested, naming General Motors and Peugeot as those who had made inquiries with the authorities in early 1973.[12]

As the moniker "Ford Decrees" suggests, much of the criticism leveled at the new rules stemmed from the view that this was an exercise of picking winners that unleveled the playing field. Ford certainly negotiated with the government and ended up benefiting from the regulations put in place. But the legislation was broad enough that others could have taken advantage of it; this was no private law. More importantly, this criticism ignores the important role that public–private coordination plays in the design of effective industrial policies. As country experiences from East Asia suggest, because much of the information relevant to policymaking is held by firms, a close coordination between the public and private sectors is needed (Page and Tarp, 2017).

A fourth advantage of the entrance of Ford in the market was the increased competition in the domestic market. This not only benefited consumers but also provided a direct competitor to the state-owned enterprise SEAT. The latter would in the end not be able to withstand the challenge and went on to incur substantial losses before it was sold in the mid-1980s. The hope may have been that increased competition would spur SEAT into shape. This was not to be the case. But, to the credit of policymakers in the late 1970s, the efforts to increase contestability in the industry were not reversed. On the contrary, they were strengthened. In 1979, the local content rules were reduced to 60 percent for all firms in the industry, prompting in short order new investments, including one by General Motors even larger than that of Ford and which in a few years would be exporting over three-quarters of its production. In an industry that worldwide was going through much technological change and a shift towards just-in-time production, the capabilities of local suppliers, spurred by the dynamism of a growing industry, became an additional competitive advantage to relatively cheap labor.

The example of the car industry is not representative of all industrial policy in the country. The evolution of iron and steel, electricity, or coal were different (Fraile, 1999). But the policy on the car industry is important to understand that, even if not across all sectors, the increase in contestability was a significant part of the practice of industrial policy. And, of course, this was not a marginal sector.

---

[12] Interview with ABC on January 18, 1973.

The car industry was large, not only in terms of exports and employment but also in terms of its role within the public sector. At the beginning of the 1980s, the state-owned enterprise with the highest number of employees was SEAT, which had over 28,000 or 30 percent of the entire workforce of state-owned enterprises. And SEAT accounted for the largest losses among state-owned enterprises (over a quarter of all losses by state-owned enterprises, Fraile, 1999, p. 248). The losses of SEAT were the result of a failure to adapt quickly enough on the face of the competition that was brought into the car industry. As such, they can be seen as evidence of a failed policy of keeping a national champion alive for too long. But, given that those losses were the result of an increased competition brought in by design, they are also evidence of the role of contestability writ large.

From vicious to virtuous circles

The success of the Ford plant in Spain would not have been possible without an adequate port from which to serve the export market. Fortunately, by the time the first Ford *Fiesta* would roll out of the Valencia factory in 1976, Spanish ports had been undergoing sustained improvements in both infrastructure and management for over a decade. A December 1963 law increased the autonomy of port authorities and a new Port Development Plan for 1964–7 set out a range of measures aimed at improving port finances, administration, and operations. Valencia's port was in fact one of almost two dozen port facilities that received some equipment financed under a $40 million loan of the World Bank signed in 1965.

The World Bank project, however, was not remarkable because of the cranes and other equipment that it financed but because of the policies it underpinned. For the World Bank loan to be declared effective, a new Ports Finances Law had to be approved by the end of January 1966. At the meeting of the Board of Executive Directors that discussed the loan, World Bank staff emphasized that the project was really about the organization and policies of port finances and management. To underscore the point, the staff noted that during the negotiations they had spent only "six hours in going through the Loan Agreement, and over 30 hours in discussing and agreeing on the associated reforms, which we felt were such an important part of this project as a whole."[13]

Just as it had done in its previous two loans, for roads and railways respectively, the World Bank was aiming at a sector where not only new investments, but also broader policy changes were needed. The issues had been diagnosed with some precision in its report on an economic mission to Spain (World Bank, 1963). In the case of ports, the World Bank mission had been concerned, above all, with

---

[13]   Transcript of meeting of the Executive Directors, World Bank, September 23, 1965.

financial losses from operations. It had also noted an imbalance among the elements of port capacity, with an emphasis on infrastructure over better equipment which resulted in many of the ports not being used to capacity. The remedies proposed had been greater decentralization of management, an end to the subsidies implicit in the lower rates charged to state-owned enterprises, and, more broadly, a new rate-setting regime that would put the ports on a better financial footing. Only then could one expect a stable flow of funds for port improvements.

On schedule, the new Ports Finances Law was enacted on January 28, 1966. The law was an important shift in the management of ports. It would now be up to the individual port authorities to propose new tariffs, with the explicit goal of covering operating costs, depreciation, as well as setting aside funds for emergency repairs and new investments. In addition, the new law ruled out the possibility of granting preferential rates to state-owned enterprises. Both were significant changes that had clear short-term losers from the reform, even if in the long run the changes were expected to lead to widespread benefits. It was precisely the type of reforms that the World Bank had been advocating. I am not arguing, however, that the policy reforms were imposed through conditionality on a reluctant Spanish government. The $40 million loan gave little leverage to the Bank given the healthy balance of payments of Spain at the time. But the timing of the enactment of the Ports Finances Law, just three days shy of the deadline set by the World Bank loan agreement, suggests that the World Bank may have helpfully nudged the process along.

Spurred by both greater demand and autonomy, new investments in port facilities took place. Crucially, these investments aimed at attracting the fastest growing segments of business, like container traffic. Valencia's port was no exception, with a series of investments starting in 1969. By the time Ford set up its factory, port facilities were greatly improved. Most remarkable of all was the emergence of new ports in what had traditionally been a very stable market. Bilbao, which had been the busiest port in Spain from 1880 to 1950, lost its position by 1970. Ports like Algeciras—located at the crossing from the Atlantic to the Mediterranean— emerged with great dynamism. Algeciras had ranked only twentieth among Spanish ports in 1950, handling only 2 percent of the volume of Bilbao. By 1970, Algeciras was the fifth busiest port in Spain, handling about three-quarters of Bilbao's volume. The volume of Algeciras would then take another leap after it premiered a container terminal in 1975. But the increased competition was in fact a source of productivity increases all around. The port of Bilbao, for example, continued to adapt, stepping up to the challenge of increasing its productivity to remain competitive and endured among the top five ports in Spain (Castillo and Valdaliso, 2017).

Changes in the shipping industry were not only limited to ports. In 1963, shipping rates were liberalized, helping further dynamize the whole industry. The number of shipping companies increased substantially, from 237 in 1950 to 405 in 1970. Importantly, the share of the tonnage handled by the five largest shippers dropped from over half to less than a third during the same period (Pastor, 1981, pp. 456, 519). This suggests that there was indeed competition for business. There was not only firm creation but also churning, which the literature over the last decade or so has increasingly identified as a necessary feature for productivity growth (Decker et al., 2014). The number of shipping firms peaked at 450 in 1965, thus at least 10 percent of firms dropped out of the market from 1965 to 1970, suggesting that exits from the marketplace took place at a fast clip. Of course, churning has no social value per se and there is no guarantee that newcomers push productivity up. Avoiding unproductive churning depends not only on removing distortions as a barrier to productivity growth but also on the capabilities of firms to adopt technologies that yield higher returns, to upgrade quality, and to identify new business opportunities that expand demand (Cusolito and Maloney, 2018). For that, the quality of entrepreneurs is critical.

Of politicians and entrepreneurs

As tourism grew in economic importance, well beyond its role as a temporary windfall that the technocrats anticipated, in 1962 Franco decided to replace his Minister of Information and Tourism. He appointed Manuel Fraga, a brilliant political scientist who had risen to prominence as the technical secretary-general of the Ministry of Education during the late 1950s. Outward-oriented like the technocrats, Fraga would nevertheless clash repeatedly with them because he had a much more political interpretation of what a ministerial job entailed. For Fraga, competence and good administration were not enough. He quickly became his own man, effectively creating a new faction within the cabinet which advocated for mild political reform to help update the regime. Appointed as minister at only 39 years of age, Fraga belonged to a new generation which had not fought in the Civil War and was widely regarded as having bigger political ambitious.[14]

Upon becoming minister, Fraga took it upon himself to advocate for any proposal that would seemingly advance the cause of tourism. Unfortunately, many initiatives lacked a sound economic reasoning. He quickly resuscitated the idea of creating a state-owned enterprise for tourism. The idea had been defeated at the cabinet twice before, in 1957 and earlier in 1962, but Fraga deployed all his political *savoir faire* to push for the National Enterprise of Tourism (ENTURSA). Fraga put forward to Luis Carrero Blanco, Franco's right hand and an extremely religious and nationalistic man, the argument that the new state-owned enterprise

---

[14] His focus on the future evolution of the regime started early; at the end of 1963 he would write in his diary that while "things are not going poorly, the imminent problem is Franco's age, a subject that no one wants to seriously discuss" (Fraga, 1980, p. 97).

could help develop the Pilgrim's Way to Santiago as well as "areas of political interest" like the surroundings of Gibraltar and Ceuta, one of the Spanish enclaves in North Africa. Even the head of INI privately admitted that such projects would incur heavy losses (Pack, 2006, p. 116). But Fraga got his way.

Once created, ENTURSA did some damage. In anticipation of a resort that ENTURSA was planning in the southern province of Almería, the government built an airport there. By the time the airport was completed, not a single flight had been scheduled to land. Near Gibraltar, a hotel school was built. It had political value to Fraga; when visiting he would give "a speech that was more political than focused on tourism, making it clear that the claim over Gibraltar would never be given up," as he himself noted in his memoirs (Fraga, 1980, p. 212). There were other initiatives too. The Ministry of Information and Tourism advocated to cut taxes on hotels and put forward a bill of Centers and Zones of National Tourist Interest, which would have submitted major resort areas under the control of the central government. Both faced stiff opposition within the cabinet.

The technocrats in the cabinet were against tax exemptions and thought that the move to centralize control over land use decisions was impractical. The irony was that those pushing for slightly more open political institutions were at odds with those technocrats pushing for more open economic institutions. In the end, the proposed tax exemption was rejected and the law of Centers and Zones of National Tourist Interest was enacted in a much watered-down form (Pack, 2007, p. 57). Importantly, differences of opinion about tourism regulation were symptomatic of broader divisions within the government. These were clear to any observers that dealt with Spanish policymakers, like the staff of international organizations. The diversity of views within the government was put in particularly vivid terms by the World Bank's special representative in Europe, which upon returning from a mission to Madrid, would report back to headquarters as follows: "In no democracy would one find such open splits between ministers or such criticism of ministers by civil servants."[15] But these conflicts often served the government well, helping it to avoid costly mistakes.

Because the law of Centers and Zones of National Tourist Interest barely limited the power of land developers, it resulted in much local variation on the extent to which building codes and other protections were enforced. But it would also lead, for better or worse, to experimentation. Under a centralized management of land use for touristic purposes, it is unlikely that a bottom-up success like that of Benidorm that we saw in the previous chapter could have occurred. Benidorm's many innovations were as much the result of the entrepreneurial spirit of a

---

[15] John Duncan Miller to S. R. Cope, Director of Operations for Europe, Africa, and Australasia, World Bank, Paris, January 25, 1960 (World Bank Archive, 1740826 Spain, General Negotiations, Volume 1).

small-town mayor as they were of an institutional set up in which the center of government could not block them. This is not to say that the institutional framework was particularly enlightened. Corrupt practices at the local level were common. Benidorm itself, with its many detractors of its architecture and approach to mass tourism, is the poster child of excesses. But regardless of where one stands on the appreciation of Benidorm, it cannot be denied that its success relied on a decentralized contest of ideas.

Perhaps even more important was that, fortunately, Almería's empty airport was the exception. It was not the case that tourism received no attention. On the contrary, in 1965 over half of roadway funds were allocated for Mediterranean provinces (Pack, 2006, p. 132). But the central government by and large avoided large mistakes. First, except for the relatively small state enterprise discussed above, it largely refrained from being an active player in the actual marketplace. Second, in the way it picked investments it was following market signals. The month after the airport in Alicante—that served Benidorm—opened in 1967, it already boasted 160 charter flights scheduled. The airport in Gerona was equally successful, as were runway expansions in Málaga, Mallorca, and Ibiza, which in all cases were investments undertaken after bottlenecks due to excess demand had become clear. Similarly, a toll highway along the Mediterranean coast helped both develop areas of high potential for tourism while limiting public outlays.

Tourism created a host of companies that quickly became competitive first in the national market and then globally. The tourist company Barceló, which opened its first hotel in Mallorca in 1962, later opened a property in Benidorm in 1970. Over time, like many other tourist companies, Barceló would turn to the international market. In 1981, it purchased Turavia, one of the Northern European tour operators that had initially helped put Benidorm on the map, and shortly thereafter it opened its first overseas hotel in the Dominican Republic. The success of hotels also helped other firms in their international expansion. A construction firm created in 1968, Ecisa, would over time leverage its experience building hotels in Benidorm into building skyscrapers and public infrastructure in Europe and the Middle East. And when the firm Riu hotels bought an undeveloped land in the Dominican Republic, it drew on a Mallorca-based company that had started wiring its hotels in Mallorca to build the infrastructure needed in the new Caribbean hotel, including power generation.

Several Spanish construction firms that would later become global players had a start during the couple of decades after 1950. An engineer in his thirties, Rafael del Pino, traveled around Europe in the early 1950s to observe how railroads were built in other countries. Del Pino bought the necessary machinery in Germany and set out to repair railroad tracks back home under the corporate name Ferrovial. The company would soon expand into other countries and eventually into sectors such as water treatment plants, highways, and airports, the latter being one of its better-known businesses because of its high-profile purchase of

British airports. Many other construction Spanish companies had been successful in expanding overseas in this period, even in the most competitive of marketplaces. As an illustration, by the early 1980s, the construction firm Entrecanales worked as a subcontractor on the restoration of New York's Statue of Liberty.

Like Ferrovial and numerous other construction firms, Entrecanales was also founded by an engineer. This is not all that surprising given the positive correlation between engineering density and subsequent technological adoption across countries. Engineers may be more likely to have the capabilities required to identify technological opportunities, and Spain had a higher number of engineers as a share of its population than Portugal or Latin American countries (Maloney and Valencia, 2017). This is no small matter because differences in the rate and intensity of adoption of new technologies have been found to be a large explanatory factor behind income differences across countries in the long run (Comin and Hobijn, 2010). But having more engineers provides only the potential for such technological catching up. Much can get in the way and prevent it from happening, as shown by the fact that Spain already had a relatively good engineering density in 1900, but it did not help the country launch its catching up in incomes for another half century.

Importantly, the successful cases of firms from the tourism and construction industries are not isolated ones. They illustrate the growing ability to adapt foreign ideas and techniques to local needs which, as business historian Núria Puig notes, became "the biggest strength" of Spanish multinationals (Puig, 2008, p. 352). This is a particularly relevant finding because a new wave of productivity analyses has emphasized the role of entrepreneurs—and their specific human capital and psychological traits—in identifying new products, techniques, or markets. For these opportunities to materialize requires individuals that are open to ideas, can evaluate and manage risk, and are driven to achieve results, adjusting and learning in the process (Cusolito and Maloney, 2018). And it is precisely the ability to identify and capitalize on opportunities that business historians have emphasized as a distinctive feature of the period: "[B]y 1986 many Spanish businesspeople and institutions had already learned to deal with change and to look for and seize investment opportunities both inside and outside the country: this is the very nature of entrepreneurship" (Puig and Alvaro, 2016, p. 31). Entrepreneurs alone, however, are not enough. An economically open access regime, or at least opening in some respects, were also necessary for the successes discussed above to materialize.

Conclusions

Juan March died in March 1962, just as the country set out on an unlikely journey of sustained productivity and economic growth that would propel it into high-income status in about a decade and a half. But the rent-seeking and extractive institutions that had made Juan March a fortune did not die with him. Therein lies a puzzle to which the literature has paid insufficient attention. If high growth follows good institutions, what is one to make of the Spanish economic takeoff during the 1960s? The traditional answer to this question is that Spain's economy grew *despite* its extractive institutions, propelled by the favorable conditions created by growth in the wider European economy. Spain could have grown even faster, the argument goes, if it had not been for its policies and regulations. Case closed it would seem.

But several pieces of evidence point to a different answer. To begin with, both output and productivity growth were at the top of the worldwide distribution. More importantly, they were sustained over a relatively long time, suggesting that the ongoing structural transformation of the economy was profound. It is possible that this could have happened without a meaningful change in economic institutions, but it is unlikely. Indicators that measure the quality of institutions over the long term are hard to find, but evidence from the historical index of economic liberty, compiled by Leandro Prados de la Escosura, confirms that economic institutions were far from frozen during the quarter-century after 1950. Not only was there a relatively steady increase in openness, as we discussed in the previous chapter, but this was closely linked to the rise in productivity. The adoption of foreign technology brought by large inflows of foreign investors attracted to the large, and protected, domestic market was a key factor in explaining this productivity growth. The increase in productivity was thus helped by public policies which aimed at openness with industrialization, much as in the case of Asia (Nayyar, 2019).

The critical role played by the evolution in policies can be seen in some of the most dynamic economic activities of the period, like car manufacturing. Initially dominated by a state-owned enterprise, with entry curtailed to a few politically connected players, price controls, and a highly protected domestic market, the exporting success of the car industry seemed highly unlikely. Over time, however, policy changes that expanded contestability in the industry played a key role in its success. Local content rules were not only imposed but also enforced, itself an example of contestability as defined here. This spurred a vibrant segment of independent car suppliers. Foreign investment helped boost their competitiveness, as did the economies of scale achieved when new foreign manufacturers set up in Spain largely to export to the rest of Europe. The latter were attracted not only by relatively cheap labor but also by rules which balanced incentives: on one hand, access to a slice of the protected domestic market, and, on the other hand, high minimum shares of production that needed to be exported. Local content rules were lowered but were still high enough to continue to help support a growing domestic industry of car suppliers.

An increase in contestability also played a role in explaining the rise of tourism. Entrepreneurs and local innovation played an even more critical role in this sector—which was effectively left unconstrained by the central government in critical aspects like land use. None of these policy measures, like local content rules or minimum export shares in the car industry or a largely decentralized approach to land use in tourist areas, were first best solutions. In the case of tourism, for example, local corruption led to lack of compliance with building codes. There remained plenty of rents and rent-seeking activity, even in the cases that we used to illustrate our argument here. But, in some cases, policy changes helped achieve a greater market discipline. Rents were enhancing the rewards of the market and can be thus thought of as economically productive in the language of the open access order framework that we have been using (North et al., 2013). In short, not all rents are created or managed equally.

In this chapter, we have shown a few selected cases where we saw increases in contestability, including the car industry, tourism, and ports. While these are not niche markets, additional examples from other aspects of economic policy management will be presented in the next chapter to further explore the argument. To readers wishing for more economy-wide analyses, let me show how existing aggregate indicators that speak to the extent of contestability in a given economic activity can mislead us. Take as an example the observed correlation in the Spanish industry of the time between the degree of regulation and the degree of concentration in an industry (Buesa and Pires, 2002, p. 183). Both were extraordinarily high for the car industry throughout this period, but the car industry became the fastest growing and achieved great success in the export market. The same can be said about the rate of protection of the domestic market, very high throughout this period for the car industry. As we have seen, there is even some evidence of regulatory capture, as most of the literature interprets the high minimum requirements for car production during the 1960s to be a measure to protect incumbents.

The case of automobiles is most remarkable because it achieved fast growth and increasing external competitiveness despite many obstacles to increased efficiency in the form of high regulation, high protection, and high concentration. This does not mean that high distortions were necessary for growth. After cars, the industrial sector with the fastest growth was chemicals, which had one of the lowest rates of regulation during the period. But the success of the car industry in overcoming those obstacles usefully highlights that it is the precise management of incentives and rents that we need to pay attention to. Given a closed domestic market, the role that openness to foreign investment played in boosting contestability was paramount. The success of the car industry also provides a practical demonstration of the second-best theory, since many of the distortions that resulted in an allocative inefficiency, such as the high rates of protection or local content rules, were precisely some of the levers used to bring about a greater market discipline and, as a result, increases in competitiveness. In conclusion, it is in the detail of both the design and implementation of policies and in their interaction with existing conditions that variation in results are likely to emerge. And for understanding those, there is no avoiding detailed case studies.

More generally, how Spain was able to infuse doses of contestability while protecting much of its industry is a relevant story that is insufficiently researched and little known. The slow and partial nature of these institutional changes call for a nuanced story. The presence of so many initial distortions also makes the assessment particularly difficult. It is possible that in the presence of existing distortions, unorthodox mechanisms can lead to positive results, as the theory of the second-best suggests. This is of course an argument on which many disastrous policies often rest. Yet, assessing general equilibrium effects of policies, which in effect is what is called for here, is a particularly challenging task. And this is not the only aspect that complicates the analysis. As we will also see in greater detail in the next chapter, sometimes the increase in market contestability was the unintended consequence of policies that did not explicitly set out to do so. Still, the evidence presented should at the very least prompt us to consider that greater contestability is a hallmark of the transformation from the Spain of Juan March to that of Amancio Ortega.

PART III
TURNING GROWTH TO DEVELOPMENT

8

Policy Tinkering

If the increase in contestability played a role in Spain's economic takeoff, as argued in the previous chapter, how do we reconcile it with the fact that much of the economy remained tightly controlled? Addressing this question is important because most analysts see the booming 1960s as a period not only lacking in reforms but as a retreat from liberal economic policies. In the conventional wisdom, the impetus for reform disappeared as soon as the crisis that is considered to be behind the 1959 Stabilization Plan subsided. The instant appeal of that interpretation is that it neatly explains both the reforms at the end of the 1950s and the alleged backtracking. Although when this view was first put forward it was openly so as a hypothesis not yet fully backed by evidence (González, 1979 and 1989), it has since become commonly accepted.[1]

Based on new evidence, however, there is much to be revised in the conventional interpretation of the political economy of the takeoff. To begin with, the adoption of reforms in the late 1950s requires a more nuanced explanation. Instead of being the consequence of economic *instability*, the adoption of reforms in the late 1950s can be better explained as the consequence of political *stability*. As the Franco regime became increasingly secure in power, it increased the time horizon of the regime and brought a new breed of technocrats into office. Those technocrats brought with them a different conception of economic policymaking, and that is what led to the reforms eventually adopted. To the extent that the crisis helped bring about the reforms, it was as a rhetorical tool, as the evidence presented in Chapter 5 shows.

As for the evidence that points to a backtracking in the freeing up of the economy in the 1960s, the picture is mixed. There was no backtracking of reforms allowing freer foreign investment. On the contrary, access to the Spanish market by foreign firms became easier over time. This proved to be crucial in bringing about more contestability. At the same time, there is evidence of capture of policymaking by private interests. One area where this has been quantitatively documented is trade policy. The best evidence in support of the capture hypothesis is the differential rates of protection, with higher rates being obtained by those closest to the policymaking (Tortella, 1994, p. 372). And in some cases, all clues point to an increasing capture by private interests as the 1960s went on. This includes

---

[1] One of the most widely used textbooks of Spanish economic history notes that "the liberalization started in 1959 was only partial, and during the 1960s there were perhaps more steps backwards than forwards in this regard" (Tortella, 1994, p. 387).

Unexpected Prosperity: How Spain Escaped the Middle Income Trap. Oscar Calvo-Gonzalez, Oxford University Press.
© Oscar Calvo-Gonzalez 2021. DOI: 10.1093/oso/9780198853978.003.0009

an increasingly revolving door between the private and the public sector, for example, former executives of steel companies would come to occupy the public offices in charge of regulating the sector (Fraile, 1999). Such capture, the argument goes, exacerbated the inefficiencies in the economy.

The case of the steel industry is illustrative of those inefficiencies. Unlike in other industries, foreign influence did not lead to large increases in productivity or competitiveness in steelmaking. US Steel took a 25 percent ownership in the industry leader, as well as a smaller stake in a new venture near Valencia. But the results were disastrous, especially after the crisis of the 1970s left an inefficient industry with excess supply of insufficient quality. In what proved to be an unsuccessful effort at safeguarding jobs, from the mid-1970s, the state took over all steel producers and absorbed losses for a decade and a half. Only after much public investment, closures of facilities, and layoffs was the restructured steel industry privatized and sustainable.

But the damage done was contained. For example, the inefficient steelmaking did not bring down the car industry with it. Ford had initially considered access to the output of the new steel plant near Valencia to be a plus. But, when the time came, the quality of steel produced was so poor that at some point it rejected 70 percent of the panels being delivered. Ford stopped buying steel panels locally and shifted to foreign suppliers.[2] By law, Ford had to buy a certain amount of local content, but crucially, it was up to the firm to decide what type of inputs it would purchase locally. By the mid-1970s, there were plenty of competitive local suppliers of other inputs, so Ford did not have to buy from the oligopolistic and inefficient domestic steel industry, no matter how politically well-connected steel executives were.[3] The question we will explore in this chapter is: How do we make sense of all this ambiguous institutional development during this critical period of fast and sustained economic growth?

A new view

My argument is not that *all* policies since 1960 continued marching towards greater liberalization. As we discussed in the previous chapter, the increase in contestability was, even if important, at the margins. And a simplistic dichotomy that sees reforms as either liberalizing or interventionist is too crude of a distinction, as it ignores the interaction with other existing policies or market structure. The regulation of the car industry was no less interventionist than that of the steel industry. But in one case, a highly interventionist stance led to an increase in

---

[2] Ford's problems with the local steel supplier are reported in a story on "The Spanish Way of Business: A Tale of 3 Companies" in the April 16, 1978 edition of *The New York Times*.

[3] The history of the steel plant near Valencia has been analyzed by Díaz Morlán et al. (2008), who argue that one of the main problems had little to do with capture: The forecasts for steel demand made when the plant was planned in 1966 proved not to materialize after the 1973 shock.

productivity and competitiveness, while it did not in the other case. The different performance cannot be accounted for by indicators like the degree of protection, the concentration of the industry, or the extent of government regulation. My argument is that some policies, including some interventionist ones like the policy for the car industry, were able to help bring about productivity gains and greater competitiveness at the margins. What truly matters is the *how* of industrial policies, as the well-known case of East Asia shows (Page and Tarp, 2017).

Besides the urge to classify policies along a simplistic interventionist–liberal dimension, our understanding of the policy landscape in Spain is also hampered by a tendency to discount heavily all but the most ambitious of reforms. Compared to the significant reforms undertaken in 1959, the policy changes in the following decade rightly appear to be minor. But public sector reforms are more complicated than macroeconomic stabilization efforts because it is not always obvious what the right policies may be (Khemani, 2020). With that in mind, an incrementalistic approach may help adapt solutions to the local context and avoid big mistakes. In fact, the mimicking of "best practice" institutional forms frequently fails, and sometimes the alleged solutions are in fact part of the problem (Andrews et al., 2017). All these cautionary voices call for a more granular analysis of how economic policies are not only designed but also implemented in practice.[4]

Economists Dani Rodrik and Murat Iyigun make a most useful distinction between institutional reforms and what they call policy tinkering. The difference between institutional reforms and policy tinkering is not an assessment of the level of ambition of a policy change.[5] Rather, the insight in Iyigun and Rodrik (2006) is to zero in on the extent to which a policy change operates neutrally, or not, between existing and new firms. Switching from one trade regime to another, for example from import substitution to export orientation, is not neutral in the sense that incumbents and new firms face sharply different consequences. Incumbents, which have an existing plant and cost structure predicated on the previous trade regime, face an adjustment cost. New entrants geared towards the export market do not. This is what Rodrik and Iyigun label a reform. In contrast, there are policy changes that do not have such a clearly different impact between existing and new firms. Take changes in taxation, which typically affect equally both incumbent and new firms. Institutional reforms create costs on incumbents but can also induce greater cost discovery. And the precise opposite is true of policy tinkering. Thus, whether reforms or tinkering would lead to better outcomes depends on the specific conditions in a country, a point to which we will return later.

I will argue here that the booming decade and a half after 1959 is best described as a period of policy tinkering. Take the case of FDI which we reviewed in

---

[4] Another voice to the chorus also comes from the rise of behavioral economics, which has shown that small changes in the choice architecture can have large effects on our behavior. That insight has yet to be fully incorporated into most analysis of public policies, and certainly to economic history.

[5] In their formal definition, an institutional reform is a draw from a new policy regime, while policy tinkering involves a new draw from an existing policy regime (Iyigun and Rodrik, 2006).

Chapter 6. Relaxing the constraints on foreign ownership, the changes were largely neutral between existing and new firms. Incumbents as much as new entrants could benefit from foreign partners bringing in technology and new management practices. And the fact that most sectors of the economy were similarly open to foreign investment further supported the neutrality of this policy change. Both exporters as well as firms focused on the domestic market benefited from the influx of foreign technology. Foreign investment indeed took hold in a diverse set of sectors and forms, from greenfield investment to strategic alliances, which had significant long-term benefits in terms of the transfer of know-how and tacit knowledge (Puig and Álvaro, 2016).

Policy tinkering also captures well the evolving regulation of the car industry, which we reviewed in the previous chapter. When requirements for local content became generalized, both existing and new firms were equally affected. It is true that the decrees passed to attract Ford lowered local content requirements only for new entrants—a case where incumbents and new firms face different costs. But much in the spirit of tinkering, the same decrees limited the market share for which the new entrants could compete to only 10 percent of the domestic market. Importantly, as we will see in the rest of the chapter, the example of FDI and the car industry were not isolated cases. What follows will be largely devoted to providing other examples of how this policy tinkering took place and, in some cases, contributed to positive development results through increased openness and contestability.

Tinkering, with results

One thing is to argue that tinkering was the dominant form of policy changes and another to suggest that such tinkering contributed positively for development. For the argument that tinkering mattered, it is important to see how it played out not only in the successful cases reviewed thus far but in a broader range of areas. But where to look for potential examples of such policy tinkering? In doing so, I will look into policy areas which have traditionally been regarded as unreformed to see if, even in those areas, we can detect some policy changes that may not qualify as reforms but can rise to the level of what we have described as policy tinkering. In this effort, I am guided by economic historians Leandro Prados de la Escosura and Blanca Sánchez-Alonso, who in their assessment of this period, conclude that the "lack of structural reforms affecting the tax system and labour and financial markets were the main shortcomings of economic policy during the 1960s" (2019, p. 24). In addition, I will also discuss key government functions such as public recruitment and procurement. Let us then first turn to exploring policy tinkering in the tax system, as it is particularly relevant to understand the Spanish experience of *how* development actually happened in a second-best world without sound institutions or significant reforms.

Increasing public revenues without tax reform

Limited progress in reforming the tax system is something that characterized not only the 1960s but pretty much every other decade before. Reliant on indirect taxes and fees, the public revenue system was inefficient, inequitable, and insufficient. This had been so for more than a century before 1950. In an average year, the Spanish state collected revenues amounting to only 10 percent of GDP (Figure 8.1). A reform of the system would not take place until 1977, when a modern personal income tax was introduced. The 1977 reform left no major tax untouched, modernizing the corporate income tax and introducing a value-added tax and a net personal wealth tax. It was part of a broader political agreement, the *Moncloa Pacts*, which was reached in the most critical of both economic and political circumstances. The country was then suffering from runaway inflation and soaring unemployment while transitioning from a dictatorship to a democracy. The results of the 1977 tax reform were remarkable. The tax-to-GDP ratio, which had been around 13 percent in the late 1970s, steadily climbed, roughly doubling over the next decade. Spain had achieved, if not full, significant convergence with the tax systems of other Western European countries.[6]

But focusing on how Spain's tax revenues compare with the levels seen elsewhere in Europe overlooks a critical question. To understand the takeoff in growth in Spain, it is more relevant to assess not if the country had a lower tax intake than the most advanced nations but if it was raising enough revenue to spur growth. Arguably, there is a minimum tax-to-GDP ratio that is linked with faster

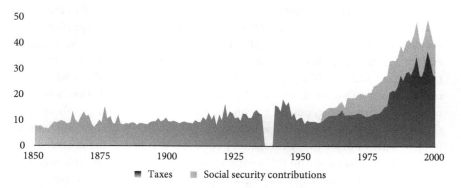

Figure 8.1   Spain's general government revenue, 1850–2000

Note: General government data is notoriously difficult to assemble over such a long period given changes in budget classifications and coverage of the available data. This indicator is therefore best interpreted as a proxy for general government revenues.

Source: Comín and Díaz (2005) and Carreras et al. (2005).

---

[6] While most of the literature on the 1977 tax reform is in Spanish, there are some outstanding contributions in English collected by Martínez-Vázquez and Sanz-Sanz (2007).

economic development because there is a minimum set of public goods the state needs to create an enabling environment. And such a tipping point is likely far below the ratios observed in Western Europe; in fact, a recent estimate puts it at between 12.5 and 13 percent of GDP (Gaspar et al., 2016a). Countries that cross that threshold tend to have a higher GDP per capita. The effect is economically significant: Crossing the threshold is associated with a per capita GDP that is 7.5 percent higher a decade later. Thus, benchmarking against the more advanced Western European countries is relevant but ignores the question of when Spain may have crossed such a tipping point. Spain hovered around this threshold on tax revenues to GDP since the mid-1960s, crossing it irreversibly from 1979 onwards.[7]

The success of the 1977 tax reform has rightly attracted much attention. But a close look at Figure 8.1 also reveals a previous development regarding public revenues, namely the introduction of social security contributions. Even though tax revenues did not increase as a share of GDP until the 1980s, total public revenues saw a steep growth starting in the 1960s thanks to a rapid rise in social security contributions. Indeed, the state was able to increase public revenues from 11 percent of GDP in 1950 to 21 percent of GDP in 1975. The latter is still a small figure when compared with the ratios commonly observed in Western European countries, but such comparisons should not make us lose sight of how significant the change at the time was.

What stands out is how social security contributions allowed for an increase in public revenues that started even before a modern reform of the tax system. Revenue from social security contributions doubled to around 6 percent of GDP by the end of the 1960s, doubling again to around 12 percent of GDP in the 1970s. Spain came to rely on social security contributions at a very early stage (González-Páramo and Hernández de Cos, 2007). At the end of the 1970s, the revenues collected from social security contributions were almost the same as those from tax revenues, 12.2 and 12.8 percent of GDP, respectively. After 1980, social security contributions stabilized at around 12 percent of GDP, lower only than a handful of Western European countries but higher than the OECD average. To see how unusual this pattern was, it is useful to benchmark social security contributions in Spain against those in the comparator countries that had a similar level of per capita GDP as Spain did in 1950—the same as discussed in the Introduction. Spain stands out as having much higher social security contributions both when compared with comparator countries at a given point in time and when we look at the importance of social security contributions recorded at the same level of development (see Figure 8.2).

---

[7] Using data from Comín and Díaz (2005). Gaspar et al. (2016b) select Spain as one of the case studies of sharp increases in the tax-to-GDP ratio and date the crossing of the tipping point in 1982.

(a) At same point in time (1990)   (b) At similar level of per capita GDP

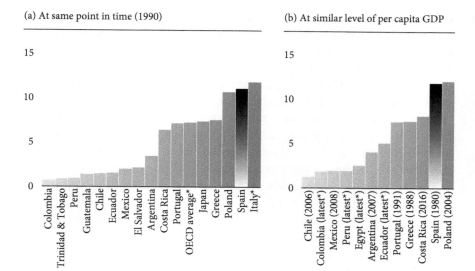

Figure 8.2   Benchmarking social security contributions in Spain vs. comparators

Notes: Social security contributions as percent of GDP. In panel (a) both the OECD average and the value for Italy, even though not in the list of comparator countries set in the Introduction, are included to provide greater context to the level of social security contributions reached in Spain. In panel (b) those countries that note "latest" as the year are comparator economies that have yet to reach the real per capita GDP of Spain in 1980 but are relatively close and therefore the comparison, while imperfect, is still informative.

Source: Own elaboration using OECD Global Revenue Statistics Database, Penn World Table 9.1, and Comín and Díaz (2005).

Social security contributions are distinct from tax revenues in that their purpose is typically earmarked to specific types of social spending. In some cases, such as contributory pensions, they may be best thought of as forced savings and the payment of benefits as deferred income. But in a pay-as-you-go system as introduced in Spain in the 1960s, the conceptual difference between tax revenues and social security contributions is much reduced. The system of social security introduced in Spain covered a broad range of benefits beyond contributory old age pensions that included healthcare, unemployment and disability insurance, and survivor pensions. Thus, much of the expenditure out of the social security contributions was more akin to transfers than to deferred income.[8]

Were social security contributions almost like taxes? The nature of the expenditure out of the social security contributions is important to assess the role they played in the economy. The literature on the links between fiscal capacity and development has argued that non-tax revenues can have a different effect on

---

[8] Treating social security contributions as transfers or as deferred income has great consequences for how one sees the incidence of fiscal policy (Lustig, 2018). In practice, however, it is hard to establish this difference with much precision, even in today's data rich world.

development than tax revenues, but the distinction is made because other non-tax revenues, such as aid or natural resource rents, typically do not require the same type of "effort" as taxes do and they can even negatively affect the incentives for the state to invest in fiscal capacity.[9] Those disincentives are not present in the case of social security contributions, further reinforcing the view that, in our case, social security contributions share the characteristics of taxes.

The capacity required to collect social security contributions is not unlike that required to collect taxes, potentially facing the same problems of evasion as taxes do. Social security contributions are applied on broad tax bases and require either voluntary compliance or strict enforcement, or both. It is also the case that social security contributions are typically not as progressive as direct taxes. Imperfect as it may have been, the increase in social security contributions allowed for a sharp rise in public social spending starting in the early 1960s. The increase in social security contributions is in large part what made possible the increase in public social spending without incurring public debt, in sharp contrast with the experience of the set of comparator countries (see panel (b) in Figure 8.3).

The unusually high reliance on social security contributions has implications for how we assess the evolution of fiscal capacity in Spain. Take the finding that the tipping point in the tax-to-GDP ratio was only reached in the early 1980s. If we were to focus on a measure of public revenues that includes both taxes and social security contributions, it is likely that any tipping point would have been reached earlier, possibly as much as a decade earlier. Of course, cross-country estimates of the tipping point would have been higher had the underlying data been not tax but general government revenues. How much higher is hard to tell, since data for general government revenues is simply not available for as long a period or as many countries as tax revenues, but given the outsized role that we have shown that social security contributions played in Spain from an early stage, it is most likely the case that the country would have crossed a "general government revenue tipping point" earlier than it crossed the "tax revenue tipping point." This is relevant because the hypothesis behind the existence of a tipping point is not about tax revenues per se, but rather about the availability of sufficient public revenues with which to fund the essential set of public goods.

Why social security contributions but not taxes?

Undoubtedly, as the existing Spanish literature has highlighted, social spending during the 1960s remained far from the European standards, and the dictatorship

---

[9] Besley and Persson (2013). As these authors put it, the "central question in taxation and development is: how does a government go from raising around 10% of GDP in taxes to raising around 40%?" See also Besley and Persson (2014).

(a) Public social spending in Spain, percent of GDP

(b) Public debt

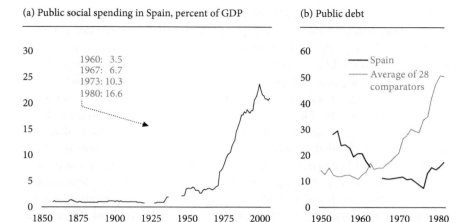

Figure 8.3 The rise of social spending (without increasing public debt)

Note: The 28 comparators are, as discussed in the Introduction, countries that had a similar per capita GDP as Spain in 1950.

Source: Espuelas (2013) and IMF Historical Public Debt Database.

retarded the growth in social spending.[10] But here we were primarily interested in a different question: How did the increases in social spending materialize, even if lagging those seen in Western European countries? Our answer that the initial turning point in social spending was made possible by the introduction of social security contributions is informative, but it prompts another question: How was it possible that social security contributions were successfully introduced when no tax reform was possible? To solve that puzzle, our argument will revolve around three elements. First, we will briefly explain previous failed efforts at reforming the tax system and how they shaped the policy options available at a later stage. Second, we will put the social security reforms of the 1960s in a longer perspective. And, third, we will consider the political economy aspects of changes to social security compared to that of tax reform.

Starting in the early 1950s, there were several efforts to reform the tax system. While these will fail to be enacted, or those that became law did not lead to increases in the tax-to-GDP ratio, the way in which they failed was significant. The tax reform of December 1957 in particular, which we noted in Chapter 5 as an effort at broadening the tax base and raising additional revenues, is worth discussing in some detail because of what it would mean for subsequent policy options.

---

[10] Espuelas (2012, 2017). The dictatorship can be said to have retarded the growth of social spending compared to a counterfactual in which a certain type of democratic government had been in place since 1939. Once social spending starting to grow, however, the pace of growth was fast despite it occurring under a dictatorship.

The 1957 tax reform is typically presented as a clear case of a failed reform. The original intention of increasing the progressivity of taxes was not achieved (Zaratiegui, 2018a, p. 65). And the legislative process was such that special interest groups effectively blocked any increases in taxes (Comín and Vallejo, 2012). The reform is widely seen as a step back from a technical point of view.[11] This is because it introduced a departure in the way taxes were assessed away from actual income to a presumptive income approach. This has often been interpreted as a measure that was out of line with the international best practice. The 1957 reform was based on the idea that instead of trying to establish the true income of a given enterprise, it would be better to determine the tax to be assessed on the basis of the average income of firms in a given industry. The underlying logic was, according to its proponents, based on both on equity and efficiency grounds. The argument for efficiency was that it would reward more productive firms. The case for equity rested on the view that, under existing failed practices, wily entrepreneurs were widely seen as outsmarting or corrupting tax inspectors. The hope was that moving away from individual assessments would reduce discretion and thus increase fairness. Significantly, under the 1957 reform, the overall tax burden was to be apportioned to different sectors of the economy, based on their contribution to national output. And within a given sector of the economy, the reform outsourced the administration of some taxes to the corporatist syndicates to which all firms in a given sector were forced to belong.

The criticism of this being a backward system appears, therefore, more than justified, but it was not without its advantages and even influential international advocates. The efficiency argument for an average income tax had been put forward by the Italian public finance scholar and politician Luigi Einaudi.[12] And the use of presumptive income was in fact quite common at the time. Presumptions based on visible signs of wealth were specified in the income tax laws not only of Spain but also France or Italy, and other middle-income countries were developing not too dissimilar systems. In Israel, beginning in 1954, a set of guidelines (*tachshiv*) using objective factors such as number of employees and other indicators, initially aimed at estimating the income of taxpayers that did not keep adequate accounting books, grew into a common practice, with more than 80 *tachshivim* for different sectors of the economy. In ways that resonate with the reform introduced in Spain, the average profitability of firms in a sector was discussed with representatives of that sector before the *tachsiv* was issued. While the

---

[11] This has been the view of all notable public finance specialists, starting with Enrique Fuentes Quintana and up to today's most distinguished scholar of the history of public finance in Spain, Francisco Comín.

[12] The equity argument was also not unheard of. Edwin Seligman, an early proponent of progressive income taxation in the US, was mindful that "the income tax is perhaps the most difficult to assess with scrupulous justice and accuracy; so that what is conceived in justice often results in crass injustice" (as quoted in Tanzi and Casanegra de Jantscher, 1987, p. 4). While Seligman was writing decades before, the conditions describe the situation in Spain at the time.

Israeli presumptive tax system had clear defects, it was in use until 1975 and imitated elsewhere, including in South Korea.[13]

More importantly, the reform had some positive incentives to surface firms as taxpayers. This was because within each sector the corporatist syndicate had the incentive to spread the total tax burden on as many taxpayers as possible. As an example, for the so-called industrial tax, within a year of the new system being in place, out of the 69,000 firms paying the tax, more than 24,000 had been newly registered since the system of sector global assessments was introduced (Comín and Vallejo, 2012, p. 160). The 1957 tax reform did not increase the tax take, but it successfully led to a greater formalization of firms on tax matters by leveraging a highly imperfect but powerful institution like the corporatist syndicates. It was a policy change that could hardly fit better the definition of policy tinkering used above: As the relative shares of taxes paid by the different sectors were unchanged, no one sector benefited disproportionately from the reform. This may have been in fact one of the keys as to why it was passed in the first place, and one of the lessons that policymakers took to heart when tackling the problem of public revenues in the following years.

The 1957 tax reform and other failed efforts showed clearly the power of corporatist interests. The corporatist syndicates had also been empowered. In that context, there would be little room for maneuver and introduction of new taxes, unless the corporate interests were confident that they could shift the burden of any new taxes. This would help explain why the introduction of social security contributions had a better chance at being enacted. Even the portion of social security contributions that were nominally the responsibility of the firm could be passed on to wages, so that it would be labor that had to bear the burden of raising more public revenues.

And while in retrospect the new system of social security put in place in the 1960s proved to be a turning point in terms of revenue mobilization, at the time of its introduction, it was a consolidation of efforts that had been built up over the previous six decades. The list of measures that aimed to introduced elements of social protection in the first decades of the twentieth century is long: workers' compensation in 1900, the first mandatory retirement pension in law in 1919 and as a constitutional right in 1931, maternity leave insurance in 1923, subsidy for large families in 1926, paid holidays in 1931, medical insurance in 1944, disability insurance in 1947, etc. But all these measures had been introduced in a piecemeal fashion, with multiple regimes and institutions in charge of managing a complex system that still had limited coverage despite the legal mandate of many of those provisions. The lack of coordination undermined their effectiveness (Comín and Díaz, 2005, p. 893). The changes in the 1960s sought to unify the system, though

---

[13] See Tanzi and Casanegra de Jantscher (1987) and Yitzhaki (2007).

it did not achieve that fully at first. The basis for contributions was also initially set below the actual amount of workers remunerations. Like the greater formalization brought about by the 1957 tax reform, such a measure may have actually helped increase the reach in the early stages and eased the process by which, after reforms in 1972 and 1974 that expanded the basis on which contributions were calculated, led to the significant increase in revenues that we discussed above.

The changes observed in the sphere of public revenues in the decade after the 1959 Stabilization Plan cannot be thought of as a major reform but fit well with the label of policy tinkering. Yet despite this lack of reforms, what we have seen is that the changes introduced in the tax system were first able to increase the number of taxpayers, and subsequently raise significantly increased public revenues through the introduction of social security contributions. And we need to remember that we were interested in the evolution of the tax system as a case study of policy tinkering not because we have a priori evidence of significant changes but precisely because the literature suggests that this is an area where reforms were lacking. To round the argument that the fast growth of the 1960s occurred not *despite* bad policies but *because of* policy changes that nudged the economy towards greater contestability, we now turn to how policy tinkering occurred in how the state itself hired staff and purchased goods. We will return to labor and finance towards the end of the chapter.

Building state capabilities

One of the reasons why assessing policy changes after 1960 is particularly challenging is that many of the efforts tried to tackle the core functions of the public administration. In this section we review two of these efforts: how the state recruits and how it procures goods and services. These are policy areas that not only account for substantial expenditures but also affect the building of state capability. Increasing the state's capability to implement public policy has long been recognized as an essential element of the process of economic development. If anything, this emphasis has increased in recent years as it has become apparent that many countries remain trapped in low state capability equilibria (Andrews et al., 2017; Woolcock, 2019).

Public recruitment

Almost 40 percent of all public expenditure in the period that mainly concerns us in this chapter, 1950–75, was spent on wages. It matters, therefore, how much and what type of value these public employees brought to their daily tasks. This makes it more relevant that public personnel policies are incorporated into our story of the takeoff. To do so, the work of political scientist Víctor Lapuente (2006) provides a particularly insightful account of public personnel policies in Spain. Lapuente's starting point is to explore the decision to bureaucratize the public administration in connection to the power of a political regime. Politicians must create incentives for public sector employees to exert effort, but civil servants may not trust politicians to keep their promises and doubt those incentives. Counterintuitively, more powerful regimes need to bureaucratize the public administration more as a way to solve the credible commitment problem (as in North and Weingast, 1989; North, 1993). Bureaucratizing here means delegating the powers to hire, fire, and promote public employees to autonomous bodies, such as corps of functionaries.

Starting in the nineteenth century, Víctor Lapuente tracks the ups and downs of the bureaucratization of the public administration in Spain. Following the example of France, corps of self-managed and self-recruiting administrators were created over time in a process that was crucially related to shifts in the political regimes of the time. The evolution during the Franco regime goes through two starkly different periods. Initially, the Franco regime sharply reduced bureaucratic autonomy. Purges of officials during and immediately after the Civil War were common and civil servants came to be selected purely based on political loyalty to the Franco regime. Ministers relied on discretionary procedures to make all appointments within their departments, including promotions. The result was an inefficient administration staffed with politically loyal but incompetent personnel. Importantly, however, all that would change from the mid-1950s onwards.

As part of a broader reform of the public administration, a 1957 decree on Competitive Examinations standardized requirements such as publication of notices of competitive examinations and, more importantly, gave corps much autonomy in the recruitment of employees. Corps of functionaries started to organize their recruitments, independently controlling conditions such as academic requirements, the periodicity of entrance exams, number of vacancies, and selection committee membership. The result was that the most common form of entry into the civil service after the late 1950s became the open competition controlled by corps. All things considered, the reforms increased the degree of bureaucratic autonomy in six dimensions: selection, tenure, promotions, disciplinary regime, incentives, and working conditions (Lapuente, 2006, p. 220).

The insight of Víctor Lapuente is in interpreting the increase in bureaucratic autonomy as a deliberate effort by the regime to tie its hands and empower the technical corps of civil servants in order to secure greater effort from the latter. It was a second-best solution. Franco had come to terms with the fact that "he could not obtain the maximum level of effort from the Engineers or the Architects of the State, but he knew they would devote at least half of their working day—generally the morning—to build public works" (Lapuente, 2006, p. 218). The pact was quite favorable to the corps, which not only enjoyed autonomy but also gained wide acceptance that their members would work part of the day at private offices. Some corps also enjoyed a form of financial independence because they were able to use fees charge to the public for their services to pay supplements on top of their regular civil servant salaries. While all this was far from ideal, it met the moment, and arguably helped to build state capacity at a critical juncture.[14]

Public procurement

How a government purchases goods and services is both a reflection of how open its economic institutions are and a factor that can contribute or harm growth. Inefficient and nontransparent systems result in rent-seeking and corruption. Fair and efficient public procurement promotes competition while ensuring value for money for scarce public resources. And the importance of public procurement for the development path of an economy stems not only from its large size. As economies develop, the purchase of simple goods and services gives way to more complex capital investment projects.

That transition happened in Spain during the two decades after 1950. The purchase of goods and services accounted for 27 percent of all government expenditures in 1950. In contrast, by 1975 this share had dropped to only 7 percent (Comín and Díaz, 2005, pp. 943, 946). This was because the state shifted its outlays towards both the provision of direct transfers and, especially relevant for our argument here, public investment. In addition to more competent and well-incentivized personnel, the shift towards public investment projects requires public procurement systems that can handle the greater complexity of large public investment projects while ensuring fairness and competition.

This would not have been possible with the procurement practices then in place. Prior to the 1950s, the main method for state purchases was a simple bidding system that only took into account the price bidders offered, without regard to other considerations like quality. Bidding had been regulated in Spain as early as 1852, and despite the introduction of other public procurement methods in 1911, it remained the default method of public procurement. The long inaction on the legal framework for public procurement is by itself revealing of how little the function of the state had changed in all those years.

But starting in the 1950s, the legal framework for public procurement would undergo significant changes. This process has attracted the attention of legal scholars but not so much of economists. For our purposes, most significant is the effort to bring in more flexibility in the way contracts are awarded. In line with a global trend that has continued since, the focus was no longer just on minimizing

---

[14] This is, however, an area where the proverbial "more research is needed" applies, in particular to evidence linking the civil service reform to the improvement in the efficiency of the public administration.

price but on maximizing value for money, although such term was not in use then. In 1953, a new regulation of local authorities' contracting laid out the principles that would later apply more widely, such as a new procurement method that considered technical bids first and then applied competitive bidding only among qualified proposals. In addition, requirements on transparency were part of this regulation, most notably the compulsory publication in the national gazette of contracts above a certain amount. These regulations would later be followed with a law of public contracting in 1963 that set out to replace the exclusive reliance on price. And a registry of technically and financially qualified contractors was established.

But how did this change contribute to greater contestability, and why is this an example of policy tinkering? At first sight, moving away from the automatic decision of contracting the lowest price bidder introduces the potential for more corruption. This is also why the strengthened independence of civil servants was important. Under these conditions, public procurement of large projects was, at times, used as an opportunity to increase openness and contestability. The largest refinery in Spain, built in 1968 near Bilbao, was the result of such a bidding process. The winning bid included Gulf Oil, with a 40 percent stake in the firm that would undertake the refinery, but the four other tenders all included foreign partners. The competition was thus effectively one between five international oil companies to present a proposal that, in line with what was described above, considered not only financial terms but also the technical strength of the proposal. In addition to limiting foreign ownership to 40 percent of the capital, the request for proposals set minimum local content for a range of activities, including construction and engineering services.

But new refineries could have threatened the position of existing ones. Thus, in yet another example of policy tinkering, the same regulations issued in March 1968 for tendering new refineries also safeguarded a minimum quantity of refined products that the state distribution monopoly would buy from each of the existing refineries. The same regulations also included an unusual requirement aimed at increasing the use of market mechanisms: The winning company would have to issue an initial public offering for at least 30 percent of its shares. Overall, the results were positive. In time, the new refinery would be successful not only in serving the domestic market but in competing overseas, exporting up to a third of its output.

Good intentions, bad outcomes ... and vice versa

Inevitably, not all policy draws succeed. And reform efforts can be captured either at the design or implementation stages. Spain was of course no stranger to any of those. In fact, we have already seen the downside of policy tinkering in some examples discussed above. For example, once the syndicate organizations were empowered to allocate the tax burden among firms in their sector, they derailed further efforts at tax reform. Similarly, the delays in unifying the social security system are sometimes attributed to the resistance of syndicate organizations to give up the special regimes that were to be replaced with a new, unified public system (Comín and Díaz, 2005, p. 893). But let us briefly review a couple of additional examples that show the range of reasons for poor results.

In the late 1960s, Spain decided to bid out the construction of some highways, largely along the Mediterranean coast.[15] Over the next decade, around two thousand kilometers of quality highways got built, appropriate tolls were collected, and, in the process, substantial amounts of private foreign capital were mobilized to support the development effort. Yet, soon thereafter, these concessions would turn into a financial disaster for the state. The contracts had been awarded with clauses that provided exchange rate guarantees, effectively amounting to borrowing in foreign currency with the risks borne by the state. With the crises of the 1970s first, and the strong dollar policy in the 1980s thereafter, the interest costs ballooned and left the state with the responsibility to pay for decades. This poor outcome was not borne out of a corrupt procurement, shoddy implementation, or poor management but out of the sheer difficulties of creating markets: There had been no appetite among foreign investors without the exchange rate guarantees that would prove so disastrous to the state. We know this because the public competition for the highway had been advertised first in August 1970 without such guarantees but elicited no bids; a few months later the government readvertised, this time including the exchange rate guarantees as part of its terms, and successfully awarded the concession.

Here is another example. In 1963, a competition law was enacted for the first time. The law created a competition tribunal and introduced in Spain principles in the defense of competition that the Treaty of Rome had enshrined. Minister Ullastres, a leading pro-liberalization figure, would say that "of all the undertakings of the Ministry of Commerce during these years [in which I have been Minister], I think this law is its most important."[16] This was, however, at the time of passing the law. It would prove to be wishful thinking on Ullastres' behalf. The law had limited impact, noting that in the following two decades the competition tribunal issued only 300 rulings (Castañeda, 2014; Fraile, 1998, p. 112). The competition law had design flaws that hampered the independence of proceedings and the power of the competition tribunal, as in fact astute analysts of the time noted (Garrigues, 1964). In the minds of the business interests that carried outsized power in parliament, those were not flaws but sought-after design features.

---

[15]   Details on the highway concessions is from Puncel (1996).
[16]   As quoted in Castañeda (2014, p. 105). This author, nevertheless, continues to emphasize that the passing of this law in 1964 occurred at a time when the return of interventionism and protectionism had started.

Unintended contestability

While the above examples could be considered cases of good intentions with bad results, the opposite can also be true. Some policy measures geared to restrict competition had at times the unintended consequence of increasing contestability. The most cited example of a reform reversal during the 1960s is the return of restrictions of entry into industrial activities. These restrictions included so-called technical conditions, like the minimum production runs that for the car industry we discussed in the previous chapters, or case-by-case prior authorization by the government. After having eased these restrictions in 1963, the share of industrial activity that would be subject to these constraints increased substantially after 1967 (Buesa and Pires, 2002).

The increased protection of these industries may have led to greater concentration but also to some positive unintended consequences. The evidence suggests that it was in fact the most regulated and concentrated sectors that acquired the most foreign technology (Cebrián, 2005). In line with Schumpeter's view, concentration led to greater innovation because the fruits of those efforts were more likely enjoyed by the innovators. Firms in those sectors sought to bring more foreign technology to gain an edge in the domestic market not *despite* the fact that they were operating in a concentrated market but *because* of it. And in the process, out of entry restrictions and concentration, we observe an increase in productivity and competitiveness. The evidence from the adoption of foreign technology presented in Cebrián (2005) questions the view that greater liberalization would have led to faster growth; but it is fully consistent with the evidence that we reviewed in Chapter 6 that foreign firms were attracted to the protected domestic market.

Marginal, slow, and ambiguous...but policy change nevertheless

The contrast between the decisiveness of the economic stabilization measures in 1959 and the policy tinkering that followed has also influenced the assessment of the latter. But this comparison is somewhat misleading. Changes in the exchange rate or tariffs as done in 1959 can take effect more quickly than the public administration reforms that were attempted in the 1960s. In both social security and public procurement, the respective framework laws were passed in 1963, but the implementing regulations would not be issued until 1966 and 1967, respectively. The time passed is often interpreted as evidence of either a government dragging its feet or of underlying tensions that blocked earlier action. Those arguments, while in part true, fail to recognize that this type of policy changes requires much implementation capacity. This, in turn, takes time to build. Regulatory changes in both public recruitment and procurement had in fact started even before the 1959 reforms.

This is not to say that there were no backtrackings. Even in tourism, a lightly regulated sector, the creation of a state-owned enterprise discussed in the previous chapter was a step back. But it was a small one. By 1970, the state-owned enterprise accounted for only 0.2 percent of hotel capacity in the country (Pellejero, 2000, p. 151). And, in another example of the ambiguity that characterized policy changes in the 1960s, while the state started its own tourist enterprise, some other regulations were eased. For example, restrictions that had blocked any privately owned hotel to open within 200 meters of a state-owned one (or within 10 kms on the open road), were lifted in late 1962.

More importantly, the state-owned enterprise for tourism would be one of the last ones ever created. As in other areas, this would be a policy change at the margin. The national development plan stated that "prior to the creation of new industrial plants of public enterprises, a competition would be advertised to allow for the private sector to undertake the respective economic activity" (Comisaría del Plan de Desarrollo Económico, 1963, p. 62). It was an effort to affirm that public enterprise would be subsidiary to private enterprise. Importantly, the mechanism envisaged to make this happen relied on an open competition. Indeed, the tender for the refinery in Bilbao that we discussed above specified that if there were no bidders, the National Institute of Industry (INI) would be awarded the concession. None of this meant a dismantling of the INI, but its growth was constrained. Compared to other countries in Western Europe, the participation of public enterprises in the economy remained relatively small (see Figure 8.4). Still, in absolute terms, INI would continue to be a highly important part of the Spanish economy with a record of performance considered mixed at best.

As in the case of the role of INI in the economy, policy changes after 1960 can best be characterized as marginal, slow, and ambiguous. Following how those changes were implemented and affected the fabric of economic activity is a daunting task that is made more difficult by the way that policymakers at the time discussed them and by the frame through which most analysts have chosen to evaluate them. The rest of this section discusses these issues.

Framing effects

When the World Bank mission tasked with writing a report on the economy in the early 1960s completed a draft, it ran into a problem. The authorities could not clear the draft and called for the mission to return to Spain.[17] Upon arriving in

---

[17] Letter from Minister of Finance Mariano Navarro Rubio to World Bank Vice President J. Burke Knapp, Madrid, May 17, 1962. World Bank Archive Folder 1740807 (Spain. General Survey Mission. Correspondence. Volume 3).

(a) Share in total employment, percent

(b) Share in gross fixed capital formation, percent

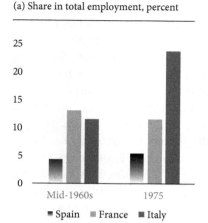
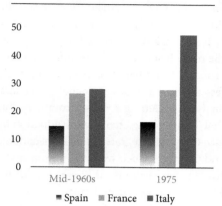

Figure 8.4 Weight of state-owned enterprises in the economy in comparative perspective
Source: Tafunell (2005).

Madrid, the Bank staff was told the draft was "quite unacceptable," but not because the authorities disagreed with the recommendations of what economic policies ought to be pursued. Surprisingly, there was wide agreement on those. Rather, as the Bank team will soon realize, the authorities "were mainly concerned with references to past action," which the Spaniards believed were presented in an overly negative fashion.[18] Suggestions that economic policies in the past were inadequate could not be tolerated, even if the criticisms seemed inconsequential to outsiders.[19]

Criticism of policies adopted in the past, even those from two decades before, did not seem trivial to the Spanish authorities. The fact that the same regime that had been in power continuously since 1939 made it more difficult for officials to regard past policies, whether their own or their predecessors', as mistaken. No politician wants to be accused of flip-flopping. This was especially true in the case of Spain, when the autarkic policies had been such a source of misery. As a result, successful operators within the regime, like the technocrats in the late 1950s and

---

[18] Memo: Richard Demuth to World Bank President Eugene Black, May 29, 1962. World Bank Archive Folder 1740807 (Spain. General Survey Mission. Correspondence. Volume 3).

[19] One of the Bank staffers in the conversations recalled them as follows: We "met with a senior official who subsequently became Prime Minister under Franco. We sat down for two days and went through the report line by line. It gradually dawned on us that the things we thought were most objectionable from their point of view were not the things that they objected to at all, but other things which we considered, for the most part, fairly trivial. So we put up a show of resistance but gave in graciously many times and as far as I'm concerned the report is more or less as we wrote it." Transcript of oral history interview with Benjamin B. King held on July 24 and 25, 1986. Available at https://oralhistory.worldbank.org/transcripts/transcript-oral-history-interview-benjamin-b-king-held-july-24-and-25-1986

1960s, learned to master the skill of praising past policies while advocating new ones. This helps to explain that most policy changes were presented as an evolution of previous policies even when there were significant departures.

It also makes for a record of policy statements full of contradictions. Separating the noise from the signal is difficult, a point that has not always been fully appreciated. It is not hard, for example, to find statements by regime officials that profess to show a persistent belief in the abandoned autarkic policies. This has led analysts, including a most prominent historian of the Franco regime, to argue that "indeed long after the introduction by the 'technocrats' of measures of liberalization and integration into international economic organizations, both Franco and Carrero Blanco were still committed to autarky" (Preston, 1994, p. 682). It is true that even the most liberalizing of measures, such as the 1959 Stabilization Plan, was presented by Franco as having its origins "in those master lines of our economic policy set from the moment in which I took on my shoulders the responsibility of leading our Homeland, and are a complement of those that have been undertaken over the last twenty years" (as quoted in Viñas, 2012, p. 687).

The statement linking the economic policies adopted in 1959 with the autarkic policies adopted 20 years before is patently false. But it is not all that surprising given the human desire for consistency—a force that social psychology has shown to be highly influential (Cialdini, 1993). Because the desire to be consistent is so strong, it is a powerful force in shaping the stories we tell others and even ourselves about the reasons for our actions.[20] Explaining the policies adopted as a "complement" of previous ones, when in fact they were in sharp opposition, can be a purposeful deception of others. But it can also be a deception of oneself. It is inevitably difficult to know if Franco believed his own lies, or the extent to which others around him did so. Either way, the main takeaway is to be cautious when interpreting statements that, as part of a narrative of the reason for the evolution of policies, stress the continuation or consistency of past policies. Interpreting those as evidence of a commitment by the authorities to past policies or as evidence of the reluctance with which reforms were undertaken is risky.

A Washington consensus lens

The effort to provide a narrative of consistent policy evolution blurred the picture of policy change. But this is not the only difficulty in assessing the nature of policy change during this critical period of fast economic convergence. The lens through which most of the literature has approached the subject adds its own distortions. To a large extent, the assessment of the policy changes in the 1960s is still the one

---

[20] Even though, paradoxically, social psychology research has long shown that people act in fact quite inconsistently across situations (Ross and Nisbett, 2011, chapter 4).

performed in the 1980s. This means that, at least for most economists that looked at economic policies in the 1960s, they did so explicit or implicitly from an emerging consensus on what was an appropriate role of the state in economic matters and what was not. And, after four decades in which criticism of those in charge was prohibited, the transition to democracy in Spain meant that at long last those in positions of authority could come under scrutiny.

All these elements play out in the assessments made of perhaps the most notable policy tools deployed in the 1960s: the national development plans. Mirroring the French practice, this was an exercise in indicative planning. They were four-year plans, the first one starting in 1967, that would serve as a loose guide for economic policy until 1975. The main tool to influence the behavior of the private sector was the granting of preferential credit to groups of private firms if they met agreed targets for investment. The plans became closely associated with Laureano López Rodó, who had been instrumental in the efforts to reform the public administration since the 1950s and had become the right-hand man of Luis Carrero Blanco, himself the right-hand man of Franco. While the idea of the plans had not originated with López Rodó, he quickly saw its potential— including for his own personal advancement—and made it his own (Zaratiegui, 2019, pp. 45–6).

One of the goals of the development plans was to create new "growth poles" of industrial activity in areas that were not traditional industrial districts. These have come under much criticism in the literature. Some consider that it was a waste of resources because the selected growth poles were in hard-to-reach areas with poor access to markets or natural resources. Others consider the very idea of place-based policies as misguided altogether. Both arguments exaggerate the importance of the growth poles in the development strategy. First, resources spent on these efforts were quite limited. Second, while it may be true that the localities chosen were far from urban markets or, in some cases, seaports, it is also the case that the development plan was in two of the most prominent cases simply following in the footsteps of the two car manufacturers, Renault and Citroen, which had set up their manufacturing facilities in Valladolid and Vigo, respectively.

Still, the development plans came under intense criticism in the 1980s. Those seeking free markets saw the plans as distortionary, those believing in the socialist planning economies saw them as toothless, and, given López Rodó's reputation for sharp elbows, there was also no shortage of those seeking to settle scores. The national development plans have been criticized for both redirecting resources to inefficient purposes and for lacking in the ability to compel the private sector. Or for being ineffective yet also distorting the allocation of resources.

The overwhelming reaction of dismissiveness to the development plans unfortunately led to a limited interest in the topic among economic historians, with notable exceptions such as Zaratiegui (2019) and De la Torre and García-Zúñiga

(2009). The latter authors point out that perhaps the most distinctive feature of the historiography on the national development plans is the "contempt" with which "clichés" about them continue to feature in the literature (p. 13). While these authors have begun to fill in many gaps, there are still many issues, such as the potential role of the plans in addressing information asymmetries between the private and the public sector, that remain largely unexplored.[21]

Much of what has been written in recent decades about Spain's industrial policies in the critical years after 1960 was explicitly or implicitly benchmarking practices against an ideal of fully competitive markets. In those assessments, the fact that the Spanish economy remained protected implied that throughout the 1960s "the main inefficiencies in the allocation of resources were not corrected" (Fuentes Quintana and Requeijo, 1984, p. 15). Yet as we saw in the previous two chapters, there is abundant evidence that productivity increased—thanks to the exposure of foreign investment and a focus on the exporting market—in industrial sectors like automobiles that were heavily protected.

Importantly, the 1980s lens on the 1960s remains firmly entrenched. Let me give an example of how the argument about the national development plans continues to be made. In a prominent account of the period, after noting the benign growth environment in Western Europe at the time, coupled with other positive developments like the growth of tourism and FDI inflows into Spain, economist Jaime Requeijo argues that it is "not difficult to suppose" that a greater liberalization of markets would have resulted in as high a rate of economic growth "without having compromised, as the development plans did, the ability of the Spanish economy to compete in open markets and, above all, its capacity to adapt to a changing environment" (Requeijo, 2005, p. 35). As the author himself recognizes, this is an assumption. And, as the account of the car industry in the previous chapter shows, it is an assumption not always borne out by the evidence.

Given the role played by protectionist measures in the development path of some manufacturing sectors, like the car industry discussed in detail the previous chapter, it is unlikely that an early full liberalization would have resulted in the growth that was observed. It is possible to imagine a scenario where a full liberalization of the economy would have resulted in a different but equally successful specialization on export products—perhaps the country would not have developed an exporting car industry but something else would have taken its place. But, at the very least, the case that the policies embedded in the development plans were a drag on growth is not as obvious as the literature suggests. Unorthodox as they may be from the perspective of later decades, the development plans proved compatible with high rates of growth of productivity, increases

---

[21] Of all the topics covered in this book, this is one that stands out as having one of the most limited specialized literature on the issue, which is surprising given how productive the output of the Spanish economic history community has been in recent decades.

in export competitiveness in some sectors, and helped increase the predictability, discipline, and growth orientation of government action.[22]

Conclusions

The fastest catching up of the Spanish economy took place in the decade and half after 1960. Yet this presents a puzzle, as it coincides with a period of lackluster reforms. After the momentous 1959 Stabilization Plan, the appetite for reforms waned to such an extent that the consensus view of the period came to think of it as one of backtracking of reforms away from openness and towards more protection and interventionist measures. Underpinning this traditional interpretation is a view of the political economy of reform that emphasizes the role of crisis in eliciting reforms. According to this view, just like the decisiveness of the 1959 stabilization measures was attributed to the severity of the crisis, the backtracking of reforms could be explained by the easing of the crisis as the 1960s progressed. Success, particularly in the form of foreign exchange reserves, kills the will to reform. Given this mental model, it was natural for the standard account to stress both the external sources of growth, such as the pull from other Western economies undergoing their own Golden Age, as well as the view that growth occurred despite bad policies and institutions. Because domestic policies are seen as slowing growth down, it follows logically, and some authors go this far, that under different policies Spain could have grown even more in the 1960s. Puzzle solved—or is it?

Relying on the external environment, no matter how positive, as the fundamental explanation for Spain's performance during this period is not convincing because what we are trying to explain is Spain's unusually good performance in a comparative perspective. It seems odd that one of the strongest growth performances of the time—among the OECD only Japan recorded faster growth—would be of interest as a case study of failure. In fact, once we begin to question this traditional interpretation, it becomes clear that it is not built on solid evidence. In previous chapters we found the crisis explanation for the adoption of the 1959 reforms to be lacking and proposed that a more plausible reason for why economic reforms were adopted was not because of *economic instability* but because of growing *political stability*. We also showed that the catching up in productivity was among the fastest in the world—which undermines the view that growth would have been much faster under alternative policies—and driven by the adoption of foreign technology. Crucially, the ease with which foreign investment could enter the country was not reversed. However, it is true, as highlighted in the

---

[22] As argued by Maluquer de Motes (2014, p. 318).

traditional account of the catching up, that policy changes were less decisive, with examples of new interventionism, protectionist measures, and some backtrackings.

In this chapter, I offer a new interpretation of the puzzle posed by the acceleration in the catching up while reforms slowed down. My argument is in four parts. First, I borrow from the literature an important distinction between reforms and policy tinkering. In this framework, reforms are disruptive to incumbents but not to new entrants because reforms entail a change in the institutional setting to which incumbents had adapted. Policy tinkering affects both incumbents and new entrants similarly and is therefore less disruptive to the status quo. Policy tinkering proves to be a fitting label for many of the policy changes during the fast catching up of Spain, including critical ones such as the regulation of foreign investment or the way that public revenues were increased. Even when policies affected new entrants differently, such as with the changes to local content rules for new car manufacturers, the impact on incumbents was cushioned by limiting the access to the domestic market of new car manufacturers.

Policy tinkering may sound dismissive, but it can lead to results.[23] Spain was able to increase public revenues from 11 to 21 percent of GDP in the quarter century after 1950, likely surpassing any tipping point in terms of minimum public revenues to fund the basics of a state that provides an adequate environment for growth. The evolution of public revenues can be understood in the terms laid out by political scientist Margaret Levi (1988) in her model of predatory rule. Having become more secure in power, the Franco regime had the incentive to increase growth-enhancing public investments but was constrained in raising revenues by the bargaining power of other social actors and high transactions costs. The effort of the 1957 reform at increasing revenues, which failed at the hands of interest groups represented in parliament, illustrates well these constraints. It was only when a new, low-transaction-cost means of raising revenues, through social security contributions, was introduced that public revenues increased.

There was also an effort to build state capabilities, which constitutes the second building block of the argument in this chapter. This is an issue of critical importance as weak state capacity had until then "severely limited" the country's ability to address core development challenges such as land reform, thus contributing to frustration, social polarization, and eventually civil war (Simpson and Carmona, 2020, p. 247). As we show here, the effort to build state capacity took many forms. There were changes in both public recruitment and procurement, areas which have not received much attention by economists analyzing this period, but which are two core processes that underpin the functioning of any state. Public

---

[23] In Iyigun and Rodrik (2006), reforms and tinkering perform best depending on the level of entrepreneurship. Under high levels of entrepreneurship, reforms do not elicit more cost discovery than tinkering. The description in previous chapters of an entrepreneurial business community would thus support, within Iyigun and Rodrik's framework, that tinkering had results.

recruitment became more independent as the professional corps of civil servants gained bureaucratic autonomy not only over the selection of personnel but also tenure and promotions. In public procurement, the move was one away from simply trying to minimize price to thinking about value-for-money, particularly important as the state composition of expenditures shifted towards more complex public investment projects. The complementarities are also clear: A more independent bureaucracy was a good complement to the efforts to introduce more complex procurement methods. Significantly, changes in both public recruitment and procurement started before the 1959 Stabilization Plan and continued long thereafter, even if changes were sometimes slow and marginal and thus not easily detectable.

Policy tinkering is also a useful label for this case because it takes us away from a simplistic dichotomy of interventionist vs. liberalizing policies. This is the third building block of our argument. Much of the literature on the Spanish takeoff saw protectionist or interventionist measures as necessarily growth reducing. But what we have seen in this and previous chapters is that, in situations far from a first-best world, it is the specifics of how policies were implemented that led to positive or negative results. Take the case of the car industry. In line with the goals of much of industrial policy in the Western world during the postwar, policies for the car industry sought to substitute imports. To that end, there was a great deal of public interventionism. This has often been interpreted as evidence not only of a protectionist policy, which it clearly was, but also of limited competition resulting in poor competitiveness. The regulation of the car industry was no less protectionist or interventionist than that of the steel industry, but the results were diametrically opposed.

An important part of the argument put forward is to recognize that there were unintended consequences of policy changes, both negative and positive. Paradoxically, some protectionist measures resulted in greater contestability. For example, more concentrated and protected industries were the ones that drew the most on foreign technology, and thus increased their competitiveness. Unintended negative consequences are also part of the story. This is to be expected, as not all policy draws would be expected to lead to positive results. And, of course, we saw examples of capture. Backtracking and delays are not unusual. Arguably, because policy tinkering does not change the balance of power, it may be particularly prone to reversals. This is because those who stand to lose out remain powerful enough to lobby against those policy changes. This creates an ambiguous policy trajectory, to the point that it makes it hard to decipher the direction of travel.

The fourth and final part of the chapter calls for an acceptance of ambiguity in the policy changes when interpreting the political economy of the period. My argument is not that all policy changes resulted in greater contestability or were never reversed. But we should not focus exclusively on the policy reversals either.

We need an account that accommodates the marginal but significant policy changes, like the restraint on the further growth of state-owned enterprises. And, finally, while making sense of ambiguous policies is always difficult in the real world, I draw attention to two aspects that make it particularly so in this case.

The political regime in Spain during this time was both dictatorial and long-lasting. These features had compounding effects. Avoiding the appearance of any criticism of past policies was an obsession of the Franco regime, as the World Bank came to learn. But the regime had been so long-lasting, and policies changed so much, that it required linguistical contortions to preserve the appearance of consistency of policies over time. This is why individual statements by policy-makers of the time, especially when made as part of a broader narrative of policy evolution, need to be interpreted with utmost care. Incidentally, this is also an argument for a more quantitative analysis of texts, as in the topic modeling of speeches performed in Chapter 5. And this is not the only difficulty in assessing the nature of policy change in our case. The lens through which most of the literature has approached policies like the national development plans, by effectively benchmarking policies against a first-best competitive market economy, is often more distorting than clarifying. Unfortunately, the account of a critical period in the evolution of economic policies remains rich in clichés and lacking in nuance.

9

Ideas and Aspirations

Like his friend Alexander Gerschenkron, Albert Hirschman did not think that the process of economic development followed a predetermined set of stages. Hirschman had come to this conclusion not from the study of European history, as Gerschenkron did, but from his role advising the government of Colombia. Hirschman, who had once shared an office with Gerschenkron at Berkeley, added one important qualification to his colleague's insights. For Gerschenkron, the mere existence of a widening gap between countries was thought to trigger action by those left behind. As backwardness became increasingly clear, countries would set out on their own path to catch up. By then the benefits of reform would clearly outweigh its costs and prompt the adoption of whatever changes may be necessary. But such a view, Hirschman pointed out, implied that decision makers really knew all along what was needed to shed backwardness and that they had chosen not to adopt those changes until countries had fallen further behind. Experience left Hirschman convinced otherwise. Just like there were no "prerequisites" for economic development, he went on, there could be no "backwardness features" because what is a hindrance in one setting may be helpful under different circumstances. Overcoming backwardness could not be reduced to a simple matter of will. Hirschman summed it up with characteristic brilliance: "The tension of development is therefore not so much between known benefits and costs as between the goal and the ignorance and misconceptions about the road to that goal."[1]

How did Spain resolve this fundamental tension of development? This chapter addresses this question, exploring how the society came to a broad consensus of what needs to be done. We will see how an important inspiration for this program was European. But this does not mean that ideas were imposed from outside. There was a great deal of local adaptation, often through mechanisms that involved a contest of ideas. And while policies were tinkered with, it is the continuity of policies over long-term horizons that stands out. A characteristic of policymaking in Spain during its sustained takeoff is therefore the balancing between adaptation and policy continuity.

The ideas of the policymaking elite evolved in parallel with a rise in aspirations of the population at large. Importantly, increasing aspirations of the people were

---

[1] Hirschman (1958, p. 10). Details about Hirschman's life are from the masterful biography by Adelman (2013).

Unexpected Prosperity: How Spain Escaped the Middle Income Trap. Oscar Calvo-Gonzalez, Oxford University Press.
© Oscar Calvo-Gonzalez 2021. DOI: 10.1093/oso/9780198853978.003.0010

both a consequence and a cause of the improvement in living conditions. But rising aspirations could have easily led to frustration or widespread social unrest. In the final part of our argument, we will explore why that was not the case. But before doing so, let us discuss the evolution of some critical ideas about policy-making and its role in bringing about prosperity in Spain.

Europe as the solution

After centuries of decline, the loss of the last overseas colonies in 1898 settled that Spain had ceased to be a global empire and had become a second-tier nation in the European periphery. Some Spanish elites of the nineteenth century had already been looking at Western Europe as a source of ideas, particularly to France because of the appeal of the revolutionary ideals. This would intensify after the loss of the colonies, which as we saw in Chapter 1 was a profound shock to Spanish society. A lively debate emerged between those who thought Spain ought to remain anchored in her own ways and those who advocated for adapting European practices. But the latter would prove much more influential over the long run. The idea of Europe, and ideas coming from Europe, would play an increasingly dominant role in Spanish society. José Ortega y Gasset, perhaps the most influential Spanish intellectual of the first half of the twentieth century, put it simply when he argued that "Spain is the problem, Europe the solution."[2]

When Ortega first made this point, in 1910, he could not have foreseen that in the following three decades, Europe would contribute to the world the likes of Nazism, Stalinism, and two world wars. From World War I to World War II, European influence on Spain was not a positive or even a moderating one. On the contrary, much of the ideological debris created in Europe during the interwar period made its way to Spain. The rise of fascism was closely followed and inspired the creation of the *Falange* party that would later be one of the constituents of the Francoist coalition (Payne, 2000, pp. 52–66). And when Europe was finally on a path to create a new postwar order in the second half of the 1940s, the Franco regime was excluded from such an effort on account of having itself been created in part thanks to the support of Nazi Germany.

None of this bode well for Ortega's hope for a Europeanization of Spain to come to pass. In fact, the sharp contrast between the postwar Western European project and the Franco regime reaffirmed a deep sense of pro-Europeanism among those opposed to the dictatorship. This will be especially true for the new generations that grew into adulthood after the Civil War. One of the sharpest

---

[2] A short account in English of Ortega's life and influence can be found in Zamora (2018). For a monograph on the broad appeal to modernize the nation after 1898 see Moreno-Luzón (2016).

analysts of the Franco regime, sociologist Víctor Pérez-Díaz, captured well this intellectual influence when he spoke about his own trajectory:

> I belong to a generation of Spaniards who first assumed professional and political responsibilities in the late 1950s and early 1960s, in the belief that the institutional framework of Francoism was both inimical to us and an impediment to solving Spain's problems [...]. We believed then that [...] western Europe and the western world as a whole provided us with keys to a better understanding of our situation and a better future for our country (1993, p. 1).

The fact that the Europeanization of Spain was a project of the opposition to the Franco dictatorship makes it even more intriguing that parts of it came to be adopted by regime insiders. If we put ourselves in the shoes of those living in 1950, it would have been hard to predict the growing influence within the Franco regime of those who looked to Europe as an inspiration for solutions or as a source of validation for policy reforms. And yet this is precisely what happened. An example will help illustrate this point. A couple of months before the Stabilization Plan was launched in July 1959, one of the men behind a similar stabilization operation in France the previous year, Jacques Rueff, was invited to speak in Madrid—surprisingly not by the technocrats but by the syndical organization that was opposed to liberal economic reforms. The speech helped, according to one of the architects of the 1959 Stabilization Plan, in strengthening the case for reforms, for which, he noted, "we could not have asked for a better recommendation" (Navarro Rubio, 1991, p. 152).

Predictably, the Spanish technocrats had a deep appreciation for Jacques Rueff. But what is more remarkable is that a French liberal technocrat like Rueff was invited by the syndical organization and that he may have had any influence in persuading his audience. This reflected in part the achievements of Jacques Rueff himself but also a broader environment more welcoming to external views. In a country that barely a decade earlier had been ostracized and that was still digesting its loss in international standing, it also reflected the desire of Spanish elites, no matter their persuasion, to be considered part of the European debate. This is also what helps to explain why the Spanish government submitted its first request to join the European Economic Community in 1962, even if it did not harbor much hope of an immediate positive response. Membership would have to wait until Spain became a democracy a quarter-century later, but by the late 1950s the Europeanization project of Ortega was already winning even among those who did not espouse it explicitly.[3]

---

[3] The habit of Spanish academics of benchmarking the experience of the country almost exclusively to that of other Western European countries is in itself a manifestation of this Europe-centric view.

The technocrats thus sought to align themselves closely to European policymakers partly because it lent them credibility. As such, it would not be uncommon for foreign leaders to be invited to Spain. And the bigger the name the better. For example, the long-time German Minister of Economic Affairs and architect of German's postwar social market economy, Ludwig Erhard, visited Madrid in May 1961 at the invitation of the reformist minister Alberto Ullastres. In some respects, this was not different from the strategy followed by the dictator himself, who derived much propaganda value during the 1950s from even the briefest of visits by dignitaries like the US president. But it would be misleading to think of the exchanges with Western policymakers as purely cosmetic. The appreciation for European ideas about policymaking was both deep and widespread—even among some constituencies of the regime that favored the least amount of change. For example, the Institute of Political Studies, a think tank initially created to support the *Falange* and which often competed with the technocrats (Sesma, 2019, p. 184), launched a "workshop on Europe" as early as 1949. This showed how important political and policy developments in Western Europe had become across the political spectrum. And European elites, even if they had been abhorred by Franco's fascist origins, went along since the early 1950s in assisting the consolidation of the Franco regime (Guirao, 2021). Symbolic gestures like the visit by Ludwig Erhard were only the tip of the iceberg of a much deeper economic and technical cooperation.

Crucially, Europe was not only the source of big ideas but also the spark for concrete policy measures that nudged the economy towards greater openness and contestability. In previous chapters we saw how the focus on boosting productivity in the car industry through increasing competition and using the export market was closely linked to the Spain–EEC agreement of 1970. That trade agreement envisaged, even if long term, declines in tariff protection that would challenge the viability of existing car producers without increases in productivity. But it also provided for access to a much larger market and with it a way to make the car industry in Spain viable. Indeed, the architect of the "Ford decrees," López de Letona, stressed in a press interview in January 1973 that greater integration in the European economy was the way to increase the competitiveness of the car industry because it "increased the size of the market [...], stimulating at the same time competition and larger production runs."[4]

The idea of using the discipline of external markets to increase competitiveness was already articulated in the first national development plan, which laid out the reasons why productivity was low and the proposed way forward. A high cost structure and a low price elasticity of output were seen as the main culprits for low productivity. The solution envisaged in the Economic and Social Development Plan for 1964 to 1967 was "greater liberalization of foreign trade, promoting

---

[4] Interview with newspaper *ABC* (January 18, 1973).

domestic competition, selected public investment projects, and the orientation of private investment" (Presidencia del Gobierno, 1963, p. 63). The extent to which each of those objectives was achieved is debatable, but the clarity of the diagnosis and the remedies is beyond doubt.

The goal of Europeanizing Spain had profound consequences for policy reforms, both big and small. We already explored many of the big reforms and policy changes in the previous five chapters, from the Stabilization Plan to policies regarding FDI. And we already discussed why the technocrats may have risen to power (see Chapter 5). What we did not touch upon above is where the policy ideas came from and how the technocrats crafted their agenda. This is what we now turn to discuss.

Policy entrepreneurs

Like most of the literature, we have so far referred to the policymakers that gained increasing responsibilities since the late 1950s as technocrats. It is time we peek behind the label. What motivated these individuals and what were they fundamentally trying to achieve? These questions are important to understand the evolution of policymaking. Although we now refer to this group of policymakers as the technocrats, it is worth stressing that, as the literature has done, they were far from a united bloc. And that the very label of technocrats did not come to be widely used until much later, almost when they were out of office. In fact, in the late 1950s, references to "technocrats" in the Spanish press referred explicitly to administrators of the European integration institutions such as the European Coal and Steel Community (Zaratiegui, 2016).

While the technocratic ministers were often personally at odds with each other, they shared three fundamental ideas. First, the goal of material progress for a greater share of society. Second, a belief in the responsibility of the state in helping to bring about such progress. And third, a clear view that the way to achieve progress was through a relentless focus on increasing efficiency and thus productivity, both in the private and in the public sector. None of this is surprising for anyone familiar with mid-twentieth century thinking on modernization. And, at some level, these three ideas were also not new in Spain either.

What was new was how these technocrats were able to implement their practical agenda over a sustained period. Above all, they relentlessly sought new ideas about policymaking from Europe and the United States to be put in practice in Spain. There had been previous technocratic efforts to emulate European practices, sometimes from reformers that reached even higher levels of government. The liberal Prime Minister José Canalejas had even attended, while in office, the first international congress of administrative sciences held in Brussels in 1910. The second congress was to take place in Madrid in 1915. But given the instability that dominated the first half of the twentieth century in Spanish politics, such efforts lacked continuity. Canalejas himself, as readers may recall from Chapter 1, was assassinated in 1912. Short tenure of governments was the norm even under less dramatic circumstances. One of the stints in office of the conservative leader, Antonio Maura, became known as "Maura's long government" even though it lasted only two years. Thus, reform efforts were typically not sustained.

Crucially, there was also continuity from the supply of practical solutions emanating from Europe. Canalejas' assassination was not the only reason why the second international congress of administrative sciences did not happen as planned in Madrid. The advent of World War I changed the nature of the European supply of ideas from which Spanish reformers could borrow. It would not be until the second half of 1940s that the technocratic dialogue about public administration that was emerging in the 1910s resumed. While the philosophy behind technocracy had originated in the United States, it was in postwar Europe that it would take root more strongly. French policymakers like Jean Monnet were first entrusted with planning the reconstruction after the war and later with the conception of new institutions for European integration. A new more activist role for the state was widely accepted. This in turn required a new cadre of public officials, imbued with a technocratic mindset, which led to the rapid establishment in the early postwar of new schools like the French *École Nationale d'Administration* (ENA) or the German *Hochschule für Verwaltungswissenschaften* in Speyer.

What was truly remarkable in the 1950s was, therefore, the confluence of both a continued demand for and supply of practical ideas from European policymakers. With an uninterrupted flow, those searching practical ideas on what the European technocratic program implied for policymaking could do so. In Spain, perhaps no one went to this well more often than the technocrat par excellence Laureano López Rodó, the advocate of the administrative reform who later became Commissioner for the development plan and influenced policymaking like no other figure during the 1960s. Compared to other technocrats like the Minister of Commerce Alberto Ullastres, who was hugely influential in the 1959 Stabilization Plan, the main advantage of tracing the technocratic program through the works and career of López Rodó is simply the sheer abundance of writing that the latter left behind.

Born in 1920, López Rodó had become a law professor by the mid-1950s but was otherwise relatively unknown. His influences included a slew of technocratic thinkers and policymakers from the US and Western Europe. In the late 1940s, López Rodó established contact first with Marcello Caetano, an authority on administrative law turned politician who later became Portugal's prime minister under the dictatorship, and thereafter with a select circle of top European professors of public law. Thanks to these contacts, López Rodó became in the 1950s a frequent speaker at leading universities in Europe, including the Sorbonne, Paris Institute of Political Studies, the London School of Economics, and University of

Oxford. Among the groups that López Rodó frequented was the International Institute of Administrative Sciences, the very organization that Canalejas had attempted to start and which flourished out of Brussels in the postwar period.[5]

López Rodó then began a rapid rise within the administration. After coming to the attention of the Minister of Justice, he was asked to produce a draft bill to help modernize the public administration. López Rodó's solution was indicative of his technocratic ideas, proposing the creation of technical secretariats in every ministry tasked with planning, technical review, and coordination across ministries. The proposal was taken to the cabinet and approved in December 1956. López Rodó himself was appointed as Technical Secretary-General of the Presidency; his first job in the administration placed him at the side of Franco's closest advisor, Luis Carrero Blanco.

Productivity was top of mind for technocrats like López Rodó. He launched a new training center for civil servants and a new journal which spelled out the details for the reform of public administration and covered at length reforms in other European countries. He penned an editorial in the new journal entitled "Towards an increase in productivity of the public administration," language that was not common in Spain in 1958. López Rodó was influenced by the ideas of scientific management and had, even before joining the administration, laid out how private sector management tools were relevant to make a more efficient state. The private sector as an inspiration for the public administration and the need to strengthen public–private partnership was another novel theme in López Rodó's work. He noted with admiration, for example, how the Administrative Staff College in Henley-on-Tames had been launched as a public–private partnership.

Nothing was too small to be optimized. Reducing waste was an important driver of these efforts. Paper sizes used in the public administration were normalized and forms simplified to save costs. The new training facility for civil servants taught completely new courses, introducing mid-level bureaucrats to new ideas of how to motivate and manage staff, and over time became a new school of public administration, inspired by the ENA in France. López Rodó stood out because he sought out both the discussions on big ideas with the most influential policymakers of the day as well as the minutiae of how those were put in practice. In his trips to the United States, for example, he visited the likes of Arthur Burns or Walt Rostow but also the training centers for US government officials, the American Management Association, or the New York Port Authority.[6]

It is hard to pinpoint the precise impact of all of this. Perhaps most important was the elevation of technical staff to decision-making roles across all ministries.

---

[5] Decades later, in the late 1970s, López Rodó would preside over this organization.

[6] López Rodó had promoted the translation of Rostow's *Stages of Growth* into Spanish and authored an introduction to it. The admiration was mutual—Walt Rostow later recalled that he "greatly admired" López Rodó (Rostow correspondence with the author, April 24, 2001).

The creation of the technical secretariats in ministries opened the door to a cadre of professionals that would prove to be instrumental in the policy reforms in subsequent years. In particular, the technical secretariats of ministries like Finance and Commerce were filled with highly trained economists. This reflected the increased credibility in public policy circles achieved by economists as a profession, who had reached in May 1956 the milestone of having their own independent corps of economists within the public administration. Some of these economists had been trained at the new dedicated faculty of economics that had only started to operate as a standalone discipline in university of Madrid in 1944. In any case, regardless of their place of training, these economists broadly shared the three technocratic ideas that would come to dominate policymaking: the goal of material progress for a greater share of society, the responsibility of the state, and the need to increase productivity as the proximate solution.

Another area of important changes was the updating of technology at the service of the public administration. A comparative perspective is difficult but shows Spain to be an early adopter in some cases. For example, the police emergency telephone number (*091*, equivalent to *911* in North America) was piloted in Madrid in 1958 and subsequently expanded nationally in 1960. This was later than in the UK (1937) but similar to Canada, where the first such number was piloted in 1959, or Australia, where it would start in 1960. The introduction of the emergency telephone line has been interpreted as an attempt to portray a police force that was at the service of citizens, ready to go wherever called (Palacios, 2018, p. 322). But it was, perhaps even more so, evidence of the high hopes that were being placed on technology as a source of economic and social progress.[7]

Conditionality or local adaptation?

In fall 1962, the World Bank, with the agreement of the Spanish authorities, released a report on the economic development of the country. To the surprise of Bank staff in Washington, it proved an immediate publishing success. The first printing, 10,000 copies, was sold out in three days. An incredulous Bank staffer in Madrid went on to explain what was going on: "The presses can turn out only 500 copies a day; a line forms at 6 a.m. to buy the daily ration when the offices of the Official Gazette opens at 9:30 a.m."[8] The World Bank report became a bestseller in part because it was widely seen as providing a credible and independent view of the Spanish economy. But this was not the only reason. The Spanish government

---

[7] The launch of the 091 police emergency telephone line was accompanied by a feature-length movie. Its trailer included the statement that "in the cold truth of statistics lies all the bare and exciting life of the big city."

[8] Warren Baum to S. Raymond Cope, October 17, 1962, in Spain—General Survey Mission Correspondence, Vol. 3, Folder 1740807, World Bank Archive.

had reviewed it line by line and agreed to its contents and publication. It could only be interpreted as also reflecting the authorities' thinking, and was regarded as such at the time.[9]

The World Bank report became influential not so much because it clashed with the program of the authorities but because of how much it was aligned with the views of many that held office. There were of course some officials that did not share the diagnostics or recommendations laid out by the Bank, but those were in the minority. This broad alignment implied that policy changes throughout the 1960s cannot be interpreted as the result of conditions imposed by the international financial institutions. In this the 1960s was no different than the 1950s, when the US was unable to extract much policy leverage from its large aid program. It was also not the case that the Bank had been able to diagnose previously intractable syndromes. The analysis of the report was actually broadly shared by most domestic analysts. In fact, most local economists who reacted to the report felt that it hit the mark—though some could not contain a feeling of unfairness at the publishing success for such a report when the World Bank had not really found anything that they had not already publicly discussed.

But if not through conditionality or new analysis, what was the impact—if any—of the World Bank on policymaking? To answer this question, it is useful to go briefly through the essence of the Bank support to Spain in this period. The position of the Bank was based on four key takeaways. First, reformists were seen as broadly sharing the Bank's agenda but recognized as only one force in the cabinet. Second, substantial amounts of public funds were being wasted through industrial state-owned enterprises. A reform program that did not address this issue was inadequate. Third, because of the differences within the cabinet, the success of any program depended on Franco's own position. This meant that there was no point for the Bank to pursue not just a lending program but even a significant analytical effort without ascertaining Franco's support for the reform agenda. And fourth, the Spanish public administration required an upgrading in their planning capacity and an improvement in the coordination between ministries. The internal documents of the Bank stress time and again these four themes. To give a sense of the language and tone used, Figure 9.1 reproduces a memo from World Bank President to the IMF Managing Director significantly from a year after the successful 1959 Stabilization Plan was launched. All four elements noted above are clearly present.

Just as we saw in the case of the IMF support in the 1959 Stabilization Plan in Chapter 5, the World Bank during the 1960s remained highly attuned to whether

---

[9] In internal Bank correspondence, it was noted that "[t]he fact that the Government has agreed to publish the report is said to have led the so-called 'man in the street' to conclude that the Government must agree with its contents." Warren Baum to S. Raymond Cope, October 17, 1962, in Spain—General Survey Mission Correspondence, Vol. 3, Folder 1740807, World Bank Archive.

Mr. Per Jacobsson   October 19, 1960

Eugene R. Black

Spain - Proposed Technical Assistance Mission

1.   The Spanish delegation to the Annual Meeting asked the Bank to
provide technical assistance in working out a development program which
they appeared to think of primarily as being a public investment program. We have agreed, in principle, to do what we can.

2.   You may remember from my letter to Mr. Navarro Rubio of July the
14th that we have serious reservations about the effectiveness of technical assistance on a development program in the absence of a responsible and influencial planning organization and, more generally, because
of the lack of coordination of economic and financial policies among
the various ministries concerned.

3.   I still have those reservations and I am therefore convinced that
we should not get into development programming unless we can agree with
the Spanish Government as a whole on satisfactory terms of reference and
conditions of work. In particular, we could not look at public investment in a vacuum, without studying existing policies and making recommendations about necessary changes. Nor could we look at public investment and economic policies affecting the rest of the economy without
taking full account of the present operations and plans of autonomous
agencies, notably INI, which are investing public funds on a large scale
with serious repercussions in the private sector.

4.   In meetings with Mr. Iliff and Mr. Knapp, Mr. Navarro Rubio and
Mr. Ullastres accepted these points in principle, if initially perhaps
with some reluctance. In view of the probably different reactions of
various other members of the Cabinet (the Minister of Industry, for
example, is most unlikely to welcome a study of INI), I think it necessary to explore the ground thoroughly and secure full Cabinet support -
which means in fact approval by General Franco - for explicit terms of
reference before we are committed to launching a large scale mission.

5.   We have, therefore, sent the attached letter to Mr. Navarro Rubio
as a first move. I will, of course, let you know what reaction we get.

Attachment

JHWilliams:mk

Figure 9.1   Memo from World Bank President to IMF Managing Director,
October 1960

Source: World Bank Archive Folder 1740805 (Spain – General Survey Mission – Correspondence 01).

the dictator supported reforms or not. In that context, the Bank sought to influence policy more by nudging the authorities and steering the agenda than by using sticks and carrots. As we saw when we discussed the evolution of ports, the Bank helped on occasion to bring change more quickly by setting deadlines for its projects. And, precisely because of the vitality of the intellectual project to Europeanize Spain, external voices like that of the World Bank lent credibility to certain views—even if, as noted above, little in the views of the Bank was truly new to the local debate. Thus, it is important to stress that the source of policy ideas, even if inspired from external experiences, was homegrown in the sense that they were distilled by local policy entrepreneurs into a program adapted to local conditions. It is also important to note that much of that local adaptation happened through contestable processes.

A contest of ideas

One of the first detailed household surveys in Spain was not conducted by the national statistical office but by a newly established foundation associated with the Catholic organization Caritas. In 1965, this foundation opened a competition on proposals for a study of the social situation in the country. The winning entry included the idea of a survey and, remarkably, it was led by a sociologist who was still in his twenties, Amando de Miguel. The survey and accompanying report would become a rich source of information on the society at the time but, for our purposes, it is its origin as part of a contest that is particularly notable. Academic institutions and even think tanks associated with the government made a point of having merit-based recruitment. For example, the courses of the Institute of Political Studies—which we discussed above—required an entrance exam, seen as "fairly assessed" even by those of a different political persuasion (Tamames, 2013, p. 107). Other types of open competitions also saw a revival. In 1969, a public competition was launched for the architectural designs for the new public universities in Madrid, Barcelona, and Bilbao. Greater competition of ideas was not limited to the market.

One of the ways to increase contestability is by enabling new actors to enter the bargaining space. Since the mid-1950s, the arrival of technocrats at progressively higher levels of government also brought greater competition in the policy arena. The decision to adopt the 1959 Stabilization Plan can be seen more as a battle of ideas more than as a conflict between competing vested interests. The technocrats deliberately framed it as such, for example by sending a questionnaire to different stakeholder groups asking for specific solutions to the economic problems of the day. As the economist Dani Rodrik (2014) has argued, ideas can—and often do—trump interests in driving policy change.

At the same time, the regime tolerated no political dissent. Competition over policy ideas was accepted and even encouraged provided the political foundation of the regime was not put in question. Individuals like Amando de Miguel could be successful in the marketplace for ideas, becoming also a professor in the public university, but the moment they stepped out of line politically they could spend some time in prison—as De Miguel did. Similarly, the economist Ramón Tamames would go from being a political prisoner in 1956 to being selected to an elite corps of officials in the Ministry of Commerce in 1957. Tamames, who was widely known to be a member of the clandestine Communist Party, would remain part of the high-level technical team in the ministry and later also obtain a professorship at a public university. It is as if the regime suffered from a type of multiple personality disorder.

Even though the contest of ideas was truncated, it can be thought of as having been beneficial because it helped increase the quality of the debate. In a model like the one presented by Rodrik (2014), policy ideas themselves can relax political economy constraints, and just as with other types of technology, policy innovation can create win–win scenarios. This is an aspect that has received little attention both in Spanish discussions on the growth takeoff and in the development economics literature at large. The Growth Commission chaired by Nobel laureate Michael Spence, having zeroed in on the experience of countries that had sustained fast economic growth over long periods, concluded that successful countries "owe a lot to an environment in which all ideas, good and bad, are exposed to review and vigorous debate" (Spence, 2008, p. 67). The Growth Commission did not elaborate on why the quality of the debate has such a positive impact on growt,h but what they describe is fully consistent with the mechanism of political innovation that Dani Rodrik points out can benefit both the elites and the rest of the population.[10]

Importantly, the country achieved both a degree of contestability in the market of ideas while preserving a large degree of stability in policy priorities. This was in part helped by the continuity of office holders. Ullastres was Minister of Commerce from 1957 to 1965. Navarro Rubio held the job as Finance Minister for the same years. López Rodó oversaw the national development plans from 1962 to 1973. But one can have continuity of leaders without continuity of policies. More significantly, there was continuity in the trajectory envisaged for the evolution policies. When López Rodó met with World Bank President Robert McNamara in January 1971 and mentioned that Spain was following the path laid out in the World Bank report—from 1962—he was not just flattering his

---

[10] Others may see the quality of debate as critical in increasing transparency and making gains and losses more salient for the population at large. We should not assume, however, that simply raising awareness of an issue will change people's views. Recent contributions from behavioral science suggest that deliberating often results in groups adopting even more extreme positions (Sunstein, 2019).

counterpart but reflecting a reality. This did not mean that policies were not adapted over time, but what remained was a sense of priorities. The Minister for Industry who negotiated with Ford in the early 1970s explained the new policy as a natural evolution of the industrial policy carried out under his predecessor in the ministry during most of the 1960s (García Ruiz, 2018, p. 38). It is true that, while instruments such as local content requirements were significantly changed under the Ford decrees, the overall objective of increasing the outward orientation of the car industry to increase its competitiveness remained unchanged.

The effect of economic policy uncertainty has attracted increasing attention in recent years. This literature has pioneered new ways of measuring the extent and impact of uncertainty, from exploiting a broad range of macroeconomic time series (Jurado et al., 2015) or a narrower set of fiscal time series (Fernández-Villaverde et al., 2015), to developing a new index of economic policy uncertainty based on newspaper coverage frequency (Bloom, 2014, and Baker et al., 2016). Importantly, one common finding across this recent literature is that the impact of policy uncertainty is large.

Unfortunately, the balancing between policy innovation and policy continuity is a topic that has received almost no attention in the existing literature on the Spanish economic takeoff. Showing the continuity of policy priorities in a comparative perspective, as many of the arguments discussed in this chapter, is no easy task. One way to approximate this is by drawing on the analysis of policy priorities as reflected in state-of-the-union-type speeches. Using the same topic modeling algorithm that we discussed in Chapter 5, we can compare the volatility of topics in Franco's end-of-year speeches with those in selected countries for which, together with my colleagues Germán Reyes and Axel Eizmendi, I have collected annual presidential speeches of a programmatic nature—most mandated by the respective constitution as a state of the union address.[11] While this is necessarily an imperfect test of the underlying argument, the emerging data confirms that Spain stands out among other countries for its continuity of policy priorities—as reflected in programmatic speeches of the countries' leaders (see Figure 9.2).

The correlation between policy volatility and economic performance, as shown by the proxies in Figure 9.2, may well be spurious or driven by the available data. But, like the recent literature on economic policy uncertainty referenced above suggests, it suggests also that there may be such a thing as a Goldilocks' sweet spot of policy changes—enough for policy innovation and adaptation to occur but not so much that it creates excessive uncertainty about the future course of policies.

---

[11] The data was collected as part of a separate research project, where coverage was limited to Spanish-speaking Latin American countries. For a methodological discussion, see Chapter 5 and Calvo-Gonzalez et al. (2018).

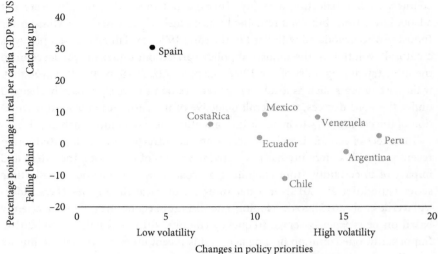

Figure 9.2 Policy volatility and convergence with US GDP per capita, 1950–75

Note: The horizontal axis shows a measure of volatility in the topics of the annual state-of-the-union type of speeches drawn from a topic modeling algorithm on each country. The volatility of each topic over 1950 to 1975 is averaged using as weights the average share of that topic over the period. The speeches from Argentina and Chile are available since 1952, Ecuador from 1951 to 1969, Venezuela from 1954 to 1975, and Spain until 1974. The vertical axis shows how each country fared compared to the US real per capita GDP, measured in percentage points. Thus, Spain's real per capita GDP converged around 30 percentage points, from 27 percent to 57 percent of the US level.

Source: Own elaboration with Axel Eizmendi and Maddison Project Database for real per capita GDP (Bolt, Inklaar, de Jong, and van Zanden, 2018).

Aspirations

In 1965, Ester Boserup was at the peak of her career. That year she published her landmark *The Conditions of Agricultural Growth* in which, very much against the prevailing Malthusian pessimism, she stressed how population growth could help unleash productivity growth through agricultural intensification. In October of that same year, Boserup traveled to Spain as Deputy Chief for a mission of the World Bank and the Food and Agriculture Organization. After traveling two months in Spain, she led the preparation of a report that saw the light in 1966 under the title *The Development of Agriculture in Spain*. The report included the familiar themes of what would later be referred to as getting prices right, noting that subsidies and preferential tax treatments resulted in uneconomic uses of resources and depressed productivity. But Boserup also managed to convey a much deeper message. Right from the first page of the executive summary, we can read:

A transformation of Spanish agriculture is thus now essential, but it would not be wise to overestimate the speed with which this can be accomplished. Much depends on the *individual initiative* of large numbers of independent farmers whose activities are based on their own intimate knowledge of *what they wish to achieve* and their own *perception of possibilities*. All these individual actions constitute the secular trend *which public policies can influence only to a limited degree.*[12]

This is one of the most insightful yet least quoted assessments of the economic takeoff in Spain. Prosperity was unexpected not only because from a statistical point of view it was unlikely or because the previous history of Spain did not bode well for a sustained period of stable development, but because it also depended on the initiative of countless individuals, and their perception of possibilities, which were not directly determined by policy.

There is a growing recognition in the economics literature that mental processes affect long-term economic outcomes for individuals and, therefore, economy-wide development. Because any human endeavor starts in the mind, psychological factors often become internal constraints that limit an individual's actions. Constraints such as the role that scarcity plays in reducing our mental bandwidth are in fact some of the more likely causes of poverty traps (Mullainathan and Shafir, 2013; Kraay and McKenzie, 2014). In today's language, we refer to the issues that Boserup was putting front and center with the term *aspirations*.[13] Although pinning down a fully satisfactory definition of aspirations is challenging, we can think of aspirations as forward-looking goals based on what people know and want. Aspirations are not unbounded wishes but are largely determined by the social environment (Ray, 2006). As Boserup herself noted in the excerpt quoted above, it matters not only what individuals want to achieve but also what they think is feasible.

While the recent literature on aspirations has shown that it can yield new insights on issues such as fertility choices, inequality, or social conflict, our ability to apply this lens to the economic takeoff in Spain is limited due to data constraints. The potential role of aspirations has not been a central topic of research by Spanish economists or historians. As a result, the stock of analyses from which to draw is rather thin. Closest to our interest in aspirations is perhaps the work on the history of mentalities, associated with the French *Annales* school, which has had some traction among scholars of Spanish social history under the Franco dictatorship. The historian Walter Bernecker, in particular, has argued that economic

---

[12] Emphasis added. Quoted from *The Development of Agriculture in Spain* (World Bank, 1966, p. 3), in World Bank Archive Folder 30030194 (Spain, Agricultural Mission Report).

[13] I am grateful to Anna Fruttero, Noel Muller, and all my colleagues at the Mind, Behavior, and Development Unit (eMBeD) of the World Bank for their insights on the link between aspirations and development.

development in the 1960s was in part the consequence of a change in attitudes and mentalities (e.g., Bernecker, 2007).

Fortunately, household and opinion surveys became more widespread in the 1960s, in part thanks to the pioneering work of sociologists like Amando de Miguel, whom we encountered earlier in the chapter. The establishment of an official Public Opinion Institute in 1963 and the professionalization of the official polling institute also contributed to the increase in surveys, which covered a wide range of subjects. The Public Opinion Institute even participated in 1967 in an unlikely collaboration with the International Peace Research Institute of Oslo in their cross-country *Mankind 2000* project, an early effort at tapping into the expectations of citizens around the world of the world at the end of the twentieth century (Alcobendas, 2006, p. 166).

On balance, the available evidence suggests two main findings about the evolution of aspirations of the Spanish people during this period. First, a large and broad-ranging shift in aspirations on issues such as family size and education, but much less so regarding gender roles. Second, many of these changes in mindsets were already noticeable in the surveys from the mid-1960s, suggesting indeed that their change may have preceded the most intense episode of economic development.

By 1965, aspirations about fertility had already shifted significantly. On average, the ideal number of children was considered to be 3.3, while respondents' mothers had on average 5.5 children each (FOESSA, 1966, p. 47). Expectations of increasing prosperity had been internalized by the majority of the population, as shown by the fact that 55 percent of survey respondents that year expected their economic situation to improve over the following five years and only 6 percent expected it to get worse. Importantly, there were no large differences between respondents in urban and rural areas about their optimism for the future. The same source also gives us clues about the wishes and expectations of parents about their children's education. Parents of boys aged less than 7 years old understood the benefits of an education for their children: 43 percent stated they wished for their boys to reach tertiary education, although the percentage of those that stated they expected it to happen to dropped to 23 percent. Still, this was a remarkably optimistic take given the existing levels of educational attainment. At the time of the survey, just 1.5 percent of the population held a degree of post-secondary education, and the average years of education of a person of labor force age in Spain was barely 5.5 (compare to, for example, 9.8 years in England; for both data points see Núñez, 2005, p. 267).

But the picture for girls was quite different. Only 23 percent of parents of girls less than 7 years old hoped their daughters would reach tertiary education and just 8 percent expected it to happen. Gender inequality remained pervasive. Single women's participation in the labor force was widely accepted, but marriage and childrearing imposed a dividing line that was solidified in social norms. In the mid-1960s, almost one in ten housewives thought it was appropriate for single women to work outside the home, but the figures dropped to just half supporting married women without children, or with grown children, working outside the home and to less than one in five supporting married women with small children working outside the home (FOESSA, 1966, p. 64). Gender norms will have to wait for over a generation to start shifting in meaningful ways. Most notably, female labor participation, which stood at 22 percent in the mid-1960s, remained below 30 percent until the mid-1980s.

That some norms and aspirations, like those about family size, had already changed by the 1960s should not surprise us. The demographic transition was well under way in the first half of the twentieth century. Life expectancy at birth for men had increased from 34 to 60 years in the first half of the twentieth century; for women it had risen even more, from 36 to 64 years during the same period. By 1950, the secular decline in overall mortality was nearly complete and, in line with the experience of the demographic transition elsewhere, fertility was also decreasing with a predictable lag.[14] And we should also be cautious not to fall for a simplistic interpretation that just because we observe fast economic growth after a shift in aspirations, the latter is a cause of the former. If we had surveyed the population three decades before the 1965 survey, we may have already observed similarly shifting aspirations about family size at that time. Yet economic growth did not take off in the first half of the twentieth century.

Also worth examining through the lens of aspirations is rural to urban migration. Like the demographic transition, this was not a new phenomenon in the second half of the twentieth century, but it intensified to such an extent in the 1950s and 1960s that it has led to recurrent questions about its drivers. Both demand and supply factors were certainly at play, as the growth of industry and services in cities attracted formerly agricultural workers who could enjoy higher wages in cities such as Barcelona, Madrid, Bilbao, or Valencia (Silvestre, 2010, p. 124). The migration to cities resulted in a significant transformation of the structure of the labor force. From 1950 to 1970, the share of the labor force engaged in agriculture dropped by half, from 48 to 23 percent.

Migration to the cities had begun immediately after the Civil War. The population of the city of Madrid doubled to around 3.1 million from 1950 to 1970. But it had already increased by 60 percent, from 1 to 1.6 million, during the 1940s. This suggests that a change in mindsets preceded the economic takeoff (Bernecker, 2007, p. 69). The best evidence for this view comes from the work of anthropologists studying rural areas. In rural ethnographies, the link between the Civil War and changes in "the way of life" is much more easily discernible than in the work of

---

[14] Population growth accelerated as infant mortality continued to decline, down from 124 per 1,000 children under one year of age in 1930 to 70 per 1,000 in 1950 and 28 per 1,000 in 1970. All demographic data from Nicolau (2005).

economists (e.g., Francisco López-Casero, 1994). In some villages of the South of Spain, the experience of the Civil War had already involved a temporary migration as populations escaped from the incoming rebels. Perhaps this earlier experience of displacement made it more likely to consider migrating after war.[15]

Another factor which could have contributed to facilitate rural to urban migration was the compulsory military service. Since Franco conceived of the army mainly as a repressive tool, he built garrisons around the large cities. Recruits from poorer rural areas were therefore often performing their military service near the booming urban centers. Many never returned to their villages after they completed their service. While this is an under-researched topic, oral history sources suggest that while the decision to migrate may have already been taken by these individuals, the very act of undertaking the service may have facilitated the act of migration if for no other reason than that it provided free transport for the conscripts and the possibility of getting acquainted with job opportunities in the area where they were serving.[16]

Conclusions

Throughout the 1960s, the Franco regime transformed into a technocratic state, an *estado de obras*—or public works state—as one of its propagandists put it. At the heyday of modernization, the rise of technocracy was far from a Spanish peculiarity. Intellectuals turned policymakers like Jacques Rueff, whose stabilization plan in France partly inspired the one in Spain, were given increasing responsibilities in governments across Europe. And the rise of technocracy was not restricted to liberal democracies. When in 1957 the Yugoslav dissident Milovan Djilas railed against a "new class," he had in the crosshairs "an educated technocracy of bureaucrats and professionals" (Judt, 2006, p. 429). The institutions for European integration were also run by technocrats, which is how the idiom came to be used in Spain, and Jacques Rueff himself had the ear of many when he visited Madrid just before the 1959 Stabilization Plan was set in motion.

But from the perspective of 1950, the rise of technocracy in Spain was hardly a foregone conclusion. This was a country ruled by a dictatorial government that included in its coalition elements that had been decidedly against the role of technical experts. The military leader of the Spanish Legion came to be known for his rallying cry of "death to the treasonous intellectual class"—first pronounced on Columbus Day 1936. More importantly, throughout the 1940s, the regime had

---

[15] This hypothesis has not yet been fully explored in the literature as far as I know.

[16] I am grateful to Professor Luis Velasco for his insights on these issues. For a broader discussion of the compulsory military service during this period see Velasco (2017).

followed policies that reflected isolationist ideas. Yet all that changed, even if gradually, after 1950.

Behind the change in economic policymaking lies a change in the ideas of the elite. And behind the change in ideas was a relentless scanning of experience outside Spain, especially in Europe. The prospect of Europeanizing Spain, a goal which had been forcefully articulated at the outset of the twentieth century, would somewhat unexpectedly kick-started after 1950. This was a slow process, which culminated in the 1986 accession of Spain to the European Communities, but which had consequential effects over several decades before entry into the EU materialized. The technocrats that held increasing power in 1960s Spain consistently sought out new ideas about policymaking from Europe and the United States. They were deliberate policy entrepreneurs.

More fundamentally, like their Western European peers, the technocrats considered a responsibility of the state to seek to advance progress for a wide spectrum of society. To pursue this objective, they considered it critical to increase efficiency and put great faith on technological progress. The latter explains some early adoption of technology. For example, Spain's nuclear energy program was early and large given the country's level of economic development (Rubio Varas and de la Torre, 2017). More generally, what truly stands out of the technocrats is that they were able to implement their practical agenda over a sustained period. There had been previous technocratic efforts to emulate European practices, sometimes from reformers that reached even higher levels of government. A long-term horizon allowed policies to evolve without unnecessary volatility.

Crucially, change was not limited to the ideas of the policy elite. The aspirations of the population at large changed too. What came first, changed aspirations or improved economic performance, is hard to establish. In some cases, mindsets started to change even before the economic transformation had yielded its fruits. Decisions about fertility, for example, were likely driven by demographic processes that were well in motion before the economic takeoff. The shock of the Civil War to the way of life of many in rural areas may also have helped jumpstart migration decisions. With rising aspirations, however, can come a sense of frustration if they are not met. As far as economic aspirations are concerned, starting from the late 1960s, a substantial increase in the state's provision of education, health, and social protection would help keep frustrations at bay. But on the political front, the story became one of increasing frustration and conflict. The technocrats had operated under the assumption that a more open polity could only be envisaged after substantial economic development. This was, of course, *the* fundamental reason why the Franco regime tolerated technocracy. But as the regime aged and political freedoms continued to be curtailed despite the substantial economic development achieved, it became increasingly obvious that technocracy had not—and could not—overcome the fundamental pitfall of the regime. Politics was about to show, again, that it reigns supreme.

10

Lucking Out

Like most Spanish people of my generation, I have a blurred but weighty memory of the evening of February 23, 1981. I remember seeing my parents in their room, sitting in their bed listening to the radio on the bedside table. They waved us away, but together with my brother and my sister, we snooped in from outside their bedroom door, which was left ajar. I was not yet 7 years old, but it was clear, even for me, that something very serious was happening. We overheard my mother mentioning that army tanks were rolling through the streets, and I remember my siblings and I resolutely looking out of the window to check if we could see tanks. Earlier that day, the Congress had been occupied by security forces. Shots were fired. The democratically elected members of parliament were ordered to lie on the floor and were told by a gun-waving member of the Civil Guard that the competent military authority would take over. Indeed, tanks rolled through the streets of the city of Valencia. It was an attempted military *coup d'état*, the forty-first in Spain since the beginning of the nineteenth century.

The coup failed when the overwhelming majority of the military obeyed the clear orders of King Juan Carlos I to stand behind the constitutional order. Four days later, there were mass demonstrations backing democracy across the country. In Madrid, an estimated million and a half people took to the streets under a single platform, agreed by all political parties, in support of freedom, democracy, and the Constitution. The unfolding of events made another coup inconceivable. The failed February 23, 1981 attempt would be the last military coup that the country has seen. The age of the *pronunciamientos* was over.

With the benefit of hindsight, it is tempting to dismiss the coup as doomed to fail. But this was far from a foregone conclusion. Fear grabbed the country. There was no immediate outpouring in the streets in support of the constitutional order. My parents' reaction was not unusual. As the novelist Javier Cercas put it, on that evening the "whole country stayed at home and waited for the coup to fail. Or to succeed."[1] The country had been awash with rumors about a military takeover for several months. The Basque separatist terrorist group ETA had killed 124 people in 1980, including many high-level military officers. Terrorism was widely seen

---

[1] Cercas (2011, p. 7). As people stayed home, electricity consumption that evening was up so much that, fearing a blackout in the city center of Madrid, the public lighting in the suburbs was cut. Inside the Congress, the assailants feared a deliberate power cut.

Unexpected Prosperity: How Spain Escaped the Middle Income Trap. Oscar Calvo-Gonzalez, Oxford University Press.
© Oscar Calvo-Gonzalez 2021. DOI: 10.1093/oso/9780198853978.003.0011

by the population as the leading problem of the day. And it was not just terrorism that weighed heavily on people's minds.

The unemployment rate had climbed from single digits to over 13 percent, resulting in a swelling of the unemployed to 1.6 million by 1981, quadrupling in just five years. For those employed, high inflation in the late 1970s eroded the purchasing power of wages to the point that real earnings growth became at best flat (Argandoña, 1999). Workdays lost to strikes soared. More broadly, sentiment about the state of the economy had kept worsening. In June 1979, when a question about the general state of the country's economy was added to the national sociological survey, around 40 percent of the population considered it either bad or very bad. This figure increased steadily to reach a high point in January 1981, when over 67 percent of the population had a similarly negative perspective of the country's economy.

Optimism about the future course of the economy also hit rock bottom in December 1980. At that time, the share of the population that thought the country's economic situation would be better in a year's time was only 8 percent, down from 30 percent in October 1978, the first time the question was asked in the national survey. This question has been asked continuously since, and the low reached in December 1980 has not yet been matched in the 40 years since, not even during the worst months of the global financial crisis. The word on the street was discontent, reflecting both political and economic concerns.

Had the coup succeeded it would have likely been on account of the response of the military leadership not involved in the coup. General Guillermo Quintana Laci, like all other captain generals of Spain, answered the call of King Juan Carlos I with a show of loyalty towards the King, "for whatever he wants." As many have pointed out, had King Juan Carlos asked the generals to fall in line behind a national unity government outside the constitutional order, the coup may have succeeded. And had the coup succeeded, we would now be stressing its connections with the long history of *pronunciamientos* that we discussed in Chapter 1. The proclamation of the rebel general in Valencia that got the tanks in the streets was a carbon copy of the one issued by the director of the coup in 1936. And the man behind it, General Jaime Milans del Bosch, was the grandson of a close collaborator of King Alfonso XIII and then the dictator Primo de Rivera, as well as a direct descendent from one of the earliest generals to launch a *pronunciamiento* in Spain in 1817.

Surprising as this may be, the failed coup of February 1981 was not even the event that came closest to derailing the transition to democracy.[2] As we will see

---

[2] The literature on the Transition (often capitalized) to democracy in Spain is voluminous and still undergoing much change. Contributions by political scientists like Maravall (1985), Linz and Stepan (1996), or Colomer (1998) remain essential, but historians have now started to delve into the period; see, for example, Soto Carmona (2005), Juliá (2017), and Molinero and Ysàs (2018).

below, there were other moments in which the outcome of the transition hung in the balance. The success of the political transition should not blind us to the fact that it could have all gone terribly wrong. In many respects, the country lucked out, as obvious risks did not materialize. The main argument in this short chapter is that the very nature of the way political power was exercised during the Franco regime implied that risks to the sustainability of prosperity could only increase as Franco aged and after his death. Much of the literature has stressed that the Franco dictatorship left an inheritance of bad economic policies. More importantly, in my view, is that the Franco dictatorship bequeathed a legacy of political risk which in turn had negative economic consequences and could have easily had disastrous ones. Fortunately, both the economy and the polity moved decisively towards an open access regime in the early 1980s.

The inevitable biological fact

Franco relentlessly promoted a personality cult. He conferred upon himself the medieval title of *Caudillo* and proclaimed he was so "by the grace of God"—as the inscription in coins reads. His face appeared on coins, stamps, and portraits hung in every public office and classroom in the country. Cinemas showed an official short newsreel before every movie, which typically showed the dictator in as positive a light as possible. Franco granted royal titles as if he were a king, he walked into every church under the *palio* or canopy that Catholics use of *Generalísimo*. Thousands of streets across Spanish cities were renamed after when taking statues of the Virgin Mary or Saints on procession, and used the title him. In such a sycophantic atmosphere, the prospect of Franco's death was not considered polite conversation and came to be known euphemistically as "the inevitable biological fact."

In 1967, Franco turned 75 years old. He had enjoyed good health for most of his life. In over thirty years, he had only missed one of the weekly cabinet meetings, in November 1959, when he suffered from the flu. But by then he had surpassed the life expectancy of men of his generation and was widely rumored to have Parkinson's disease. The question in everyone's mind was: After Franco, what? Our interest in this question stems mainly from how the nature of the dictatorship compromised the sustainability of economic gains once Franco died— we will return to this issue below. But the life cycle of Franco's personal dictatorship also had important consequences for policymaking while Franco was still alive.

As Franco aged, intrigues and disputes between and within factions of the regime took a new meaning. In 1969, Franco appointed Prince Juan Carlos, then 31 years old, as his successor with the title of king, in line with the Law of Succession of 1947 that we discussed in Chapter 3. While this clarified who would be the new head of the state, it settled very little else. Some examples will help illustrate this power struggle which, importantly, could only escalate as Franco's demise appeared closer. For some time, the technocrats had gotten the upper hand, with a swelling of their numbers in the cabinet throughout the 1960s. The appointment of Prince Juan Carlos was also seen as evidence of the hold on power by the technocrats, and in particular by their sponsor Luis Carrero Blanco.

But days after the appointment of Prince Juan Carlos as successor, a major scandal broke out. In order to collect on public loans meant to incentivize exports, a firm named Matesa had been fraudulently misrepresenting its sales abroad. The Ministers of Finance and Commerce and a former Minister of Finance were implicated, if not for outright corruption, for negligence. They were all technocrats. The Minister of Information, Manuel Fraga, who as we know from the last chapter was opposed to the technocrats, thought it an opportune time to let the press discuss the scandal freely. In letting this happen, Fraga was conveniently applying a recent law which had inched the press towards slightly greater freedoms, including the elimination of prior censorship. The attacks in the press were an indictment not only of specific individuals but also of the technocrats as a group.

Fraga's gamble, however, boomeranged. After a couple of months, Carrero convinced Franco of the need to move forward with a more unified government. In characteristic fashion, Franco removed not only those implicated in the scandal but also those who had let it be discussed in the press, like Fraga, or who appeared to be critical of the technocrats. The new government, pejoratively named monochromatic by its critics within the regime because of its uncharacteristic lack of representation of different factions, was a complete victory for Carrero. After 1969, Franco delegated to Carrero much of the day-to-day running of the cabinet. Carrero's ascent would culminate in June 1973 when he was promoted to prime minister, a position which the 1967 Organic Law of the State had clearly differentiated from that of the head of state. Franco, who had been both head of state and prime minister since 1936, appeared to have clarified the way forward that he envisaged after his death.

Then, on December 20, 1973, Carrero was assassinated by the Basque terrorist group ETA. The news shocked the country. Carrero was killed by an explosion detonated under his car shortly after he left the church in which he attended his daily morning mass. Carrero's car, which always used the same route, was blown up with such force that it ended up on the roof a five-story building. The news left the government momentarily paralyzed. ETA had used assassinations as part of its tactics since 1968 but had only killed half a dozen people before the terrorist attack on Carrero. Radio stations stopped their regular programming, switching to play classical music instead, but the rumor of Carrero's death spread during the day over the phone. The vacuum of news sparked serious concerns. Initially thought of as an accident due to a gas explosion, the realization that it had been a terrorist attack quickly took hold.

Worried citizens rushed home early, afraid of what these events could imply. Many parents showed up at their children's schools to pick up their children early, and some schools dismissed class altogether. The trial of leaders of an illegal trade union was temporarily suspended because the authorities in charge feared uncontrolled groups of extreme right-wingers in search of targets on which to exercise revenge. The director of the Civil Guard put the entire corps in a state of emergency and called for zero restraint on the use of force. Not knowing what the Civil Guard was reacting to, some local authorities feared a more serious civil conflict had broken out.

The country had been experiencing strikes and demonstrations demanding political freedoms. In many respects, these demands were the upshot of the economic betterment of large swaths of the population, but many in government saw it as a social upheaval that called for repression. Carrero himself saw it that way, as he told Henry Kissinger, whom he met in Madrid just the day before he was killed. The assassination perhaps made an even tougher repressive posture of the regime more likely. As we noted in Chapter 1, cross-country evidence suggests that the assassinations of leaders tend to enflame low-scale conflicts (Jones and Olken, 2009). In any event, Carrero's assassination was a clear demonstration that the country had not superseded the era of political violence. It drew a straight line back to those other Spanish prime ministers in office in 1870, 1897, 1912, and 1921 (see Figure 1.1 in Chapter 1).

It was only late in the evening of December 20, 1973, close to midnight, that it was confirmed on national TV that Carrero had been assassinated. The message was conveyed by Torcuato Fernández-Miranda, who as deputy prime minister had automatically become acting prime minister. Fernández-Miranda, a constitutional law professor who had been a teacher and close advisor of Prince Juan Carlos, would perform on the day of Carrero's assassination the first of many acts of political poise. With limited instructions from Franco, who barely conveyed to him that he felt the ground under their feet was shaken, and facing calls from within the government to exact revenge, Fernández-Miranda kept cool, and decided that there would be no declaration of a state of exception. His message on TV that night stressed how "our pain does not cloud our calmness. Our calm in these moments is our best show of force." The government appeared in control.[3]

Franco, who had just turned 81 and whose Parkinson's had clearly advanced, was in shock. The day of Carrero's funeral mass, he was seen sobbing in public. Over the following days, he seemed unable to decide on who to name as prime minister, changing his mind at the very last minute. The new prime minister,

---

[3] There would be flare-ups of tension provoked by the far right, including during Carrero's funeral. The far right was upset with what they thought was an ungrateful Catholic Church that had been putting distance between itself and the regime, particularly the Archbishop of Madrid, who presided over the funeral: Vicente Enrique Tarancón, the same man who, as we saw in the Introduction, had complained in 1950 about bread shortages and the corrupt management of food rationing.

Carlos Arias Navarro, replaced 12 of 18 ministers and appointed a new cabinet where old factions such as the *Falange* regained a measure of power. The technocrats were wiped out of the cabinet. They had risen to power promising the Franco regime legitimacy on account of its success in bringing about economic development and an ensuing "twilight of ideologies"—the title of a 1961 book by Gonzalo Fernández de la Mora, a technocratic minister for whom success was "political apathy," which for him was "not a symptom of social disease but of health."[4] The assassination of Carrero was the final proof that the technocrats' program of securing political apathy had failed.

The technocrats had lost, but under the weak leadership of Arias, it was not clear that there were any winners. The weakness of the regime and the divisions within it, which were fully reflected in the cabinet, had major consequences for economic policymaking. That autumn of 1973, the first oil shock had been set in motion. Crude oil prices, which had already almost doubled in the second half of 1973 to close the year at $4.70 per barrel, more than tripled to $13 per barrel in January 1974. The response of the embattled Spanish government was what one would expect of policymakers with the most short-sighted of horizons: Consumer prices of oil products were kept unchanged, and the public budget picked up the bill.

Policy tinkering became policy dithering. Over the next five years, economic management gave way to mismanagement. Subsidizing oil was particularly detrimental, not only fiscally, but also because it led to an increase in the energy intensity of the economy—all in the middle of repeated shocks to the oil price! Uncertainty took hold, interest rates and inflation shot up, asset prices became depressed, and growth flatlined. Job creation came to a halt, precisely at a time when larger demographic cohorts started to reach the labor market. In 1981, youth aged 15–29 years surpassed 3 million, about half a million more than a decade earlier. It is in these years that the main features that would come to characterize the Spanish labor market for decades took shape, such as protection of insiders, extremely high youth unemployment, and low participation rates.

Turkeys voting for Christmas

After a long illness, Franco died on November 20, 1975. In his political testament, read on national TV, the late dictator called on all Spaniards to profess loyalty to the new head of state, the 37-year-old Prince Juan Carlos. Two days later, the new King is sworn in, with an oath to uphold the fundamental laws of the Franco

---

[4] As quoted in Gilmour (1985, p. 18). Revealingly, he would end up as Minister of Public Works from 1970 to 1973. He was, incidentally, the minister that tendered the highway concessions that would end up costing a fortune due to the exchange rate guarantee.

regime. It was Franco's own vision to leave his successor constrained, unable to exercise the type of power that he had enjoyed. For the new King, this presented a true Catch-22. Large swaths of the country demanded political freedoms, and he had hinted at his desire to move in that direction when in his first speech as king that he wanted to be the king of all Spaniards. But how could reform take place if he was bound to simply follow existing laws? How could he break with the past without appearing disloyal, and thus risking being seen as illegitimate by the regime insiders? How could he placate the Francoists that occupied all state institutions without alienating the pro-democracy forces? Members of the political opposition already saw him with great suspicion as a king that had been installed by Franco. The exiled leader of the Spanish Communist Party would famously prognosticate that the new King would become known as Juan Carlos *el breve* (the brief, as he was not expected to be able to hold onto power for long).[5]

After asking for the resignation of Carlos Arias, to which the latter could have technically refused to submit, the new King engineered the appointment of Adolfo Suárez as new prime minister in July 1976.[6] The appointment of Suárez, who at 43 years of age was of the same generation as the monarch but lacked the distinguished accomplishments of others who were in the running, was considered initially by many in the press as an outright rookie mistake by the new King. The new government was so inexperienced that early reactions dismissed it as a cabinet of undersecretaries or untenured professors. But the new government set out on a daring course to reform the entire Francoist institutional framework. Caught between the demands of the political opposition for a break with the past and the immobilism of the Francoist institutions, the new government unveiled a strategy to reform the political institutions from within the law. Torcuato Fernández-Miranda, whom we have met above and who was strategically named the new President of the Congress, prepared a draft of a Law for the Political Reform.

The law did not mince words. It envisaged a new, fully democratic regime in which the existing parliament would dissolve itself to give rise to a constitutional process. It effectively asked the parliamentarians to put themselves out of power. An intense and targeted effort of lobbying each of the congressmen ensued. Each member of parliament probably had their own reasons for going along with what many deemed political suicide. Some may have fancied their chances in an open political competition. Others, like the Minister of Labor, later explained—or

---

[5] At the other end of the political spectrum, the one-time leader of the Conservatives during the Republic and later a prominent advocate of a restoration under Don Juan, wondered whether, under the conditions that it was being installed, the monarchy had any chance of consolidation. He was cautious enough to acknowledge that in politics all predictions are very risky, but he left no doubt that the course of events had resulted in the "failure of the restoration of the monarchist legitimacy" (Gil-Robles, 1976, p. 10).

[6] The King could not choose his own prime minister freely but had to select him from a list of three names proposed by the Council of the Realm, an institution created by the Law of Succession and a stronghold of conservatism.

perhaps rationalized—their vote in favor of the Law for the Political Reform as a conscious decision to build a new future (De la Fuente, 1998, p. 272). Either way, the end result was a milestone in the transition to democratic rule. Two days before the first anniversary of Franco's death, the Francoist Congress approved with a convincing majority of 80 percent of the chamber to dismantle the entirety of the Francoist institutional architecture. The law was then to be voted by the public in a referendum.

The specter of violence

Around the time that the Law for the Political Reform was being considered, in October 1976, the marketing campaign for the launch of a new newspaper got off to a rocky start when the official censorship banned the song that was to accompany the radio and TV ads for the newspaper. The censors relented and the song *Sin Ira Libertad* (Freedom Without Anger), possibly aided by the additional publicity of the initial censorship, shot to number one of the billboards in December and stayed there for over a month. Its seven singers, decked in bell-bottom pants, the men sporting long hair and, some, beards, captured the moment. The song became an anthem for those demanding political freedom. The very first lines of the song went like this:

> Old folks say that in this country
> There was a war
> That there are two Spains that still keep
> The grudge of old debts.

As a work of art, the song is hardly noteworthy, but its lyrics are revealing of its time. The song is a dare to a cynical viewpoint held by a strawman—the "old folks" with which the song starts—that dismisses political freedom as impossible because "we are all quick to resort to violence here." In contrast, the song argues that a new generation, sufficiently removed from old grievances, can be trusted to handle political disagreements without the resort to violence. This was essentially the affirmation of a new generation with a message of hope.

It was the same hope with which an overwhelming majority of 94 percent of voters approved the Law for the Political Reform in a referendum in mid-December 1976. More important, over three quarters of eligible voters had showed up at the polls. But, while the consensus was broad, there were pockets of those prepared to use violence. Days before the referendum took place, a Marxist terrorist group had kidnapped the conservative politician and businessman Antonio María Oriol Urquijo, member of the Council of the Realm, former Minister of Justice, and one of the richest men in the country. The government lived in fear that the hostage would be killed and his body found just as the referendum got under way.

That winter things got worse. In the particularly tragic month of January 1977, extremists from both the right and the left entered into a dangerous escalation of violence. Right-wing extremists opened fire in a trade union legal aid clinic, killing five. Marxist terrorists killed police officers and undertook another high-profile kidnaping—a lieutenant general no less. A student demonstrating was killed by police. The funerals of slain police officers were chilling moments in which extreme right-wingers openly called for violence and a military takeover. Violence was not just a potential threat but a political reality (Molinero and Ysàs, 2018). The legalization of the Communist Party in Easter 1977 created another tense moment, as many military leaders felt betrayed after having understood from the Suárez government that such a move was off the table.

Fortunately, the violence did not get out of hand. Restraint by the organized political opposition proved helpful. After decades of persecution, what animated the opposition leaders was not revenge but turning the page. The pro-democracy demonstrators' cry throughout the 1970s had been *Amnesty and Freedom*, in that order. This has sometimes been misunderstood as amnesia. On the contrary, the memories from the violent past were very present in the collective psyche. There was trepidation in the population as a whole. A few days ahead of the first free elections on June 15, 1977, a local leader of the Socialist Party in Toledo, a psychiatrist, intimated that "[a]s soon as the elections became a reality, the psychosomatic symptoms of the general population grew. Many people don't realize they are suffering mentally...no name has been put on the ailments we are treating during this period...obsessive rememberings of the past."[7] On the eve of election night, the leader of the Communist Party, Santiago Carrillo, used the free national TV time allocated to his party to give a reassuring message: "What us communists wholeheartedly want is that in Spain there be no more civil wars."

The economic consequences of Francoism

The research question that lies beneath much of the Spanish economic history literature of the second half of the twentieth century revolves around who to assign credit for the prosperity that the country attained. Often the question is implicit, which muddles the discussion even more. When asked explicitly, it tends to be put in terms such as the following: "Should Franco and his regime be credited with the economic success of the country?" (Martín Aceña and Martínez Ruiz 2007, p. 38). Posed that way, this research question can trip us in several ways.

---

[7] As quoted in Probst Solomon (1983, p. 258).

First, it nudges researchers away from exploring the "how" of economic development. As a result, some topics have gone under-researched. We encountered this, for example, when we discussed the role of indicative planning in Chapter 8. Reflecting on the issue, a leading economic historian notes that "with the passing of time, and without the pressure to necessarily condemn the acts of the Franco regime, we can state that through the plans, the 'technocrats'...increased the transparency of projects and decision-making" (Maluquer de Motes, 2014, p. 318). Scholars still feel the need to go out of their way to caveat that any positive assessment of developments during the Franco dictatorship is not to be interpreted as an endorsement of the dictator or his regime.[8] I too stress that acknowledging the economic growth that took place and exploring its underlying factors should not be interpreted as a vindication of the regime whatsoever. But it should go without saying.

It also puts too much emphasis on the individual figure of the dictator. Franco was the ultimate decision maker for close to 40 years, but he is not the key to understand the period, any more than Narváez—the general with whom we started Chapter 1 and who in his deathbed could not forgive his enemies because he had shot them all—is the key to understand the nineteenth century. What is key is that both Narváez and Franco used violence to achieve and stay in power. In many ways, Franco was the last rebel general of the nineteenth century, "anachronistically inserted in the twentieth" (Reig Tapia, 2012, p. 917).

In earlier chapters, we have noted that the economic success can be attributed to increases in openness and contestability, and thus a limited opening of access to economic opportunities. We have also noted that there was some competition of ideas within the government. But none of that qualifies in any form that the regime was a classic limited access order regime as far as political opportunities are concerned. Not only were there no free and fair elections or other forms of political contestability, but most groups in society were precluded from participating in political life. Perhaps this is clearest in the case of women, who were fully excluded, but it applies to most socioeconomic groups (see Figure 10.1 for two de facto measures of exclusion). It would only be in the early 1980s that the Spanish polity would become a fully open access order.

As a personal dictatorship, the Franco regime had an inevitable succession problem. That political uncertainty increased as the dictator grew into old age and died was the natural consequence of the way political power was exercised in that regime. This harmful political legacy had negative consequences for the conduct of economic policy and ultimately for growth. But, more importantly, it also exposed the country to extraordinarily large downside risks. While the worst

---

[8] These caveats are common even in highly technical and specialized assessments. One such example regarding the role of engineers stresses that "[a]cknowledging the significance of science and technology in the making of Francoism is not a vindication of the regime" (Camprubí, 2014, p. 161).

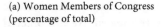

(a) Women Members of Congress
(percentage of total)

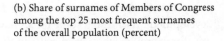

(b) Share of surnames of Members of Congress
among the top 25 most frequent surnames
of the overall population (percent)

Figure 10.1 Two de facto measures of open access

Note: The distribution of surnames in Spain is highly skewed. The top 25 most frequent surnames are so common that they account for 58 percent of peoples' surnames. Because more frequent surnames are on average more likely to be associated with lower socio-economic backgrounds the distance to the 58 percent benchmark can be interpreted as a measure of how open access to political organizations really was for an average citizen. An increase in this indicator indicates that the distribution of surnames of parliamentarians is closer to that of the overall population and thus suggests a more open access regime.

Source: Own elaboration based on data on parliamentarians from the Spanish Congress and surname frequency by the National Institute of Statistics.

outcomes of widespread violence and the unraveling of the transition to democracy did not materialize, those contingent liabilities would need to be included in any evaluation, even if one were to be solely interested in assessing the economic consequences of the dictatorship.

Conclusions

The eight years between the assassination of Prime Minister Carrero in December 1973 and the unsuccessful coup in February 1981 was most consequential. These two violent bookends underscore that the transition from the Franco regime to a constitutional democracy was not devoid of political violence. Ultimately, the successful transition from a dictatorial regime to a democratic one set in motion the longest run of peaceful transfers of power the country has ever seen. The transition to an open access society in the political sphere also will be essential to the sustainability of the prosperity that was initially unleashed under closed access institutions.

Such a positive outcome was not preordained. Beyond the failed coup with which we started the chapter, the risk of additional political violence was very real. History is always contingent, and this chapter has shown several instances when the country got very close to veering off the precipice into political violence. These uncomfortably high risks to the peaceful political transition were not the result of poor management of the transition process but were the direct result of the nature of the Franco dictatorship. Just as Franco's death was the "inevitable biological fact," in the euphemistic language of Francoist circles, uncertainty about who would hold power after Franco was inevitable given the nature of the regime. In fact, the succession problem of the Franco dictatorship started to have significant consequences even before Franco died.

In previous chapters, I took issue with a common argument in the literature that suggests that the economic takeoff in Spain happened despite its bad economic policies and that the country could have grown faster in the absence of such poor policies. Growth could have perhaps been faster, and the economy could have certainly taken off earlier had policies that promoted openness and increased contestability been adopted earlier. But for those interested in assessing the economic consequences of the Franco regime, that is not the biggest economic liability of the dictatorship. It was not the economic policy legacy of Francoism but the inevitable legacy of uncertainty that was the biggest drag on economic prosperity in the late 1970s. The economic consequences of Francoism cannot be disentangled from its politics.

Conclusion

When one looks for reasons why a glass is half empty, it is easy to fail to notice how it got half full in the first place. Likewise, most of the discussion on Spanish economic development in historical perspective has long focused on its short-comings. Yet, despite its shortfalls, today Spain is a prosperous society solidly established among the high-income economies and with not insignificant achievements in terms of human development. How did it become so? Instead of focusing on relative failures, the purpose here has been to explain how Spain's economy grew and developed. In doing so, it provides a new perspective, one that uncovers growth after 1950 as fast, sustained, and unexpected.

The glass had been filling quite rapidly, not only in absolute terms but when compared to the leading economies in the world. At the midpoint of the twenti-eth century, Spain's real per capita GDP was only 27 percent of that in the US. By 1980, it had caught up almost 30 percentage points, jumping to 56 percent of US real per capita GDP. Importantly, while growth slowed down in the last two decades of the twentieth century, the catching up continued even if in a more subdued form. Thanks to recent scholarship that has produced historical output estimates for many economies, we can now compare Spain not just with the lead-ing countries but with a much broader set of countries. As of the time of writing, there are almost three dozen countries in the world with output data for every half-century milestone since the beginning of the nineteenth century. When we compare Spain with those countries, the pattern of convergence is even more pronounced and sustained. After diverging for a century and a half, Spain caught up around 50 percentage points vis-à-vis the median of those countries in the half-century after 1950.

Yet the story of how Spain escaped the middle income trap does not feature prominently in the development literature. It is a story that, paradoxically, feels both too old and too recent. Spain graduated from being a borrowing member of the World Bank in 1977. The landscape of development today certainly feels much different than during the roughly three decades, from the early 1950s to the mid-1980s, when Spain transitioned into a high-income economy. In other respects, however, the period of fast and sustained economic growth is still too recent. Economic growth took off under the cruel dictatorship of General Franco, who gained power after rebelling against a democratically elected government, plunged the country into a vicious civil war, and held onto power through a

Unexpected Prosperity: How Spain Escaped the Middle Income Trap. Oscar Calvo-Gonzalez, Oxford University Press.
© Oscar Calvo-Gonzalez 2021. DOI: 10.1093/oso/9780198853978.003.0012

brutal repression. Both the Civil War and the Franco regime remain very much current in today's Spain. Faced with the risk that any positive assessment of economic developments during the Franco regime could be misconstrued as support for the latter, most of the historiography has perhaps unconsciously focused on the shortcomings of the economic path—the half-empty part of the glass. And given the few accounts of Spain's rise to high-income status, the demand for learning about the unlikely story of Spain's economic development remains latent. This is particularly so when compared to other success stories, such as the case of South Korea or other East Asian Tigers, which continue to be top of mind among development practitioners.

This relative neglect of Spain's path to prosperity is a pity. Not only are there just a handful of economies that have successfully transitioned from middle to high income in recent decades, but Spain's experience provides a treasure trove of insights that, contrary to expectations, are relevant for today's world. Like in other countries that achieved sustained economic takeoffs, the intensity of the convergence that Spain accomplished was unexpected. This is a point that is not sufficiently stressed in the literature, which tends to focus on the positive external environment and the advantages of Spain being in Europe as critical factors behind the country's success in reaching high-income status. A common misconception about Spain's rising prosperity is that it was largely achieved thanks to its membership of what is now the European Union. While EU membership helped solidify many of its gains, and the idea of Europeanizing Spain helped create a political and social consensus around certain reforms, the path to prosperity depended on many institutional developments that took place well before EU membership.

The external context was mostly favorable at the time of Spain's intense catching up, but the country had failed to translate similarly good external conditions into sustained growth on previous occasions. In fact, the economy had been losing ground in relative terms over the century and a half before 1950. This divergence was not due to inadequate rates of growth during spells of growth but to the short-lived nature of those spurts and the disastrous consequences of all too frequent economic contractions. The frequency of economic shrinking, as opposed to economic growth, was tightly linked to the precariousness of political settlements. During the period 1800–1950, there were over fifty coups—including over a dozen successful ones—and four civil wars. However, within this long span, we can differentiate before and after 1875. The use of violence as the norm to resolve political disputes became partially controlled since the Restoration of the monarchy in 1876 when the two main political parties agreed to take turns in government.

Violence was reduced, but through political and economic institutions that reflected entrenched narrow interests. In the framework of Douglass North and coauthors used throughout the analysis, Spain simply evolved from a fragile to a basic limited access order during the century and a half before 1950. And, as the unraveling of the Restoration settlement showed, repeated bouts of political violence were not unthinkable from the perspective of 1950. Both the limited control of violence and the characteristics of what Douglass North and coauthors refer to as a limited access order contributed to the economy suffering frequent shrinking episodes in the long period that preceded 1950. Yet, over the next three decades or so, the country would transform towards an increasingly open access regime. How did the country evolve from a closed access order in 1950 to an open access one by 1985? Our answer to this critical question is in four parts.

Ring the bells that still can ring

When the Civil War broke out in 1936, Albert Hirschman was quickly drawn to Spain. He was not alone amidst the intellectuals of his generation. Among many others, Ernest Hemingway, André Malraux, and Arthur Koestler would also fight for the Spanish Republic or report on the war from the Republican side. They have left us with powerful accounts of events and deep insights drawn from the conflict. In contrast, Hirschman would not put pen to paper on his experiences in Spain. He would not return to the country until 1989 and would never publicly discuss his views on developments in Spain since he fought as a soldier. Yet, of all the intellectuals that poured into Spain in the late 1930s, his voice could have been most enlightening, especially given Hirschman's appreciation for unintended consequences.

The first bell that rang for Spain was one it had little to do with. The Civil War, with all its devastation and the resulting dictatorial regime of Franco, did not bode well for Spain in the second half of the twentieth century. The regime that emerged victorious from the war succeeded, through a brutal repression, to achieve a monopoly of violence in Spain, but it lacked legitimacy. Having been installed in power with the help of Nazi Germany and Fascist Italy, Franco's regime found itself isolated at the end of World War II. Many thought the regime's days were numbered. But the Cold War created the conditions for an American rapprochement to Spain. Military interests dominated American foreign policy-making. The key was the geographic location of the Iberian Peninsula, far enough from what was expected to be the main theater of operations in Western Europe, but close enough for fighter jets to reach into the Soviet Union out of military bases in Spain. An aid-for-bases agreement sealed the end of the Franco regime as an international pariah and secured the regime once and for all. American support proved important to buttress business confidence, leading to a rise in private investment and economic growth.

But political stability also had domestic roots. Franco was able to secure a monopoly on the use of violence for political purposes. He did so by a brutal repression against the left and by co-opting and playing against each other the members of his coalition. Because Franco was prepared to kill to stay in power, anyone who would have wanted to oust him was forced to resort to violence. The opposition was ultimately unprepared to do so, either because they were benefiting from the regime, were afraid of reprisal, or worse, plunging the country into yet another civil war. Yet, political stability by itself would not be enough to explain the sustained nature of the economic takeoff. Economic growth took off after political stability was achieved, but it also required significant economic policy reforms.

Macroeconomic stability was the second bell that rang, in this case not so much pushed by the outside winds but by the pull of the policymakers. The country performed a drastic turnaround in economic policymaking, from an autarkic to a more open one. The growth dividend from correcting bad macroeconomic policies was large. A Stabilization Plan with the support of the international financial institutions in 1959 was an important milestone in this regard, but early reforms undertaken before 1959 played almost as much of a role in boosting growth. A simple empirical model suggests that the combined impact of improved economic policies boosted growth in per capita output by 3.7 percentage points annually. The main benefits came from removing acute distortions in the fiscal and monetary policy arenas, as well as getting the external price of the peseta right.

While much of the literature argues that the adoption of reforms was the result of a worsening economic situation in the late 1950s, drawing on archival evidence, I argue that the shift in economic policies can be best understood not as the result of economic instability but of political stability. Just as the autarkic policies had been adopted in the 1940s largely for political reasons, their progressive abandonment in the 1950s was also because of a change in the political environment. In short, the increase in political stability reduced the perception of threats, and the regime shifted its attention increasingly to economic issues. As the analysis of policy priorities captured in the text-mining of Franco's speeches undertaken here, this process took place gradually.

Forget your perfect offering

After the landmark liberalization in 1959, subsequent reforms pale in comparison. Thereafter, most accounts of Spain's economic development suggest that there was a reversal of policies, with a new interventionism and protectionism creeping in. The economy went on growing, in fact it accelerated its pace of growth, but—the standard argument maintains—this growth took place despite bad policies and institutions. The list of suboptimal policy choices is not short, as it includes persistently high tariff protection, excessive regulatory requirements, insufficient public revenue collection, limited support for innovation, inefficient public spending and development planning, etc. On closer inspection, however, the conventional wisdom falls short.

For example, the large car industry that developed in Spain did so not despite protection and regulation but because of them. Foreign companies that brought new technology and set up in the country were attracted to the fact that the domestic market was highly protected. The setting of requirements on local content, and most crucially their enforcement, helped develop a vibrant car parts manufacturing sector. But tariff protection on cars—which remained high—gives an incomplete picture of the extent to which the industry was subject to the contestability that comes from exposure to competition. To attract a new Ford plant, the authorities reduced the requirement of local content in exchange of a minimum amount of investment, set an export ratio of at least two-thirds of their new output, and capped the number of cars that the new manufacturer would be allowed to sell domestically equivalent to a percentage of the units sold in the national market the previous year. Overall, the incentives were aligned to ensure a competitive operation.

The opening up of Spain to the international economy helps to explain much of the growth spurt in the 1960s. Foreign investment continued to be made easier, not harder, and the country benefited from opening up to tourism and from migrants' remittances. Spain's openness ratio doubled in the 1950s to 15 percent of GDP and continued to increase to 22 percent of GDP by 1970. Crucially, in addition to greater openness, there was also an increase in export diversification—a development that has until recently gone largely unnoticed due to the lack of comparable data across countries. The key to the increased diversification is the rise in productivity that occurred, and it is our first hint that more contestability in markets may also be a factor behind the takeoff in economic growth. Indeed, we documented increases in contestability in a range of settings, from public procurement to critical infrastructure such as ports or the tourist sector. Often, the policy measures in question were far from best practices or first bests, but they were well adapted to the local context.

Efficiency gains accounted for two-thirds of the growth in output per capita. During the quarter-century after 1950, total factor productivity grew at a rate of 3.7 percent annually, up from an average of only 0.3 percent annually over the previous century. This was not just Spain benefiting from the worldwide increases in productivity during the Golden Age of postwar growth. A comparative analysis across countries for which labor productivity data is available over the long term shows Spain crawling up 30 percentile ranks in the three decades after 1950. The transfer of technology through foreign investment is a significant factor behind this performance. A sharp rise in imports of equipment and machinery, made possible by the inflows of foreign capital combined with tourism revenues and migrants' remittances, was also helpful. Although more difficult to quantify, there was also a greater focus on management techniques and the existence of a well-trained cadre of local professionals and entrepreneurs that was ready to adopt and adapt the new technology to the realities of Spain.

The evolution of economic policy after 1959 can be described as policy tinkering. The term is fitting because policy changes after 1959 were often at the margin, typically limiting the impact on existing players—just like the reduction of local content negotiated for new car plants did not affect existing ones. Most importantly, as suggested by the example of the car industry and others that we have reviewed, increases in openness and contestability continued despite the absence of major reforms. Arguably, the increases in efficiency occurred not despite the existing bad policies but rather *because* policy and institutional changes were well adapted to the country's conditions. We documented this not just in the case of the car industry but elsewhere. For example, public revenues began to increase significantly through the introduction of social security contributions when previous efforts at increasing taxation had been successfully resisted. Similarly, public recruitment became more competitive as the professional corps of civil servants were given greater bureaucratic autonomy. These are of course examples, but they refer to core functions of government and, moreover, they are not isolated. The simple lesson remains that Spain traveled its own distinct path to prosperity, just like Gerschenkron emphasized any backward country would.

There is a crack in everything

The fact that we have detected an increase in openness and contestability over time should not be interpreted as evidence that Spain had ceased to be what Douglass North and coauthors refer to as a limited access order—a society where access to economic opportunities and political organizations is restricted to certain groups. What we saw in Spain after 1950 was the maturing of a limited access order where elites increasingly competed nonviolently with each other for economic and political power and were increasingly subject to the rule of law. But undoubtedly, access not only to political power but also to economic opportunities remained limited.

The extent to which the country remained a limited access society can be illustrated by simply connecting some individuals named in this book with each other. Let me give just one example. José María López de Letona, the Minister of Industry that brought Ford back to Spain in 1972, had attended the same high school as Alberto Ullastres, the Minister of Commerce who was arguably the most instrumental figure behind the change of economic policies in the late 1950s. López de Letona was a cousin of Rafael del Pino, who became one of the richest men in Spain thanks to his construction firm, and a second cousin of

Jaime Milans del Bosch, one of the generals behind the failed coup on February 23, 1981. Milans del Bosch came from a long line of military men, including one responsible for one of the earliest *pronunciamientos* in the nineteenth century. His grandfather had been the civil governor for Barcelona under the dictator Miguel Primo de Rivera in the 1920s. Miguel Primo de Rivera was himself a marquis and a count. His son founded the *Falange* fascist party that inspired one of the political families throughout the Franco regime. One of Primo de Rivera's grandsons would sponsor, as a member of parliament, the Law for the Political Reform in 1977...and we could go on and on.

The above exercise is easier to do than the size of the population of the country, over 30 million, would suggest. It is nevertheless just an illustrative example that calls for a more thorough analysis. While much is still unknown in this regard, in the search for a quantitative indicator to assess how limited access evolved over time, we analyzed here the frequency of surnames among members of parliament. This analysis, which draws on the fact that more common names in Spain are associated with lower socioeconomic backgrounds, confirms that not only was the political regime nondemocratic but that de facto access to political power did not increase over the decades prior to the transition to a constitutional democracy in the late 1970s. Behind the impressive economic performance of the quarter-century after 1950 was a political order full of cracks, most notably a succession problem that could simply not be avoided given the personalistic nature of the Franco dictatorship.

That's how the light gets in

The maturing of the limited access order in Spain in the three decades after 1950 had several upshots—some lights that shone through its cracks.[1] First, there were some outright unintended positive consequences. We saw this, for example, when we discussed how the most regulated and concentrated manufacturing sectors turned out to be those that acquired the most foreign technology, as firms in those sectors had the most to gain from efficiency gains given their privileged position in the domestic market. Similarly, the limited control of local elites as they promoted tourism created not only many abuses of urban planning but also a great amount of innovation—like Benidorm. Or the exposure to management techniques and ideas that resulted from the increased contact with Western economies, with benefits for innovation and entrepreneurship.

A second set of positive consequences came from the competition, even if limited, among those groups that did have access to power. And I am referring in

---

[1] The headings in this Conclusion are indeed from a verse in poet Leonard Cohen's song "Anthem."

particular to the competition of ideas. Economists, just like other technocrats, were elevated to power on account of their technical expertise and their low political profile. As Hirschman argued, the fundamental tension of development is between the goal and the lack of understanding about how to get there. The technocrats will prove to be increasingly influential within the Franco regime on account of their ideas and the clarity of their thinking. They did not represent a specific narrow interest group, but they were themselves the product of an intellectual climate that had come to see "Europe as the solution" for Spain's problems. They got support from international figures and institutions like the World Bank and the International Monetary Fund, but their policy program was fully homegrown.

Lastly, one crack in the political order under which the economic takeoff occurred could have derailed much of the prosperity that was achieved. The unavoidable succession problem of the Franco regime put at risk the very foundation on which the economic catching up had rested, the control of violence. The inevitable political uncertainty undermined confidence and introduced policy volatility. The unraveling of the regime started to occur, predictably, even before the demise of the dictator. The true poisoned legacy of the Franco regime was not bad economic policies but bad politics. Fortunately, the risks of slipping back did not materialize, and the country was able to successfully transition into an open access society in the 1980s.

Overall, Spain's unexpected prosperity hinged on firmly anchoring expectations of both political and macroeconomic stability, harnessing ideas and aspirations, and striking a balance between policy adaptation and continuity that allowed for course corrections and exploiting opportunities. My hope is that these insights may be of some relevance across geographies and time. After all, as Eric Hobsbawm (1997, p. 108) put it, "as a historian, I am always concerned about the future."

References

Abramovitz, Moses. 1993. "The search for the sources of growth: Areas of ignorance, old and new." *The Journal of Economic History*, 53(2): 217–43.

Acemoglu, Daron and James A. Robinson. 2000. "Why did the west extend the franchise? democracy, inequality and growth in historical perspective." *The Quarterly Journal of Economics*, 115(4): 1167–99.

Acemoglu, Daron and James A. Robinson. 2012. *Why Nations Fail. The Origins of Power, Prosperity, and Poverty*. New York: Crown Publishers.

Acheson, Dean. 1969. *Present at the Creation. My Years at the State Department*. New York and London: W.W. Norton.

Adelman, Jeremy. 2013. *Worldly Philosopher. The Odyssey of Albert O. Hirschman*. Princeton: Princeton University Press.

Agénor, Pierre-Richard. 2016. "Caught in the middle? The economics of middle-income traps." *Journal of Economic Surveys*, 31(3): 771–91.

Aghion, Philippe and Steven Durlauf (eds.). 2005. *Handbook of Economic Growth*, 1. Amsterdam: North Holland, Elsevier.

Aixalá Pastó, José. 1999. *La peseta y los precios*. Zaragoza: Prensas Universitarias de Zaragoza.

Alcobendas Tirado, María Pilar. 2006. *Historia del Instituto de la Opinión Pública, 1963-1977*. Madrid: Centro de Investigaciones Sociológicas.

Alesina, Alberto, and Romain Wacziarg. 1998. "Openness, country size and government." *Journal of Public Economics*, 69(3): 305–21.

Alonso, Gregorio. 2018. "The Crisis of the Old Regime: 1808-33." In *The History of Modern Spain. Chronologies, Themes, Individuals*, edited by Adrian Shubert and José Álvarez Junco. London: Bloomsbury Academic.

Álvarez Fernández, José Ignacio. 2007. *Memoria y trauma en los testimonios de la represión franquista*. Barcelona: Anthropos Editorial.

Alvarez Nogal, Carlos and Leandro Prados de la Escosura. 2013. "The rise and fall of Spain (1270-1850)." *The Economic History Review*, 66(1): 1–37.

Álvaro Moya, Adoración. 2011. "*Hízose el milagro*. La inversión directa estadounidense y la empresa Española c. 1900-1975." *Investigaciones de Historia Económica*, 7(3): 358–68.

Álvaro Moya, Adoración. 2014. The globalization of knowledge-based services: Engineering consulting in Spain, 1953-1975." *Business History Review*, 88(4): 681–707.

Andrews, Matt, Lant Pritchett, and Michael Woolcock. 2017. *Building State Capability. Evidence, Analysis, Action*. Oxford: Oxford University Press.

ANFAC. 2019. "Informe Annual 2018." Asociación Española de Fabricantes de Automóviles y Camiones.

Ang, Yuen Yuen. 2016. *How China Escaped the Poverty Trap*. Ithaca and London: Cornell University Press.

Anson, Luis María. 1994. *Don Juan*. Barcelona: Plaza & Janés Editores.

Argandoña Rámiz, Antonio. 1999. "Una historia del desempleo en España." Discurso de ingreso en la Real Academia de Ciencias Económicas y Financieras. Barcelona: Publicaciones de la Real Academia de Ciencias Económicas y Financieras.

Aróstegui, Julio (ed.). 1994. *Violencia y política en España*. Ayer. Madrid: Marcial Pons.

Avni, Haim. 1982. *Spain, the Jews, and Franco*. Philadelphia: Jewish Publication Society.

Babiano, José and Ana Fernández Asperilla. 2003. "Elementos del proceso de la emigración española de los años sesenta. La voz de un pasado reciente." *Gaceta Sindical. Reflexión y Debate*, 279–94.

Bajo-Rubio, Oscar and Simón Sosvilla-Rivero. 1994. "An econometric analysis of foreign direct investment in Spain, 1964–89." *Southern Economic Journal*, 61(1): 104–20.

Baker, Scott R., Nicholas Bloom, and Steven J. Davis. 2016. "Measuring economic policy uncertainty." *The Quarterly Journal of Economics*, 131(4): 1593–636.

Balcells, Laia. 2017. *Rivalry and Revenge. The Politics of Violence during Civil War*. Cambridge: Cambridge University Press.

Balfour, Sebastian. 1997. *The End of the Spanish Empire, 1898–1923*. Oxford: Oxford University Press.

Banco de España. 2019. "60° Aniversario del Plan de Estabilización de 1959." Sucursal de Barcelona, Conference proceedings. 3 October 2019.

Bandura, Albert. 2016. *Moral Disengagement. How People Do Harm and Live with Themselves*. New York: Worth Publishers, Macmillan Higher Education.

Barciela, Carlos (ed.). 2003. *Autarquía y mercado negro. El fracaso económico del primer franquismo, 1939–1959*. Barcelona: Editorial Crítica.

Bardavío, Joaquín and Justino Sinova. 2000. *Todo Franco. Franquismo y antifranquismo de la A a la Z*. Barcelona: Plaza & Janés Ed.

Bar-Tal, Daniel and Phillip L. Hammack. 2012. "Conflict, Delegitimization, and Violence." In *The Oxford Handbook of Intergroup Conflict*, edited by Linda R. Tropp. Oxford: Oxford University Press.

Baumol, William J. 1982. "Contestable markets: An uprising in the theory of industry structure." *American Economic Review*, 72(1): 1–15.

Beaulac, Willard L. 1986. *Franco: Silent Ally in World War II*. Carbondale: Southern Illinois University Press.

Belletini, Giorgio, Carlotta Berti Ceroni, and Giovanni Prarolo. 2013. "Political persistence and economic growth." *European Journal of Political Economy*, 31: 165–79.

Beltrán Tapia, Francisco J. 2012. "Commons, social capital, and the emergence of agricultural cooperatives in early twentieth century Spain." *European Review of Economic History*, 16(4): 511–28.

Beltrán Tapia, Francisco J. 2013. "Enclosing literacy? Common lands and human capital in Spain, 1860–1930." *Journal of Institutional Economics*, 9(4): 491–515.

Beltrán Tapia, Francisco J. 2015. "Commons and the standard of living debate in Spain, 1860–1930." *Cliometrica*, 9: 27–48.

Bernàcer, Óscar. 2016. *El hombre que embotelló el sol*. Nakamura Films and RTVE.

Bernecker, Walter L. 2007. "The Change in Mentalities during the Late Franco Regime." In *Spain Transformed. The Late Franco Dictatorship, 1959–75*, edited by Nigel Townson. Basingstoke and New York: Palgrave Macmillan.

Bertier de Sauvigny, Guillaume de. 1962. *Metternich and His Times*. London: Darton, Longman, & Todd.

Besley, Timothy and Torsten Persson. 2011. "Fragile states and development policy." *Journal of the European Economic Association*, 9(3): 371–98.

Besley, Timothy and Torsten Persson. 2013. "Taxation and Development." In *Handbook of Public Economics*, vol. 5, edited by Alan J. Auerbach, Raj Chetty, Martin Feldstein, and Emmanuel Saez. Amsterdam: North Holland, Elsevier.

Besley, Timothy and Torsten Persson. 2014. "Why do developing countries tax so little?" *Journal of Economic Perspectives*, 28(4): 99–120.

Blattman, Christopher, and Edward Miguel. 2010. "Civil war." *Journal of Economic Literature*, 48(1): 3–57.

Blei, David M. 2012. "Probabilistic topic models." *Communications of the ACM*, 55(4): 77–84.

Bloom, Nicholas. 2014. "Fluctuations in uncertainty." *Journal of Economic Perspectives*, 28(2): 153–76.

Bolt, Jutta, Robert Inklaar, Herman de Jong, and Jan Luiten van Zanden. 2018. "Rebasing 'Maddison': New Income Comparisons and the Shape of Long-Run Economic Development." Maddison Project Working Paper 10.

Boserup, Ester. 1965. *The Conditions of Agricultural Growth. The Economics of Agrarian Change under Population Pressure*. London: G. Allen and Unwin.

Bowen, Wayne H. 2000. *Spaniards and Nazi Germany: Collaboration in the New Order*. Columbia and London: University of Missouri Press.

Bradley, Omar N. and Clay Blair. 1983. *A General's Life. An Autobiography*. New York: Simon & Schuster.

Brenan, Gerald. 1951. *The Face of Spain*. New York: Farrar, Straus & Cudahy. Published previously by Turnstile Press in London in 1950.

Broadberry, Stephen and John Wallis. 2017. "Growing, Shrinking, and Long Run Economic Performance: Historical Perspectives on Economic Development." National Bureau of Economic Research Working Paper No. 23343.

Brooks, John. 1980. *The Games Players. Tales of Men and Money*. New York: Truman Talley Books/Times Books.

Bruno, Michael and William Easterly. 1998. "Inflation crises and long-run growth." *Journal of Monetary Economics*, 41(1): 3–26.

Brydan, David. 2019. *Franco's Internationalists. Social Experts and Spain's Search for Legitimacy*. Oxford: Oxford University Press.

Buesa, Mikel and Luis E. Pires. 2002. "Intervencionismo estatal durante el franquismo tardío: la regulación de la inversión industrial en España (1963–1980)." *Revista de Historia Industrial*, 21: 159–98.

Cabrera, Mercedes. 2011. *Juan March (1880–1962)*. Madrid: Marcial Pons.

Cahalan, Margaret Werner. 1986. *Historical Corrections Statistics in the United States, 1850–1984*. Rockville: U.S. Department of Justice, Bureau of Justice Statistics.

Calvo-Gonzalez, Oscar. 2001. "'¡Bienvenido, Míster Marshall!' La ayuda económica americana y la economía española en la década de 1950." *Revista de Historia Económica*, 19: 253–75.

Calvo-Gonzalez, Oscar. 2002. "The Political Economy of Conditional Foreign Aid to Spain, 1950–1963. Relief of Input Bottlenecks, Economic Policy Change and Political Credibility." Unpublished PhD dissertation, London School of Economics.

Calvo-Gonzalez, Oscar. 2007a. "American military interests and economic confidence in spain under the franco dictatorship." *The Journal of Economic History*, 67(3): 740–67.

Calvo-Gonzalez, Oscar. 2007b. "Conditionality and ownership in IMF programs: Back to Per Jacobsson's time." *Review of International Organizations*, 4(2): 329–43.

Calvo-Gonzalez, Oscar. 2008. "La liberalización de las inversiones extranjeras durante el franquismo." In *La inversión extranjera en España*, edited by Julio Tascón. Madrid: Ed. Minerva.

Calvo-Gonzalez, Oscar, Axel Eizmendi, and German Reyes. 2018. "Winners Never Quit, Quitters Never Grow: Using Text Mining to Measure Policy Volatility and Its Link with Long-Term Growth in Latin America." World Bank Policy Research Working Paper No. 8310.

Camprubí, Lino. 2014. *Engineers and the Making of the Franco Regime*. Cambridge, Massachusetts and London: The MIT Press.

Canal, Jordi. 2003. "El carlismo crepuscular 1939–2002." In *El carlismo y las guerras carlistas. Hechos, hombres e ideas*, edited by Julio Aróstegui, Jordi Canal, and Eduardo González Calleja. Madrid: La esfera de los libros.

Cañellas Mas, Antonio (coord.). 2016. *La tecnocracia hispánica. Ideas y proyecto político en Europa y América*. Gijón: Ediciones Trea.

Carmona, Juan, Markus Lampe, and Joan Rosés. 2017. "Housing affordability during the urban transition in Spain." *The Economic History Review*, 70(2): 632–58.

Carmona, Xoán. 2018. "Fabricando el 2 CV para el mercado español: los primeros años de Citroën Hispania, S.A., 1958–1972." In *La industria del automóvil de España e Italia en perspectiva histórica*, coordinated by Carlos Barciela and Giovanni Luigi Fontana and edited by Rafael Vallejo and Margarita Vilar. Alicante: Publicacions Universitat d'Alacant.

Carr, Raymond. 1980. *Modern Spain, 1875–1980*. Oxford: Oxford University Press.

Carr, Raymond. 1994. "A Seemingly Ordinary Man." *The New York Review*, November 17.

Carreras, Albert, Leandro Prados de la Escosura, and Joan R. Rosés. 2005. "Renta y riqueza." In In *Estadísticas Históricas de España, siglos XIX–XX*, coordinated by Albert Carreras and Xavier Tafunell. Bilbao: Fundación BBVA.

Carreras, Albert and Xavier Tafunell. 2004. *Historia económica de la España contemporánea*. Barcelona: Editorial Crítica.

Carreras, Albert and Xavier Tafunell (coord.). 2005. *Estadísticas históricas de España, siglos XIX–XX*. Bilbao: Fundación BBVA.

Carreras, Albert and Xavier Tafunell. 2010. *Historia económica de la España contemporánea (1789–2009)*. Updated first edition. Barcelona: Editorial Crítica.

Carreras, Albert and Xavier Tafunell. 2021. *Between Empire and Globalization. An Economic History of Modern Spain*. Palgrave Studies in Economic History. Palgrave Macmillan.

Caruana, Leonard and Hugh Rockoff. 2003. "A Wolfram in sheep's clothing: Economic warfare in Spain, 1940–1944." *The Journal of Economic History*, 63(1): 100–26.

Caselli, Francesco and Silvana Tenreyro. 2005. "Is Poland the Next Spain?" National Bureau of Economic Research Working Paper No. 11045.

Castañeda Boniche, Antonio. 2014. "Algunos recuerdos y reflexiones en el cincuentenario de la primera Ley de Competencia en España." *Información Comercial Española*, 876: 105–23.

Castillo, Daniel and Jesús M. Valdaliso. 2017. "Path dependence and change in the Spanish port system in the long run 1880–2014: An historical perspective." *International Journal of Maritime History*, 29(3): 569–96.

Catalán, Jordi. 1995. *La economía española y la segunda guerra mundial*. Barcelona: Ariel.

Catalan, Jordi. 2010. "Strategic policy revisited: The origins of mass production in the motor industry of Argentina, Korea and Spain, 1945–87." *Business History*, 52(2): 207–30.

Cazorla Sánchez, Antonio. 2000. *Las políticas de la victoria: la consolidación del Nuevo Estado Franquista, 1938–1953*. Madrid: Marcial Pons.

Cazorla-Sánchez, Antonio. 2010. *Fear and Progress. Ordinary Lives in Franco's Spain, 1939–1975*. Chichester: Wiley-Blackwell.

Cebrián, Mar. 2005. "La regulación industrial y la transferencia internacional de tecnología en España (1959–1973)." *Investigaciones de Historia Económica*, 1(3): 11–40.

Cebrián, Mar and Santiago López. 2005. "Economic Growth, Technology Transfer and Convergence in Spain, 1960–73." In *Technology and Human Capital in Historical Perspective*, edited by Jonas Ljungberg and Jan-Pieter Smits. London: Palgrave Macmillan.

Cercas, Javier. 2011. *The Anatomy of a Moment: Thirty-Five Minutes in History and Imagination*. New York: Bloomsbury USA.

Chislett, William. 2013. *Spain. What Everybody Needs to Know*. Oxford: Oxford University Press.

Christiansen, Thomas. 2012. *The Reason Why: The Post Civil-War Agrarian Crisis in Spain*. Zaragoza: Prensas Universitarias de Zaragoza.

Cialdini, Robert B. 1993. *Influence. The Psychology of Persuasion*. Revised edition, 2007. New York: Harper Business.

Clavera, Joan, Joan M. Esteban, M. Antònia Monés, Antoni Montserrat, and Jacint Ros Hombravella. 1973. *Capitalismo español: De la autarquía a la estabilización (1939-1959)*. Madrid: Editorial Cuadernos para el Diálogo.

Colomer, Josep. 1998. *La transición a la democracia: el modelo español*. Barcelona: Editorial Anagrama.

Comín, Diego and Bart Hobijn. 2010. "An Exploration of Technology Diffusion." *American Economic Review*, 100(5): 2031–59.

Comín, Francisco. 2016. *La crisis de la deuda soberana en España (1500-2015)*. Madrid: Editorial Catarata.

Comín, Francisco. 2018. "La corrupción permanente: el fraude fiscal en España." *Hispania Nova/Revista de Historia Contemporánea*, 16: 481–521.

Comín, Francisco and Daniel Díaz. 2005. "Sector público administrativo y estado del bienestar." In *Estadísticas Históricas de España, siglos XIX-XX*, coordinated by Albert Carreras and Xavier Tafunell. Bilbao: Fundación BBVA.

Comín, Francisco and Rafael Vallejo Pousada. 2012. "La reforma tributaria de 1957 en las cortes franquistas." *Investigaciones de Historia Económica*, 8(3): 154–63.

Comisaría del Plan de Desarrollo Económico. 1963. *Plan de Desarrollo Económico y Social 1964-1967*. Madrid: Presidencia del Gobierno.

Coser, Lewis. 1956. *The Functions of Social Conflict*. New York: The Free Press.

Costa, Daniela, Timothy J. Kehoe, and Gajen Raveendranathan. 2016. "The Stages of Economic Growth Revisited: Part 1. A General Framework and Taking Off into Growth." Economic Policy Paper 16-5, Federal Reserve Bank of Minneapolis.

Crafts, Nicholas and Gianni Toniolo (eds.). 1996. *Economic Growth in Europe since 1945*. Cambridge: Cambridge University Press.

Crespo MacLennan, Julio. 2000. *Spain and the process of European integration, 1957-1985*. Basingstoke: Palgrave.

Cruz, Jesús. 2000. "The Moderate ascendancy, 1843-1868." In *Spanish History since 1808*, edited by José Álvarez Junco and Adrian Shubert. London: Bloomsbury Academic.

Cuéllar, Domingo. 2018. "Razones y maravedís: una mirada crítica a los negocios del ferro-carril en España (1844-1943)." *Hispania Nova/Revista de Historia Contemporánea*, 16: 522–57.

Curto-Grau, Marta, Alfonso Herranz-Loncán, and Albert Solé-Ollé. 2012. "Pork-Barrel politics in semi-democracies: The Spanish 'parliamentary roads,' 1880-1914." *The Journal of Economic History*, 72(3): 771–96.

Cusolito, Ana Paula and William Maloney. 2018. *Productivity Revisited. Shifting Paradigms in Analysis and Policy*. Washington, DC: World Bank.

Daniele, Vittorio and Renato Ghezzi. 2017. "The impact of World War II on nutrition and children's health in Italy." *Investigaciones de Historia Económica/Economic History Research*, 15(2): 119–31.

Dawidoff, Nicholas. 2002. *The Fly Swatter. How My Grandfather Made His Way in the World*. New York: Pantheon Books.

Decker, Ryan, John Haltiwanger, Ron Jarmin, and Javier Miranda. 2014. "The role of entrepreneurship in US job creation and economic dynamism." *Journal of Economic Perspectives*, 28(3): 3–24.

De la Dehesa, Guillermo. 1993. "Spain." In *The Political Economy of Policy Reform*, edited by John Williamson. Washington, DC: Institute for International Economics.

De la Fuente, Licinio. 1998. *Valió la pena. Memorias de Licinio de la Fuente*. Madrid: Edaf.

De la Torre, Joseba and Mario García-Zúñiga (eds.). 2009. *Entre el Mercado y el Estado. Los planes de desarrollo durante el franquismo*. Pamplona: Universidad Pública de Navarra.

De Mariana, Juan. 1845[1599]. *Del Rey y de la dignidad real*. Spanish translation of *De rege et regis institutione*. Madrid: Imprenta de la Sociedad Tipográfica y Literaria.

De Miguel, Amando. 1975. *Sociología del Franquismo. Análisis ideológico de los Ministros del Régimen*. Barcelona: Editorial Euros.

Del Arco Blanco, Miguel Angel. 2006. "'Morir de Hambre'. Autarquía, escasez y enfermedad en la España del primer Franquismo." *Pasado y Memoria. Revista de Historia Contemporánea*, 5: 241–58.

Del Cura, María Isabel and Rafael Huertas. 2007. *Alimentación y Enfermedad en Tiempos de Hambre. España, 1937–1947*. Madrid: CSIC.

Devarajan, Shantayanan and Delfin S. Go. 2003. "The 123PRSP Model." In *The Impact of Economic Policies on Poverty and Income Distribution: Evaluation Techniques and Tools*, edited by François Bourguignon and Luiz A. Pereira da Silva. Washington, DC: World Bank and Oxford University Press.

Díaz Morlán, Pablo, Antonio Escudero Gutiérrez, and Miguel Ángel Sáez García. 2008. "¿Proyecto faraónico o chivo expiatorio? La IV Planta Siderúrgica Integral de Sagunto (1966–1977)." *Investigaciones de Historia Económica*, 4(11): 137–64.

Dixon, Arturo. 1985. *Señor monopolio: La asombrosa vida de Juan March*. Barcelona: Editorial Planeta.

Domènech, Jordi. 2011. "Legal origin, ideology, coalition formation or crisis? The emergence and evolution of labor law in a civil law country, Spain, 1850–1936." *Labor History*, 52(1): 71–93.

Domènech, Jordi. 2013. "Rural labour markets and rural conflict in Spain before the Civil War (1931–6)." *The Economic History Review*, 66(1), 86–108.

Durá, Juan. 1985. *U.S. Policy Toward Dictatorship and Democracy in Spain, 1931–1953. A Test Case in Policy Formation*. Sevilla: Arrayán.

Easterly, William. 2005. "National Policies and Economic Growth: A Reappraisal." In *Handbook of Economic Growth*, edited by Philippe Aghion and Steven Durlauf. Amsterdam: North Holland, Elsevier.

Edwards, Jill. 1999. *Anglo-American Relations and the Franco Question, 1945–1955*. Oxford: Clarendon Press.

Eichengreen, Barry, Donghyun Park and Kwanho Shin. 2012. "When fast-growing economies slow down: international evidence and implications for China." *Asian Economic Papers*, 111: 42–87.

Enrique Tarancón, Vicente. 1950. "El pan nuestro de cada día dánosle hoy…Carta pastoral del Dr. D. Enrique Vicente y Tarancón." Tárrega: F. Camps Calmet.

Enrique Tarancón, Vicente. 1996. *Confesiones*. Madrid: PPC Editorial.

Espuelas Barroso, Sergio. 2012. "Are dictatorships less redistributive? A comparative analysis of social spending in Europe (1950–1980)." *European Review of Economic History*, 16(2): 211–32.

Espuelas Barroso, Sergio. 2013. "La evolución del gasto social público en España, 1850–2005." Banco de España, Estudios de Historia Económica no. 63.

Espuelas Barroso, Sergio. 2017. "Political regime and public social spending in Spain: A time series analysis (1850–2000)." *Revista de Historia Económica/Journal of Iberian and Latin American Economic History*, 35(3): 355–86.

Estapé, Fabián. 2000. *Sin acuse de recibo*. Barcelona: Plaza & Janés Ed.

Estevadeordal, Antoni and Alan Taylor. 2013. "Is the Washington Consensus dead? Growth, openness, and the Great Liberalization, 1970s–2000s." *The Review of Economics and Statistics*, 95(5): 1669–90.

Feenstra, Robert C., Robert Inklaar, and Marcel P. Timmer. 2015. "The next generation of the Penn World Table." *American Economic Review*, 105(10): 3150–82.

Felipe, Jesús, Utsav Kumar, and Reynold Galope. 2017. "Middle-income transitions: trap or myth?" *Journal of the Asia Pacific Economy*, 22(3): 429–53.

Fernández de la Mora, Gonzalo. 1965. *El crepúsculo de las ideologías*. Madrid: Editorial Rialp.

Fernández-Miranda, Juan and Jesús García Calero. 2018. *Don Juan contra Franco. Los archivos secretos de la última conspiración monárquica*. Barcelona: Plaza & Janés, Penguin Random House.

Fernández Navarrete, Donato. 2005. "La política económica exterior del Franquismo: Del aislamiento a la apertura." *Historia Contemporánea*, 30: 49–78.

Fernández Santander, Carlos. 1985. *Tensiones militares durante el Franquismo*. Barcelona: Plaza & Janés Ed.

Fernández-Villaverde, Jesús, Pablo Guerrón-Quintana, Keith Kuester, and Juan Rubio-Ramírez. 2015. "Fiscal volatility shocks and economic activity." *American Economic Review*, 105(11): 3352–84.

FOESSA. 1966. *Informe sociológico sobre la situación social en España 1966*. Madrid: Fundación FOESSA, Fomento de Estudios Sociales y de Sociología Aplicada.

Fontana, Josep. 2003. "Prólogo." In *Una inmensa prisión. Los campos de concentración y las prisiones durante la guerra civil y el franquismo*, edited Carme Molinero, Margarida Sala, and Jaume Sobrequés. Barcelona: Editorial Crítica.

Foxley, Alejandro and Fernando Sossdorf. 2011. *Making the Transition. From Middle-Income to Advanced Economies*. Washington, DC: Carnegie Endowment for International Peace.

Fraga, Manuel. 1980. *Memoria breve de una vida pública*. Barcelona: Editorial Planeta.

Fraile Balbín, Pedro. 1991. *Industrialización y grupos de presión: La economía política de la protección en España, 1900–1950*. Madrid: Alianza Universidad.

Fraile Balbín, Pedro. 1998. *La retórica contra la competencia en España (1875–1975)*. Madrid: Fundación Argentaria.

Fraile Balbín, Pedro. 1999. "Spain: Industrial Policy under Authoritarian Politics." In *European Industrial Policy. The Twentieth-Century Experience*, edited by James Foreman-Peck and Giovanni Federico. Oxford: Oxford University Press.

Franco Salgado-Araujo, Francisco. 2005. *Mis conversaciones privadas con Franco*. Barcelona: Editorial Planeta.

Fuentes Quintana, Enrique. 1984. "El Plan de Estabilización económica de 1959, veinticinco años después." *Información Comercial Española*, 612–613: 25–40.

Fuentes Quintana, Enrique and Jaime Requeijo. 1984. "La larga marcha hacia una política económica inevitable." *Papeles de economía española*, 21: 2–39.

Fukuyama, Francis. 2010. "Transitions to the rule of law." *Journal of Democracy*, 21(1): 33–44.

Fukuyama, Francis. 2011. *The Origins of Political Order: From Prehuman Times to the French Revolution*. New York: Farrar, Straus and Giroux.

Fukuyama, Francis. 2014. *Political Order and Political Decay: From the Industrial Revolution to the Present Day*. New York: Farrar, Straus and Giroux.

Fusi, Juan Pablo. 1995. *Franco*. Madrid: Taurus Santillana. First published in 1985.

Gaddis, John Lewis. 1997. *We Now Know. Rethinking Cold War History*. Oxford: Oxford University Press.

Gallego, Elena and Estrella Trincado. 2020. "Debates on Development in the Spanish Economy, 1848–1960." In *Ideas in the History of Economic Development. The Case of Peripheral Countries*, edited by Estrella Trincado, Andrés Lazzarini, and Denis Melnik. London and New York: Routledge.

García Carrero, Francisco Javier. 2019. "La Guardia Civil como institución en la búsqueda del control social." In *Mecanismos de control social y político en el primer franquismo*, coordinated by Julián Chaves Palacios. Barcelona: Anthropos Editorial.

García Delgado, José Luis. 1989. "La industrialización y el desarrollo económico de España durante el franquismo." In *La economía española en el siglo XX. Una perspectiva histórica*, edited by Jordi Nadal, Albert Carreras, and Carles Sudrià. Barcelona: Ariel.

García Ormaechea, Pedro. 1965. "Don Agustín Betancourt y Molina." *Revista de Obras Públicas*, 1(2997): V–VI.

García Ruiz, José Luis (coord). 2003. *Sobre ruedas. Una historia crítica de la industria del automóvil en España*. Madrid: Editorial Síntesis.

García Ruiz, José Luis. 2018. "Luces y sombras de las políticas industriales en España." In *La industria del automóvil de España e Italia en perspectiva histórica*, coordinated by Carlos Barciela and Giovanni Luigi Fontana and edited by Rafael Vallejo and Margarita Vilar. Alicante: Publicacions Universitat d'Alacant.

Garicano, Luis. 2014. *El dilema de España. Ser más productivos para vivir mejor*. Barcelona: Ediciones Península.

Garriga, Ramón. 1971. *La España de Franco. De la División Azul al pacto con los Estados Unidos (1943 a 1951)*. Puebla, México: Editorial Cajica.

Garrigues Díaz-Cañabate, Joaquín. 1964. *La defensa de la competencia mercantil*. Madrid: Sociedad de Estudios y Publicaciones.

Garrigues Walker, Antonio. 1965. "Análisis crítico del sistema vigente." *Boletín de estudios económicos*, 20(65): 433–48.

Gaspar, Vitor, Laura Jaramillo, and Philippe Wingender. 2016a. "Tax Capacity and Growth: Is there a Tipping Point?" IMF Working Paper No. 16/234.

Gaspar, Vitor, Laura Jaramillo, and Philippe Wingender. 2016b. "Political Institutions, State Building, and Tax Capacity: Crossing the Tipping Point." IMF Working Paper No. 16/233.

Gerschenkron, Alexander. 1962. *Economic Backwardness in Historical Perspective: A Book of Essays*. Cambridge, Massachusetts: Belknap Press of Harvard University Press.

Gill, Indermit and Homi Kharas. 2007. *An East Asian Renaissance: Ideas for Economic Growth*. Washington, DC: World Bank.

Gill, Indermit and Martin Raiser. 2012. *Golden Growth: Restoring the Lustre of the European Economic Model*. Washington, DC: World Bank.

Gilmour, David. 1985. *The Transformation of Spain: From Franco's Dictatorship to the Constitutional Monarchy*. London: Quartet Books.

Gilovich, Thomas and Lee Ross. 2016. *The Wisest One in the Room. How You Can Benefit from Social Psychology's Most Powerful Insights*. New York: The Free Press.

Gil-Robles y Quiñones, José María. 1976. *La Monarquía por la que yo luché. Páginas de un Diario 1941–1954*. Madrid: Taurus Ediciones.

Glawe, Linda and Helmut Wagner. 2016. "The middle-income trap: definitions, theories and countries concerned. A literature survey." *Comparative Economic Studies*, 58(4): 507–38.

Goldstein, Robert J. 1983. *Political Repression in 19th Century Europe*. Totowa, New Jersey: Barnes & Noble Books.

Gómez-Mendoza, Antonio. 2000. *De mitos y milagros. El Instituto Nacional de Autarquía (1941–1963)*. Barcelona: Universitat de Barcelona, Monografías de Historia Industrial.

González-Bueno y Bocos, Pedro. 2006. *En una España cambiante. Vivencias y recuerdos de un ministro de Franco*. Barcelona: Áltera.

González Duro, Enrique. 1992. *Franco. Una biografía psicológica*. Madrid: Ediciones Temas de Hoy.

González González, Manuel-Jesús. 1979. *La economía política del franquismo (1940–1970). Dirigismo, mercado, y planificación*. Madrid: Tecnos.

González González, Manuel-Jesús. 1989. "La autarquía económica bajo el régimen del General Franco: una visión desde la teoría de los derechos de propiedad." *Información Comercial Española*, 676: 19–31.

González González, Manuel-Jesús. 1999. "La economía española desde el Plan de Estabilización hasta la transición política." In *La historia económica de España. Siglos XIX y XX*, edited by Gonzalo Anes. Barcelona: Galaxia Gutenberg.

González-Páramo, José Manuel and Pablo Hernández de Cos. 2007. "Tax Reform in Perspective: The Role of the Public Sector in Spain along the Process of European Integration." In *Fiscal Reform in Spain Accomplishments and Challenges*, edited by Jorge Martínez-Vázquez and José Félix Sanz-Sanz. Northampton: Edward Elgar.

Grafe, Regina. 2012. *Distant Tyranny: Markets, Power, and Backwardness in Spain, 1650–1800*. Princeton: Princeton University Press.

Graham, Helen. 2005. *The Spanish Civil War: A Very Short Introduction*. Oxford: Oxford University Press.

Guillén, Mauro. 1994. *Models of Management. Work, Authority, and Organization in a Comparative Perspective*. Chicago: The University of Chicago Press.

Guillén, Mauro. 2001. *The Limits of Convergence. Globalization and Organizational Change in Argentina, South Korea, and Spain*. Princeton: Princeton University Press.

Guirao, Fernando. 1998. *Spain and the Reconstruction of Western Europe, 1945–57*. Basingstoke and New York: Macmillan, St. Martin's Press.

Guirao, Fernando. 2021. *The European Rescue of the Franco Regime, 1950–1975*. Oxford: Oxford University Press.

Hausmann, Ricardo, César Hidalgo, Sebastián Bustos, Michele Coscia, Alexander Simoes, and Muhammed A. Yıldırım. 2013. *The Atlas of Economic Complexity: Mapping Paths to Prosperity*. 2nd edition. Cambridge, Massachusetts: The MIT Press.

Hausmann, Ricardo, Lant Pritchett, and Dani Rodrik. 2005. "Growth accelerations." *Journal of Economic Growth*, 10(4): 303–329.

Herr, Richard. 1974. *An Historical Essay on Modern Spain*. Berkeley, Los Angeles, and London: University of California Press.

Herranz-Loncán, Alfonso. 2007. "Infrastructure investment and Spanish economic growth, 1850–1935." *Explorations in Economic History*, 44(3): 452–68.

Hills, George. 1967. *Franco. The Man and His Nation*. New York: Macmillan.

Hirschman, Albert O. 1958. *The Strategy of Economic Development*. New Haven and London: Yale University Press.

Hobsbawm, Eric. 1998. *On History*. New York: The New Press.

Huberman, Michael, and Wayne Lewchuk. 2003. "European economic integration and the labor compact, 1850–1913." *European Review of Economic History*, 7(1): 3–42.

Huntington, Samuel P. 1968. *Political Order in Changing Societies*. New Haven and London: Yale University Press.

Im, Fernando and David Rosenblatt. 2015. "Middle-income traps: a conceptual and empirical survey." *Journal of International Commerce, Economies and Policy*, 6(3): 1–39.

International Monetary Fund. 2014. "Sustaining Long-Run Growth and Macroeconomic Stability in Low-Income Countries. The Role of Structural Transformation and Diversification." IMF Policy Paper. Washington, DC: IMF.

Irwin, Douglas A. 2019. "Does Trade Reform Promote Economic Growth? A Review of Recent Evidence." National Bureau of Economic Research Working Paper No. 25927.

Iyigun, Murat and Dani Rodrik. 2006. "On the Efficacy of Reforms: Policy Tinkering, Institutional Change, and Entrepreneurship." In *Institutions, Development, and Economic Growth*, edited by in Theo S. Eicher and Cecilia Garcia-Peñalosa. Cambridge, Massachusetts: The MIT Press.

James, Harold. 1996. *International Monetary Cooperation since Bretton Woods*. Washington, DC: International Monetary Fund and Oxford University Press.

Jarque, Arturo. 1998. *Queremos esas bases." El acercamiento de Estados Unidos a la España de Franco*. Alcalá de Henares: Universidad de Alcalá.

Jones, Benjamin F., and Benjamin A. Olken. 2009. "Hit or miss? The effect of assassinations on institutions and war." *American Economic Journal: Macroeconomics*, 1(2): 55–87.

Jones, Edward E. and Steven Berglas. 1978. "Control of attributions about the self through self-handicapping strategies: The appeal of alcohol and the role of underachievement." *Personality and Social Psychology Bulletin*, 4(2): 200–6.

Jong-A-Pin, Richard and Jakob De Haan. 2011. "Political regime changes, economic liberalization and growth accelerations." *Public Choice*, 146: 93–115.

Jordana, Jacint and Carles Ramió. 2005. "Gobierno y administración." In *Estadísticas Históricas de España, siglos XIX–XX*, coordinated by Albert Carreras and Xavier Tafunell. Bilbao: Fundación BBVA.

Judt, Tony, 2006. *Postwar. A History of Europe since 1945*. Penguin Books.

Juliá, Santos. 2010. *Hoy no es ayer. Ensayos sobre historia de España en el siglo XX*. Barcelona: RBA Libros.

Juliá, Santos. 2017. *Transición: historia de una política española (1937–2017)*. Barcelona: Galaxia Gutenberg.

Jurado, Kyle, Sydney C. Ludvigson, and Serena Ng. 2015. "Measuring Uncertainty." *American Economic Review*, 105(3): 1177–216.

Khemani, Stuti. 2020. "Political economy of reform." *Oxford Research Encyclopedia of Economics and Finance*, January.

Kindelán, Alfredo. 1981. *La verdad de mis relaciones con Franco*. Barcelona: Ed. Planeta.

Kraay, Aart and David McKenzie. 2014. "Do Poverty Traps Exist? Assessing the Evidence." *Journal of Economic Perspectives*, 28(3): 127–48.

Lapuente, Víctor. 2006. "A Political Economy Approach to Bureaucracies." DPhil dissertation, Oxford University.

Leffler, Melvyn. 1992. *A Preponderance of Power. National Security, the Truman Administration, and the Cold War*. Stanford: Stanford University Press.

Leitz, Christian. 1999. "Nazi Germany and Francoist Spain, 1936–1945." In *Spain and the Great Powers in the Twentieth Century*, edited by Sebastian Balfour and Paul Preston. London: Routledge.

Levi, Margaret. 1988. *Of Rule and Revenue*. Berkeley and Los Angeles: University of California Press.

Levine, Ross and David Renelt. 1992. "A sensitivity analysis of cross-country growth regressions." *American Economic Review*, 82(4): 942–63.

Liedtke, Boris N. 1998. *Embracing a Dictatorship. US Relations with Spain, 1945–53*. London and New York: Macmillan/St Martin's Press.

Linz, Juan J. 1964. "An Authoritarian Regime: The Case of Spain." In *Cleavages, Ideologies and Party Systems*, edited by Eric Allard and Yrjo Littunen. Helsinki: Academic Bookstore.

Linz, Juan J. and Alfred Stepan. 1996. *Problems of Democratic Transition and Consolidation: Southern Europe, South America, and Post-Communist Europe*. Baltimore and London: Johns Hopkins University Press.

Linz, Juan J., José Ramón Montero, and Antonia M. Ruiz. 2005. "Elecciones y política." In *Estadísticas Históricas de España, siglos XIX–XX*, coordinated by Albert Carreras and Xavier Tafunell. Bilbao: Fundación BBVA.

López-Casero, Francisco. 1994. "La redefinición del pueblo. Entorno sociológico del desarrollo local en la España meridional." In *El precio de la modernización. Formas y retos del cambio de valores en la España meridional*, edited by Francisco López-Casero, Walter L. Benecker, and Peter Waldmann. Frankfurt am Main: Iberoamericana Editorial Vervuert.

López Ortiz, M. Inmaculada and Joaquín Melgarejo. 2018. "Zonas francas e industria del automóvil." In *La industria del automóvil de España e Italia en perspectiva histórica*, coordinated by Carlos Barciela and Giovanni Luigi Fontana and edited by Rafael Vallejo and Margarita Vilar. Alicante: Publicacions Universitat d'Alacant.

López Rodó, Laureano. 1990. *Memorias*. Barcelona: Plaza & Janés Ed.

Lustig, Nora (ed.). 2018. *Commitment to Equity Handbook. Estimating the Impact of Fiscal Policy on Inequality and Poverty*. New Orleans and Washington, DC: CEQ Institute at Tulane University and Brookings Institution Press.

Madariaga, Salvador de. 1958. *Spain. A Modern History*. New York: Praeger.

Malefakis, Edward. 2015. "The Second Republic: A Noble Failure?" In *Is Spain Different? A Comparative Look at the 19th and 20th Centuries*, edited by Nigel Townson. Brighton: Sussex Academic Press.

Maloney, William and Felipe Valencia. 2017. "Engineering Growth: Innovative Capacity and Development in the Americas." CESifo Working Paper No. 6339.

Maluquer de Motes, Jordi. 2014. *La economía española en perspectiva histórica*. Barcelona: Pasado & Presente.

Maravall, José María. 1985. *La política de la transición*. Madrid: Ed. Taurus.

Martín Aceña, Pablo. 2004. "¿Qué hubiera sucedido si Franco no hubiera aceptado el Plan de Estabilización?" In *Historia virtual de España 1870–2004. ¿Qué hubiera pasado si…?*, directed by Nigel Townson. Madrid: Ed. Taurus.

Martín Aceña, Pablo and Francisco Comín. 1991. *INI: 50 años de industrialización en España*. Madrid: Espasa Calpe.

Martín Aceña, Pablo and Elena Martínez Ruiz. 2007. "The Golden Age of Spanish Capitalism: Economic Growth without Political Freedom." In *Spain Transformed. The Late Franco Dictatorship, 1959–75*, edited by Nigel Townson. Basingstoke and New York: Palgrave Macmillan.

Martinez-Galarraga, Julio, Joan R. Rosés, and Daniel A. Tirado. 2015. "The long-term patterns of regional income inequality in Spain, 1860–2000." *Regional Studies*, 49(4): 502–17.

Martínez González-Tablas, Angel. 1979. *Capitalismo extranjero en España*. Madrid: Cupsa editorial.

Martínez Ruiz, Elena. 2003. "El sector exterior durante la autarquía: Una reconstrucción de las balanzas de pagos de España (1940–1958)." Banco de España, Estudios de Historia Económica no. 43.

Martínez Ruiz, Elena. 2008. "Autarkic policy and efficiency in the Spanish industrial sector. An estimate of domestic resource cost in 1958." *Revista de Historia Económica/Journal of Iberian and Latin American Economic History*, 26(3): 439–69.

Martínez Ruiz, Elena and Pilar Nogues-Marco. 2014. "Crisis cambiarias y políticas de intervención en España (1880–1975)." Banco de España, Estudios de Historia Económica no. 66.

Martínez Serrano, José Antonio. 1982. *Economía española: 1960–1980. Crecimiento y cambio estructural.* Madrid: Ed. Blume.

Martínez-Vázquez, Jorge and José Félix Sanz-Sanz (eds.). 2007. *Fiscal Reform in Spain Accomplishments and Challenges.* Northampton: Edward Elgar.

Martorell, Miguel and Santos Juliá. 2012. *Manual de historia política y social de España (1808–2011).* Barcelona: RBA Libros.

Mauro, Paolo, Rafael Romeu, Ariel Binder, and Asad Zaman. 2013. "A Modern History of Fiscal Prudence and Profligacy." IMF Working Paper No. 13/5.

McDermott, Rose. 2004. "Prospect theory in political science: Gains and losses from the first decade." *Political Psychology,* 25(2): 289–312.

McGuire, Martin C. and Mancur Olson. 1996. "The economics of autocracy and majority rule: The invisible hand and the use of force." *Journal of Economic Literature,* 24(1): 72–96.

McKechnie, Alastair, Andrew Lightner, and Dirk Willem te Velde. 2018. "Economic Development in Fragile Contexts. Learning from Success and Failure." Supporting Economic Transformation. London: Overseas Development Institute.

McMillan, Margaret, John Page, David Booth, and Dirk Willem te Velde. 2017. "Supporting Economic Transformation. An Approach Paper." London: Overseas Development Institute.

Merrill, Dennis (ed.). 1988. *Documentary History of the Truman Presidency.* Bethesda: University Publications of America.

Miranda Encarnación, José Antonio. 2004. "La Comisión Nacional de Productividad Industrial y la 'americanización' de la industria del calzado en España." *Revista de Historia Económica,* 22(3): 637–68.

Mokyr, Joel and Hans-Jochim Voth. 2010. "Understanding Growth in Europe, 1700–1870: Theory and Evidence." In *The Cambridge Economic History of Modern Europe,* 1. Cambridge University Press.

Molinas, César. 2013. *Qué hacer con España. Del capitalismo castizo a la refundación de un país.* Barcelona: Ediciones Destino.

Molinero, Carme and Pere Ysàs. 2018. *La Transición. Historia y relatos.* Madrid: Siglo XXI.

Moreno, Xavier. 2015. *The Blue Division: Spanish Blood in Russia, 1941–1945.* Sussex Academic Press.

Moreno-Luzón, Javier. 2016. *Modernizing the Nation. Spain during the Reign of Alfonso XIII, 1902–1931.* Sussex Academic.

Moreno-Luzón, Javier. 2018. "The Restoration: 1874–1914." In *The History of Modern Spain. Chronologies, Themes, Individuals,* edited by Adrian Shubert and José Álvarez Junco. Bloomsbury Academic.

Mullainathan, Sendhil and Eldar Shafir. 2013. *Scarcity: Why Having Too Little Means So Much.* Times Books/Henry Holt and Co.

Muñoz Jofre, Jaume. 2016. *La España corrupta. Breve historia de la corrupción (de la Restauración a nuestros días, 1875–2016).* Granada: Editorial Comares.

Muns, Joaquín. 1986. *Historia de las relaciones entre España y el Fondo Monetario International (1958–1982).* Madrid: Alianza Editorial.

Nadal, Jordi. 1975. *El fracaso de la revolución industrial en España, 1814–1913.* Barcelona: Ariel.

Navarro Rubio, Mariano. 1976. "La batalla de la estabilización." *Anales de la Real Academia de Ciencias Políticas y Morales,* 53: 173–202.

Navarro Rubio, Mariano. 1991. *Mis memorias. Testimonio de una vida política truncada por el 'Caso MATESA.* Plaza & Janés.

Nayyar, Deepak. 2019. *Resurgent Asia. Diversity in Development.* Oxford University Press.

Nicolau, Roser. 2005. "Población, salud y actividad." In *Estadísticas Históricas de España, siglos XIX–XX,* coordinated by Albert Carreras and Xavier Tafunell. Bilbao: Fundación BBVA.

North, Douglass C. 1993. "Institutions and credible commitment." *Journal of Institutional and Theoretical Economics,* 149(1): 11–23.

North, Douglass C., John Joseph Wallis, and Barry R. Weingast. 2009. *Violence and Social Orders. A Conceptual Framework for Interpreting Recorded Human History.* Cambridge University Press.

North, Douglass C., John Joseph Wallis, Steven B. Webb, and Barry R. Weingast. 2013. *In the Shadow of Violence. Politics, Economics, and the Problems of Development.* Cambridge University Press.

North, Douglass C. and Barry R. Weingast. 1989. "Constitutions and commitment, evolution of institutions governing public choice in seventeenth-century England." *The Journal of Economic History,* 49(4): 802–32.

Núñez, Clara Eugenia. 2005. "Educación." In *Estadísticas Históricas de España, siglos XIX–XX,* coordinated by Albert Carreras and Xavier Tafunell. Bilbao: Fundación BBVA.

Olmeda, José Antonio. 1988. *Las Fuerzas Armadas en el estado franquista. Participación política, influencia presupuestaria y profesionalización, 1939–1975.* Madrid: El Arquero.

Olson, Mancur. 2000. *Power and Prosperity. Outgrowing Communist and Capitalist Dictatorships.* New York: Basic Books.

Organisation for Economic Co-operation and Development. 1971. *Mercado de capitales en España.* Madrid: Instituto de Estudios Económicos.

Oto-Peralías, Daniel and Diego Romero-Ávila. 2016. "The economic consequences of the Spanish Reconquest: The long-term effects of medieval conquest and colonization." *Journal of Economic Growth,* 21(4): 409–64.

Özden, Çağlar, Christopher R. Parsons, Maurice Schiff, and Terrie L. Walmsley. 2011. "Where on earth is everybody? The evolution of global bilateral migration 1960–2000." *World Bank Economic Review,* 25(1): 12–56.

Pabón, Jesús. 1983. *Narváez y su época.* Madrid: Espasa-Calpe.

Pack, Sasha D. 2006. *Tourism and Dictatorship: Europe's Peaceful Invasion of Franco's Spain.* New York: Palgrave.

Pack, Sasha D. 2007. "Tourism and Political Change in Franco's Spain." In *Spain Transformed. The Late Franco Dictatorship, 1959–1975,* edited by Nigel Townson. Basingstoke and New York: Palgrave Macmillan.

Page, John and Finn Tarp (eds.). 2017. *The Practice of Industrial Policy. Government-Business Coordination in Africa and East Asia.* Oxford University Press.

Page Fortna, Virginia. 2004. *Peace Time: Cease-Fire Agreements and the Durability of Peace.* Princeton University Press.

Palacios Cerezales, Diego. 2018. "The State." In *The History of Modern Spain. Chronologies, Themes, Individuals,* edited by in Adrian Shubert and José Álvarez Junco. London: Bloomsbury Academic.

Pastor Prieto, Santos. 1981. "El transporte marítimo en España : crecimiento, crisis y política económica: bases para una ordenación económica del sector." Unpublished PhD dissertation, Universidad Complutense de Madrid, Facultad de Derecho.

Patel, Dev, Justin Sandefur, and Arvind Subramanian. 2018. "Everything You Know about Cross-Country Convergence Is Now Wrong." October 15. Washington, DC: Center for Global Development.

Payne, Stanley. 2000[1987]. *The Franco Regime, 1936–1975*. London: Phoenix Press.

Pellejero Martínez, Carmelo. 2000. *El Instituto Nacional de Industria en el Sector Turístico. Atesa (1949–1981) y Entursa (1963–1986)*. Universidad de Málaga.

Perdices de Blas, Luis and Thomas Baumert. 2010. *La hora de los economistas*. Madrid: Ecobook.

Pérez-Díaz, Víctor. 1993. *The Return of Civil Society. The Emergence of Democratic Spain*. Harvard University Press.

Pérez Sanchó, Miguel. 2003. "La industria del automóvil en la Comunidad Valenciana: el caso de Ford España." In *Sobre ruedas. Una historia crítica de la industria del automóvil en España*, coordinated by José Luis García Ruiz. Madrid: Editorial Síntesis.

Perpiñá Grau, Román. 1936. *De Economía Hispana*. Barcelona: Editorial Labor.

Perry, Theodore A. 1987. *The Moral Proverbs of Santob de Carrión. Jewish Wisdom in Christian Spain*. Princeton University Press.

Piatkowski, Marcin. 2018. *Europe's Growth Champion. Insights for the Economic Rise of Poland*. Oxford University Press.

Portero, Florentino. 1989. *Franco aislado. La cuestión Española (1945–1950)*. Aguilar Maior.

Prados de la Escosura, Leandro. 2003. *El progreso económico de España 1850–2000*. Bilbao: Fundación BBVA.

Prados de la Escosura, Leandro. 2007. "Growth and structural change in Spain, 1850–2000: A European perspective." *Revista de Historia Económica/Journal of Iberian and Latin American Economic History*, 25(1): 147–81.

Prados de la Escosura, Leandro. 2008. "Inequality, poverty and the Kuznets curve in Spain, 1850–2000." *European Review of Economic History*, 12(3): 287–324.

Prados de la Escosura, Leandro. 2016. "Economic freedom in the long run: Evidence from OECD countries (1850–2007)." *Economic History Review*, 69(2): 435–68.

Prados de la Escosura, Leandro. 2017. *Spanish Economic Growth, 1850–2015*. Palgrave Studies in Economic History. Palgrave Macmillan.

Prados de la Escosura, Leandro and Joan R. Rosés. 2009. "The sources of long-run growth in Spain, 1850–2000." *The Journal of Economic History*, 69(4): 1063–91.

Prados de la Escosura, Leandro, Joan R. Rosés, and Isabel Sanz-Villarroya. 2011. "Economic reforms and growth in Franco's Spain." *Revista de Historia Económica/Journal of Iberian and Latin American Economic History*, (30)1: 45–89.

Prados de la Escosura, Leandro and Blanca Sánchez-Alonso. 2019. "Economic Development in Spain, 1815–2017." European Historical Economics Society Working Paper 163.

Prados de la Escosura, Leandro and Vera Zamagni. 1992. *El desarrollo económico en la Europa del sur: España e Italia en perspectiva histórica*. Madrid: Alianza Editorial.

Presidencia del Gobierno. 1963. *Plan de Desarrollo Económico y Social para el periodo 1964–1967*. Madrid: Comisaría del Plan de Desarrollo Económico.

Preston, Paul. 1990. *The Politics of Revenge. Fascism and the military in 20th century Spain*. London and New York: Routledge.

Preston, Paul. 1994. *Franco. A Biography*. New York: Basic Books.

Preston, Paul. 2008. *El gran manipulador. La mentira cotidiana de Franco*. Barcelona: Ediciones B.

Preston, Paul. 2012. *The Spanish Holocaust. Inquisition and Extermination in Twentieth-Century Spain*. New York: W.W. Norton & Company.

Preston, Paul. 2019. *Un pueblo traicionado. España de 1874 a nuestros días: corrupción, incompetencia política y division social*. Debate. Penguin Random House Grupo Editorial.

Probst Solomon, Barbara. 1983. *Short Flights*. New York: The Viking Press.

Puell de la Villa, Fernando. 2009. "El devenir del Ejército de Tierra, 1945–1975." In *Fuerzas Armadas y políticas de defensa durante el Franquismo*, IV Congreso de Historia de la Defensa, Madrid, 3–5 de noviembre, Instituto Universitario General Gutiérrez Mellado.

Pueyo Sánchez, Javier. 2006. "El comportamiento de la gran banca en España (1921–1974)." Banco de España, Estudios de Historia Económica, 48.

Puig, Nuria. 2005. "La ayuda económica de Estados Unidos y la americanización de los empresarios españoles." In *España y Estados Unidos en el siglo XX*, edited by M. Dolores Elizalde and Lorenzo Delgado. Madrid: CSIC.

Puig, Nuria. 2008. "Business education in Spain." *Business History Review*, 82(2): 348–53.

Puig, Núria and Adoración Álvaro-Moya. 2016. "The long-term impact of foreign multinational enterprises in Spain: new insights into an old topic." *Journal of Evolutionary Studies in Business*, 2(1): 14–39.

Puig, Núria and Adoración Álvaro-Moya. 2018. "The long-term effects of foreign investment on local human capital: Four American companies in Spain, 1920s–1970s." *Business History Review*, 92(3): 425–52.

Puncel Chornet, Alfonso. 1996. *La autopista del Mediterráneo. Cesiones, Concesiones, Servicios y Servidumbres*. Valencia: Universitat de Valencia.

Radosh, Ronald, Mary R. Habeck and Grigory Sevostianov. 2011. *Spain Betrayed: The Soviet Union in the Spanish Civil War*. Yale University Press.

Ray, Debraj. 2006. "Aspirations, Poverty, and Economic Change." In *Understanding Poverty*, edited by Abhijit V. Banerjee, Roland Bénabou, and Dilip Mookherjee. Oxford University Press.

Reig Tapia, Alberto. 2012. "La pervivencia de los mitos franquistas." In *En el combate* por *la historia. La República, la Guerra Civil, el Franquismo*, edited by Ángel Viñas. Barcelona: Pasado & Presente.

Requeijo, Jaime. 2005. "La era del quantum: 1960–1974." *Información Comercial Española*, 826: 25–37.

Richards, Michael. 1998. *A Time of Silence. Civil War and the Culture of Repression in Franco's Spain, 1936–1945*. Cambridge University Press.

Rico, Eduardo G. 1994. *Yo, José de Salamanca, el "Gran Bribón."* Barcelona: Ed. Planeta.

Ridruejo, Dionisio. 1976. *Casi unas memorias: Con fuego y con raíces*. Barcelona: Ed. Planeta.

Rodríguez, Francisco and Dani Rodrik. 2001. "A re-examination of the relationship between trade policy and economic growth and a critical review of the literature." In *Macroeconomics Annual 2000*, edited by Ben Bernanke and Kenneth S. Rogoff. MIT Press for NBER.

Rodrik, Dani. 1996. "Understanding economic policy reform." *Journal of Economic Literature* 34(1): 9–41.

Rodrik, Dani. 2014. "When ideas trump interests: Preferences, worldviews, and policy innovations." *Journal of Economic Perspectives*, 28(1): 189–208.

Rodrik, Dani. 2015. "Premature deindustrialization." *Journal of Economic Growth*, 21: 1–33.

Romeo Mateo, María Cruz. 2015. "The Civil Wars of the 19th Century: An Exceptional Path to Modernization?" In *Is Spain Different? A Comparative Look at the 19th and 20th Centuries*, edited by Nigel Townson. Sussex Academic Press.

Ros Hombravella, Jacint. 1979. *Política económica Española (1959–1973)*. Madrid: Ed. Blume.

Rosés, Joan R. 2003. "Why isn't the whole of Spain industrialized? new economic geography and early industrialization, 1797–1910." *The Journal of Economic History*, 63(4): 995–1022.

Rosés, Joan R., Julio Martínez-Galarraga, and Daniel A. Tirado. 2010. "The upswing of regional income inequality in Spain (1860–1930)." *Explorations in Economic History*, 47(2): 244–57.

Rosés, Joan R. and Blanca Sánchez-Alonso. 2004. "Regional wage convergence in Spain (1850–1930)." *Explorations in Economic History*, 41(3): 404–25.

Ross, Lee, and Richard Nisbett. 2011. *The Person and the Situation Perspectives of Social Psychology*. Pinter & Martin. First published in 1991 by McGraw-Hill.

Rostow, Walt W. 1960. *The Stages of Economic Growth. A Non-Communist Manifesto*. Cambridge University Press.

Rubio, Mariano. 1968. "El Plan de Estabilización de 1959." *Moneda y crédito*, 105(June): 3–38.

Rubio Varas, Mar and Joseba de la Torre (eds.). 2017. *The Economic History of Nuclear Energy in Spain. Governance, Business and Finance*. Palgrave.

Rubottom, R. Richard and J. Carter Murphy. 1984. *Spain and the United States since World War II*. New York: Praeger.

Rumeu de Armas, Antonio. 1968. *Agustín de Betacourt, fundador de la Escuela de Caminos y Canales: nuevos datos biográficos*. Madrid: Colegio Oficial de Ingenieros de Caminos, Canales y Puertos.

Runciman, W. Leslie. 1927. "The World Economic Conference at Geneva." *The Economic Journal*, 37(147): 465–72.

Sala-i-Martin, Xavier. 2002. "15 Years of New Growth Economics: What Have We Learnt?" In *The Challenges of Economic Growth*, edited by Norman Loayza. Central Bank of Chile.

San Román, Elena. 1999. *Ejército e industria: el nacimiento del INI*. Barcelona: Editorial Crítica.

Sánchez-Alonso, Blanca. 2000. "Those who left and those who stayed behind: Explaining emigration from the regions of Spain, 1880–1914." *The Journal of Economic History*, 60(3): 730–55.

Sánchez Lissen, Rocío and María Teresa Sanz Díaz. 2015. "The Spanish Stabilization Plan of 1959: Juan Sarda Dexeus and the social market economy." *Investigaciones de Historia Económica*, 11(1): 10–19.

Sánchez Sánchez, Esther M. 2006. *Rumbo al Sur. Francia y la España del Desarrollo*. Madrid: CSIC.

Santesmases, María Jesús. 2018. *The Circulation of Penicillin in Spain. Health, Wealth and Authority*. Palgrave Macmillan.

Sardá, Joan. 1970. "El Banco de España, 1931–1962." In *El Banco de España: una historia económica*, edited by in Felipe Ruiz Martín/Madrid: Banco de España. Reprinted in *El Fondo Monetario Internacional, el Banco Mundial y la economía española*, coordinated by Manuel Varela Parache. Madrid: Pirámide.

Sardá, Joan. 1973. "Prólogo." In *Capitalismo español: de la autarquía a la estabilización (1939–1959)*, edited by Joan Clavera, Joan M. Esteban, M. Antònia Monés, Antoni Montserrat, and Jacint Ros Hombravella. Madrid: Editorial Cuadernos para el Diálogo.

Sarkees, Meredith Reid and Frank Wayman. 2010. *Resort to War: 1816–2007*. Washington DC: CQ Press.

Schmitz, David F. 1999. *Thank God They Are on Our Side*. Chapel Hill: University of North Carolina Press.

Schumpeter, Joseph A. 1994. *History of Economic Analysis*. Routledge. First published in 1954.

Seco Serrano, Carlos. 2000. *Historia del conservadurismo español. Una línea política integradora en el siglo XIX*. Madrid: Ediciones Temas de Hoy.

Serrano, Rodolfo and Daniel Serrano. 2016. *Toda España era una cárcel. Memoria de los presos del Franquismo*. Ed. MueveTuLengua.

Sesma Landrín, Nicolás. 2019. "Paving *the Way* for the Transition? The Administrative Reform of the late 1950s." In *From Franco to Freedom. The Roots of the Transition to Democracy in Spain, 1962–1982*, edited by Miguel Ángel Ruiz Carnicer. Sussex Academic Press.

Shiller, Robert R. 2019. *Narrative Economics. How Stories Go Viral and Drive Major Economic Events*. Princeton University Press.

Shubert, Adrian and José Álvarez Junco (eds.). 2018. *The History of Modern Spain. Chronologies, Themes, Individuals*. London: Bloomsbury Academic.

Silvestre Rodríguez, Javier. 2010. "Las emigraciones interiors en España, 1860–2007." *Historia y Política*, 23(1): 113–34.

Simpson, James and Juan Carmona. 2020. *Why Democracy Failed. The Agrarian Origins of the Spanish Civil War*. Cambridge: Cambridge University Press.

Smyth, Denis. 1999. "Franco and the Allies in the Second World War." In *Spain and the Great Powers in the Twentieth Century*, edited by Sebastian Balfour and Paul Preston. London and New York: Routledge.

Sojo, Kepa. 2011. "La nueva imagen de los Estados Unidos en el cine español de los cincuenta tras el Pacto de Madrid 1953." *Ars bilduma: Revista del Departamento de Historia del Arte y Música de la Universidad del País Vasco*, 1: 39–54.

Soto Carmona, Álvaro. 2005. *Transición y cambio en España, 1975–1996*. Alianza Editorial.

Spence, A. Michael. 2008. *The Growth Report: Strategies for Sustained Growth and Inclusive Development*. Report of the Commission on Growth and Development chaired by Michael Spence. Washington, DC: World Bank.

Spolaore, Enrico and Romain Wacziarg. 2009. "The diffusion of development." *The Quarterly Journal of Economics*, 124(2): 469–529.

Spolaore, Enrico and Romain Wacziarg. 2013. "How deep are the roots of economic development?" *Journal of Economic Literature*, 51(2): 325–69.

Staw, Barry M. 1981. "The escalation of commitment to a course of action." *Academy of management Review*, 6(4): 577–87.

Sunstein, Cass R. 2019. *Conformity. The Power of Social Influences*. NYU Press.

Svensson, Jakob. 1998. "Investment, property rights and political instability: Theory and evidence." *European Economic Review*, 42(7): 1317–41.

Swyngedouw, Erik. 2015. *Liquid Power. Water and Contested Modernities in Spain, 1898–2010*. The MIT Press.

Tafunell, Xavier. 2005. "Empresa y Bolsa." In *Estadísticas Históricas de España, siglos XIX–XX*, coordinated by Albert Carreras and Xavier Tafunell. Bilbao: Fundación BBVA.

Tamames, Ramón. 2013. *Más que unas memorias. Años de aprendizaje, la edad de la razón*. Barcelona: RBA Libros.

Tanzi, Vito and Milka Casanegra de Jantscher. 1987. "Presumptive Income Taxation: Administrative, Efficiency, and Equity Aspects." IMF Working Paper No. 87/54.

Tedde de Lorca, Pedro. 1994. "Cambio institucional y cambio económico en la España del siglo XIX." *Revista de Historia Económica*, 12(3): 525–38.

Tena, Antonio. 2005. "Sector exterior." In *Estadísticas Históricas de España, siglos XIX–XX*, coordinated by Albert Carreras and Xavier Tafunell. Bilbao: Fundación BBVA.

Thomas, Hugh. 2009. *Eduardo Barreiros and the Recovery of Spain*. Yale University Press.

Tirado, Daniel A., Elisenda Paluzie, and Jordi Pons. 2002. "Economic integration and industrial location: The case of Spain before World War I." *Journal of Economic Geography*, 2(3): 343–63.

Toft, Monica Duffy. 2009. *Securing the Peace. The Durable Settlement of Civil Wars*. Princeton University Press.

Tommasi, Mariano and Andrés Velasco. 1996. "Where are we in the political economy of reform?" *Journal of Policy Reform*, 1(2): 187–238.

Tortella, Gabriel. 1994. *El desarrollo de la España contemporánea. Historia económica de los siglos XIX y XX*. Alianza Universidad.

Tortella, Gabriel. 2011. "José Salamanca Mayol 1811–1883" in *Cien empresarios andaluces*, edited by José Antonio Parejo Barranco. Madrid: LID Editorial.

Townson, Nigel. 2007. "Introduction." In *Spain Transformed. The Late Franco Dictatorship, 1959–75*, edited by Nigel Townson. Basingstoke and New York: Palgrave Macmillan.

Townson, Nigel. 2015. "Spain. A Land Apart?" In *Is Spain Different? A Comparative Look at the 19th and 20th Centuries*, edited by Nigel Townson. Brighton: Sussex Academic Press.

Townson, Nigel. 2018. "The Contested Quest for Modernization: 1914–36." In *The History of Modern Spain. Chronologies, Themes, Individuals*, edited by Adrian Shubert and José Álvarez Junco. London: Bloomsbury Academic.

Treglown, Jeremy. 2013. *Franco's Crypt. Spanish Culture and Memory since 1936*. New York: Farrar, Straus and Giroux.

Truman, Harry S. 1955. *Memoirs of Harry S. Truman. Volume I: Year of Decisions, 1945. Volume II: Years of Trial and Hope, 1946–1952*. Garden City, NY: Doubleday & Co.

Tullock, Gordon. 1967. "The welfare costs of tariffs, monopolies, and theft." *Western Economic Journal*, 5(3): 224–32.

Tusell, Javier. 1989a. "Prólogo." In *Franco aislado. La cuestión Española (1945–1950)*, by Florentino Portero. Madrid: Aguilar Maior.

Tusell, Javier. 1989b. *La España de Franco*. Madrid: Historia 16.

Tusell, Javier. 1991. "La conspiración y el golpe de estado de Primo de Rivera (Septiembre 1923)." Working Paper 1991/15. Madrid, Instituto Juan March.

Tusell, Javier. 1993. *Carrero. La eminencia gris del régimen de Franco*. Madrid: Temas de Hoy.

Tusell, Javier. 2011. *Spain: From Dictatorship to Democracy*. Chichester: Wiley-Blackwell.

Ullastres Calvo, Alberto. 1994. "La estabilización contada por un protagonista de excepción." In *El Fondo Monetario Internacional, el Banco Mundial y la economía española*, coordinated by Manuel Varela Parache. Madrid: Ed. Pirámide.

Urquijo y Gotia, José Ramón de. 2008. *Gobiernos y ministros españoles en la edad contemporánea*. Madrid: Editorial CSIC.

Varela Parache, Manuel. 1989. "El Plan de Estabilización como yo lo recuerdo." *Información Comercial Española*, 676–677: 41–56.

Varela Parache, Manuel (coord.). 1994. *El Fondo Monetario Internacional, el Banco Mundial y la economía española*. Madrid: Ed. Pirámide.

Velarde Fuertes, Juan. 1999. "Stackelberg y su papel en el cambio de la política española." In *Economía y economistas españoles*, volume 7 ("La consolidación académica de la economía"), coordinated by Enrique Fuentes Quintana. Barcelona: Galaxia Gutenberg.

Velarde Fuertes, Juan. 2019. "Sexagésimo aniversario de un nuevo modelo económico para España." Banco de España, Conference proceedings. 3 October 2019.

Velasco Martínez, Luis. 2017. "¿Uniformizando la nación?: el servicio militar obligatorio durante el franquismo." *Historia y Política*, 38: 57–89.

Viñas, Ángel. 1980. "Autarquía y política exterior en el primer franquismo." *Revista de Estudios Internacionales*, January–March: 61–92.

Viñas, Ángel. 1981. *Los pactos secretos de Franco con Estados Unidos. Bases, ayuda económica, recortes de soberanía*. Barcelona: Grijalbo.

Viñas, Ángel. 1984. "Spain, the United States, and NATO." In *Spain: Conditional Democracy*, edited by Christopher Abel and Nissa Torrents. Beckenham: Croom Helm.

Viñas, Ángel. 1999. "Franco's Dreams of Autarky Shattered. Foreign Policy Aspects in the Run-up to the 1959 Change in Spanish Economic Strategy." In *Spain in an International*

Context, 1936–1959, edited by Christian Leitz and David J. Dunthorn. New York: Berghahn Books.

Viñas, Ángel. 2003. *En las garras del águila. Los pactos con Estados Unidos de Francisco Franco a Felipe González (1945–1995)*. Barcelona: Editorial Crítica.

Viñas, Ángel. 2012. "El Plan de Estabilizacion y Liberalización. De la suspensión de pagos al mito." In *En el combate por la historia. La República, la Guerra Civil, el Franquismo*, edited by Ángel Viñas. Barcelona: Pasado & Presente.

Viñas, Ángel. 2015. *La otra cara del Caudillo: Mitos y realidades en la biografía de Franco*. Barcelona: Editorial Crítica.

Viñas, Ángel. 2016. *Sobornos. De cómo Churchill y March compraron a los generales de Franco*. Barcelona: Editorial Crítica.

Viñas, Ángel, Julio Viñuelas, Fernando Eguidazu, Carlos Fernández Pulgar, and Senén Florensa. 1979. *Política comercial exterior en España (1939–1975)*. Madrid: Banco Exterior de España. In two volumes.

Wacziarg, Romain and Karen Horn Welch. 2008. "Trade Liberalization and Growth: New Evidence." *The World Bank Economic Review*, 22(2): 187–231.

Wang, Xuerui and Andrew McCallum. 2006. "Topics over time: a non-Markov continuous-time model of topical trends." Proceedings of the 12th ACM SIGKDD international conference on Knowledge discovery and data mining (KDD '06): 424–33.

Waugh, Michael and Bala Ravikumar. 2016. "Measuring openness to trade." *Journal of Economic Dynamics and Control*, 72: 29–41.

Weber, Max. 1919. *Politics as a Vocation*. Reprinted in 2004 as *The Vocation Lectures*, edited by David Owen and Tracy B. Strong and translated by Rodney Livingstone. London: Hackett Classics. Hackett Publishing Inc.

Weingast, Barry R. 1995. "The economic role of political institutions, market-preserving federalism and economic development." *Journal of Law, Economics and Organizations*, 11(1): 1–31.

Wood, Adrian. 1988. "Global Trends in Real Exchange Rates, 1960–1984." World Bank Discussion Papers. No. 35.

Woods, Randall B. 1995. *Fulbright: A Biography*. Cambridge: Cambridge University Press.

Woolcock, Michael. 2019. "Why Does Hirschmanian Development Remain Mired on the Margins? Because Implementation (and Reform) Really is 'a Long Voyage of Discovery.'" CID Working Papers 347, Center for International Development at Harvard University.

World Bank. 1963. *The Economic Development of Spain. Report of a Mission Organized by the International Bank for Reconstruction and Development at the Request of the Government of Spain*. Baltimore: The Johns Hopkins Press.

World Bank. 1966. *The Development of Agriculture in Spain*. Report of a Mission Organized by the International Bank for Reconstruction and Development and the Food and Agriculture Organization of the United Nations at the request of the Government of Spain. Washington, DC: World Bank.

World Bank. 2011. *Conflict, Security, and Development*. World Development Report. Washington, DC: World Bank.

World Bank. 2017. *Governance and the Law*. World Development Report. Washington, DC: World Bank.

World Bank. 2018a. *Fair Progress? Economic Mobility Across Generations Around the World*. Washington, DC: World Bank.

World Bank. 2018b. *Argentina: Escaping Crises, Sustaining Growth, Sharing Prosperity. Systematic Country Diagnostic*. Washington, DC: World Bank.

Yitzhaki, Shlomo. 2007. "Cost-benefit analysis of presumptive taxation." *FinanzArchiv/ Public Finance Analysis*, 63(3): 311–26.

Zamora Bonilla, Javier. 2018. "José Ortega y Gasset." In *The History of Modern Spain. Chronologies, Themes, Individuals*, edited by Adrian Shubert and José Álvarez Junco. London: Bloomsbury Academic.

Zaratiegui, Jesús M. 2016. "Los orígenes ideológicos de la tecnocracia en España (1940–1962)." In *La tecnocracia hispánica. Ideas y proyecto político en Europa y América*, coordinated by Antonio Cañellas Mas. Gijón: Ediciones Trea.

Zaratiegui, Jesús M. 2018a. *Cuéntame cómo pasó. El bienio pre-estabilizador 1957–1958.* Pamplona: Ediciones Universidad de Navarra S.A.

Zaratiegui, Jesús M. 2018b. *Del rosa al amarillo. El plan de estabilización español (1959).* Pamplona: Ediciones Universidad de Navarra S.A.

Zaratiegui, Jesús M. 2019. *Bienvenido, míster Marshall. Los planes de desarrollo (1964–1973).* Pamplona: Ediciones Universidad de Navarra S.A.

Index

For the benefit of digital users, indexed terms that span two pages (e.g., 52–53) may, on occasion, appear on only one of those pages.